# REMEMBERING RECONSTRUCTION

# REMEMBERING RECONSTRUCTION

## STRUGGLES OVER THE MEANING OF AMERICA'S MOST TURBULENT ERA

EDITED BY

Carole Emberton AND Bruce E. Baker

INTRODUCTION BY

W. Fitzhugh Brundage

LOUISIANA STATE UNIVERSITY PRESS

BATON ROUGE

Published by Louisiana State University Press

Manufactured in the United States of America
First printing

DESIGNER: Michelle A. Neustrom
TYPEFACE: Sina Nova
PRINTER AND BINDER: McNaughton & Gunn, Inc.

LIBRARY OF CONGRESS CATALOGING-IN-PUBLICATION DATA

Names: Emberton, Carole, editor. | Baker, Bruce E., editor.
Title: Remembering Reconstruction : struggles over the meaning of America's most turbulent era / edited by Carole Emberton and Bruce E. Baker ; Introduction by W. Fitzhugh Brundage.
Description: Baton Rouge : Louisiana State University Press, 2017. | Includes index.
Identifiers: LCCN 2016044793| ISBN 978-0-8071-6602-4 (cloth : alk. paper) | ISBN 978-0-8071-6603-1 (pdf) | ISBN 978-0-8071-6604-8 (epub) | ISBN 978-0-8071-6605-5 (mobi)
Subjects: LCSH: Reconstruction (U.S. history, 1865–1877)—Historiography. | Collective memory.
Classification: LCC E668 .R426 2017 | DDC 973.8—dc23
LC record available at https://lccn.loc.gov/2016044793

The paper in this book meets the guidelines for permanence and durability of the Committee on Production Guidelines for Book Longevity of the Council on Library Resources. ♾

# Contents

Introduction
W. FITZHUGH BRUNDAGE 1

I. WHITE SUPREMACY AND THE MEMORIES OF RECONSTRUCTION

1. Jim Crow Memory
*Southern White Supremacists and the Regional Politics of Remembrance*
K. STEPHEN PRINCE 17

2. Causes Lost and Found
*Remembering and Refighting Reconstruction in the Roosevelt Era*
JASON MORGAN WARD 35

II. BLACK COUNTER-MEMORIES OF RECONSTRUCTION

3. T. Thomas Fortune, Racial Violence of Reconstruction, and the Struggle for Historical Memory
SHAWN LEIGH ALEXANDER 59

4. Facts, Memories, and History
*John R. Lynch and the Memory of Reconstruction in the Age of Jim Crow*
JUSTIN BEHREND 84

5. The Freedwoman's Tale
*Reconstruction Remembered in the Federal Writers' Project Ex-Slave Narratives*
CAROLE EMBERTON 109

III. RECONSTRUCTION AND THE CREATION OF AMERICAN EMPIRE

6. The Lessons of Reconstruction
*Debating Race and Imperialism in the 1890s*
MARK ELLIOTT 139

7. A New Reconstruction for the South
NATALIE J. RING 173

8. "A Bitter Memory Upon Which Terms of Peace Would Rest"
*Woodrow Wilson, the Reconstruction of the South, and the Reconstruction of Europe*
SAMUEL L. SCHAFFER 203

IV. REMEMBERING RECONSTRUCTION IN THE POST–CIVIL RIGHTS ERA

9. The Cultural Work of the Ku Klux Klan in US History Textbooks, 1883–2015
ELAINE PARSONS 225

10. Wade Hampton's Last Parade
*Memory of Reconstruction in the 1970 South Carolina Tricentennial*
BRUCE E. BAKER 262

Contributors 281

Index 285

# REMEMBERING RECONSTRUCTION

# Introduction

W. FITZHUGH BRUNDAGE

Had the freed people of the American South given a name to the postwar era they might have called it Jubilee. Like the Old Testament Jubilee, when slaves were freed, debts forgiven, and God's mercy was manifest, the freed people discerned in the Civil War and its aftermath a transcendent moment in human history. The injustice of slavery was lifted and now African Americans, to the full extent of their native abilities and in accordance with God's design, stood poised to participate fully and equally in modern civilization.[1]

The postwar era, however, acquired a less evocative label: Reconstruction. In narrowest terms, President Abraham Lincoln and his contemporaries applied the name to the process of restoring the states of the former Confederacy to the Union. It entailed the litany of federal policies, revisions to state constitutions and laws, and amendments to the federal constitution that subsequent generations of students have been coerced into memorizing. If something less than the Jubilee of the Old Testament, this thicket of acts, laws, and amendments still represented a redefinition of the American state and its relationship with its citizens. No revision of comparable breadth and impact would occur again until the so-called "rights revolution" of the 1950s and 1960s.[2]

But Americans used the term *Reconstruction* to describe far more than the political and legal measures involved in reuniting the nation. Unlike many names that subsequently are attached to historical periods—the antebellum era, for instance—Reconstruction was used by contemporaries to demarcate the epoch in which they lived. It extended from the war until the disputed election of 1876 and "Redemption," when conservative white southerners regained control of the region. The term suggested an intentional refashioning of the nation; it implied innovation, regeneration, rehabilitation, and reorganization. In a nation marked by a tradition of episodic, gradual, and piecemeal reform,

Reconstruction stood out as a historical rupture when blacks experienced rapid and unprecedented empowerment, northerners exercised pervasive influence over southern institutions, white southerners suffered a dramatic diminution of their power within the region and nation, and the southern economy experienced profound upheaval.

That the period of Reconstruction was exceptional was in part a reflection of the extraordinary and far-reaching consequences of the war that preceded it. When considering the Reconstruction era, it is important to begin with the scale of the bloodshed unleashed by the Civil War. An entire generation of men either participated in or was indirectly exposed to its unprecedented violence. Perhaps as many as 3 million men saw duty in the Union and Confederate armies, out of a total population in 1860 of roughly 31.5 million. More than half of the 5.6 million American men of military age served during the war. (By comparison less than one-third of military-age men served during World War II.)[3]

The character of the war also defined the postwar era. Across the South and far from the frontlines, the familiar rhythms of day-to-day life had been broken. Simultaneously the allure of freedom had inspired slaves everywhere in the region to test the limits of their bondage. Although epic battles such as Antietam and Gettysburg loomed large in the memory of the war, swathes of Arkansas, Missouri, Kentucky, Tennessee, and Virginia bore the scars of the brutal guerrilla warfare that had been waged there. And all southerners experienced the severe scarcity of essentials brought on by the conflict. At the war's close, the South was riven by deep divisions; southern courts were clogged with legal wrangling over wartime disputes, and aggrieved southerners took to settling scores through extralegal means. Against this background, whatever peace prevailed after the war was necessarily brittle. Restoring order in the defeated Confederacy and reunited nation was in itself an ambitious and uncertain undertaking.[4]

The architects of the postwar settlement aspired to do more than merely restore order. At the very least, postwar visionaries recognized the need to address the future of both the freed people and the economy of the South. The postwar settlement could not be a restoration of the antebellum order. The wartime process of emancipation unequivocally precluded the revival of slavery even while it otherwise left unresolved the status of former slaves.

The postwar settlement also had to address the urgent need for a system of labor to replace slavery and a system of finance to succeed antebellum credit networks. Thus even the most pinched scenario for the postwar order entailed substantial innovation in statecraft, law, and economic affairs.[5]

Republican visions of Reconstruction were far more audacious. While moderate Republicans entertained postwar plans that were far-reaching, the radical wing of the party proposed one of the most imposing programs of social engineering since the nation's founding. Moderate and radical Republicans alike believed that under their leadership the United States was finally poised to consolidate its grip over the entire North American continent. With the debate over slavery in the territories resolved by the war, the nation need no longer be riven by intractable regional divisions and cultures. Free labor, progressive civilization, and the modern market could prevail everywhere, fulfilling the promise of American civilization. Reconstruction would establish the nation on a more secure, modern, and progressive foundation than had the revolution concluded by the nation's founders. We do not have to subscribe to white southern critiques of Reconstruction to recognize that the Republican vision for the postwar nation was extravagantly ambitious, even utopian.[6]

For other Americans, especially former Confederates, the postwar reconstruction they had in mind was much less sweeping in scope. Some hankered for a reconstruction, to the extent possible, of the antebellum order. Others acknowledged that the war and emancipation rendered any resurrection of the old order impossible, but they envisioned no more than incremental change to southern institutions. Above all, most were committed, even to a greater degree than many had been before the war, to regional autonomy. The cohesive national economy and polity that Republicans strove to fashion was anathema. For conservative white southerners especially, Reconstruction was the crucible of a new regional identity. Indeed, conservative southern whites would derive a greater source of racial and regional unity in response to Reconstruction than the Confederacy or the Civil War had ever fostered.[7]

The competing visions of Reconstruction were inextricably bound up in competing interpretations of the sectional crisis that had precipitated the Civil War. As Reconstruction was unfolding, participants strove to align their preferred versions of the past with their preferred scenario for the nation's reconstruction. Competing plans for Reconstruction went hand in hand with competing historical narratives; pitched political contests were accompanied by vigorous disputes in the cultural arena. From the outset, participants in Reconstruction viewed themselves as not only competing to control the course of reunion, but also the historical memory of the war and of the reunion that followed.[8]

This collection of essays is a testament to the extent and import of this contest over the memory of Reconstruction to the present day. They demonstrate the myriad ways in which Americans have produced, disseminated, and consumed divergent renderings of Reconstruction. This volume moves far beyond the familiar ground of historiographical debates that have engaged the interest of scholars since the late nineteenth century. Within these pages we see the struggle to define the meaning of Reconstruction unfold in autobiographies of politicians, late nineteenth-century gatherings of reformers, local commemorative celebrations, textbooks, and the pages of popular novels. The diversity of these manifestations of the memories of Reconstruction reminds us of our enduring preoccupation with making sense of Reconstruction.[9]

This volume also is evidence of the interest in the study of historical memory during the past quarter-century. Historians working on all regions and eras have taken up the question of historical memory, which has become shorthand for the notion of the social construction of historical identity. As part of a larger blurring of disciplinary boundaries between intellectual and cultural history and other subdisciplines of history, the current approach to historical memory melds semiotics, material culture, and social, cultural, and political history. The overarching ambition of scholars has been to explicate how historical meaning has been assigned through discourse, with due attention to forms of both elite and popular cultural expression (ranging from images and ritual to material culture). Scholars of historical memory face the challenge of apparent capaciousness of historical memory, which extends from acts of self-reflection and family lore to ritualized commemorative observances. The authors of these essays adroitly provide a glimpse of the breadth of the historical memories of Reconstruction without producing an exhaustive catalog of its endless particularities. Throughout the volume, they focus our attention on how individuals and various groups of Americans self-consciously sought to fashion a recalled past that made larger claims on the nation for recognition and legitimation. By insinuating their memory of Reconstruction into public life, these individuals and groups sought to exert cultural authority, forge and express collective solidarity, and achieve a measure of permanence for their preferred version of the past.[10]

This volume highlights several important themes in the historical memory of Reconstruction. Most observers, whether they lamented or celebrated the era, portrayed Reconstruction as a distinct era with a clear beginning and end. As Steve Prince explains in his essay, the architects of white supremacy during the late nineteenth century were at pains to depict Reconstruction as a tragic historical aberration that should not be repeated. Likewise, for the mid-twentieth century defenders of Jim Crow that Jason Ward's essay addresses, it was a trauma survived and remembered but never to be experienced again. And Natalie Ring's contribution demonstrates that early twentieth-century reformers in the South were intent on distinguishing their campaigns from any Reconstruction-era precedents. To the extent that Reconstruction was somehow a deviation from the nation's regular trajectory of development, it was viewed by opponents as illegitimate and by advocates as a singular and ephemeral moment.

Yet even after the era's perceived conclusion with the restoration of "white rule" in the South, Reconstruction remained living history. Every essay in this volume underscores the diverse ways subsequent generations of Americans found in Reconstruction a useable past. The memory of Reconstruction proved to be salient to pressing debates regarding, for instance, the rights of citizens, the measure of patriotism, and the appropriate exercise of national power in the century after Appomattox.

Reconstruction was so valuable as a useable past because, despite its seemingly ambiguous resolution, Americans drew unequivocal lessons from it. For white southerners, whether comparative moderates on racial issues or strident champions of white supremacy, the era provided abundant evidence of the folly of the extension of voting rights and full citizenship to former slaves. In this telling, Reconstruction had been a nightmarish subversion of the natural racial hierarchy.[11] The memory of Reconstruction also taught lessons about northern hypocrisy and perfidy. Motivated by both envy of antebellum southern civilization and greed, northerners used force and graft to implement irresponsible reforms in the South. Democracy had been trammeled by the self-interested wheeling and dealing of northern politicos and their African American allies.

The resulting bacchanalia of corruption and lawlessness in the South exposed northerners' true intentions. The lessons were clear: blacks were unfit in every regard for equality with whites; northern civilization was corrupt and corrupting; and the ill-conceived reconstruction of southern institutions was a case study of illegitimate and destructive government overreach. Permutations of this version of the Reconstruction past are explored in the essays by Bruce Baker, Mark Elliott, Elaine Parsons, Steve Prince, Sam Schaffer, and Jason Ward in this collection.

African Americans and whites sympathetic to their ambitions gleaned very different lessons from Reconstruction. It confirmed that black voters and elected officials were good stewards of democracy. Former congressman John R. Lynch, Justin Behrend explains, used his autobiography to demonstrate the effectiveness, probity, and resolve of Reconstruction-era black politicians like himself. By recounting instances of successful collaborations between white and black politicians across party lines, Lynch sought to dispel the falsehood that black politicians and voters voted as a bloc along lines of narrow self-interest. T. Thomas Fortune, a tireless black agitator and man of letters, found in Reconstruction overwhelming evidence of the hypocrisy and duplicity of white southerners. Shawn Alexander traces how Fortune used his talents as a poet, essayist, polemicist, and editorialist to insist that there was almost no form of violence or political skullduggery that they were not willing to employ to wrest power and rights from African Americans.

African Americans and some white allies also concluded that Reconstruction was an example of well-intentioned but lamentably incomplete American reform. Fortune, as Alexander's essay reveals, linked the horrors of Reconstruction-era violence and the violent oppression of African Americans at the end of the nineteenth century in the same chain of historical events. Reconstruction may have been over, but the issues of the era remained unresolved and pressing. Some prominent white Republicans agreed and when they had a chance, a decade and a half after the "end" of Reconstruction, they sought to provide federal protection of the right to vote and federal funding for black education. The resulting Blair Bill and Federal Elections Bill of 1890, Elliott explains, were intended to address the unfinished business of Reconstruction. The defeat of both measures marked the end of meaningful action by the federal government to address the status of African Americans in the American South for at least two generations.

Far from the corridors of power in the nation's capital, African Americans drew from Reconstruction other important lessons about surviving the vicissitudes of freedom. Carole Emberton's essay offers a richly textured account of one black woman's memory of Reconstruction. Here we can see the dialectic between Hannah Irwin's personal experience, her personal memory, and the broader forces that shaped both her life and memory. Although imprecise about dates and seemingly a contradictory jumble of crisp, murky, and nostalgic recollections, Irwin's account of Reconstruction made it clear that the freedpeople could not take for granted that either white northerners or southerners held their best interests to heart. Instead, blacks had to evaluate their circumstances and judge, as best they could, which whites, if any, were trustworthy. In this regard, her memory of Reconstruction compounded the lessons of slavery that blacks existed in a state of existential vulnerability and could take little for granted.

Natalie Ring's contribution to this collection highlights another cadre of commentators and activists who argued for the continuing reconstruction of the South decades after the so-called Compromise of 1877. For these men, Reconstruction had not gone far enough in its refashioning of the South. Its conclusion was a manifestation of the lack of American resolve and stamina. Yet so tainted was the memory of Reconstruction that they and other advocates of new government activism avoided any language or programs that would either invoke or evoke Reconstruction. For these would-be reformers, Reconstruction was a case study of ill-conceived, badly executed, and counterproductive government activism. The lesson they drew was that reform and innovation could never be imposed from above or from without. Instead, lasting reform was possible only if it was initiated and embraced by the objects of the reform. Such an understanding of the failures of Reconstruction necessarily encouraged twentieth-century reformers in the South to pursue incremental transformation and to recoil from more ambitious goals or aggressive reform tactics.

The lessons that Americans drew from Reconstruction extended far beyond the realm of domestic politics and race relations. In the hands of many commentators, Reconstruction was a powerful complement to the laissez-faire ideology of the late nineteenth and early twentieth centuries. For sceptics of government activism, the folly of Reconstruction was an American counterpart to the Paris Commune—a dangerous threat to the foundations of civilization itself.[12] Property rights, the natural ordering of society on the basis of innate talent and abilities, and the respect for order had all been subverted in the cause of naïve social and racial uplift. The memory of Reconstruction, both Ring and Elliott persuasively argue, also informed debates at the end of the nineteenth century about how best to deal with "dependent peoples" in the expanding American empire, including in Cuba, Puerto Rico, and the Philippines. Ignoring the tradition of biracial collaboration during Reconstruction that Lynch recounted in his autobiography, most white commentators resolved that the full measure of citizenship henceforth would be earned, not granted outright as natural or inalienable rights. Less advanced and dependent peoples, the argument went, were like the former slaves of the American South—naive, childlike, and incapable of self-rule. And Schaffer makes a compelling case that the memory of Reconstruction was never far from President Woodrow Wilson's mind when he considered the best possible outcome of World War One. He wanted to avoid what he believed to be the errors of the harsh post–Civil War settlement imposed on the South. Not only did Wilson seek to ensure that Germany was not subjected to a "vindictive" peace, but also to prevent the folly of empowering races not yet capable of self-rule. To extend self-rule to the colonized peoples of the world would be to replicate the errors of Reconstruction.

This collection goes far to explain how and why the white conservative critique of Reconstruction exerted powerful influence throughout the nation. All of the essays demonstrate that the search for the meaning of Reconstruction was much more than an academic exercise conducted by professional historians. It was one of the major American cultural projects of the late nineteenth and first half of the twentieth centuries. White southerners came to understand that in an age of emerging mass culture, they could wield influence as consumers even if they could not control the production of culture. They could demand the censoring of provocative movies, such as black filmmaker Oscar Micheaux's *Within Our Gates* (1919), which portrayed the postwar South in a less than flattering light. They could boycott textbooks that deviated from the white southern orthodoxy about slavery, the Civil War, and Reconstruction. And they could put pen to paper and craft plays, poems, and fiction that transformed the white southern memory of Reconstruction into popular culture for national (and international) audiences.

White southerners proved uncommonly skillful at this craft. For example, Thomas Dixon, the author of best-selling novels and highly successful plays, was a master of turn-of-the-century melodrama. Moreover, his highly dramatic and visual prose style was well suited for adaptation to the film screen. Beginning even before D. W. Griffith's adaptation of Dixon's play *The Clansman,* the newest and most influential technology of mass culture—film—became a powerful means to disseminate the white southern memory of Reconstruction. Dixon, Griffith, and their ilk tapped into a deep vein of antiblack popular culture, including the insidious Zip Coon character made familiar by antebellum blackface minstrelsy. Filmmaker D. W. Griffiths's notorious vignette of the South Carolina legislature in *Birth of a Nation* (1915), in which garishly dressed and buffoonish black legislators bloviate and chomp on chicken bones, was blackface minstrelsy masquerading as historical documentary. In this instance and countless others, familiar tropes of the romantic South and of black primitivism in popular culture were yoked to a deeply conservative memory of Reconstruction.[13]

Professional historians, as many of the essayists here remind us, also had an outsized role in legitimating the conservative white narrative of Reconstruction. Parsons's essay exposes the ideological orientations and narrative choices made by history textbook writers that severely circumscribed understandings of Reconstruction, especially Reconstruction violence. The American historians who built the foundations for twentieth-century historical scholarship embraced a nationalist perspective that discouraged any sympathy for the ambitions of radical Republicans or blacks. At the same time, many historians, including a large cohort of influential scholars of southern descent, espoused conventional racist attitudes of the era. Consequently, these scholars were predisposed to sympathize with the "plight" of white southerners during Reconstruction and to dismiss Republican policies as misguided at best, dangerous at worst. Finally, anxious to establish their cultural authority over the interpretation of the past, professional historians cast doubt upon any historical accounts that were not the product of professional scholars of a similar cast of mind. Consequently, they cavalierly dismissed or ignored the work of African American scholars or other outliers whose interpretations challenged the prevailing historical wisdom.[14]

Parsons's and the other essays underscore how enduring the conservative narrative of Reconstruction has been. It is evident in the muted acknowledgment of Reconstruction-era violence in most American history textbooks. The violence of the Klan is sprinkled in some textbooks, but far more pervasive and chronic violence, ranging from assassinations, lynchings, riots, and arson, are seldom described. It is striking that until the 1960s, historians paid scant attention to the remarkably full and rich record of racist and anti-Republican violence cataloged by the congressional hearings on the Ku Klux Klan in 1871. To this day the published testimony from the hearings provides one of the most complete portraits of terrorist violence in the United States. Instead, the focus of much of the discussion of Reconstruction-era violence was on black violence against whites, especially white women. Conservative whites littered their accounts of Reconstruction with lurid accounts of black criminality, and in the process contributed to fashioning the shibboleth of the black rapist that would justify lynching for decades to come.[15]

Yet even while these essays demonstrate the persistence of some tropes of Reconstruction memory, they simultaneously alert us to the erosion of the power of Reconstruction memory to mobilize Americans. Ward's essay demonstrates the facility with which conservative white southern politicos invoked Reconstruction to justify opposition to almost any New Deal era program that posed a threat to white southern power in Congress or over the region. Even so, the more prescient members of the anti–New Deal vanguard, such as John C. Stennis, came to recognize that invocations of Reconstruction and white southern pride were inadequate to protect the "southern way of life" after World War II. The specter of a "second Reconstruction" was sufficient to mobilize some resistance to the civil rights activists of the 1950s and 1960s, but, as Stennis predicted, too few white southerners were willing to take the drastic steps advocated by the most defiant white supremacists in the South. Similarly, Baker's essay on the representation of Reconstruction in South Carolina's Tricentennial celebrations highlights the continuing relevance of Reconstruction in one South Carolina community and its waning significance elsewhere in the state. Herein is a case study of the relationship between place and historical memory. The contrasting renderings of Reconstruction in the celebrations in Anderson and Orangeburg underscore how local conditions and politics nourish local historical memory, which in turn works to sustain those distinctive local politics and conditions.

No single volume on the historical memory of Reconstruction could exhaust the topic. For all the evident strengths of this collection, there is still work to be done, questions still to be asked and answered. Can we, for example, unearth long-overlooked alternative memories of reunion and reconstruction? What of the memory of the Readjuster movement in Virginia, a biracial political experiment that survived the "end" of Reconstruction? What of the memory of the "other" southerners, including Civil War–era Unionists and dissenters, white Republicans, Cherokees, and other Indians? For all of these groups Reconstruction was a time of wrenching and lasting change. Yet we know very little about their participation in the contest over memory during and after Reconstruction.[16]

It is striking that we still lack an intellectual history of the concept of "reconstruction" within the Republican party. Before the Civil War, Republicans in Illinois had already begun advocating the "reconstruction" of southern Illinois, or "Egypt." Their plans to refashion backward and reactionary southern Illinois, where the residents seemed to display all of the worst failings of the slave South, failed to transform the inhabitants of the region or to pry them away from the Democratic Party. Given the failure of the prewar and wartime efforts to reconstruct "Egypt," we might wonder how Republicans were so sanguine that the purportedly inherent virtues of their program would appeal to white southerners. We need, in sum, to connect the Republican experience with prewar and wartime "reconstruction" with their postwar project.[17]

Despite the excellent scholarship on postwar organizations that became de facto postwar guardians of memory, such as the Grand Army of the Republic, the United Confederate Veterans, and the United Daughters of the Confederacy, we lack robust comparative work on their handiwork.[18] Such scholarship may reveal that many northerners had much less investment in defending Reconstruction than they did in defending their memory of the Civil War. They may have ceded some of the ground on Reconstruction to conservative white southerners because the memory of it did not advance their cultural and political preoccupations. Yet it is worth noting that some northerners tenaciously challenged conservative renderings of Reconstruction.[19] Moreover, historians for too long have dismissed the penchant of some northern politicians to "wave the bloody shirt" (as a way of drawing attention to white southern violence and persisting incorrigibility) as shrill political posturing. To the contrary, they were engaged in the important work of compiling and sustaining a counter-memory to the ascendant conservative memory of Reconstruction.

Finally, we know altogether too little about the relationship between the memories of Reconstruction and of the simultaneous conquest of the West. In recent years historians have exposed the interrelated processes of pacifying the postwar South and wresting the American West from its previous inhabitants. Soldiers who had battled rebels and terrorists in the Deep South subsequently found themselves fighting Indians in the West; issues of national power and citizen rights that were contested in the South would also arise in the West.[20] Yet, curiously, Americans both then and since seem to have quarantined the memories of Reconstruction and the conquest of the West from each other. Somehow the Reconstruction of the South stands outside of the national narrative while the conquest of the West is enfolded within it. This curious bifurcation of the memory of these two contemporaneous processes awaits revision. This collection is certain to perform a valuable service as it inspires readers and scholars to wrestle with this and other lingering questions about Reconstruction and its memory.

NOTES

1. Reginald F. Hildebrand, *The Times Were Strange and Stirring: Methodist Preachers and the Crisis of Emancipation* (Durham: Duke University Press, 1995); Matthew Harper, *End of Days: African American Religion and Politics in the Age of Emancipation* (Chapel Hill: University of North Carolina Press, 2016).

2. The best overview of the era remains Eric Foner, *Reconstruction: America's Unfinished Revolution, 1863–1877* (New York: Harper & Row, 1989).

3. The scale of destruction of human life and property during the war can be gleaned from James M. McPherson, *Battle Cry of Freedom: The Civil War Era* (New York: Oxford University Press, 1988).

4. The disorder at the close of the war is explored in Dan T. Carter, *When the War Was Over: The Failure of Self-Reconstruction in the South, 1865–1867* (Baton Rouge: Louisiana State University Press, 1985); Michael Fellman, *This Terrible War: The Civil War and Its Aftermath* (New York: Longman, 2003); Daniel E. Sutherland, *A Savage Conflict: The Decisive Role of Guerrillas in the American Civil War* (Chapel Hill: University of North Carolina Press, 2009); Gregory P. Downs, *After Appomattox: Military Occupation and the Ends of War* (Cambridge: Harvard University Press, 2015); Carole Emberton, *Beyond Redemption: Race, Violence, and the American South After the Civil War* (Chicago: University of Chicago Press, 2013); and Adam Domby, "War Within the States: Loyalty, Dissent, and Conflict in Southern Piedmont Communities, 1860–1876" (PhD diss., University of North Carolina, 2015).

5. For insights into Reconstruction and labor in the South, see Eric Foner, *Nothing but Freedom: Emancipation and Its Legacy* (Baton Rouge: Louisiana State University Press, 1984); Gerald David Jaynes, *Branches Without Roots: Genesis of the Black Working Class, 1862–1882* (New York: Oxford University Press, 1986); and Laura F. Edwards, *Gendered Strife and Confusion: The Political Culture of Reconstruction* (Chapel Hill: University of North Carolina Press, 1997).

6. Foner, *Reconstruction,* esp. 228–316.

7. Charles Reagan Wilson, *Baptized in Blood: The Religion of the Lost Cause, 1865–1920* (Athens: University of Georgia Press, 1980); George C. Rable, *But There Was No Peace: The Role of Violence in the Politics of Reconstruction* (Athens: University of Georgia Press, 1984); Carter, *When the War Was Over;* W. Scott Poole, *Never Surrender: Confederate Memory and Conservatism in the South Carolina Upcountry* (Athens: University of Georgia Press, 2004); Arthur Remillard, *Southern Civil Religion: Imagining the Good Society in the Post-Reconstruction Era* (Athens: University of Georgia Press, 2011), esp. 15–44.

8. Nancy Cohen, *The Reconstruction of American Liberalism, 1865–1914* (Chapel Hill: University of North Carolina Press, 2002); K. Stephen Prince, *Stories of the South: Race and the Reconstruction of Southern Identity, 1865–1915* (Chapel Hill: University of North Carolina Press, 2014); Elaine Frantz Parsons, *Ku-Klux: The Birth of the Klan during Reconstruction* (Chapel Hill: University of North Carolina Press, 2016).

9. Bruce E. Baker, *What Reconstruction Meant: Historical Memory in the American South* (Charlottesville: University of Virginia Press, 2007).

10. The scholarship on historical/collective memory is now voluminous. Good starting points are W. Fitzhugh Brundage, ed., *Where These Memories Grow: History, Memory, and Southern Identity* (Chapel Hill: University of North Carolina Press, 2000); and Astrid Erll, ed., *Cultural Memory Studies: An International and Interdisciplinary Handbook* (Berlin: Walter de Gruyter, 2008).

11. Poole, *Never Surrender;* Baker, *What Reconstruction Meant.*

12. Cohen, *Reconstruction of American Liberalism.*

13. David W. Blight, *Race and Reunion: The Civil War in American Memory* (Cambridge: Belknap Press of Harvard University Press, 2001); Karen L. Cox, *Dreaming of Dixie: How the South Was Created in American Popular Culture* (Chapel Hill: University of North Carolina Press, 2011); and Caroline E. Janney, *Remembering the Civil War: Reunion and the Limits of Reconciliation* (Chapel Hill: University of North Carolina Press, 2013).

14. See Kenneth M. Stampp, "The Tragic Legend of Reconstruction," in Kenneth M. Stampp and Leon F. Litwack, eds., *Reconstruction: An Anthology of Revisionist Writings* (Baton Rouge: Louisiana State University Press, 1969); and Peter Novick, *That Noble Dream: The "Objectivity Question" and the American Historical Profession* (New York: Cambridge University Press, 1988).

15. Allen W. Trelease, *White Terror: The Ku Klux Klan Conspiracy and Southern Reconstruction* (New York: Harper & Row, 1971); Richard Zuczek, *State of Rebellion: Reconstruction in South Carolina* (Columbia: University of South Carolina Press, 1996); Diane Miller Sommerville, *Rape & Race in the Nineteenth-century South* (Chapel Hill: University of North Carolina Press, 2004); Hannah Rosen, *Terror in the Heart of Freedom: Citizenship, Sexual Violence, and the Meaning of*

*Race in the Postemancipation South* (Chapel Hill: University of North Carolina Press, 2009); Kate Côté Gillin, *Shrill Hurrahs: Women, Gender, and Racial Violence in South Carolina, 1865–1900* (Columbia: University of South Carolina Press, 2013); Emberton, *Beyond Redemption.*

16. Jane Elizabeth Dailey, *Before Jim Crow: The Politics of Race in Postemancipation Virginia* (Chapel Hill: University of North Carolina Press, 2000); Carl N. Degler, *The Other South: Southern Dissenters in the Nineteenth Century* (New York: Harper & Row, 1974); Victoria E. Bynum, *The Long Shadow of the Civil War: Southern Dissent and Its Legacies* (Chapel Hill: University of North Carolina Press, 2010); Domby, "War Within the States"; Malinda Maynor Lowery, *Lumbee Indians in the Jim Crow South: Race, Identity, and the Making of a Nation* (Chapel Hill: University of North Carolina Press, 2010).

17. For the Republican Party's prewar southern strategy, see Eric Foner, *Free Soil, Free Labor, Free Men: The Ideology of the Republican Party Before the Civil War* (New York: Oxford University Press, 1970); Richard H. Abbott, *The Republican Party and the South, 1855–1877: The First Southern Strategy* (Chapel Hill: University of North Carolina Press, 1986); and Susan-Mary Grant, *North over South: Northern Nationalism and American Identity in the Antebellum Era* (Lawrence: University Press of Kansas, 2000).

18. Gaines M. Foster, *Ghosts of the Confederacy: Defeat, the Lost Cause, and the Emergence of the New South, 1865 to 1913* (New York: Oxford University Press, 1987); Stuart C. McConnell, *Glorious Contentment: The Grand Army of the Republic, 1865–1900* (Chapel Hill: University of North Carolina Press, 1992); Karen L. Cox, *Dixie's Daughters: The United Daughters of the Confederacy and the Preservation of Confederate Culture* (Gainesville: University Press of Florida, 2003); Barbara A. Gannon, *The Won Cause: Black and White Comradeship in the Grand Army of the Republic* (Chapel Hill: University of North Carolina Press, 2011); M. Keith Harris, *Across the Bloody Chasm: The Culture of Commemoration Among Civil War Veterans* (Baton Rouge: Louisiana State University Press, 2014).

19. Janney, *Remembering the Civil War.*

20. Heather Cox Richardson, *West from Appomattox: The Reconstruction of America after the Civil War* (New Haven: Yale University Press, 2007).

# I

# WHITE SUPREMACY AND THE MEMORIES OF RECONSTRUCTION

1

# Jim Crow Memory

## *Southern White Supremacists and the Regional Politics of Remembrance*

K. STEPHEN PRINCE

Jim Crow took shape in southern state conventions and city streetcars, at restaurants and polling places, at general stores and in capitol buildings, along sidewalks and at spectacle lynchings. Between 1890 and 1910, white southerners established an adaptable and flexible system of oppression and control that would maintain white supremacy almost inviolate until the mid-twentieth century. Through the systematic revision of southern state constitutions and the careful deployment of such antidemocratic means as the grandfather clause and the white primary, white supremacists turned the South's electoral politics lily-white.[1] The rise of spatial segregation and the definition of certain spaces as "white" and others as "colored" built the reality of white supremacy into the very landscape of the region.[2] The lynchings and race riots that convulsed the South after 1890 bespoke a single truth: black bodies—corporeal, just as surely as political—had no rights that the southern white man was bound to respect.[3] Jim Crow segregation, disfranchisement, and systematic racial violence were neither natural nor inevitable. They were, instead, the result of a planned and coordinated attack on African American civil and political rights. As historian Stephen Kantrowitz puts it, "white supremacy was hard work."[4]

But the establishment of Jim Crow also required a different sort of work, one that took place in the auditoriums and print culture of the North rather than the streets and convention halls of the South. For all the system's violence and injustice, the birth of Jim Crow occurred in a remarkably forthright and open manner. Southern white supremacists did not try to hide their handiwork from the rest of the nation—far from it. As they trampled black lives and livelihoods in the South, Jim Crow propagandists actively made their case to the rest of the nation.[5] These overtures form a part of a longer tradition of southern regional self-definition, a "rage to explain" also reflected in the postwar efforts of New South boosters like Henry Grady and in the Lost Cause apologetics of the United Daughters of the Confederacy.[6] And yet, the missionaries of Jim Crow had an agenda all their own. Turn-of-the-century white supremacists sought to explain and naturalize racial murder and political domination. They worked to make the unnatural seem natural, the discriminatory seem charitable, and the hard work of white supremacy appear inevitable and barely conscious. This nationwide campaign of explanation was inseparable from the campaign for racial domination in the South. Disfranchisement, segregation, and lynching may have been largely southern phenomena, but they were constructed before a national audience.

In this campaign, the memory of Reconstruction played a starring role. Between 1890 and 1910, the architects of segregation and disfranchisement produced and disseminated a history of Reconstruction carefully tailored to serve the needs of turn-of-the-century white supremacy. Though this popular memory anticipated many of the arguments advanced by William Archibald Dunning and his students at Columbia University, Jim Crow's propagandists avowed purposes more political than historical. In speeches delivered at lyceums, courthouses, and town greens, in partisan histories, in articles published in widely circulated northern periodicals, and in best-selling novels, white southerners systematically rewrote the memory of Reconstruction in full view of the nation. As they looked to the past, white supremacists always had one eye on the present. In remembering Reconstruction, they were actually advancing Jim Crow.

As historians Grace Elizabeth Hale, Bruce E. Baker, and Glenn Feldman have noted, late nineteenth-century southern elites used the memory of Reconstruction to enforce racial unity and to take the teeth out of biracial Populist and Fusionist political movements.[7] I will argue, however, that along with the obvious *racial* politics of Reconstruction memory, historians need to recognize the *regional* politics at work. The turn-of-the-century white supremacist memory of Reconstruction was never exclusively about black domination; it was also about northern control of the South. With the benefit of hindsight, historians recognize that the federal government largely declined to respond to the white South's systematic destruction of African American civil and political rights after 1890.[8] Such assurance, however, was denied to late nineteenth- and early twentieth-century Americans. The fact that the federal government *did not* intervene during the 1890s and 1900s should not be construed as evidence that it *could not* have intervened. Popular treatments of Reconstruction highlight a real fear on the part of Jim Crow's architects, who were desperate to ensure northern inaction and acquiescence as they segregated public space and drafted disfranchising constitutions. Indeed, why continue to drag up the corpse of Reconstruction if the issues at play were no longer relevant? In their overtures to the northern public, white southerners consistently reminded Yankees of the guiding role that the North had played in spawning the nation's darkest era. This reading of history pointed to a single, inevitable conclusion: northerners did not understand the idiosyncrasies of southern race politics, and must leave matters to the white southerners who did.

Since Pierre Nora, scholars have emphasized the role of memory in creating and sustaining group identities.[9] This was certainly true in the South, where collective memory of the Civil War and Reconstruction played a central role in the postwar reformulation of white identity.[10] But memory also proved itself to be an extraordinarily powerful political tool when aimed beyond the Mason-Dixon line. The white South actually waged two concurrent campaigns in the 1890s and 1900s. The first was a determined and vicious push for political domination that produced disfranchisement, segregation, and spectacle lynching. The second campaign was not waged with grandfather clauses, nooses, and "whites only" placards, but with words. Turn-of-the-century white supremacists used the memory of Reconstruction as a bludgeon—a blunt rhetorical tool that worked best through sheer repetition. It was indelicate, but the specter of Reconstruction arguably offered the most powerful weapon that southern white supremacists had in their campaign to ward off renewed federal intervention. Less than two decades after the close of Reconstruction, white southerners systematically and self-consciously reimagined the history of Reconstruction in an attempt to overthrow the remaining legislative and judicial enactments of the period. To secure white supremacy at home, the white South needed to justify it to the rest of the nation. A white supremacist rewriting of Reconstruction was an indispensable corollary to the rise of Jim Crow.

+ + +

In early 1890, congressional Republicans began discussion of the Lodge Federal Elections Bill. The measure, sponsored by Massachusetts congressman Henry Cabot Lodge, would have allowed a small number of voters to trigger a federal investigation of an election deemed suspect or fraudulent. Designed to ensure the sanctity and impartiality of federal elections in the South, the Lodge Bill appeared to herald a renewed Republican commitment to African American voting rights.[11] Though the Lodge Bill stalled in the Senate, southern Democrats recognized the grave threat that the legislation posed to the maintenance of white supremacy. The so-called "Force Bill" represented an intolerable imposition into local affairs. It would have reinvigorated southern Republicanism and boosted black voting totals in one fell swoop. More than this, it portended a return to the dark days of Reconstruction, when native southern whites lost control of the region's race relations.

It is in this context that Alabama congressman Hilary A. Herbert and a coterie of like-minded southerners produced a book called *Why the Solid South?* The text was an extended brief against the sort of federal interventionism that the Lodge Bill represented. Significantly, however, *Why the Solid South?* did not criticize the Lodge bill directly. Instead, Herbert and his coauthors turned to the memory of Reconstruction.[12] The text offered state-by-state histories of the Reconstruction period penned by notable residents. The narratives vary, but all repeat familiar tropes of ignorant black voters, rampant corruption, and crushing state debt. Though Herbert insisted that contributors had been instructed to "write as impartially as possible," the presentist orientation of *Why the Solid South?* is clear on every page. "The lessons drawn from recent experience," Herbert explained, "offer the most valuable that history can teach."[13] Since "like causes produce like effects," the nation must learn from Reconstruction in order to avoid repeating it.[14]

An underlying regional logic unifies the essays in *Why the Solid South?* As Congress considered renewed federal oversight of southern elections, Herbert and company used the history of Reconstruction to prove to northerners just how little they knew about southern race relations. As Hilary Herbert put it, the book highlighted "the consequences which once followed an interference in the domestic affairs of certain states by those, who either did not understand the situation or were reckless of results."[15] Other contributors offered similar warnings. North Carolinian Zebulon Vance hoped that "this recital of these unhappy events may tend in some degree to soften the opinion and mitigate the judgment of many of my impartial countrymen in the Northern portion of our Union."[16] The "blunder" of the northern-led Reconstruction effort, Ethelbert Barksdale of Mississippi wrote, "must be clear to the authors themselves." In the future, therefore, northerners must "permit us to control our domestic affairs . . . according to our own judgment."[17] South Carolina congressman John J. Hemphill was even more blunt: "All we ask is to be let alone, and that, surely, is not so great a request that it cannot or ought not be granted."[18] *Why the Solid South?* dramatized all that was at stake in the battle over the Federal Elections Bill. More than this, it highlighted the political salience of popular memory in the decades that followed the overthrow of the Reconstruction regimes. In the 1860s, northern involvement in southern racial affairs had spawned the nightmare of Reconstruction. In the 1890s, Herbert and his coauthors hoped that a chastened northern population would take a lesson from the past, willfully ceding control to the white South.

The defeat of the Lodge Bill in 1890 did not slow the white South's engagement with the memory of Reconstruction, nor did it fundamentally alter the regional logic introduced in *Why the Solid South?* In their discussions of Reconstruction and elsewhere, turn-of-the-century white supremacists claimed an inborn expertise on racial issues, simply by virtue of their southern upbringing. Proximity to African Americans, they argued, imparted an intimate understanding necessarily denied to those who lived outside the South. Such arguments turned southernness into a credential. On the basis of a knowledge rooted in years of experience and lifelong proximity to black people, white southerners insisted upon their own ability to speak authoritatively on racial matters. "The South claims the possession of knowledge superior to that of the North with regard to the negro's wants, character, and condition," a Tuscaloosa, Alabama resident named Walter Guild explained in the *Arena* in 1900. "The Southerner is 'on the ground' with generations of experience and with every facility for accurate information."[19] North Carolina senator Furnifold Simmons professed a "more or less intimate acquaintance with the character and adaptation and capabilities of the negro," while South Carolina's Ben Tillman "claimed by birth, education, long residence in the south, and opportunity for and constant application to the study of the topic, to be peculiarly fitted to discuss this gravest problem before the nation."[20] A deep knowledge of African American character was a part of a southern upbringing; race knowledge was an organic outgrowth of the South's rich soil. "I am a Southern woman, thirty-five years of age, married, and the mother of one child," a contributor to the *Independent* wrote. "I know the negro from tradition and experience."[21]

The logical flip side to the notion of white southern racial expertise was a firm conviction that northerners were incapable of understanding the idiosyncrasies of southern race relations. "It is hardly possible for any one, no matter how great his intellect or resplendent his genius, to reach a correct conclusion without understanding the conditions that surround the subject," Alabama governor Joseph F. Johnston said. "And yet many who never set foot in the South are ready to solve this question without study or reflection."[22] Northerners might pick up a book or make a journey through the South, but they could never know the region's black population in the way that native whites did. "Reasoning from abstract philanthropy at the distance of a thousand miles," journalist John Temple Graves told a Chicago audience, the North "cherishes a fixed faith in the unity of race and the equality of man."[23] From such a distance, racial democracy and political equality might have their appeal. Those who were on the ground in the South had no such illusions. Tulane University professor William Benjamin Smith was equally dismissive of the northern point of view. "The testimony of the North and of Europe is hardly more relevant than would be that of the Martians," Smith wrote. "Their treatment of the subject is merely academic and sentimental. They have generous ethical ideas, respectable but well-worn and overworked maxims, high humanitarian principles," but "the practical problem never confronts them in its unrelieved difficulties and dangers."[24] At its heart, the question was an epistemological one. Jim Crow propagandists insisted that their own racial knowledge, rooted in firsthand experience, was of a purer, higher, and truer stripe than northern racial thought. African American citizenship might seem reasonable to those safely ensconced in their northern homes. To those on the ground in the South, black inferiority was an undeniable fact.

White southerners found ample evidence for their claims to a monopoly on race knowledge in their study of the immediate postwar period. The evils of Reconstruction, Jim Crow–era white supremacists argued, flowed directly from wrongheaded northern intervention in southern racial policy. "What, then, is this thing which we call 'Reconstruction'?" Mississippian Alfred Holt

Stone asked in his 1908 book *Studies in the American Race Problem*. "In the South it is that period of misery which covered the decade or more between 1865 and 1875 or 1880, and measured the time during which the control of their domestic affairs was lost and regained by Southern white men."[25] Stone cast Reconstruction as an unparalleled crisis of authority, juxtaposing northern abstraction and idealism with white southern knowledge and realism. The "misery" of the period was directly related to the failure of southern white men to control the region's domestic (that is, racial) affairs. In the aftermath of the Civil War, northern Radicals and demagogues had nearly destroyed the South. Flying by the seat of their collective pants as they ruled the South from afar, northern Republicans had overturned the South's racial order and imperiled the region's very existence. Less than thirty years later, as southern white supremacists took steps to limit black political participation and overturn what remained of the constitutional legacies of Reconstruction, they set out to ensure that the nation would not make the same mistake again.

When they were feeling charitable, white southern commentators argued that the northern architects of Reconstruction simply had not known any better. *Uncle Remus* author Joel Chandler Harris believed that any injustice suffered by an African American since the war "has been almost entirely due to the unwise and unnecessary crusade inaugurated in his behalf by the politicians of the North, who neither knew nor cared anything for the situation at the South."[26] Others cited more sinister motives. Mississippi's James K. Vardaman was not one to mince words. "The crime of all crimes," he claimed, "was committed when, in the agonizing spasm of infuriated men, just after the Civil War, the North expressed its hatred of the white people of the South in the amendments to the Constitution which vested the negro with all the rights and privileges of citizenship."[27] Whether they chalked it up to ignorance or malice, however, two points were particularly salient. First, Jim Crow propagandists cast Reconstruction as the most wrongheaded and unnatural experiment in US history. Second, they uniformly agreed that northern control of southern race relations was a defining characteristic of the period. This reading of Reconstruction vindicated the conduct of the white supremacist South and presented a powerful argument against further federal interventionism.

Thomas Dixon Jr.'s 1902 novel *The Leopard's Spots* offers a striking sketch of northern racial ignorance in the figure of Miss Susan Walker, a Boston philanthropist who appears in the novel only long enough to get the worst of an encounter with John Durham, a preacher whose southern chivalry does not extend to ignorant Yankees. In the wake of the Civil War, Miss Walker arrives in the fictional North Carolina town of Hambright, prepared to devote her "life and fortune" to the "education and the elevation of the Negro race."[28] In typical northern fashion, however, Miss Walker's philanthropy combines an inflated sense of self-worth with an almost total lack of firsthand experience with black people. Her half-baked plans, Durham fears, will only exacerbate southern racial strife. "In the settlement of this Negro question you are an insolent interloper," he thunders. "You're worse; you are a [willful], spoiled child of rich and powerful parents playing with matches in a powder-mill."[29] Durham, the white southerner, plays the role of the hardened realist, fearful for the future of the South and entirely pessimistic regarding the possibility of African American improvement. Miss Walker is the flighty northern idealist, an impulsive philanthropist whose previous good works include the construction of a "home for homeless cats" in Boston.[30] Reconstruction proved that white southern knowledge must triumph over northern theories, Dixon insisted. In the midst of its racial crisis, the South could little afford to indulge in sentiment and philanthropy.

Dixon was not the only southern propagandist to evoke the scourge of meddlesome postwar interlopers in an attempt to ward off latter-day interventionism. A number of commentators turned to the memory of the carpetbaggers—northern migrants who, according to the prevailing mythology of Reconstruction, moved south after the war to rob, plunder, and sow racial strife. As historian Ted Tunnell has shown, a concerted campaign of character defamation and propaganda in the 1860s produced most of the negative images that consigned the carpetbagger to historical infamy.[31] The 1890s and 1900s would see the rebirth and solidification of the "terrible carpetbagger" stereotype. At a symposium on race relations held in Montgomery, Alabama, Clifton R. Breckenridge of Kentucky critiqued the "locusts of Egypt," the "professional patriot, the mountebank, the harpy, the carpet-bagger."[32] At the same conference, Hilary Herbert insisted that "it was the carpet-bagger that drew the color line."[33] Virginian Myrta Lockett Avary offered a similar treatment in her 1906 memoir. "The carpet-bagger was the all-important figure in Dixie after the war. He was lord of our domain; he bred discord between races, kept up war between sections, created riots and published the tale of them, laying all blame on whites."[34] The carpetbagger stereotype proved well suited to the political needs of turn-of-the-century white supremacy. To raise the specter of the carpetbagger was to none-too-subtly remind northern readers of the sordid history of northern involvement in the racial affairs of the South.

Thomas Nelson Page and Joel Chandler Harris, two of the most popular southern authors of the postwar era, each published Reconstruction-themed novels around the turn of the twentieth century. Both Page's *Red Rock* (1898) and Harris's *Gabriel Tolliver* (1902) took scheming, conniving carpetbaggers as their central villains. In Harris's novel, the arrival of the carpetbagger Gilbert Hotchkiss signals the onset of Radical Reconstruction in Shady Dale, Georgia. An abolitionist and philanthropist, Hotchkiss sees in Reconstruction an opportunity to put his theories to the test. After doing all he can to promote a "spirit of incendiarism among the negroes," however, the "ill-informed emissary of race hatred and sectional prejudice" is summarily shot by one of his black constituents.[35] If Harris at least accorded his carpetbag villain the benefit of a sincere (though misguided) belief in racial equality, Page's Jonadeb Leech proves to be every bit the odious bloodsucker that his name suggests. Leech has no particular regard for black rights or citizenship, but finds in the Reconstruction of the South a perfect opportunity for self-aggrandizement. Leech is the embodiment of corrupt carpetbagger rule, the "vampire, sucking the life-blood of the people; the harpy, battering on the writhing body of the prostrate State."[36] In each case, northern involvement in southern race politics was figured as corrupt, cynical, and dangerous. Though Harris and Page wrote about Reconstruction, their warnings about outside interference retained their salience. The carpetbaggers had been chased from the scene, but their memory lived on.

+ + +

On one level, white supremacist treatments of Reconstruction strove to set the period apart from the mainstream of US political and social history. By consigning Reconstruction to the distant (or not so distant) past, Jim Crow propagandists hoped to contain its radicalism. They argued that Reconstruction was an aberration, a tragic mistake, a dark era to be studied at a distance but never repeated. By extension, the issues that animated the sectional struggle of the postwar decades—notably federal support of African Americans' civil and political rights—became relics of a bygone age, fossils with little relevance in the turn-of-the-century world. At the same time, however, white supremacist commentators claimed that the all-too-real legacies of Reconstruction continued to haunt the South. In the imaginative landscape of southern white supremacy, Reconstruction was very much alive, a matter to be treated in the *present tense* rather than the past. In this guise, it offered a one-size-fits-all explanation for the violent excesses of Jim Crow. Disfranchisement, segregation, and racial violence were simply the fruit of the lessons learned during Reconstruction. White southerners still lived in a world indelibly shaped by Reconstruction.

Since the most tangible legacies of Reconstruction were constitutional, it is unsurprising that some turn-of-the-century white supremacists called for an end to the United States' experiment in universal manhood suffrage via the overturning of the Fifteenth Amendment. Alfred Moore Waddell, who spearheaded the 1898 Wilmington, North Carolina racial massacre, argued that "the true remedy" for southern political turmoil "is to be found in the repeal, or modification, of the Fifteenth Amendment."[37] Relying on the familiar distinction between southern race knowledge and northern abstraction, Waddell scoffed that "'Doctrina[ir]es' and moralists may theorize and dogmatize forever, but they can not convince an Anglo-Saxon that Negroes ought to participate in the government of white men and a statesman will always recognize this insuperable fact in dealing with the Negro problem in the South."[38] Mississippi's James K. Vardaman was equally forthright. "The nation should correct the error—this stupendous solecism," Vardaman said with reference to the Fifteenth Amendment. "Now is the time to do it, and I believe the Southern people should take the initiative. They are familiar with all the facts; they alone are capable of informing the world of the profound, God-stamped, time-fixed and unalterable incompetency of the negro for citizenship in a white man's country . . . the nation should act in this matter, and act now."[39]

Most recognized, however, that the official repeal of the Fifteenth Amendment was highly unlikely. More to the point, it was unnecessary. Though the Amendment remained in force, it had been practically annulled in most southern states by the first years of the twentieth century. In rehashing the history of Reconstruction, southern white supremacists did not need to convince Yankees to formally abrogate the Reconstruction amendments. They required only tacit acquiescence from the federal government as the southern states systematically invalidated the Fifteenth Amendment in practice. "The simple truth is that Negro suffrage was the most artificial creation ever known to our history," racial theorist Alfred Holt Stone explained.[40] "The South did not disfranchise this ignorant and helpless horde in order to get control of political affairs," but to bring an unnatural state of affairs to a merciful end.[41] "What the Negro needs just now is a political 'rest cure,'" Stone concluded. "His daily litany should include a prayer to be let alone."[42] Black suffrage was an anomaly, a naïve experiment foisted upon the defeated South during the stormy days of Reconstruction. This fact could no longer be denied. Southern race knowledge must rule, free from outside interference. "The folly and the futility of Northern tutelage is now fully demonstrated; and the Negro is again under the tutelage of the South, to remain there until the race problem is finally settled," North Carolina educator George T. Winston told a national political science conference. Winston urged his audience to recognize the inevitable: "The withdrawal of the Negro from politics is now being accomplished by legislation in the various Southern States." Disfranchisement was a tempered and rational response to untenable circumstances, one that was in the best interests of all southerners, black and white. If left to their own devices, white southerners would soon solve the race problem. He warned, however, that "if this is interrupted by the North, and the old battle of Reconstruction fought again, the result will be the complete and final estrangement of the two races."[43]

By the first years of the twentieth century, therefore, white supremacists felt that they had found a solution to the vexing race problem. The systematic disfranchisement of black voters solved the political crisis born during Reconstruction, while the rise of street-level segregation reserved the pleasures of modernity for the exclusive benefit of the white South. All that remained was to convince the North and the federal government to refrain from interference. This was the explicit goal of Thomas Nelson Page's 1904 treatment of the race question, a book whose title—*The Negro: The Southerner's Problem*—perfectly captured its larger arguments. Though he clearly wrote with a northern audience in mind, Page was adamant that the resolution of the race question must be left to the white South. It is no surprise that much of Page's evidence for these claims was drawn from Reconstruction. "The chief trouble that arose between the two races in the South after the war grew out of the ignorance at the North of the actual conditions at the South," Page claimed.[44] Incapable of understanding the complexities of southern race relations, northern partisans and ideologues attempted to legislate impossibilities. Reconstruction "was a subject which called for the widest knowledge and the broadest wisdom," but "both knowledge and wisdom appeared to have been resolutely banished in the treatment of the subject."[45] The Reconstruction Amendments, according to Page, were the "offspring of ignorance and passion. They were adopted partly to punish the South, partly to arm the Negroes with a weapon which would enable them to hold their own against the whites, and partly to perpetuate the ascendancy of the radical wing of the Republican party."[46] Page concluded that "the whole country owes a debt to the Southern people who withstood to the end the policy of the misguided fanatics and politicians who would have put the South permanently under Negro domination."[47]

Of course, Page's engagement with the history of Reconstruction was merely a means to an end. Like his contemporaries, Page mobilized Reconstruction precisely because it proved politically effective and intellectually useful in discussing turn-of-the-century racial affairs. Page's argument about Reconstruction—that it was a nightmarish period of racial chaos brought about by northern ignorance and federal overreach—fed naturally into his treatment of political disfranchisement and Jim Crow segregation. Toward the end of the book, Page reiterated that "many, if not most, of the difficulties of the race problem since the war have been caused, or at least increased, by the ignorance of those outside the South, who, most cocksure of their positions where they were most in error, have tried to force a solution on lines contrary to natural and unchangeable laws."[48] Free of the "continual harping" of "the Northern press and the politicians," Page insisted, native southerners of both races would find a satisfactory solution to the race question. "When the self-righteous shall be fewer than they are now and the teachings which have estranged the races shall become more sane," Page concluded, "the great Anglo-Saxon race, which is dominant, and the Negro race, which is amiable, if not subservient, will adjust their differences more in accordance with the laws which must eventually prevail, and the old feeling of kindness, which seems, under the stress of antagonism, to be dying away, will once more reassert itself."[49] The race question, Page insisted, must be left to those who understood it; the black man was the southerner's problem.

+ + +

*The Clansman* (1905), Thomas Dixon's second Reconstruction novel, can be fruitfully read as a capstone to the memorial practices of Jim Crow–era white supremacy. Though the novel is well known for its virulent racism, the politics of region are every bit as central to Dixon's message as the politics of race.[50] Ben Cameron, Confederate veteran and the founder of the Ku Klux Klan, receives top billing in the novel. However, the journey of Austin Stoneman—the Radical Republican architect of Reconstruction and a thinly veiled proxy for Pennsylvania congressman Thaddeus Stevens—is at the heart of *The Clansman*'s political vision. *The Clansman* opens in Washington, DC, where Stoneman almost single-handedly presides over Radical Reconstruction. Though the precise motivation for his actions is never made entirely clear—Dixon cites insanity, zealotry, a raging ego, hatred for the South, elevated notions of black capability, and the malicious influence of a mixed-race housekeeper, among others—Stoneman seizes upon the power vacuum left after Abraham Lincoln's assassination and immediately begins "planning a reign of terror for the South."[51]

Halfway through the novel, a doctor advises an ailing Stoneman to retire to the warmer climes of Dixie for rest and recuperation. Joined by his grown children Phil and Elsie, Stoneman settles upon the town of Piedmont, South Carolina, where the remainder of the novel takes place. Delegating responsibility for the day-to-day control of Reconstruction South Carolina to a mixed-race crony, Austin Stoneman falls into a coma, sparing him direct contact with the chaos he has unleashed. The white people of the South are not so lucky. Dixon's Reconstruction is an extended nightmare, complete with bullying black soldiers, illiterate legislators, rampant corruption, and a brutal attack on the womanhood of the South. The horrors of Reconstruction force Ben Cameron to drastic measures. He founds the Ku Klux Klan, a secret order dedicated to ridding the South of Reconstruction and its black menace.

Upon his recovery, Austin Stoneman remains unswerving in his support for black domination. He uses his substantial political clout to wage war on the Klan, rescinding habeas corpus and secretly engineering the execution (without trial) of Klan leader Cameron. It is only when Stoneman discovers that his guards do not have Cameron, but his own son Phil, in their custody, that he begins to see the light. Suddenly, the horrors of Reconstruction—the unjust rule, the incapable management, the constant danger to life and limb—come crashing down on the program's own architect. Stoneman has only one option: to put his faith in the Ku Klux Klan. A coordinated Klan assault, led by Ben Cameron, frees the falsely condemned Phil Stoneman and ends black Republican rule in South Carolina in a single spasm of racial violence. In his last line of the novel, Stoneman announces his conversion: "The Klan!—The Klan! No? Yes! It's true—glory to God, they've saved my boy!—Phil—Phil!"[52]

Dixon's decision to move the Austin Stoneman/Thaddeus Stevens character to the South—an ingenious, if ahistorical, flourish of authorial license—is central to the message of *The Clansman.* Throughout, the novel deploys a predictable sort of regional arithmetic. When exposed to the South's race problem firsthand, northerners come to recognize the wisdom and necessity of southern-style white supremacy. Phil Stoneman grasps the matter almost immediately, even asking to join the Ku Klux Klan. Elsie Stoneman, out of love for her father, resists for a while longer, before finally submitting to the essential truth of white supremacy (and the charms of Ben Cameron). It is Austin Stoneman himself, however, who is the great prize. Early in the novel, safely ensconced in his Washington office and relying on abstract notions of equality and democracy in lieu of any sort of actual knowledge, Stoneman foments a racial revolution. The move to the South brings Stoneman closer to the belly of the beast, but his seclusion allows him to continue to ignore reality and cultivate his lofty theories. Finally, however, Phil's false imprisonment forces Stoneman to confront the actual facts. With his son's life in the balance, he comes to understand the position of the white South. He has seen the light, grasping the race conflict for what it is. Dixon's novel insists that notions of black equality are only tenable if accompanied by a complete divorce from actual conditions. Introduce a Yankee to the true face of the Negro Problem, and he could not help but embrace the tenets of white supremacy.

In *The Clansman,* Dixon reimagined Reconstruction through the lens of Jim Crow. Rather than imposing its racial theories on the South, Dixon's North (in the person of Stoneman) accepts the dictates of white supremacy. The lesson Stoneman learns is precisely that which Dixon hoped to teach all turn-of-the-century northerners: when it came to race relations, southerners simply knew better. The rest of the nation should defer to their expertise. The tragedy of Reconstruction had been rooted in a failure to understand this timeless truth. The success of Jim Crow demanded the acceptance of it.

+ + +

In discussing Reconstruction, turn-of-the-century white southerners were largely speaking about their own place and time. Popular memory reflected and advanced the needs of the nascent Jim Crow regime, producing a narrative of Reconstruction that had as much to say about region as it did about race. As southern white supremacists sought to overturn the democratic structures erected during Reconstruction, they kept a wary eye on the North. Though historians tend to follow Michael Perman in declaring the failure of the Lodge Federal Elections Bill "the end of an era" for the northern Republican Party, this view assumes a critical distance that turn-of-the-century Americans did not possess.[53] Contemporary southerners had no way of knowing that the days of northern involvement in southern racial affairs were over. Their partisan memory of Reconstruction served as a sort of cultural inoculation against further federal interventionism. As Jason Morgan Ward's essay in this volume suggests, the memory of Reconstruction would continue to do so for decades to come. Juxtaposing their own adept handling of the Negro Problem in the 1890s with the North's abortive attempts to legislate equality in the 1860s and 1870s, turn-of-the-century southern white supremacists insisted that history had borne out their status as the self-appointed arbiters of the region's racial norms. The sheer frequency with which Jim Crow propagandists turned to Reconstruction highlights the centrality of this cultural work to the destruction of racial democracy. In the end, this white supremacist memory of Reconstruction was less a reflection of the past than an attempt to shape the future.

NOTES

1. Portions of this chapter appeared in *Stories of the South: Race and the Reconstruction of Southern Identity, 1865–1915,* by K. Stephen Prince (Chapel Hill: University of North Carolina Press, 2014). For an overview of disfranchisement, see Michael Perman, *Struggle for Mastery: Disfranchisement in the South, 1888–1908* (Chapel Hill: University of North Carolina Press, 2000).

2. See Grace Hale, *Making Whiteness: The Culture of Segregation in the South* (New York: Vintage, 1999), esp. 121–99.

3. For an overview of southern lynching, see W. Fitzhugh Brundage, *Lynching in the New South: Georgia and Virginia, 1880–1930* (Urbana: University of Illinois Press, 1993); for spectacle lynching as a tool of white supremacy, see Hale, *Making Whiteness,* 199–240, and Amy Louise Wood, *Lynching and Spectacle: Witnessing Racial Violence in America, 1890–1940* (Chapel Hill: University of North Carolina Press, 2009).

4. Stephen Kantrowitz, *Ben Tillman and the Reconstruction of White Supremacy* (Chapel Hill: University of North Carolina Press, 2000), 3. Kantrowitz's claim recalls Stuart Hall's notion that "hegemonizing is hard work," quoted in George Lipsitz, "The Struggle for Hegemony," *Journal of American History* (June 1988): 146–47. For other studies that emphasize the "work" of white supremacy, see C. Vann Woodward, *The Strange Career of Jim Crow* (New York: Oxford University Press, 1955). See also Glenda Elizabeth Gilmore, *Gender and Jim Crow: Women and the Politics of White Supremacy in North Carolina, 1896–1920* (Chapel Hill: University of North Carolina Press, 1996), esp. 61–118.

5. In *The Crucible of Race,* Joel Williamson offers a brief analysis of this aspect of southern white supremacy, noting the existence of "a virtual crusade in which the South undertook to explain itself to the North." Joel Williamson, *The Crucible of Race: Black/White Relations in the American South Since Emancipation* (New York: Oxford University Press, 1984), 330.

6. See Fred Hobson, *Tell About the South: The Southern Rage to Explain* (Baton Rouge: Louisiana State University Press, 1983); Angie Maxwell, *The Indicted South: Public Criticism, Southern Inferiority, and the Politics of Whiteness* (Chapel Hill: University of North Carolina Press, 2014); Jennifer Rae Greeson, *Our South: Geographic Fantasy and the Rise of National Literature* (Cambridge, MA: Harvard University Press, 2010). On Grady, see William A. Link, *Atlanta, Cradle of the New South: Race and Remembering in the Civil War's Aftermath* (Chapel Hill: University of North Carolina Press, 2013), esp. 136–68. On the United Daughters of the Confederacy, see Karen L. Cox, *Dixie's Daughters: The United Daughters of the Confederacy and the Preservation of Confederate Culture* (Gainesville: University Press of Florida, 2003).

7. Glenn Feldman has dubbed this process the "Reconstruction syndrome." Glenn Feldman, *The Disfranchisement Myth: Poor Whites and Suffrage Restriction in Alabama* (Athens: University of Georgia Press, 2004), esp. 37–42. See also Hale, *Making Whiteness,* 75–84; Bruce E. Baker, *What Reconstruction Meant: Historical Memory in the American South* (Charlottesville: University of Virginia Press, 2007), 21–43.

8. See Perman, *Struggle for Mastery,* 224–44; Charles W. Calhoun, *Conceiving a New Republic: The Republican Party and the Southern Question, 1869–1900* (Lawrence: University Press of Kansas, 226–59).

9. Pierre Nora, "Between Memory and History: Les Lieux des Memoire," *Representations* (Spring 1989): 7–24.

10. For studies that focus on memory and the creation of southern identity (or identities), see Charles Reagan Wilson, *Baptized in Blood: The Religion of the Lost Cause* (Athens: University of Georgia Press, 1980); Gaines Foster, *Ghosts of the Confederacy: Defeat, the Lost Cause, and the*

*Emergence of the New South, 1865–1915* (New York: Oxford University Press, 1987); W. Fitzhugh Brundage, ed., *Where These Memories Grow: History, Memory, and Southern Identity* (Chapel Hill: University of North Carolina Press, 2000); David W. Blight, *Race and Reunion: The Civil War in American Memory* (Cambridge, MA: Harvard University Press, 2001), esp. 255–99; Cox, *Dixie's Daughters;* W. Fitzhugh Brundage, *The Southern Past: A Clash of Race and Memory* (Cambridge, MA: Harvard University Press, 2005), 12–137; Baker, *What Reconstruction Meant;* Caroline E. Janney, *Burying the Dead But Not the Past* (Chapel Hill: University of North Carolina Press, 2008).

11. On the Lodge Bill, see Calhoun, *Conceiving a New Republic,* 226–59; Perman, *Struggle for Mastery,* 38–43.

12. On the relationship between the Lodge Bill and *Why the Solid South?,* see Baker, *What Reconstruction Meant,* 22–27.

13. Hilary A. Herbert, et al., *Why the Solid South?; or, Reconstruction and Its Results* (Baltimore: R. H. Woodward, 1890), xv.

14. Herbert, *Why the Solid South?,* xvi.

15. Herbert, *Why the Solid South?,* xvii.

16. Herbert, *Why the Solid South?,* 84.

17. Herbert, *Why the Solid South?,* 348.

18. Herbert, *Why the Solid South?,* 111.

19. Walter Guild, "A Plea from the South," *Arena,* November 1900, 40.

20. Furnifold Simmons, "The Political Future of the Southern Negro," *Independent,* 28 June 1906, 1525; clipping, unknown newspaper, Series 5, Box 2, Scrapbook 11, Benjamin Ryan Tillman Papers, Clemson University Special Collections, Clemson, SC.

21. "The Negro Problem: How it Appeals to a Southern White Woman," *Independent,* 18 September 1902, 2224.

22. *Race Problems of the South. Report of the Proceedings of the First Annual Conference Held Under the Auspices of the Southern Society for the Promotion of the Study of Race Conditions and Problems in the South. At Montgomery, Alabama, May 8, 9, 10 A.D. 1900* (Richmond, VA: B. F. Johnson, 1900), 21.

23. *The Possibilities of the Negro in Symposium* (1904; repr., New York: Negro Universities Press, 1969), 9.

24. William Benjamin Smith, *The Color Line: A Brief in Behalf of the Unborn* (New York: McClure, Phillips, 1905), 23.

25. Alfred Holt Stone, *Studies in the American Race Problem* (New York: Doubleday, Page, 1908), 265.

26. Joel Chandler Harris, "The Negro of To-Day: His Prospects and His Discouragements," *Saturday Evening Post,* 30 January 1904, 3.

27. "Governor Vardaman on the Negro," *Current Opinion,* March 1904, 271.

28. Thomas Dixon Jr., *The Leopard's Spots: A Romance of the White Man's Burden, 1865–1900* (1902; repr., New York: A. Wessels, 1908), 44.

29. Dixon, *Leopard's Spots,* 47.

30. Dixon, *Leopard's Spots,* 49.

31. Ted Tunnell, "Creating the 'Propaganda of History': Southern Editors and the Origins of *Carpetbagger* and *Scalawag,*" *Journal of Southern History* 72, no. 4 (November 2006). See also Richard N. Current, *Those Terrible Carpetbaggers: A Reinterpration* (New York: Oxford University Press, 1988).

32. *Race Problems of the South,* 172.

33. *Race Problems of the South,* 35.

34. Myrta Lockett Avary, *Dixie After the War: An Exposition of Social Conditions Existing in the South, in the Twelve Years Succeeding the Fall of Richmond* (New York: Doubleday, Page, 1906), 325.

35. Joel Chandler Harris, *Gabriel Tolliver: A Story of Reconstruction* (1902; repr., Ridgewood, NJ: Gregg Press, 1967), 182, 176.

36. Thomas Nelson Page, *Red Rock: A Chronicle of Reconstruction* (New York: Charles Scribner's Sons, 1898), 564.

37. *Race Problems of the South,* 44.

38. *Race Problems of the South,* 47.

39. "Governor Vardaman on the Negro," *Current Opinion,* March 1904, 271.

40. Stone, *Studies in the American Race Problem,* 359.

41. Stone, *Studies in the American Race Problem,* 384.

42. Stone, *Studies in the American Race Problem,* 420.

43. George T. Winston, "The Relation of the Whites to the Negroes," *Annals of the American Academy of Political and Social Science* (July 1901): 116–17.

44. Thomas Nelson Page, *The Negro: The Southerner's Problem* (New York: Charles Scribner's Sons, 1904), 32.

45. Page, *The Negro,* 34.

46. Page, *The Negro,* 130.

47. Page, *The Negro,* 124.

48. Page, *The Negro,* 293.

49. Page, *The Negro,* 203–4.

50. On Dixon, see Williamson, *Crucible of Race,* 140–76. See also Michele K. Gillespie and Randal L. Hall, eds., *Thomas Dixon, Jr. and the Birth of Modern America (Baton Rouge: Louisiana State University Press, 2006).* For northern responses to Dixon and *The Clansman,* see Akiyo Ito Okuda, "'A Nation is Born': Thomas Dixon's Vision of White Nationhood and his Northern Supporters," *Journal of American Culture* 32, no. 3 (September 2009): 214–31.

51. Thomas Dixon Jr., *The Clansman* (1905; repr., Lexington: University of Kentucky Press, 1970), 17.

52. Dixon, *The Clansman,* 373.

53. Perman, *Struggle for Mastery,* 41.

2

# Causes Lost and Found

## *Remembering and Refighting Reconstruction in the Roosevelt Era*

JASON MORGAN WARD

They can't reform us and they can't reconstruct us. . . . I like the unchangeable character of the South. I like her ability to withstand criticism and to repel the advances of uplifters.

—Josiah Bailey, North Carolina senator, 1938

The negroes are not going to vote in La. and Miss. The KKKs are not extinct. They put down carpetbag rule 70 years ago, and they will put it down again.

—B. W. Morgan, white Louisianan, 1942

In October 1942, the United States House of Representatives voted—by a three-to-one margin—to outlaw the poll tax. Eight southern states still required it. Combined with a host of other disfranchisement tactics, the poll tax had effectively barred most southern blacks from casting ballots since the turn of the century. By the outbreak of World War II, the national campaign to abolish the tax had become a liberal cause célèbre and a flashpoint for racial controversy. Anti–poll tax advocates emphasized the measure's role in depressing white *and* black voter turnout while entrenching a disproportionately powerful southern bloc on Capitol Hill, but many diehards down South interpreted the campaign as a direct assault on white supremacy. The same week that the anti–poll tax bill passed the House, Mississippi mobs lynched three victims in a single week. In Georgia, the state public safety commissioner and other prominent allies of race-baiting governor Eugene Talmadge sanctioned the backlash by calling on white men to join their newly formed "Vigilantes, Inc." If the federal government insisted on "waging war against the white people of the South," a Mississippi congressman warned, they could expect more of the same.[1]

As racial backlash surged across the southern home front, filibustering senators—not marauding mobs—ultimately saved the poll tax. Barely a month after the unprecedented House vote, the anti–poll tax bill died an inglorious death on the Senate floor. For his role in the filibuster, Mississippi senator Theodore Bilbo—by then the Senate's most infamous and outspoken white supremacist—received hearty congratulations from like-minded diehards. One of them, a white lawyer from eastern Arkansas, praised Bilbo's fierce defense of the poll tax and shared his father's memories of a time before Jim Crow. At 87 years old, Judge E. D. Robertson grew up in Helena, a bustling river port in the black-majority, cotton-covered Arkansas Delta. "He tells me that he was a big boy when the Civil War was over," the judge's son explained, "that negroes used to line up for two blocks long... waiting for the polls to open." Resentful whites used tricks and terrorism—from "fake pistol fight[s]" at the polls to Ku Klux Klan attacks—to intimidate black voters. "He said that they soon caught on to these things," the son explained, "but when they put the $1.00 poll tax to them they faded out of politics like dew in August before the morning sun." For father and son, the story summed up the stakes of civil rights struggles past and present. "Lots of Southern people would die and go to Hell . . . ," the younger Robertson warned, "before they would become subject to the negro race."[2]

This lesson in white supremacy, handed down from father to son, reveals that the distance between post–Civil War racial struggles and the modern civil rights movement is shorter than many realize. For white southerners in the Roosevelt era, Reconstruction represented more than a mystic memory. Men like James Robertson—the region's political and economic elite—were not only steeped in Lost Cause mythology but also raised by a generation that lived through Reconstruction and Redemption. Their direct link to the decades before Jim Crow—itself a political project designed to thwart another experiment in interracial democracy and civic equality—informed how white southerners responded to the perceived racial threats of the New Deal and the civil rights revolution that followed. Judge Roberston's memories dramatize the lessons that white southerners derived from Reconstruction and applied to contemporary racial politics. More importantly, these memories reveal a keen understanding of Jim Crow's constructed and contingent nature. If white supremacy could be won, it could be lost. If their fathers had built a new racial caste system in the wake of emancipation and enfranchisement, then black activists and their allies could tear it down.

Southern white supremacists traded in plantation nostalgia and claims of black contentment under Jim Crow, and frequently defended their racial order as organic and divinely ordained. However, Reconstruction memory served as a reminder of black determination and resistance. Rather than characterize civil rights activism as unprecedented and unnatural, Jim Crow's defenders resurrected the fears of "carpetbag rule" and "Negro domination" to awaken southern whites to the threat of a "second" Reconstruction. Faced with legislative and judicial challenges to poll taxes, white primaries, and segregated facilities, elites and everyday southerners frequently drew parallels between post–Civil War racial struggles and the controversies of the Roosevelt era. Meanwhile, they pondered the irony that the next "tragic era" would be ushered in not by radical Republicans, but by a Democratic Party hijacked by "carpetbagging" New Dealers.[3]

White supremacists invoked a distorted and contradictory strain of historical memory, in which "outside" forces threatened to undermine the dual myths of white unity and racial harmony in the Solid South. Since its inception in Reconstruction, white supremacists had mobilized the specter of the "carpetbagger" to exaggerate the threat of outsiders and downplay the role of native white southerners in challenges to the political status quo. Yet during the New Deal, as during Reconstruction, diehard white supremacists contended with internal challenges and rival factions as well as external threats. In the most solidly pro-Roosevelt corner of the country, they faced the reality that the memory of Reconstruction failed to fully account for the political transformations around them. Yet they persisted in this rhetoric precisely because of the power that it still held in southern political culture.[4]

During the 1930s and 1940s, when many could still recall a time before Jim Crow, the memory of Reconstruction gave shape and meaning to white supremacist politics. Anti–New Deal southerners invoked Reconstruction imagery and Lost Cause mythology to argue that new federal programs and policies would undermine the racial caste system. Furthermore, southern diehards lamented black voters' shifting party loyalties and rising clout in national politics as "Negro domination" redux. As African Americans abandoned the Republican Party in favor of Roosevelt, Solid South Democrats lamented their waning clout in the "white man's party" of their fathers. By World War II, southern white supremacists interpreted civil rights controversies as signs that another round of federal meddling and race militancy had arrived. In the decade before Dixiecrats and segregationists launched a white supremacist crusade draped in battle flags and drenched in Lost Cause rhetoric, a potent blend of myth and memory helped to dramatize gathering racial threats in a region still overwhelmingly loyal to Roosevelt. This racialized critique—popularized by southern elites and reflected in grassroots resentment—recast the New Deal as a repudiation of Redemption and a harbinger of another "carpetbag era." By examining how southern white supremacists understood the stakes of Reconstruction, we discover that they—like the black activists they battled—viewed the racial skirmishes of the Roosevelt era as a continuation of struggle rather than as echoes of a bygone era.[5]

From the earliest stirrings of anti–New Deal sentiment in the South, Roosevelt's critics raised the specter of federal intrusion and misguided social engineering. Southern critics, who traded in Reconstruction imagery and Lost Cause mythology, stressed from the outset the racial consequences of new federal policies. For example, the National Recovery Administration's (NRA) attempt to standardize wages and working conditions alarmed southern industrialists who rallied in defense of the region's segregated, low-wage labor system. Any codes and regulations that required equal pay, conservative businessmen argued, would not only undermine southern industry's competitive edge but also endanger their workers' "racial purity." These fears fueled the establishment of the Southern States' Industrial Council (SSIC), a regional network of right-wing businessmen who lobbied against New Deal reforms they deemed a threat to economic growth and the segregated status quo. From its founding in 1933, the SSIC invoked Reconstruction as an era of federal interference and economic stagnation. Comparing the NRA to a second "March to the Sea," SSIC executives warned that an administration representing the interests of the industrialized North would force southern industrialists to "again . . . eat the crumbs that drop from the tables of our richer neighbors."[6]

While some southern elites soured quickly on the New Deal, they faced an uphill battle convincing everyday folks to turn on their wildly popular president. The concerns of wealthy industrialists did not trickle down to mill villages and sharecropper cabins. For William Watts Ball, an early and outspoken anti-New Dealer, Roosevelt's class-based politics portended a return to Reconstruction-era radicalism. "It seems to me a conclusion of mathematical precision," the champion of "aristocratic" democracy lamented in 1936, "that if the propertyless shall number enough to decide the elections for president, governors and legislatures they will in time take the possessions of others for their own use. That, of course, was what the carpetbaggers and negroes tried to do and did." For Ball, a Confederate colonel's son, the emerging New Deal coalition of working-class whites and blacks harkened back to the interracial Republican and "fusion" governments that white Democrats had fought so hard to defeat in the late nineteenth century. Now, that threat emanated from within the "white man's party" of his father's generation.[7]

During the early years of the New Deal, such allusions to the horrors of Reconstruction failed to resonate. But by the late 1930s, the region's anti–New Deal hard core started to gain some political traction. Controversies over court-packing and the "Roosevelt recession" eroded the president's aura of invincibility, while the fight over federal antilynching legislation opened the door for white southerners to rally around race and region. In April 1937, as the US House debated an antilynching bill authored by New York congressman Joseph Gavagan, a Mississippi newspaper blasted northern Democrats for attempting to "threaten us with the Federal Government, as in Reconstruction days, when they forgot their White Brothers for others."[8] While the Gavagan Bill passed the House by a three-to-one margin, southern senators killed the companion bill with a record-breaking six-week filibuster replete with allusions to the "tragic era."[9]

Roosevelt refused to endorse antilynching legislation, but he championed an expanded program of regional development and openly challenged conservative southern Democrats who stood in his way. As the president attempted to reform the South's "feudal system," southern politicians decried the "Roosevelt purge" with more racially charged allusions to Reconstruction.[10] While right-wing businessmen still led the attack, their economic critique increasingly overlapped with charges that the New Deal posed a direct threat to white supremacy. That convergence of economic and racial anxieties compelled North Carolina senator Josiah Bailey to draft a "manifesto" of free enterprise, fiscal conservatism, and "state's rights" in 1937. The only southern senator to tout his role in the creation of the secretive, bipartisan Conservative Manifesto, Bailey instantly earned the admiration of anti-Roosevelt diehards. At an SSIC banquet in May 1938, the Confederate colonel's son delighted his "fellow feudalists" with a rousing and unreconstructed tribute to the "unchangeable character of the South." Every reformer, Bailey declared, "from 1865 to this good hour, and more in the last four years than in all the other years put together, has come down there to uplift us, and we have refused to be uplifted." As some of the region's wealthiest businessmen hooted and clapped their approval, the North Carolina senator boasted, "They can't reform us and they can't reconstruct us."[11]

While Bailey embraced his role as the South's poster boy for principled conservatism, he readily conceded that there were others in Washington more unreconstructed than he. Ellison "Cotton Ed" Smith, South Carolina's five-term senior senator, personified the intransigence that anti–New Deal southerners celebrated. A perennial thorn in the president's side, Smith had famously stormed out of the 1936 Democratic National Convention when a black minister rose to deliver the opening invocation. "Every power on earth of every administration has been exhausted on him," Bailey bragged at the Washington banquet, "but he is the same old southern democrat that Ed Smith was when he first came here.... They can't change him."[12] First elected to the Senate in 1908, Cotton Ed turned his sixth senatorial campaign into a Lost Cause extravaganza after President Roosevelt endorsed a pro–New Deal challenger. "Senator Smith is a white supremacy Democrat," read a typical campaign pamphlet, "his reelection will be a wholesome warning to the East." On the campaign trail, Cotton Ed reminded voters that "outside organizations" wanted him to lose. "Every red-blooded white man," he warned, should make sure that did not happen.[13]

He might have added *red-shirted,* as well. In one of the most dramatic invocations of Reconstruction memory in the Roosevelt era, some of Smith's most fervent supporters donned red shirts on Election Day in a tribute to the white vigilantes who had helped to oust the state's Reconstruction government in 1876. Sixty-two years later, Cotton Ed's Red Shirts patrolled polling places around Orangeburg and escorted ballot boxes to the courthouse for tallying. Later that night, two hundred Red Shirts drove to Columbia to celebrate with Cotton Ed. Standing under Wade Hampton's monument, wearing a red shirt, Smith urged his followers to stand guard against "the mongrel breed who would take us back to the horrid days of reconstruction." For now, though, they could celebrate another victory for white supremacy. "We conquered in '76 and we conquered in '38," Smith boomed. "We fought with bullets then, but today, thank God, we fought with ballots."[14]

As the New Deal stalled in the late 1930s, Reconstruction's lessons proved to be as malleable as they were resilient. White supremacists updated tragic-era narratives of Yankee persecution and Negro domination to reflect contemporary controversies and new foes. When Cotton Ed spoke of outside organizations and mongrel breeds taking aim at the white South, he conjured up the kind of images that haunted Thomas Dixon. Earlier and more emphatically than most southern diehards, the aging novelist had turned against Roosevelt. Convinced that Communists had infiltrated the New Deal, and horrified that northern Democrats were welcoming black voters into the Democratic fold, Dixon joined a smattering of disaffected southerners on a battle-flag-draped dais at the 1936 Grass Roots Convention. Quietly bankrolled by a few right-wing magnates, and rumored to be a springboard for Georgia governor Talmadge's presidential run, the gathering featured a barrage of rhetoric aimed at "Negroes, the New Deal, and Karl Marx." For Dixon and his ilk, that unholy trinity threatened to unleash a second Reconstruction more horrible than the first. After stumping for Republican presidential candidate Alf Landon—Talmadge's bid to unseat Roosevelt never materialized—Dixon devoted himself fully to a new trilogy aimed at exposing the intertwined evils of socialism and social equality.

Famous for his turn-of-the-century "Trilogy of Reconstruction"—*The Leopard's Spots, The Clansman,* and *The Traitor*—Dixon essentially updated his tragic-era plotlines by trading carpetbaggers and scalawags for New Dealers, NAACP activists, and Marxist agitators. In the *Flaming Sword,* the first and only volume of the planned trilogy, Dixon vented his political disgust through conservative southern "patriots" like Captain Tom Collier. "There has been since the Civil War but two classes of white men in the South, Southerners and renegades," the fictional Collier explains to a young lawyer who has spoken out against lynching. "In Reconstruction time . . . the renegades were called 'Scalawags.' . . . Today they're called Liberals. God save the mark! They're the same breed of pups." As for civil rights activists, Dixon described "a new Reconstruction Bill," authored by the NAACP, "which would destroy the sovereignty of the States and put the South under the rule of Federal bayonets." Liberalism and racial agitation set the stage for the novel's climactic scene, where a Communist-led "Nat Turner Legion" launches "a reign of terror—burning, murdering, and raping" its way across the South.[15]

Dixon's apocalyptic final novel, while widely panned as a "nightmare melodrama," illustrates a persistent trope of Reconstruction memory. Whether carpetbagger or Communist, the white South's enemies played the pied piper for hordes of impressionable and irrepressibly savage blacks. Just two decades after D. W. Griffith's *Birth of a Nation* brought to life Dixon's scenes of Reconstruction-era upheaval and embedded scenes of carpetbaggers and their marauding black minions in America's collective consciousness, anticommunists played on this fear that outside agitators and homegrown "renegades" would again work otherwise contented blacks into a frenzy. Of course, pushers of the prewar Red Scare engaged in some outside agitation as well. The Constitutional Educational League (CEL), an anticommunist clearinghouse based in New Haven, Connecticut, set up its southern beachhead in the Birmingham offices of Charles DeBardeleben's coal company. Alarmed by rising labor and civil rights activism in the region, and backed by Birmingham's "Big Mules," the CEL churned out antilabor and anti–civil rights propaganda replete with Reconstruction imagery. "A dangerous alien-bred and alien-minded Fifth Column has invaded an unsuspecting Southland," the CEL warned. Through labor unions, interracial meetings, and traveling puppet shows "on the problems of Negro farmers," southern subversives were working toward "the destruction of time-honored southern traditions." In a hyperbolic flourish that would have fit well in *The Flaming Sword,* the CEL warned of coming "race riots" and "revolutionary uprisings" that "would make Sherman's march to the sea seem tame and trivial."[16]

Like Dixon, anticommunists traded in apocalyptic Reconstruction rhetoric and imagery. But they also pointed out that their adversaries had derived very different lessons from Reconstruction. In *The Fifth Column in the South,* CEL head Joseph P. Kamp quoted a Congress of Industrial Organizations (CIO) organizer who argued that "Reconstruction, when the Negro freedmen and the poor white masses of the South stepped forward to take their place, in the government, was the most democratic period the South has ever seen." To Marxist subversives, Kamp suggested, Reconstruction provided a glimpse of interracial class consciousness and a blueprint for the overthrow of the South's "white ruling class." In rhetoric aimed squarely at readers steeped in tragic-era mythology, Kamp branded leftist subversives and reform-minded fellow travelers as "modern carpet-baggers."[17]

Both Dixon and Kamp could point to a smattering of leftist publications—authored by American Communists and assorted radicals—that did indeed celebrate Reconstruction as a blueprint for reforming a reactionary and racist South. Prominent politicians joined the attack by highlighting parallels between Reconstruction and the Communist Party's advocacy of self-determination for the Black Belt, most notably during the 1938 Senate filibuster against a federal antilynching bill. As concerns about domestic subversion mounted in the wake of the 1939 nonaggression pact between Hitler and Stalin, this Lost Cause–inflected anticommunist rhetoric moved from the Senate to the House. East Texas congressman Martin Dies, head of the Special House Committee on Un-American Activities, charged in 1940 that the northern wing of the Democratic Party was "politically controlled by foreigners and transplanted negroes." Having steered his committee from investigations of domestic fascists to an all-out search for Communists in civil rights, labor groups, and New Deal agencies, Dies concluded that progressive reform movements provided a "Trojan Horse" for Marxist revolutionaries. Dies devoted an entire chapter of his prewar anticommunist tract, *The Trojan Horse in America,* to the group he deemed most susceptible to Communist appeals—"Negroes." Like Dixon, Kamp, and other anticommunist propagandists, Dies portrayed reform-minded liberals and leftists as reincarnated carpetbaggers bent on manipulating impressionable southern blacks for selfish and nefarious ends.[18]

Emboldened by an anticommunist backlash, southern white supremacists stepped up their racialized critique of the New Deal as the nation mobilized for war. The establishment of the Committee on Fair Employment Practice (FEPC), which resulted from Roosevelt's 1941 executive order banning employment discrimination in federal agencies and defense industries, sparked widespread talk of another Reconstruction. Thomas Dixon's nephew Frank, Alabama's wartime governor, turned down a $2 million defense contract rather than submit to the new fair employment mandate. Such policies, he argued, would "break down the principle of segregation under which the white and Negro races have lived in peace together in the South for all the years since Reconstruction." By scuttling that hard-won racial truce, Dixon warned, the federal government sought once again to "set the Negro astride the necks of the white people of the South." Years before civil rights historians appropriated the term, Alabama newspaper editors lambasted the FEPC for attempting to "force a second reconstruction upon us" and applauded the governor for standing up to "New Deal radicals." Speaking before the Southern Society of New York, the governor updated his uncle's Reconstruction-era scenes for a new generation of Redeemers. "True patriots of the South," he pledged, "will drive out . . . negro using and [negro] loving Southerners . . . just as they did sixty odd years ago."[19]

The FEPC struck at the economic and social imperatives that drove Jim Crow, but attacks on disfranchisement measures threatened the system's political foundation. And while white supremacists could mystify de jure segregation as instinctive and timeless tradition, they defended disfranchisement as a necessary bulwark against the reentry of blacks into southern political life. If "social equality" lacked a clear historical precedent, civic equality most certainly did not. The Reconstruction nightmare, white southerners learned from an early age, proved that blacks were unfit to participate in political life. Their validation came not only from southern apologists, but from professional historians and textbooks as well. "One fact and one fact alone explains the attitude of most recent writers toward Reconstruction," W. E. B. Du Bois lamented in his pioneering and searing indictment of the reigning scholarly consensus. "They cannot conceive Negroes as men." Henry Lee Moon, a veteran black activist and perceptive political strategist, added that the image of the black voter as "singularly ignorant, venal, and corrupt" pervaded mid-century American politics.[20]

Electoral imperatives and egalitarian war aims compelled many non-southern politicians to back voting reforms. While fair employment directives emanated straight from the White House, the poll tax fight revealed a deeper sectional split. In the House, southern poll-tax defenders found themselves outnumbered three-to-one. Sobered by their colleagues' seeming indifference to their obsession with "negro domination," Dixie congressmen took solace in the inevitable southern filibuster in the Senate. For his prominent role in derailing the legislation, Mississippi senator Theodore Bilbo received congratulations from unreconstructed admirers across the South. "Pres. and Mrs. Roosevelt are always trying to put the bottom rail on top," ranted an Alabama leader of the United Confederate Veterans. "A race only a few years from the jungle of Africa can't be placed in the social plane with a race of higher culture."[21] Although he lived in a southern state that had already repealed its poll tax, a white Louisianan understood the stakes of the fight in Congress. "The KKK's are not extinct," he warned, "they put down carpetbag rule 70 years ago, and they will put it down again."[22]

Given how frequently white supremacists compared wartime racial reformers to carpetbaggers, it is striking how rarely they used those analogies to describe the totalitarian armies rampaging across Europe and Asia. Southern conservatives frequently blamed racial unrest on an Axis-inspired "fifth column" conspiracy, but most drew a distinction between federal incursion and foreign invasion. If forced to choose between a Nazi takeover and a second Reconstruction, some diehards flatly admitted that they would rather take their chances with Hitler. "I feel as do many thousands of true Southerners," a father of two soldiers declared, "that it might be better to lose this war, than to have victory with Negro equality and black domination." Like Senator Bilbo, who declared himself "as much a soldier in the preservation of the American way . . . as the boys fighting and dying on Guadalcanal," grassroots white supremacists perceived no conflict between battling the Axis and preserving white supremacy. "We the people of the south are as patriotic and determined to win this World War as any body . . . ," a white Louisianan argued during the poll tax fight, "but we might as well be under Hitler rule as to be under the rule of these boneheaded niggers here."[23]

In Mississippi, memories of "negro domination" and white counterrevolution fueled wartime defiance. The river port of Vicksburg, Mississippi's largest city during Reconstruction, dramatized this convergence of historical memory and diehard white supremacy. In 1875, white vigilantes fired on a Fourth of July rally and rampaged through the city in pursuit of fleeing black Republicans. A month later, the "white man's party" swept the local elections. The "Vicksburg troubles" provided the blueprint for a statewide campaign of terror and fraud by white Democrats that ousted the state's interracial Republican government.[24] Sixty-seven years later, the birthplace of the "Mississippi plan" maintained its hard-edged commitment to white rule. After the House voted to abolish the poll tax, Vicksburg's mayor lamented "the beginning of another carpet bag era." Blasting the bill as "an outright invasion of state rights" and "a knife plunged into the very heart of local self government by what we thought was *our party*," Mayor J. C. Hamilton maintained that Vicksburg blacks—"the happiest people in the world"—wanted no part in politics. Local whites echoed the mayor's claim that federal civil rights legislation would provoke "another civil war in this country."[25]

As racial tensions rose in the months after Pearl Harbor, gory predictions moved from the fringe to the front page. White moderates attempted to chart a middle ground between reform and reaction, and they invoked Reconstruction memory to stress the stakes of wartime racial turmoil. Blaming the crisis on "negro agitators" and "white rabble-rousers," Richmond newspaperman Virginius Dabney appropriated the latter faction's sanguinary rhetoric in an *Atlantic Monthly* editorial. "Unless saner counsels prevail," the prominent southern liberal warned in early 1943, "we may have the worst internal clashes since Reconstruction, with hundreds, if not thousands, killed and amicable race relations set back for decades." University of North Carolina sociologist Howard Odum, who spent the early months of the war compiling a "catalogue of rumors, tensions, conflicts, and trends," concluded in 1943's *Race and Rumors of Race* that the South stood at the brink of "the greatest crisis since the days of reconstruction." Civil rights advocates had resurrected "many of the same symbols of conflict and tragedy," Odum argued, and had inspired among white supremacists "a new unity in resisting, to the end they went to extremes reminiscent of the old days of reconstruction."[26]

The racial warnings from prominent southern moderates reveal that the use—and abuse—of history spanned the political spectrum. Embattled white moderates, who positioned themselves between the extremes of "race prejudice" and wartime egalitarianism, proved just as likely to deploy Reconstruction memories against civil rights advocates as diehard white supremacists did. Despite their progressive leanings, white moderates were schooled in the same Reconstruction mythology as the demagogues they denounced. In the fall of 1942, when the NAACP commissioned a native white Mississippian to survey southern "racial attitudes," the ghost of Reconstruction reared its head. Craigen Kennedy, a recent University of Alabama graduate, reported the "most bitterness and resentment" against "northern agitation" emanated from "the more liberal people . . . who are trying to do something constructive on this race problem."[27]

Indeed, several weeks of "liberal" lament had taken their toll on the young woman, who ultimately lapsed back into the tragic era narrative herself.

"I came down into the South this trip expecting to gather evidence to prove that this bitterness towards . . . ideas of racial equality was a result of anti-New Deal propaganda," she reported. "But it is not. It is pure and simple the result of this traditional strong emotional feeling for Northerners who try to tell Southerners how to run their problems." In a gloomy dispatch, typed "for irony's sake" on letterhead from Jackson, Mississippi's Robert E. Lee Hotel, Kennedy concluded that Reconstruction "is the root of the trouble now." White resentment of wartime racial change, she informed her NAACP contacts, "stems directly from the bitterness created 80 years ago." NAACP executive secretary Walter White deemed the Reconstruction analogies "absurd" and upbraided Kennedy for her "apparent capitulation to a way of thinking which is not even up to that of the more enlightened Southern white point of view." But if the young investigator's conclusions exasperated the NAACP head, her ambitious and revealing interviews reveal how deeply Reconstruction memory pervaded the racial politics of the wartime South.[28]

Histrionics and historical analogies belied how easily southern senators fended off wartime civil rights bills. Yet the legal challenge to the white primary, originating in Texas in 1938 and taken up by the US Supreme Court in early 1944, suggested that all three branches of the federal government had thrown in with the carpetbaggers. The court's ruling in *Smith v. Allwright* invalidated the chief bulwark against black participation in the Solid South's single-party politics. Unsurprisingly, the decision sparked a new round of Reconstruction analogies. South Carolina governor Olin Johnston, whose 1938 senatorial bid had crumbled in the face of "Cotton Ed" Smith's Red Shirt theatrics, wielded the memory of Reconstruction in a particularly evocative show of white supremacist defiance. On the heels of the Supreme Court decision, Johnston convened a special joint session of the state legislature. "Where you now sit," he reminded the legislators, "there sat a majority of negroes." South Carolina's legislators—all white, all Democrats—hardly needed a reminder. Many likely recalled D. W. Griffith's "historical facsimile" in *Birth of a Nation*—lifted directly from Thomas Dixon's *Clansman*—which depicted barefooted, leering, and chicken leg–clutching black legislators running amuck in the legislative chamber. "The records will bear me out," Johnston continued, "that fraud, corruption, immorality, and graft existed during that regime that has never been paralleled in the history of our State." Invoking the rhetoric and imagery of a "Second Reconstruction," Johnston argued that "the representatives of these agitators, scalawags, and unscrupulous politicians that called themselves white men . . . are in our midst today, and history will repeat itself unless we protect ourselves against this new crop of carpetbaggers and scalawags, who would use the colored race to further their own economic and political gains."[29]

By the final months of the war, invocations of Reconstruction memory became even more shrill and apocalyptic. As this rhetoric moved from the margins to the mainstream, white supremacists increasingly argued that the second Reconstruction would be far worse than the first. The FEPC, the most direct federal challenge to legalized segregation since Reconstruction, heightened fears that black activists and their white allies desired more than civic equality and economic opportunity. Combined with a wartime upsurge in egalitarian rhetoric and a shifting scholarly consensus on race, fair employment convinced white supremacists that the "new carpetbaggers" wanted to obliterate the color line altogether. Georgia senator Richard Russell, who like Olin Johnston had faced off against race-baiting Roosevelt critics during the 1930s, deemed the FEPC "the most sickening manifestation of the trend that is now in effect to force social equality and miscegenation of the white and black races on the South." One of the most powerful southerners in Washington, Russell predicted darker days ahead. "The real suffering and the heavy blows to our Southern civilization did not fall either during or immediately after the Civil War, despite Sherman's march and the terrors of Reconstruction," he lamented in mid-1944. "It seems that they were reserved for a few generations."[30]

Appeals for interracial unity and understanding disturbed southern white supremacists. The wartime campaign to lessen home-front friction and discredit Axis "super race" ideology enjoyed scholarly support, celebrity endorsements, and—in some cases—government funding. As Gene Weltfish, a Columbia University anthropologist and coauthor of the USO-commissioned pamphlet *The Races of Mankind,* explained to her southern critics, "the facts of science" would equip American soldiers and civilians to resist "the lies of Hitler and his henchmen." Such arguments not only called into question Jim Crow practices and southern patriotism, but also fueled fears that a second Reconstruction would wipe out the white race. "The historical Carpet Bag Politicians attempted to get the Negro's support by offering them 'Forty Acres of Land and a Mule,'" lamented Earnest Sevier Cox, a Richmond propagandist who had spent two decades lobbying the federal government to resettle black Americans in Africa. "The New Carpetbagger proposes to throw in a white wife with the mule and the land."[31]

Southern critics of the "cult of equality" complained that the war emergency had significantly weakened white supremacy's hold on national politics and culture. They had a point. But the claim that "social equality" represented a "new" threat or an expanded neo-carpetbagger agenda conveniently ignored both Reconstruction-era white supremacists' obsession with miscegenation, and historical depictions of carpetbaggers and scalawags as promiscuous race-mixers. Indeed, even as Cox lamented the fusion of "miscegenation ideals" with "war ideals," his most notorious political ally penned a segregationist call to arms that rehashed timeworn tales of Reconstruction regimes' "degenerate" sexual mores. To thwart the charge that southern slaveholders were "solely responsible for the racial mixture which has occurred in the United States," Theodore Bilbo claimed in *Take Your Choice: Separation or Mongrelization* that "many of the Northern carpet-baggers who came to the South following the war lived with Negro women." Scalawags, a constituent and admirer reminded the senator, "also believed in intermarriage and practiced it when one of them could find a negro woman low down enough to unite with them."[32]

To the extent that the wartime civil rights movement represented a second Reconstruction, the South's carpetbagger complex had primed the region for a furious postwar Redemption. A series of events—the ongoing FEPC fight, a wave of postwar racial attacks, and the 1948 Dixiecrat revolt against Truman's civil rights program—all suggested that the specter of Reconstruction would continue to overshadow white supremacist politics. Jim Crow apologists, from filibustering senators to Deep South scholars, continued to invoke the lessons of Reconstruction. Some familiar themes, like the parallels between carpetbaggers and Communists, seemed particularly adaptable to Cold War–era civil rights debates. Mississippi senator James O. Eastland, who spent the postwar months battling the establishment of a permanent FEPC and touring occupied Germany, equated those who attempted "to destroy the white race" during Reconstruction with the "Oriental hordes . . . stalking the streets of Western civilization as conquerors." Another outspoken FEPC opponent, Mississippi congressman William Colmer, argued that "the Soviet super minds" pined for a repeat of the "Carpet Bag days of the Reconstruction period," when "the White man was to become the slave of his Negro master."[33]

The Dixiecrat revolt—perhaps more than any event before or since—revealed both the lingering power and political limitations of Reconstruction memory. Conventions and campaign rallies, to quote the most authoritative history of the movement, were "historical pageants" replete with Reconstruction-era trappings. From planters' hats to Confederate garb to red shirts—to say nothing of battle flags—Dixiecrats "resurrected the symbols" of southern defiance. They cheered elderly attendees who, as one reporter explained, "remember the Reconstruction period and the strenuous campaign which ended the rule of the carpet-baggers."[34] But these paeans to causes lost and found obscured important tactical shifts that began well before the Dixiecrats came and went. Indeed, even as his Mississippi colleagues—and an overwhelming majority of his constituents—caught Dixiecrat fever after President Truman announced an ambitious civil rights program in early 1948, rookie senator John C. Stennis recognized the limits of segregationist arguments that revolved around race, region, and Reconstruction. Having succeeded the race-baiting Theodore Bilbo in 1947, Stennis personified the strategic and stylistic shift in anti–civil rights politics. In order to win the sympathy and support for "States Rights as a principle of government," Stennis argued, "we must divorce our thinking from (a) the so-called racial question, (b) the war between the States, (c) the South as a geographical region." In private conversations and constituent correspondence, Stennis still drew timeworn parallels between the civil rights struggle and "the unfortunate carpetbagger days," but publicly he stressed the movement's threat to "sound American constitutional government." Rather than pine for the idyllic antebellum order that Reconstruction had overturned, the postwar segregationists focused on preserving the "constitutional" counterrevolution that ushered in the Jim Crow era.[35]

Carpetbagger analogies failed to unite white southerners around a neo-Redeemer agenda. Furthermore, the civil rights movement's most perceptive opponents candidly admitted that Reconstruction's demise had not ushered in decades of racial harmony but rather a constant struggle to blot out its dangerous precedent. The violent white supremacist campaigns of the late nineteenth century, the racial backlash that followed World War I, and the explosive politics of the New Deal era all seemed to confirm North Carolina governor Charles B. Aycock's warning, in 1900, that the race issue was "a question that will not stay settled." In the wake of a legislative session that stripped the state's black citizens of their voting rights, Aycock grimly predicted, "Every generation will have the problem on their hands, and they will have to settle it for themselves." As K. Stephen Prince reminds us in this very collection, white southerners at the turn of the century did not interpret the federal government's failure to intervene against their white supremacist schemes in the 1890s and 1900s as evidence that the federal government could not or would not intervene eventually. If the question would not stay settled, then white southerners had to stand at post.[36]

Clyde Hoey, the youngest member of North Carolina's turn-of-the-century legislative session, lived long enough to see Governor Aycock's worst fears realized. Born in 1877—the year that Reconstruction ended—and elected to the US Senate in 1945, the former congressman and governor embodied—as one admirer remembered—"the things of the past." Hoey's father, a Confederate captain and heir apparent to a sprawling South Carolina plantation, struggled to navigate the turmoil of emancipation and Reconstruction. The younger Hoey, who remembered vividly his father's postwar economic troubles and imbibed his Lost Cause nostalgia, resented black Republicans' political resurgence in the 1890s. An advocate of "disfranchising all the Negroes possible," the rookie campaigner rode a wave of white supremacist backlash into the legislative session that adopted a grandfather clause, literacy tests, and poll-tax requirements. A half-century later, the US senator provided a living link to a time before Jim Crow. With his flowing white hair and antebellum bearing, Hoey embodied the unreconstructed southern statesman for a new generation of civil rights opponents. Yet Hoey's death in May 1954, the same week as the *Brown* decision, dramatized how far civil rights advocates and their white supremacist adversaries had come. Hoey may have died facing a portrait of Robert E. Lee, as the papers reported, but his southern colleagues had already concluded that the lessons of the past could neither fully explain their present nor help them navigate an uncertain future.[37]

Perhaps the greatest testament to Reconstruction's promise, Redemption's incomplete victory, and white supremacy's tenuous reign is that some of those present at Jim Crow's birth lived to witness its death throes. Far more kept alive the memory of a mythic past as they stood guard against ongoing threats to the racial status quo. While these "lessons" continued to infuse southern politics, their impact decreased as postwar segregationists ran up against the limits of racial and regional appeals. Yet the white supremacist strains of Reconstruction memory—a profoundly pessimistic view of black civic fitness, a pathological mistrust of interracial democracy, and a never-ending narrative of southern persecution—pervaded the civil rights era and persisted in its wake. A fitting legacy, perhaps, for an era that symbolized so much, yet settled so little.

NOTES

1. Glenda E. Gilmore, *Defying Dixie: The Radical Roots of Civil Rights, 1919–1950* (New York: Norton, 2008), 336–41; Linda Reed, *Simple Decency and Common Sense: The Southern Conference Movement, 1938–1963* (Bloomington: Indiana University Press, 1991), 65–78; "Defiant Dixie In Poll Tax Rout, Lynches 2, Forms Vigilantes," *New York Amsterdam Star-News,* 17 October 1942, 1; "This Is Utter Foolishness Which Will Do Harm Rather Than Good," *Tupelo (Miss.) Daily Journal,* 12 September 1942, 4; *Congressional Record,* 77th Cong., 2nd sess., 8078.

2. James Robertson to Theodore G. Bilbo, 31 May 1943, Box 1076, Folder 6, Theodore Gilmore Bilbo Papers, Special Collections, McCain Library and Archives, University of Southern Mississippi, Hattiesburg.

3. On the roots of "carpetbagger" rhetoric, see Ted Tunnell, "Creating 'The Propaganda of History': Southern Editors and the Origins of Carpetbagger and Scalawag," *Journal of Southern History* 72 (November 2006): 792. Tunnell notes that for whites in the Reconstruction era and beyond, the term *carpetbagger* "shaped southerners' worldview and formed the 'building blocks' of an ideology of resistance" that both helped inspire the overthrow of Reconstruction and that lived on for a century in politics and culture. Tunnell builds on the work of an earlier generation of historians who challenged the villainous stereotype of the carpetbagger. For the most comprehensive reappraisal, see Richard Nelson Current, *Those Terrible Carpetbaggers: A Reinterpretation* (New York: Oxford University Press, 1988).

4. Tunnell notes that anti-Reconstruction southerners first invoked "carpetbagger" and "scalawag" rhetoric in response to the 1867 constitutional conventions that occurred after the passage of the Reconstruction Act—meetings dominated not by northern-born whites but by an interracial coalition of native-born white and black southerners. Nevertheless, despite the scalawags' preponderance in postwar politics, the southern press preferred denunciations of carpetbaggers precisely because it exaggerated the role of outsiders in the region's Reconstruction regimes. Tunnell, "Creating 'The Propaganda of History,'" 794, 813.

5. In his recent survey of southern racial politics from the end of the Civil War through World War II, Glenn Feldman emphasizes how the white South's "Reconstruction syndrome" shaped the region's political culture through the Roosevelt era. "The most persistent product of

the Reconstruction trauma," Feldman argues, "was a lasting southern conception of the central government as something strange, powerful, menacing, and foreign, a voraciously tax-hungry alien force prone to meddlesomeness, never to be trusted, and only rarely to be complied with." See Feldman, *The Irony of the Solid South: Democrats, Republicans, and Race, 1865–1944* (Tuscaloosa: University of Alabama Press, 2013), 180. For the most exhaustive examination of how southerners understood and invoked the lessons of Reconstruction, see Bruce E. Baker, *What Reconstruction Meant: Historical Memory in the American South* (Charlottesville: University of Virginia Press, 2007).

6. George Brown Tindall, *The Emergence of the New South, 1913–1945* (Baton Rouge: Louisiana State University Press, 1967), 444; Katherine Rye Jewell, "As Dead as Dixie: The Southern States Industrial Council and the End of the New South, 1933–1954" (PhD diss., Boston University, 2010), 96–97.

7. W. W. Ball to J. Heyward Gibbes, 25 March 1936, Folder "1936, March–April"; W. W. Ball to Fitz Hugh McMaster, 27 June 1936, Folder "Letters, 1936, June"; both in Box 26, William Watts Ball Papers, Special Collections, Duke University, Durham, North Carolina.

8. "Lynching," Biloxi, Mississippi *Daily Herald,* 16 April 1937, 4.

9. Keith M. Finley, *Delaying the Dream: Southern Senators and the Fight against Civil Rights* (Baton Rouge: Louisiana State University Press, 2008), 30–33.

10. Franklin Delano Roosevelt, "The United States Is Rising and Is Rebuilding on Sounder Lines," 168; "Fireside Chat on Party Primaries," 395; both in Samuel I. Rosenman, ed., *The Public Papers and Addresses of Franklin Delano Roosevelt,* vol. 7 (New York: Macmillan, 1941).

11. "Southern States Industrial Council-Dinner Session Minutes," Washington, DC, 2 May 1938, 8, Box 1, Folder 4, Southern State Industrial Council Records, Tennessee State Library and Archives, Nashville, Tennessee; James T. Patterson, *Congressional Conservatism and the New Deal: The Growth of the Conservative Coalition in Congress, 1933–1939* (Lexington: University Press of Kentucky, 1967), 198–210; Douglas Carl Abrams. *Conservative Constraints: North Carolina and the New Deal* (Jackson: University Press of Mississippi, 1992), 243–44.

12. "SSIC-Dinner Session Minutes," 8.

13. "Race is Issue of Primaries in the South," *Chicago Defender,* 3 September 1938, 4; Susan Dunn, *Roosevelt's Purge: How FDR Fought to Change the Democratic Party* (Cambridge: Harvard University Press, 2010), 179–90.

14. Baker, *What Reconstruction Meant,* 101–2; "Midnight in Columbia," *Time,* 12 September 1938, 26.

15. Thomas Dixon, *The Flaming Sword,* ed. John David Smith (Lexington: University Press of Kentucky, 2005), 172, 272, 462; John David Smith, "'My Books are Hard Reading for a Negro': Tom Dixon and his African American Critics, 1905–1939," in Michelle K. Gillespie and Randal L. Hall, *Thomas Dixon Jr. and the Birth of Modern America* (Baton Rouge: Louisiana State University Press, 2006), 46–79.

16. K. W., "A Novel of Conflict," *New York Times Book Review,* 20 August 1939, BR10; Diane McWhorter, *Carry Me Home: Birmingham, Alabama, The Climactic Battle of the Civil Rights Revolution* (New York: Simon & Schuster, 2001), 51–55; Robert J. Norrell, "Labor at the Ballot

Box: Alabama Politics from the New Deal to the Dixiecrat Movement," *Journal of Southern History* 57 (May 1991): 217; Joseph P. Kamp, *The Fifth Column in the South* (New Haven, CT: Constitutional Educational League, 1940), 5, 8.

17. Kamp, *The Fifth Column in the South,* 6. When the CIO launched a post–World War II southern organizing drive, Kamp churned out a thirty-two-page pamphlet entitled *Communist Carpetbaggers in Operation Dixie* (New Haven, CT: Constitutional Educational League, 1946).

18. Baker, *What Reconstruction Meant,* 110–44; David Daniel Potenziani, "Look to the Past: Richard B. Russell and the Defense of Southern White Supremacy" (PhD diss., University of Georgia, 1981), 25–26; *Congressional Record,* 75th Cong., 3rd sess., 1098–1103; Martin Dies, *The Trojan Horse in America* (New York: Dodd, Mead, 1940), 118–29. The Molotov-Ribbentrop Pact, historian Glenda Gilmore has noted, was a boon to southern white supremacists. Civil rights advocates had argued that their collaboration with leftists was part of the Popular Front struggle against fascism at home and abroad, but the pact between Hitler and Stalin blurred the lines between the various "isms" that southern racial conservatives railed against. See Gilmore, *Defying Dixie,* 301.

19. John Temple Graves II, *The Fighting South* (New York: Putnam, 1943), 135; Glenn Feldman, *The Irony of the Solid South: Democrats, Republicans, and Race, 1865–1944* (Tuscaloosa: University of Alabama Press, 2013), 180–81; Frank M. Dixon, "Crossroads Democracy," typescript, Box 3, Folder 2, Frank Murray Dixon papers, LPR33, Alabama Dept. of Archives and History, Montgomery, Alabama.

20. W. E. B. Du Bois, *Black Reconstruction in America* (New York: Transaction, 2013), 648; Henry Lee Moon, *Balance of Power: The Negro Vote* (New York: Doubleday, 1949), 39.

21. James W. Moore to Theodore G. Bilbo, n.d., Box 1076, Folder 1; A. W. Morgan to Theodore G. Bilbo, n.d., Box 1076, Folder 7, Bilbo Papers.

22. Theodore G. Bilbo to A. M. Jones, 23 November 1942, Folder 1; James W. Moore to Theodore G. Bilbo, n.d., Folder 1; A. W. Morgan to Theodore G. Bilbo, n.d., Folder 7; all in Box 1076, Bilbo Papers.

23. A. W. Morgan to Theodore G. Bilbo, n.d., Box 1076, Folder 7, Bilbo Papers.

24. Nicholas Lemann, *Redemption: The Last Battle of the Civil War* (New York: Farrar, Straus, and Giroux, 2006), 63–99.

25. J. C. Hamilton to Theodore G. Bilbo, 17 October 1942, Folder 10; E. M. Pace to TGB, 19 November 1942, Folder 1; both Box 1077, Bilbo Papers.

26. Virginius Dabney, "Nearer and Nearer the Precipice," *Atlantic Monthly* 171 (January 1943), 94; Howard W. Odum, *Race and Rumors of Race: Challenge to American Crisis* (Chapel Hill: University of North Carolina Press, 1943), 4, 17.

27. Craigen Kennedy to Walter White, 5 October 1942; Craigen [Kennedy] to Odette [Harper], 1 December 1942, p. 6; both in Box II: A859, Folder "Kennedy, Craigen, Study, 1942–43"; Papers of the National Association for the Advancement of Colored People, Library of Congress, Washington, DC [cited hereafter as NAACP Papers].

28. Craigen [Kennedy] to Odette [Harper], 1 December 1942, pp. 1, 5, 7; Walter White to Craigen Kennedy, 15 December 1942, p. 1; both in Box II: A859, Folder "Kennedy, Craigen, Study, 1942–43," NAACP-LOC.

29. Olin D. Johnston, untitled typescript, n.d., Box 3, Folder "Negro Question (2)," Johnston Gubernatorial Papers, South Carolina Department of Archives and History, Columbia; Melvyn Stokes, *D. W. Griffith's The Birth of a Nation: A History of "The Most Controversial Motion Picture of All Time"* (New York: Oxford University Press, 2007), 197–99; Thomas Dixon Jr., *The Clansman: An Historical Romance of the Klu Klux Klan* (New York: Doubleday, 1905), 263–75; Baker, *What Reconstruction Meant*, 107–8.

30. Richard B. Russell to Cobb C. Torrance, 31 May 1944, Series X, Box 108, Folder 2, Richard B. Russell Papers, Russell Library for Political Research and Science, University of Georgia, Athens.

31. Gene Weltfish to Theodore G. Bilbo, 9 March 1944, Box 1067, Folder 2, Bilbo Papers; Cox to Bilbo, 8 May 1944, Box 6, Folder "1944," Earnest Sevier Cox Papers, Special Collections, Perkins Library, Duke University, Durham, North Carolina; Ruth Benedict and Gene Weltfish, *The Races of Mankind*, 1st edition (New York: Public Affairs Committee, 1943); Earnest Sevier Cox, *The Races of Mankind: A Review* (Jellico, TN: Arthur Daugherty, 1951); John P. Jackson, *Science For Segregation: Race, Law, And The Case Against Brown V. Board Of Education* (New York: New York University Press, 2005), 38–40. On the wartime egalitarian campaign and the white supremacist response, see Glenda E. Gilmore, *Defying Dixie*, 396–97.

32. Stuart Omer Landry, *The Cult of Equality: A Study of the Race Problem* (New Orleans: Pelican, 1945); Theodore G. Bilbo, *Take Your Choice: Separation or Mongrelization* (Poplarville, MS: Dream House Publishing, 1947); A. S. Coody to Theodore G. Bilbo, 9 July 1945, Box 4, Folder 50, Archibald S. Coody Papers, Mississippi Department of Archives and History, Jackson.

33. Chris Myers Asch, "Revisiting Reconstruction: James O. Eastland, the FEPC, and the Struggle to Rebuild Germany, 1945–1946," *Journal of Mississippi History* 67 (Spring 2005): 1–28; William Colmer, "Congressional Sidelights," 27 April 1949, Box 422, Folder 3, Colmer Papers, USM. For a scholarly attempt to apply the lessons of Reconstruction to Truman's civil rights program, see Alfred Holt Stone, "A Mississippian's View of Civil Rights, States Rights, and the Reconstruction Background," *Journal of Mississippi History* 10 (October 1948): 181–239.

34. Kari Frederickson, *The Dixiecrat Revolt and the End of the Solid South, 1932–1968* (Chapel Hill: University of North Carolina Press, 2001), 173.

35. "Memorandum on Statement Given to the Press in New Orleans," September 17, 1948, Box 3, Folder 13; John Stennis to William F. Winter, May 26, 1954, Box 1, Folder 32; both in Series 29, John C. Stennis Collection, Congressional and Political Research Center, Mitchell Memorial Library, Mississippi State University, Starkville. In his study of southern senators in the civil rights era, Keith M. Finley contends that Reconstruction "received far less attention than one would expect" in postwar anti–civil rights arguments because "the mythology of the Old South did not necessarily aid individuals formulating arguments in support of a new and different mythology . . . based not on chattel slavery but on the constitutionality of de jure segregation." Realizing that they "could not dwell indefinitely on matters of race or region," southern senators "balanced their rhetoric between placating constituents and winning over nonsoutherners with the latter objective given first priority." See Finley, *Delaying the Dream*, 9. Beyond Capitol Hill, as Bruce Baker contends, by the 1950s the memory of Reconstruction "no longer explained the world in which white southerners found themselves living. . . . The

white supremacist narrative of Reconstruction changed from a confident jeremiad to an elegiac recollection, often skirting dangerously close to nostalgia and sentimentality." See Baker, *What Reconstruction Meant,* 160.

36. Josephus Daniels to John Temple Graves, 21 December 1942, Box 1, Folder 5, John Temple Graves II Papers, Birmingham Public Library, Birmingham, Alabama.

37. Susan Tucker Hatcher, "A Last Gasp: Clyde R. Hoey and the Twilight of Racial Segregation, 1945–1954," in *The South Is Another Land: Essays on the Twentieth Century South,* ed. Bruce Clayton and John A. Salmond (New York: Greenwood Press, 1987), 29–48.

# II

# BLACK COUNTER-MEMORIES OF RECONSTRUCTION

# 3

# T. Thomas Fortune, Racial Violence of Reconstruction, and the Struggle for Historical Memory

SHAWN LEIGH ALEXANDER

The chief witness in Reconstruction, the emancipated slave himself, has been largely barred from the court. His written Reconstruction record has been largely destroyed and nearly always ignored.

—W. E. B. Du Bois, *Black Reconstruction,* 1935

Reconstruction, from its initial stages well into the twentieth century, has fueled American historical and literary imagination. Writers and historians have debated in their works whether Reconstruction preserved the democratic principles and ideals on which this nation was founded, or, on the contrary, it ushered in a dark period of political anarchy and social barbarity in the South, a period that saw an entire social order virtually turned upside down. As part of an interdisciplinary, intertextual dialogue where individuals revise, again and again, the story of Reconstruction, historians and writers have used the postwar historical moment to strengthen, challenge, and sometimes create ideologies that give a sense of understanding and order to the country's experiences.[1]

In the years directly following Reconstruction, and on into the twentieth century, whites crafted a reassessment of slavery and the Reconstruction era in both public and academic discourses that was used, along with social Darwinism more generally, to provide cover for racial terrorism and the national rise of white supremacy. Many whites, especially those in the postbellum South, mourned the death of slavery. They described the antebellum period as a time when whites and blacks lived in harmony, and they asserted that slavery was a constructive, civilizing school for African Americans. Slavery increasingly came to be viewed as a paternalistic relationship, in which blacks benefited from their exposure to masters who were neither abusive nor inhumane.[2]

During the same period, historians also began to reexamine Reconstruction, producing a number of state studies exposing the horrors of "radical rule." James W. Garner published *Reconstruction in Mississippi* (1901); William A. Dunning, *Essays on Civil War and Reconstruction* (1898; rev. edition 1904); Walter Lynwood Fleming, *Civil War and Reconstruction in Alabama* (1905); and J. C. Lester and D. L. Wilson, *Ku Klux Klan: Its Origin, Growth and Disbandment* (repr. 1905). In addition, the periodical press published numerous articles, stories, and poems on the subject by individuals such as Thomas Nelson Page, Joel Chandler Harris, and Thomas Dixon that supported these studies in popular culture.[3] As W. Fitzhugh Brundage has pointed out, whether an individual or a group erected a statue, staged a reunion of Confederate veterans, or wrote a novel, poetry, or a historical study, it all "provided crucial ideological ballast for white supremacy by rooting the contemporary racial hierarchy in a historical narrative and in a manner that naturalized it."[4]

This popular drive to rewrite the history of slavery and Reconstruction reached a zenith in the early part of 1905 with the release of Thomas Dixon's *The Clansman. The Clansman* casts a highly critical gaze at the "tragic" Reconstruction era while romanticizing the antebellum, plantation South as an edenic world where the feudalistic social hierarchy was maintained by the harmonious relationship between kind, paternalistic gentlemen and contented, hard-working, and docile slaves. The turning of the South on its head, in Dixon's depiction, could only be thwarted by the emergence of the Ku Klux Klan, which was an "institution of Chivalry, Humanity, Mercy and Patriotism," created to uphold the constitution, protect southern white women, and restore order to the South.[5] Ten years later in D. W. Griffith's hugely successful 1915 film adaptation of Dixon's novel, *The Birth of A Nation,* the saving of the South on the silver screen was transformed into multitudes of patriotic, mounted Ku Klux Klansmen. Its climactic, and most notorious, scene shows a lustful black soldier chasing a young white woman who jumps from her cliffside pedestal rather than succumbing to black personal or political rule. Justice, however, is not complete until the woman's death is avenged by a lynching.[6]

African Americans during and after the Reconstruction period used their newspapers, poetry, and literature, as well as the pulpit, lectern, and street corners to create a counter-public discourse that challenged the growing white supremacist memory of the period.[7] Extremely important in this group was the large crowd of journalists, such as T. Thomas Fortune, Ida B. Wells-Barnett, John E. Bruce, John Mitchell, and William Calvin Chase, among others, who were gaining more respect during the period. As African American elected officials progressively lost the fragile footing they held in the political arena during the post- Reconstruction era, the black press increasingly became the voice of the race, expressing racial pride and encouragement as well as attacking all forms of racism and exploitation. From the late 1880s into the first decade of the twentieth century, the black press became more and more important as a voice in the community, and the editors of the increasing number of black newspapers and journals commanded more respect and gained a greater following because of the perspicacity and range of their analysis. Among the issues they took up were the history of slavery and the Reconstruction period, to remind the community, and the nation, of what had occurred during more than two hundred fifty years of slavery and the brutal decade of Reconstruction, when nearly twenty thousand people were killed and many more were terrorized.[8] These publications, individually and collectively, provided a counter-narrative to the white supremacist narrative that was gaining control of the national consciousness

Chief among those who were not simply chronicling the historical facts of the period, but creating and refashioning images and ideas that would play a role in the development of an African American consciousness and the attempt to rewrite the American narrative being written, was T. Thomas Fortune. Fortune, born a slave in Florida, watched his father, Emanuel Fortune, and his Republican colleagues struggle against nefarious forces during Reconstruction. The Fortune family was frequently threatened by the Ku Klux Klan and ultimately had to flee their home for the relative safety of Jacksonville, Florida. Soon after the election of Rutherford B. Hayes and the end of Reconstruction, T. Thomas Fortune left the South, settled in New York, and founded the New York *Globe* (subsequently named the *Freeman* and the *Age*), which quickly became the most widely read black paper of the era. Using the memory of his youth in Reconstruction Florida and his newspaper as his pulpit, the sometimes-contentious Fortune became one of the most outspoken critics of southern racism, a promoter of racial solidarity and race pride, and an uncompromising advocate for the civil and political rights of African Americans.

Throughout his fight for black rights and equality Fortune would return to his childhood, and the memory of Reconstruction violence, to accentuate his arguments and remind his readers that violence and injustices of the present moment were not new, but had a history—in particular, a history that was different from the one that had become the most commonly understood within the country.[9] It was not a history of "benevolent paternalism" and missteps by an inferior race thrust into power, the white supremacist memory that historian David Blight argues took over the national memory of the period by the turn of the nineteenth century.[10] Instead, Fortune's counter-public discourse was one that used the memories of himself and others living through the period to stress the violence of Reconstruction while demonstrating the resiliency of the black community in the wake of that brutality and terrorism. Equally important to Fortune was that this counter-memory of the period could be used to help individuals understand and resist the violence and restrictions of the developing Jim Crow system.

+ + +

In the remaining space, I will begin the process of investigating these counter-memories by looking, briefly, at a few of the writings of T. Thomas Fortune and the way he treated Reconstruction—a period that he described as an era of "horrors."[11] Fortune was born on October 3, 1856, in Marianna, Jackson County, Florida, one of seven children born to Sarah Jane and Emanuel Fortune. It was a time, as he described it, "when the conflicting forces were fronting each other in a death struggle, with John Brown stirring up the fighting spirit and Chief Justice Roger B. Taney . . . shocking the moral sense of the Nation."[12] Fortune's parents were slaves of Ely P. Moore—Sarah Jane was a child of a Seminole Indian and an African American woman of mixed ancestry, while Emanuel was the son of an Irishman, Timothy Fortune, and an African American woman who claimed Anglo-Saxon and Spanish Indian descent as well. After Emancipation, Emanuel took the family name, began working as a shoemaker and a tanner, and was soon swept into Reconstruction politics.[13]

Emanuel Fortune, like many of his peers, was terrorized for his political activity. During the Ku Klux Klan hearings, the 1871 congressional investigation into violence in the southern states following the Civil War, he testified that he heard an "indirect expression made by the crackers" that "those damned politicians should be got rid of." He also recalled that he once spoke of John Brown at a political rally and had a pistol pulled on him by a member of the audience. The situation became so ominous that Fortune stopped leaving his home at night. He also taught his wife and children how to protect themselves and their home in the event of an attack.[14]

The anticipated attack did not happen, but during the Reconstruction years young Timothy Fortune continually witnessed the frustrations of his father and others in the community as they struggled for their rights as citizens. A total of 153 individuals were murdered in Jackson County during these years, a striking contrast to neighboring Gadsden County, which had no killings.[15] The frustrations and fears of the Fortune family and their community were heightened during the year of 1869 when Jackson County, and Marianna in particular, experienced some of the bloodiest months of the Reconstruction era.[16]

One evening in February, W. J. Purman, the local Freedman's Bureau agent and a friend of the Fortunes, was walking home with a friend when an assassin ambushed them from the public square, seriously wounding Purman and killing his associate. The attempted assassination of Purman signaled the complete breakdown of law and order in Marianna and the beginning of a reign of terror that lasted for months. The sheriff of Jackson County told Purman that he would not investigate the murder because he feared for his own life. After the sheriff's announcement, an armed committee of black residents, including Emanuel Fortune, approached Purman, claiming that they were ready to destroy the town in reprisal, but Purman dissuaded them.[17]

In the wake of the Purman assassination attempt, attacks in the county on both blacks and whites continued for months. In early March, a white farmer was shot to death in his home. A few days later a black corpse was found floating in the Chipola River. Another white man was killed on a rural farm in April.[18] In accordance with this rise of violence there were persistent rumors that Tom Barnes, a local farmer and known member of the Klan, was the individual responsible for the attempt on Purman's life. With no official action forthcoming, Green White gathered a small band of friends who set out to apprehend Barnes on their own. As the redressers approached Barnes's home near Chattahoochee, a furious gun battle ensued. Green and another man in his party were killed during the shooting, while a third was seriously wounded. Barnes, on the other hand, escaped unharmed.[19]

In May, racial tensions in the region were inflamed even more when a group of young white women went to the cemetery and removed flowers from the graves of Union soldiers that had been buried in the town. African Americans had placed the flowers on the graves during their local May Day festival. Upon being reported to a local Freedmen's Bureau the culprits were ordered into the Bureau court by Jonathan Q. Dickinson, another agent in the region who was drawing just as much ire of the white residents as Purman. According to reports, Dickinson publicly reprimanded the women before a mixed audience.[20]

Within this environment another individual was beginning to draw resentment from the white community, Calvin Rogers, a former slave who had been elected constable of Marianna. The only official elected by popular vote, Rogers was disliked by many whites simply because he symbolized the new political order, but he had also incurred their wrath merely because he was carrying out his duties. By the fall of 1869, he was singled out by the Klan as their next target.[21]

On September 28, Rogers and a group of friends were headed to a picnic when they were ambushed from the dense thicket along the roadside. A man named Wyatt Scurlock and a small boy were killed instantly, but Rogers was unharmed. A posse was assembled to apprehend the bushwhackers, but they were unable to locate them as they dispersed back into the community. The following day "unknown parties" killed two more blacks near Marianna. These acts of violence were just the preliminary skirmishes in what has been referred to as the "Jackson County War."[22]

The third violent incident in as many days took place on the porch of a local boarding house. On the veranda sat Attorney James F. McClellan (who had previously had some run-ins with Calvin Rogers), his daughter Maggie, and James P. Cocker. Both McClellan and Cocker, along with Tom Barnes, were believed to be ringleaders of the county's Klan activity. According to reports, a group of blacks "strolled down the street and into the shadows" just before they opened fire upon the individuals sitting on the balcony. McClellan was seriously wounded and Cocker escaped unharmed, but the bullet intended for him struck Maggie McClellan and killed her instantly.[23]

During questioning of witnesses of the shooting, several observers recalled seeing Calvin Rogers among the group of alleged black assailants. Though the black community had been discussing reprisal for the recent acts of violence, this action does not seem like a very clever attempt at undetected assassination. However, the murder of Maggie McClellan, "an innocent white women," and the possibility of the black community plotting the assassination of McClellan and Cocker, was enough to throw Marianna into a frenzy.

A mob was quickly assembled with the intention of killing Calvin Rogers and all others suspected of complicity in the shooting. When the group did not find Rogers they focused their ire on two suspected accomplices, Oscar Granbury and Matt Nichols, taking them out of town where Granbury was shot while Nichols managed to escape. His reprieve, however, was short. Three days later the Klan met on Marianna's main street and vowed to resume their hunt. That night Matt Nichols, his wife, and their son were killed and their bodies were tossed into a nearby lime sink. On the same evening it was rumored that Calvin Rogers was arming the black community for an attack on the city of Marianna and the white community was reported to have "slept on its arms." This was only the beginning. Tensions continued to rise amid recurring murders and attempted murders. No law was operative beyond that of the mob, and by the second weekend of October, Marianna had witnessed at least one murder each day.[24]

After the bloody days of October the murder rate slowed down, but tensions remained high. Calvin Rogers managed to elude capture and continued to perform many of his duties throughout the fall. In February, however, the Klan finally caught up with him and his body was found in his home filled with bullet holes.[25] Moreover, in the wake of this violence many fled the city, including Purman and Emanuel Fortune. Fortune had actually been in temporary hiding since the attempted Purman assassination, leaving his wife and children to protect their home in the manner in which he had taught them. By the year's end, however, Emanuel decided it was time for the family to move. He did not believe that he would be as free as he was before the violence, when there was "freedom of speech" and he could "act in politics as a man would want with his own people . . ."[26]

+ + +

These experiences formed T. Thomas Fortune's political outlook and informed his memory of the years immediately after emancipation. These lived experiences also gave him the ability to advocate for a counter-memory of the period as whites attempted to solidify their grasp on the public memory of Reconstruction. The violence that Fortune and his family experienced in Marianna, and of the period in general, always haunted him. As he explained in his only book-length work, *Black and White:* "As I stand before the thirteen bulky volumes, comprising the 'Ku Klux Conspiracy'... my blood runs cold at the merciless chronicle of murder and outrage, of defiance, inhumanity and barbarity on the one hand, and usurpation and tyranny on the other."[27]

The haunting volumes that Fortune referenced were the *Report* of the *Joint Select Committee to Inquire into the Condition of Affairs in the Late Insurrectionary States,* popularly known as the Ku Klux Klan hearings, which yielded over eight thousand pages of firsthand testimony of the realities of the post-emancipation South. This testimony revealed to the country then, and still reveals today, what one Mississippi resident described as a "reign of terror" affecting blacks and whites alike.[28]

Individuals from every segment of the southern population appeared before the committee. Governors, members of the US Congress, state legislators, mayors, law enforcement officials, veterans (Union and Confederate), planters, doctors, editors, merchants, artisans, teachers, and clergymen—black and white, male and female, all presented their cases.

Suspected members of the Klan, and former Confederates in general, gave little helpful information about the violence, generally denying membership in the Klan or any knowledge of its activities. African American witnesses proved to be better sources. Hundreds of black women and men played a remarkable role, coming forward to testify during the hearings. Democratic committee members attempted to discredit their testimony, equating the two-dollar-a-day allowance that witnesses received to bribery and accusing local Republicans of coaching them; nevertheless, these witnesses' testimony offers abundant evidence of the impact of Klan violence upon the South. As historian Kidada Williams has argued, the testimony is important because it "was some African Americans' only means of having a public record of the violence they endured and the losses they sustained."[29]

Fortune urged the readers of *Black and White* to read the reports, stating that they were "accessible to the reading public." He also argued they were central to understand what happened during Reconstruction. The testimony before the congressional committee, according to Fortune, tells

> the bloody story of the terrible miscarriage of the "Reconstruction policy"; they show how cruel men can be under conditions favorable to unbridled license, undeterred by the strong arm of constituted authority; they show how helpless the freed people were; how ignorant, how easily led by unscrupulous adventurers *pretending to be friends* and how easily murdered and overawed by veterans inured to the dangers and the toils of war; and, lastly, they show how powerless was the national government to protect its citizens' rights, specifically defined by the Federal Constitution.[30]

Seeing the value of the hearings, Fortune understood in 1884, as more historians are discovering today, that the evidence witnesses provided yields important insights into the nature—the motivation and effects—as well as the end results of the systematic violence that was used to turn back the Reconstruction revolution and reassert white supremacy. Finally, it gives one a better understanding of what it was like to be a victim of or a witness to orchestrated violence. The testimony of the survivors of nightrider violence, as well as victims' relatives and friends, revealed the tactics of the assailants and the types of individuals who became their targets.[31]

Unlike those pushing a white supremacist memory of Reconstruction, Fortune, in the vindicationist tradition, wanted to expose the barbaric, inhuman realities of the period and revive the history of black Americans righteously struggling against violent opposition. Such an argument was vastly different from the developing interpretation of Reconstruction as that "tragic era" when the Radical Republicans rammed black supremacy upon the defeated South, and corruption in the hands of unscrupulous carpetbaggers, traitorous scalawags, and ignorant freedmen ran rampant throughout the region. Or as Thomas Dixon would later describe it, Reconstruction was the attempt of Thaddeus Stevens and his "radical cohorts" to "Africanise ten great states of the American Union."[32]

Fortune's discussion of the southern response to Reconstruction also challenged the developing national narrative: the notion that the white community eventually overthrew misgovernment and regained control of their region, or—again in Dixon's words—how "the young South . . . went forth . . . against overwhelming odds, daring exile, imprisonment, and a felon's death, and saved the life of a people."[33] For Fortune, "southern redemption" was neither benign nor an act of destiny; rather, the southern response was criminal, violent, and barbaric.

"If the shot upon Fort Sumter was treason," he argued, "what shall we call the bloody conflict which the white men of the South have waged against the Constitutional amendments from 1866 to the murder of innocent citizens at Danville, Virginia, in 1883, even unto the present time? If the shot upon Fort Sumter drew down upon the South the indignation and the vengeance of the Federal government, putting father against son, and brother against brother, what shall we say the Federal Government should have done to put a period to the usurpations and the murders of these leagues of horror?"[34]

For Fortune, the horrors of the Ku Klux period were directly connected to the present conditions and he did not want his readers to forget such a fact. "The horrors of the Klan period," he explained, "are a link in the chain; and though to-day's links are different in form and guise, *the chain is the same.*"[35] Fortune's friend Booker T. Washington shared this sentiment. While fiction writer and journalist Joel Chandler Harris and others were shaping the nation's view of slavery, emancipation, and Reconstruction, Fortune and Washington were actively discussing how to counter the hegemonic racist images portrayed by these white writers. In 1899, after reading *The Chronicles of Aunt Minervy Ann,* Washington wrote to Fortune and asked for a response.[36]

In contrast to his well-known Uncle Remus stories in which he recounted folktales, Harris attempted in *Minervy Ann* to give a genuine depiction of life in a small Georgia town during Reconstruction.[37] In *Minervy Ann,* just as in his Uncle Remus collections, Harris used the literary device of a white narrator eliciting anecdotes from a sympathetic, older black storyteller. The protagonist, Minervy Ann, a former slave, was an outspoken house servant—a stereotypical "mammy" figure—devoted to the family of her former owners, who continued to employ her after emancipation. Harris represented her speech with the same literary dialect he used for Uncle Remus, in contrast with the standard English he used for the white narrator. Consistent with his other works, Harris conveyed a patronizing, paternalistic liking toward his black protagonist.

Harris's story mirrors, in a burlesque manner, the experiences of many southern African Americans during the period, including Fortune's own family's life in Florida. Minervy Ann's husband, Hamp, is depicted as an uneducated former slave who is elected to the state legislature, where the carpetbaggers easily manipulate him for their own gain. Whites in the community threaten Hamp's life because of his political activity, but Harris depicts the Klan as comically inept and easily thwarted by Minervy Ann's compassionate employer, who altruistically comes to Hamp's defense.[38]

Although superficially similar, the experiences of the Fortune family—and blacks throughout the South during Reconstruction—were markedly different from the events described in Harris's stories. In stark contrast to the passive Hamp caricature, the self-educated Emanuel Fortune, like many other African Americans in Florida who attained elected office, was a savvy, well-read politician. Whereas Harris depicted all carpetbaggers as gluttonous schemers who manipulated their black constituents, Purman and his colleague, Charles M. Hamilton, worked closely with Fortune's father and maintained a close relationship with the entire family. Finally, the Klan that terrorized the Fortunes and Jackson County was not a maladroit band of brothers, but rather a brutal, competent paramilitary force.[39]

T. Thomas Fortune was troubled by the distortions of *Minervy Ann* and concurred with Washington that someone must respond to Harris by presenting an accurate record of the daily life of African Americans in the South during Reconstruction. He wrote back to Washington, explaining that the only way "[we] can meet this sort of thing is to go into fiction and do it, and I shall go in and do my share if possible." He further argued that his "After War Times" would alter the discussion. It would "be an eye opener," he explained."[40]

+ + +

Fortune had already entered the debate and entered it often. Since the end of Reconstruction, southern states, backed by violence, intimidation, and the invocation of white supremacist racial politics, continued to pass legislation stripping African American citizens of their civil, social, and political rights. At the same time, black citizens' rights in the North were also being increasingly curbed, with the active collusion of the federal government. In a series of rulings the Supreme Court first gave impetus to the legalizing of segregation in public accommodations by invalidating the Civil Rights Act of 1875 a short eight years after its passage in the *Civil Rights Cases* decision. Then, in 1896 the court confirmed its 1883 ruling with its famous *Plessy v. Ferguson* decision, which legalized segregation on railway cars as long as the accommodations were separate but equal. Finally, in 1898, the year before the publication of *Minervy Ann,* the court upheld efforts to disfranchise the southern black electorate with its decision in *Williams v. Mississippi.*[41]

The slow, methodical creation of a system of de jure and de facto segregation now known as Jim Crow was accompanied by a reign of terror against black individuals and the community. As historian Edward Ayers noted, unprosecuted white lawlessness and the "violence of lynching was a way for white people to reconcile weak governments with a demand for an impossibly high level of racial mastery, a way of terrorizing blacks into acquiescence."[42] Additionally, during this period sociological, psychological, and physiological "certainty" rather than biblical authority now proved racial inferiority.

African Americans responded to this crippling discrimination and violence in several ways. Black men and women organized: unions of industrial workers and farmers; educational, cultural, historical, social welfare, legal aid, and fraternal benefit societies; civil rights and antilynching leagues; associations of club women, businessmen, editors, teachers, and doctors; schools for higher education as well as industrial and agricultural training; and churches that were active in all areas of social and economic improvement.[43]

Fortune was at the forefront of this activity. In 1884, the year after the Supreme Court decision in the Civil Rights Cases, he called for the black community to create a national civil rights organization to fight against this flourishing racial hostility and mob terrorism. The proposed group would ultimately form on the national stage in 1890 and be reborn the year before the publication of Harris's *Minervy Ann.* In addition, in the pages of his papers and from the lectern, whenever an audience would listen, Fortune castigated disfranchisement, election fraud, both of the political parties, mob violence, the convict lease system, inequities in school funding, and the rise of segregation.[44]

In particular, Fortune responded to the popular white literature, including pieces like *Minervy Ann* and Thomas Nelson Page's *Red Rock* (1898), which presented a paternalistic image of Reconstruction and portrayed African Americans as childlike "darkies" who were forced into freedom and ultimately Reconstruction politics too soon. These were works that longed for the mythical good old days of the slave plantation, when blacks knew their places, were happily subservient, and never crossed the lines of social separation. Throughout the nearly twenty years of publishing his newspaper, Fortune had taken every opportunity to challenge this memory of Reconstruction. In Fortune's memory, Reconstruction was a period when African Americans righteously struggled to better themselves after the horrors of slavery, but paid the price in suffering and blood of trying to create their own definition of freedom and citizenship during Reconstruction.

Throughout the years Fortune was always calling on his readers to remember this counter-narrative of Reconstruction. In the pages of the *Globe, Freeman* and the *Age* he often evoked the violence of the period, referencing massacres and riots, such as those at Hamburg and Danville, and condemning the Republican Party for its abandonment of the African American community and the "treachery of Hayes." In reference to the former president, he asserted that the nation should hold him in "scorn and contempt" and remember him as a "traitor and coward." It was Hayes and the cowardly Republican Party, according to Fortune, that allowed the "assassins and incendiaries" to "resume control." Moreover, he often reminded his readers that "no Federal Election law" would "repair that monumental blunder." The "rebel" would remain "in the saddle" "until dislodged by violent revolution."[45] Finally, as early as 1883 the editor called on his readers to "remember the blood which has dyed the soil of the South for two hundred years; remember the heartless cruelties of the slave regime, and guiltless blood which has flowed since the war. . . . The ignominious cognomens of the Ku-Klux Klan—bloody assassins!—and white Liners, midnight raiders and banditti generally."[46]

One of Fortune's most lasting contributions to the historic memory of Reconstruction, however, came in 1886, the year after he published *Black and White*. During this year, Fortune contributed a poem to the *AME Church Review* entitled "Bartow Black." Throughout the fight for emancipation poetry had become a popular form of protest, but literary scholar Joan Sherman has argued that "Reconstruction sounded the death knell of militant protest poetry." According to Sherman, in the wake of emancipation and the failure of Reconstruction, "African American poets would lower their voices, mask discontents, and write sober, genteel verse largely indistinguishable from their white contemporaries' art. They would portray noble black men and women for the race to emulate and for whites to recognize as capable, reasonable citizens worthy of integration into American society."[47]

In the late nineteenth century a number of black periodicals and newspapers began to flourish and all of them provided space for African American literary artists to publish their work. Most of the poets produced "inspirational, descriptive, or sentimental verses about love, poetic art, religion, nature, children, death, and the old, romanticized South."[48] Those who did speak about race and rights, according to Sherman, "swipe weakly at the establishment; or cautiously plead for black civil rights."[49]

One of the few exceptions was Fortune's "Bartow Black."[50] In the poem Fortune directly counters the perceived idea of Reconstruction, moving beyond sentimentalism and the romanticized paternalistic South. Fortune uses the poem to refashion images and ideas of the period to create a new consciousness and a new national history of Reconstruction. In "Bartow Black," he evokes the hopes and dreams of the period, the success of the community and the backlash and violent reaction of the whites, while providing a window into the "thoughts and strivings" and memories that guided African Americans.

In the first two stanzas of the poem the aspiring poet/activist Fortune captures that immediate moment of emancipation that a number of historians, including Herbert Gutman, Leon Litwack, and Tera Hunter, have tried to explain in recent years.[51] Upon hearing the Emancipation Proclamation, Fortune's poetic protagonist leaves his plantation, changes his name, and abandons the old world of agricultural labor.

> 'Twas when the Proclamation came,—
> Far in the sixties back,—
> He left his lord, and changed his name
> To "Mister Bartow Black."
>
> He learned to think himself a man,
> And privileged, you know,
> To adopt a new and different plan,—
> To lay aside the hoe.

Mirroring the lives of many freedmen, including his own father, Fortune then chronicles Bartow's rise in local Reconstruction politics.

> He took the lead in politics,
>     And handled all the "notes,"
> For he was up to all the tricks
>     That gather in the votes;
>
> For when the war came to a close
>     And negroes "took a stand,"
> Young Bartow with the current rose,
>     The foremost in command.
>
> His voice upon the "stump" was heard;
>     He "Yankeedom" did prate;
> The "carpet-bagger" he revered;
>     The Southern did hate.
>
> He now was greater than the lord
>     Who used to call him slave,
> For he was on the "County Board,"
>     With every right to rave.

But like Emanuel Fortune and so many of his peers, Bartow's success brought the attention of the local Ku Klux Klan and he was soon terrorized for his political activity.

> But this amazing run of luck
>     Was far too good to stand:
> And soon the chivalrous "Ku-Klux"
>     Rose in the Southern land.
>
> Then Bartow got a little note,—
>     'Twas very queerly signed,—
> It simply told him not to vote,
>     Or be to death resigned.

Like Fortune, himself, his Bartow knew "his rights and had the courage to defend them."[52] Bartow stood up to the Klan and continued to perform his duties.

Young Bartow thought this little game
Was very fine and nice
To bring his courage rare to shame
And knowledge of justice.

"What right have they to think I fear?"
He to himself did say.
"Dare they presume that I do care.
How loudly they do bray?

"This is my home, and here I die.
Contending for my right!
Then let them come! My colors fly!
*I'm ready now to fight!*

"Let those who think that Bartow Black,—
An office-holder, too!—
Will to the cowards show his back,
Their vain presumption rue!"

Bartow pursued his office game,
And made the money, too,
But home at nights he wisely came
And played the husband true.

The nightriders however, would not be stopped. Under the cloak of darkness they cowardly snuck into the home of the man they feared.

When they had got their subject tame,
And well-matured their plan.
They at the hour of midnight came,
And armed was every man!

They numbered fifty Southern sons,
    And masked was every face;
And Winfield rifles were their guns,—
    You could that plainly trace.

One Southern brave did have a key,
    An entrance quick to make;
They entered all but meek, you see,
    Their victim not to wake!

Poor Bartow could not reach his gun,
    Though quick his arm did stretch,
For twenty bullets through him spun,
    That stiffly laid the wretch.

And then they rolled his carcass o'er,
    And filled both sides with lead;
And then they turned it on the floor,
    And shot away his head!

Ere Black his bloody end did meet
    His wife had swooned away;
The Southern braves did now retreat,—
    There was no need to stay![53]

This poem, "Bartow Black," is Fortune's real effort of going into "fiction"—which he defined broadly—to challenge the developing memory of Reconstruction. Fortune further urged his readers to go into this history by explaining to them in a footnote, "Black was well known to me, by his proper name, Calvin Rogers."[54] He then urged the readers to learn more about his murder by looking at volume thirteen of the Klan Conspiracy report. If the readers did investigate further they would have discovered the testimony was that of Emanuel Fortune, Fortune's father.[55]

With Fortune using Calvin Rogers as a literary character, and supplementing his "fiction" with historical authentication, he staked claim to the history that he was telling. Furthermore, his use of the Klan hearing testimony adds primacy to Fortune's belief that the evidence found in the pages of the hearings offered an insight into the experiences of African Americans in the South after emancipation that you cannot find in other sources. The testimonies are memories of those on the ground, personally experiencing the horrors of Reconstruction, and for Fortune these voices were essential to understand what happened during the period. As W. E. B. Du Bois would argue in *Black Reconstruction,* these voices, these witnesses could not be ignored.[56] Furthermore, by using his father's testimony as authentication of his memorialization of Reconstruction, Fortune claimed personal ownership to the memory, telling his reader that he lived this experience, while individuals such as Joel Chandler Harris and others did not. Fortune was not just fighting over the "facts" and myths of the era, he was creating a fuller history and national consciousness, a new history. With this type of remembering, Fortune was also urging his readers to recall their own experiences, or incidents involving their family and friends, and to pass them along to add to the new history. The editor followed a similar pattern with the publication of "After War Times," his second fully conceived attempt to assert his memory of Reconstruction into the consciousness of his readers.

Fortune finally published "After War Times: A Boy's Life in Reconstruction Days," the "eye opener" that he discussed with Booker T. Washington in 1899, as a serialized autobiography in the Norfolk *Journal and Guide* and the Philadelphia *Tribune* in 1927, one year before his death. After nearly fifty years of journalism, the creation of the nation's first civil rights organization, the Afro-American League, and his countless other activities during his seventy-plus years, Fortune returned to the story of his youth—the story of Reconstruction—as the period of his life that he believed needed to be told, needed to be remembered.[57]

In the story of his years as a "manchild" growing into an Afro-American, Fortune emphasized the "horrors" of the period.[58] He was returning to these acts of terror because they had a profound effect on him and he never wanted his readers or the nation to forget. Fortune powerfully juxtaposes the fond nostalgia of an old man for his childhood with scenes of shocking, abrupt violence. He repeatedly confronts the reader with the brutality of daily life, particularly for the African American who found little, if any, protection in the rule of law. As he explained, "There is no condition one can live in which strains the nerves and confuses thought more than a lawless one; a condition in which a person knows that his life is at the mercy of any assassin who can catch him off his guard." His family, and southern blacks in general, asserted Fortune, "lived in that sort of condition all through the Reconstruction period, when none could call his life his own, and fear and demoralization dominated the lives of all men."[59]

In one startling episode, Fortune describes a beating he received as a young boy at the hands of his owner. Sarah Jane, provoked by the abuse of her child, physically defended her son and then fled to escape the severe retribution certain to follow. In several articles, in a direct attack on the "benevolent paternalism" myth of Reconstruction propagated by white writers and historians, Fortune described an idyllic rural life interrupted by murders and outrages. In one such episode he retold the story of the shocking murder of John Gilbert, the first African American killed in the county.[60] In another he told the "horror of horrors!," a Klan attack upon a group of teachers and children at a picnic. Describing the "ghastly business" that left the ground "littered with dead and maimed children and grown-ups," he pleaded with his readers to imagine the shameful act of "grown-up white persons deliberately shooting into a crowd of Sunday school teachers and children!"[61] He also retold the story of the assassination attempt on Purman, the death of McClellan's daughter, and the murder of Calvin Rogers. Further, in a particularly ominous incident, young Fortune, in search of a stray calf, stumbled across a notorious Klansman lying in ambush to assassinate his father. The period was one of such lawlessness, explained Fortune, that "every Negro and Southern loyalist and carpet-bagger in Jackson county lived in constant fear of assassination."[62]

This is the story of Reconstruction that Fortune wanted his readers to remember. It is with "Bartow Black," "After War Times," countless editorials, and other writings that Fortune, along with others, laid the foundation for the counter-memory of the era that survived over the years and was pushed by William Sinclair in his 1905 classic *Aftermath of Slavery* and made famous by W. E. B. Du Bois in *Black Reconstruction*.[63] It is this counter-memory that he and his cohorts pleaded with the country to remember. He wanted the community and the nation to remember the strong leadership of his father and individuals such as Calvin Rogers, but he also understood the necessity of understanding the violence of the period and the psychological impact that it had on individuals, families, and communities.

The memory of Reconstruction for Fortune was not one of redemption, but rather survival, resiliency, and perseverance amidst a life of terror. Furthermore, the South was not, as Harris and others portrayed, grievously wronged during the Reconstruction era and was therefore not justified in taking sometimes harsh measures against African Americans and errant white politicians to correct the extravagant mistakes of the Republicans who briefly controlled southern politics after the Civil War. By contrast, Fortune anticipated the work of African American historians, including A. A. Taylor, W. E. B. Du Bois, and John Hope Franklin, who began to question the fundamental assumptions underlying dominant Reconstruction historical and literary portrayals, and positioned former slaves as neither a problem to be solved by the correctives of benevolent whites nor a violent force that threatened the well-being of white southerners. Rather, they were a community of proud, hardworking people intent on being recognized and valued as American citizens in the face of overwhelming resistance and adversity.[64] Violence used in Reconstruction and beyond was brutal, not a corrective or deterrent, as whites believed. Moreover, as Fortune wanted his readers to understand, the community has, and can again, resist these forms of brutality.

For Fortune the nation's history had to include the violence, past and present, that was used to subjugate the African American community as well as the struggles and resiliency of the community to endure, survive, and resist that violence. Fortune believed that the black community and the nation as a whole could and should never forget the violence of Reconstruction. Nor should the violence and the African American community's resolve to survive be stripped from the national narrative. As he stated in 1884, "it is not necessary . . . to recapitulate the incidents of Reconstruction history which naturally led up to the finality of 1876. It is sufficient to know that anarchy prevailed in every Southern State; that a black man's life was not worth the having; that armed bodies of men openly defied the Constitution of the United States and nullified each and every one of its guarantees of citizenship to the colored man."[65] More importantly, Fortune reminded his readers that while "thousands of black men . . . were shot down like sheep . . . not *one* of the impudent assassins was ever hung by the neck until he was dead."[66] This is the memory of Reconstruction and the national history that Fortune continued to tell his readers and anyone who would listen. Such was the history of Bartow Black, Jackson County, Florida, the Fortune family, and so many others throughout the South.

NOTES

1. Some of the key works informing the narrative of Reconstruction today include W. E. B. Du Bois, *Black Reconstruction* (1935; repr., Millwood, NY: Kraus-Thomson Organization, 1976); Leon F. Litwack, *Been in the Storm So Long: The Aftermath of Slavery* (New York: Knopf, 1979); Eric Foner, *Reconstruction: America's Unfinished Revolution, 1863–1877* (New York: Harper & Row, 1988); Steven Hahn, *A Nation under Our Feet: Black Political Struggles in the Rural South, from Slavery to the Great Migration* (Cambridge, MA: Belknap Press of Harvard University Press, 2003).

2. See John David Smith, *An Old Creed for the New South: Proslavery Ideology and Historiography, 1865–1918* (Athens: University of Georgia Press, 1991).

3. To examine the historiography and general discussion of how Reconstruction has been treated over the years, see Smith, *An Old Creed for the New South;* Eric Foner, "Reconstruction Revisited," *Reviews in American History* 10, no. 4 (1982): 82–100; Thomas J. Brown, *Reconstructions: New Perspectives on the Postbellum United States* (Oxford and New York: Oxford University Press, 2006); K. Stephen Prince, *Stories of the South: Race and the Reconstruction of Southern Identity, 1865–1915* (Chapel Hill: University of North Carolina Press, 2014); Sharon D. Kennedy-Nolle, *Writing Reconstruction: Race, Gender, and Citizenship in the Postwar South* (Chapel Hill: University of North Carolina Press, 2015); and Michele Gillespie and Randal L. Hall, *Thomas Dixon Jr. and the Birth of Modern America* (Baton Rouge: Louisiana State University Press, 2006).

4. W. Fitzhugh Brundage, "White Women and the Politics of Historical Memory," in Jane Elizabeth Dailey, Glenda Elizabeth Gilmore, and Bryant Simon, eds., *Jumpin' Jim Crow: Southern Politics from Civil War to Civil Rights* (Princeton, NJ: Princeton University Press, 2000), 126.

5. Thomas Dixon, *The Clansman: An Historical Romance of the Ku Klux Klan* (New York: Doubleday, 1905), 320.

6. D. W. Griffith and Thomas Dixon, *Birth of a Nation* (Los Angeles: Triangle Film Corp., 1915). For more on Dixon, see Gillespie and Hall, *Thomas Dixon Jr. and the Birth of Modern America;* and Prince, *Stories of the South,* 244–46. For a contemporary response to Dixon's depiction of Reconstruction, see William Albert Sinclair, *The Aftermath of Slavery: A Study of the Condition and Environment of the American Negro* (1905; repr., Columbia: University of South Carolina Press, 2012), 97.

7. David William Blight, *Race and Reunion: The Civil War in American Memory* (Cambridge, MA: Harvard University Press, 2001). See also David William Blight, *Beyond the Battlefield: Race,*

*Memory, and the American Civil War* (Amherst: University of Massachusetts Press, 2002); and Bruce E. Baker, *What Reconstruction Meant: Historical Memory in the American South* (Charlottesville: University of Virginia Press, 2007).

8. Twenty thousand is the number most historians use today. In the years following the brutal violence of the Ku Klux Klan period, a number of African Americans pushed the number much higher. For example, William Sinclair estimated the number at closer to fifty thousand. See Sinclair, *The Aftermath of Slavery,* 97.

9. For more on T. Thomas Fortune, see *T. Thomas Fortune the Afro-American Agitator: A Collection of Writings, 1880–1928,* ed. Shawn Leigh Alexander (Gainesville: University Press of Florida, 2008); Shawn Leigh Alexander, *An Army of Lions: The Civil Rights Struggle before the NAACP* (Philadelphia: University of Pennsylvania Press, 2012); and Emma Lou Thornbrough, *T. Thomas Fortune: Militant Journalist* (Chicago: University of Chicago Press, 1972).

10. See Blight, *Race and Reunion.*

11. T. Thomas Fortune, "After War Times: A Boy's Life in Reconstruction Days," Part 1, *Norfolk Journal and Guide,* 16 July 1927.

12. Fortune, "After War Times."

13. Fortune, "After War Times," Part 1, 16 July 1927, and Part 2, 23 July 1927; Alexander, ed., *T. Thomas Fortune, the Afro-American Agitator;* and Thornbrough. *T. Thomas Fortune: Militant Journalist.*

14. Joint Select Committee to Inquire into the Condition of Affairs in the Late Insurrectionary States, *Report of the Joint Select Committee to Inquire into the Condition of Affairs in the Late Insurrectionary States: Made to the Two Houses of Congress February 19, 1872,* vol. 13 (Washington, DC: US Government, 1872), 94; T. Thomas Fortune, "After War Times: A Boy's Life in Reconstruction Days, Part 3," *Norfolk Journal and Guide,* 30 July 1927; and T. Thomas Fortune, "After War Times: A Boy's Life in Reconstruction Days, Part 4," *Norfolk Journal and Guide,* 6 August 1927.

15. *Report of the Joint Select Committee to Inquire into the Condition of Affairs,* 13:222, 75–93. See also Daniel R. Weinfeld, *The Jackson County War: Reconstruction and Resistance in Post–Civil War Florida* (Tuscaloosa: University of Alabama Press, 2012).

16. See Ralph L. Peek, "Lawlessness in Florida, 1868–1871," *Florida Historical Quarterly* 60 (1961), and Allen W. Trelease, *White Terror: The Ku Klux Klan Conspiracy and Southern Reconstruction* (Baton Rouge: Louisiana State University Press, 1995). See also Weinfeld, *The Jackson County War.*

17. *Report of the Joint Select Committee,* 13:100, 144, 155, 205–6, and 281.

18. *Report of the Joint Select Committee,* 13:81.

19. *Southern Sun,* 12 August 1869.

20. *Report of the Joint Select Committee,* 13:232, 282, 285.

21. Report of the Joint Select Committee, 148 and 192.

22. Report of the Joint Select Committee, 290; *Southern Sun,* 7 October 1869; and *Banner,* 15 October 1869. See also Weinfeld, *The Jackson County War.*

23. *Report of the Joint Select Committee,* 13:78–82, 140, 145, 188–92, 283, and 289–91. See also *Banner,* 15 October 1869; *Semi-Weekly Commercial,* 15 October 1869; and *Florida Peninsular,* 20 October 1869.

24. Peek. "Lawlessness in Florida, 1868–1871."

25. *Florida Peninsular,* 16 February 1870.

26. *Report of the Joint Select Committee,* 13:94.

27. Timothy Thomas Fortune. *Black and White; Land, Labor, and Politics in the South.* (1884; repr., Chicago: Johnson Publishing, 1970), 59.

28. *Report of the Joint Select Committee,* 12:1029.

29. Kidada E. Williams, *They Left Great Marks on Me: African American Testimonies of Racial Violence from Emancipation to World War I* (New York: New York University Press, 2012), 51.

30. Fortune, *Black and White,* 61. Emphasis in original.

31. Some works that have looked at the hearings and violence of the period more generally include Carole Emberton, *Beyond Redemption: Race, Violence, and the American South after the Civil War* (Chicago: University of Chicago Press, 2013); Williams, *They Left Great Marks on Me;* Hahn, *A Nation Under Our Feet;* and before them, Trelease, *White Terror.*

32. Thomas Dixon, *The Clansman: An Historical Romance of the Ku Klux Klan* (New York: Grossett & Dunlap, 1905), iv.

33. *Dixon,* The Clansman,, iii.

34. Fortune, *Black and White,* 59.

35. Fortune, *Black and White,* 61.

36. T. Thomas Fortune to Booker T. Washington, *Booker T. Washington Papers,* 5:233–34. Fortune also criticizes Washington for his "habit of apologizing for the shortcomings of white men," especially in relation to the Reconstruction deviltry." He explains that he qualified Washington's comments whenever possible in the proofs of the *Future of the American Negro.* For the published words by Washington on Reconstruction in the *Future of the American Negro,* see *Booker T. Washington Papers,* 5:307–9. Joel Chandler Harris, *The Chronicles of Aunt Minervy Ann,* was the fictional reminiscences of a black cook in Georgia and her husband Hamp. Minervy Ann was cast as a black mammy and her husband was a comic African American who wore fancy clothes, including a stovepipe hat, and served in the Georgia legislature during Reconstruction. Joel Chandler Harris, *The Chronicles of Aunt Minervy Ann* (New York: Charles Scribner's Sons, 1899.)

37. For more on Joel Chandler Harris's *Uncle Remus* tales and historical memory, see Jennifer Ritterhouse, "Reading, Intimacy, and the Role of Uncle Remus in White Southern Social Memory," *Journal of Southern History* 69, no. 3 (2003): 585–622. See also K. Stephen Prince, *Stories of the South: Race and the Reconstruction of Southern Identity, 1865–1915* (Chapel Hill: University of North Carolina Press, 2014).

38. Harris, *The Chronicles of Aunt Minervy Ann.* See also Timothy Thomas Fortune and Daniel R. Weinfeld, *After War Times: An African American Childhood in Reconstruction-Era Florida* (Tuscaloosa: University of Alabama Press, 2014).

39. Fortune and Weinfeld, *After War Times,* xxvii. See also Harris, *The Chronicles of Aunt Minervy Ann.*

40. T. Thomas Fortune to Booker T. Washington, *Booker T. Washington Papers,* 5:233. Fortune, descended from European, African, and Seminole forebears, probably objected to derogatory comments about "mulatters" and the especially harsh disparagement of an "Injun mulatter" in *Minervy Ann.* See Harris, *The Chronicles of Aunt Minervy Ann.*

41. C. Vann Woodward, *Origins of the New South, 1877–1913* (Baton Rouge: Louisiana State University Press, 1951); C. Vann Woodward, *The Strange Career of Jim Crow* (New York: Oxford University Press, 1966); Edward L. Ayers, *The Promise of the New South: Life After Reconstruction* (New York: Oxford University Press, 1992); and Michael Perman, *Struggle for Mastery: Disfranchisement in the South, 1888–1908* (Chapel Hill: University of North Carolina Press, 2001).

42. Ayers, *The Promise of the New South,* 157.

43. Alexander, *An Army of Lions;* August Meier, *Negro Thought in America, 1880–1915: Racial Ideologies in the Age of Booker T. Washington* (Ann Arbor: University of Michigan Press, 1963); and Steven Hahn, *A Nation under Our Feet.*

44. See Alexander, *An Army of Lions.*

45. *New York Age,* 15 March 1890.

46. *New York Globe,* 10 November 1883.

47. Joan R. Sherman, ed., *African-American Poetry of the Nineteenth Century: An Anthology* (Urbana: University of Illinois Press, 1992), 8.

48. Sherman, *African-American Poetry of the Nineteenth Century,* 10.

49. Sherman, *African-American Poetry of the Nineteenth Century,* 10.

50. Sherman, *African-American Poetry of the Nineteenth Century,* 10. See also Joan R. Sherman, *Invisible Poets; Afro-Americans of the Nineteenth Century* (Urbana: University of Illinois Press, 1974), 141–53.

51. Litwack, *Been in the Storm So Long;* Herbert George Gutman, *The Black Family in Slavery and Freedom, 1750–1925* (New York: Vintage Books, 1977); Tera W. Hunter, *To 'Joy My Freedom: Southern Black Women's Lives and Labors after the Civil War* (Cambridge, MA: Harvard University Press, 1997); and Heather Andrea Williams, *Help Me to Find My People: The African American Search for Family Lost in Slavery* (Chapel Hill: University of North Carolina Press, 2012).

52. *New York Age,* 25 January 1890.

53. T. Thomas Fortune, "Bartow Black," *A.M.E. Church Review* 3 (October 1886): 158–59.

54. Fortune, "Bartow Black," 159.

55. See *Report of the Joint Select Committee,* 13:94–101.

56. Du Bois, *Black Reconstruction,* 210.

57. Alexander, *An Army of Lions,* and Alexander, ed., *T. Thomas Fortune the Afro-American Agitator.*

58. Fortune, "After War Times," Part 1, *Norfolk Journal and Guide,* 16 July 1927.

59. Fortune, "After War Times," Part 12, *Norfolk Journal and Guide,* 1 October 1927.

60. Fortune, "After War Times," Part 3, *Norfolk Journal and Guide,* 30 July 1927.

61. Fortune, "After War Times," Part 5, *Norfolk Journal and Guide,* 13 August 1927.

62. Fortune, "After War Times," Part 12, *Norfolk Journal and Guide,* 1 October 1927.

63. Sinclair, *The Aftermath of Slavery.*

64. See for example, Alrutheus Ambush Taylor, *The Negro in Tennessee, 1865–1880* (Washington, DC: Associated Publishers, 1941); Alrutheus Ambush Taylor, *The Negro in South Carolina During the Reconstruction* (New York: Russell & Russell, 1969); Alrutheus Ambush Taylor, *The Negro in the Reconstruction of Virginia* (New York: Russell & Russell, 1969); Du Bois, *Black Reconstruction;* and John Hope Franklin, *Reconstruction after the Civil War* (Chicago: University of Chicago Press, 1961).

65. *New York Freeman,* December 6, 1884.

66. *New York Freeman,* December 6, 1884. Emphasis in original.

# 4

# Facts, Memories, and History

## *John R. Lynch and the Memory of Reconstruction in the Age of Jim Crow*

JUSTIN BEHREND

In the summer of 1913 an unlikely author sought to turn the emerging popular and scholarly consensus of Reconstruction on its head. John R. Lynch humbly aimed, in his book *The Facts of Reconstruction,* "to present the other side."[1] He wanted to bring to the public's attention the praiseworthy achievements of "the most important and eventful period in our country's history."[2] And he was uniquely positioned to do so. Born into slavery fourteen years before the beginning of the Civil War, Lynch rose to become an influential Republican congressman during Reconstruction. His experience as a local, state, and federal officeholder gave him incomparable insight into the triumphs and tragedies of the Reconstruction period. But he was not stirred to publish his experiences until his sixty-sixth year, or thirty-one years after he left elective office. The timing of the publication of this well-regarded book is as significant as the message that it conveys.

*The Facts of Reconstruction* was published fifty years after Lincoln's Emancipation Proclamation—and, just as important, fifty years after Lynch's own emancipation—but by then few remembered the remarkable achievements of African Americans in securing their freedom.[3] Instead, white America tended to think of Reconstruction as one of the darkest periods in US history, one in which a reckless federal government pushed aside traditional white southern leaders and handed over the reins of government to illegitimate usurpers, namely scalawags, carpetbaggers, and "Negro politicians." The result was "mongrelism, ignorance and depravity," raged Ethelbert Barksdale, a white Mississippi Democrat who in 1890 sought to educate "the business men of the North" on the evils of Reconstruction.[4]

This popular memory gained new validity and legitimacy in the early twentieth century when Columbia University professor William A. Dunning and his students began to analyze Reconstruction from a scholarly perspective. The so-called Dunningites argued that carpetbaggers and scalawags tricked illiterate and inexperienced African American men to vote with the Republican Party. And once in power, these corrupt northerners and unsophisticated freedmen provoked racial conflicts and emptied public treasuries to line their own pockets. Only the intimidating influence of white paramilitary forces saved the South by driving the Republicans from power and restoring white rule. The Dunningites based their arguments on documentary evidence and were more even-tempered in their prose than southern Democratic politicians; nevertheless, their interpretations did not divert much from popular renderings.[5] Two years after Lynch published his book, the groundbreaking film *Birth of a Nation,* directed by D. W. Griffith, was released to wide acclaim. Although a fictional account based on the novel *The Clansman* by Thomas Dixon Jr., the film interlaced historical facsimiles into the story line to lend a degree of credibility to the view that Klansmen rescued the nation from the sexual and political depravity of African American men.[6]

In this intense white supremacist environment, Lynch hoped to reach a broad audience of black and white readers and offer an alternative history. Joining him in this effort were a cohort of African American scholars such as W. E. B. Du Bois and Carter G. Woodson who also sought to debunk the myths of Reconstruction.[7] Yet it was not until the mid-twentieth century that the viewpoints expressed in *The Facts of Reconstruction* began to take hold.[8] Currently, Lynch's book is considered one of the best firsthand accounts of Reconstruction and is cited in numerous historical studies, in part because Lynch's interpretations concur with the revisionist view of Reconstruction. Yet few historians have bothered to examine the book's unorthodox structure or address the significant time lapse between the events described and when the book was published.[9]

By titling the book "Facts" and endeavoring to write an "objective" account, Lynch situated himself within the emerging professionalization of historical writing.[10] But *The Facts of Reconstruction* is not, nor are any of his other writings, works of historical scholarship. Lynch based his interpretation almost exclusively on his memory, not on the documentary record, which explains, in part, why some turn-of-the-century scholars wrote him off.[11] Yet neither is the book a "race history" or a typical autobiography. In contrast to most race histories that were often written by ministers, Lynch did not ascribe any role to providence in the unfolding of Reconstruction, nor did he intend to unite people of African descent in the United States under a common religious and racial identity.[12] Unlike in most autobiographies, Lynch's personal life is all but absent from this account. He had little to say about his family or his formative years and only included information about himself as it related to Reconstruction and partisan politics.[13]

Like many African Americans living in the age of Jim Crow, Lynch used his personal experiences to attack the popular memories and scholarly consensus on Reconstruction. His political and ideological motives were similar to those of many African American autobiographers such as Alexander Crummell and Ida B. Wells-Barnett, writing in the race vindicationist tradition.[14] Like T. Thomas Fortune, the great African American journalist, they both turned to autobiography late in life and wrote explicitly to black audiences. But unlike Fortune, Lynch deliberately downplayed political violence.[15] And similar to the vernacular memories of ex-slaves, Lynch foregrounded his personal encounters to better make sense of the disparities in his present world.[16] Although his scholarly tone differs substantially from the oral traditions, fictional accounts, and autobiographical approaches utilized by his contemporaries, Lynch's story is similarly rooted in a counter-memory of Reconstruction.

Lynch clearly directed his book, in one sense, at the flawed and biased histories produced by academic historians. Contrary to the Dunning school, he contended that Reconstruction produced the best governments that the South had ever seen; that black and white people worked together in mutual accord; that white Democrats, not black Republicans, created the color line in politics; that "Negro Domination" was a myth; and that extending suffrage rights to African American men was a wise decision. Yet even as he strove to emphasize the balance in his historical interpretation, he hoped that his conclusions would influence contemporary debate over African Americans' citizenship rights. In emphasizing the "moderate" tone of the book, "devoid of bitterness, . . . sectional animosity, or partisan bias," Lynch hoped that the public would take notice of the "commendable and meritorious" aspects of Reconstruction.[17]

He believed that a better—a more factual—history would vindicate the race and lead to an improved social and political position for black people in American society. It is evident that he regarded federal intervention in the South after the Civil War as a necessary and shrewd move, yet he qualified the more controversial features of Reconstruction and instead offered an alternative interpretation of postbellum southern politics, one in which segregation and white supremacy did not determine public life. His repeated discussions of internal party debates and preparations for political campaigns, almost to the exclusion of policies and public opinion, suggest an effort to undermine the premise of legal segregation. He returned to his personal experiences, time and again, because they show how a previous generation of African American politicians worked seamlessly with white politicians on terms of mutual respect. Lynch, in other words, deployed his memory against the popular conception of Reconstruction history in order to show how memory could loosen history's powerful grip on the present. His memories were careful excavations of the past, designed to address the contemporary problem of Jim Crow in American society.[18] This perspective helps explain both what he included in his text as well as the important omissions.[19]

Comparing the historical record to Lynch's memory demonstrates that he pulled his punches. Reconstruction was far more radical than he let on. His own experiences undermine some of the book's arguments, and yet his memory served as a useful counter-narrative to white supremacist histories, demonstrating the contingent nature of the color line. Understanding the historical context of *The Facts of Reconstruction,* then, helps to separate the constructed memories from the lived experiences of African Americans during Reconstruction. And the silences shed light on the limited possibilities, fifty years after emancipation, for democracy and equality in the age of Jim Crow.

## REPUBLICAN GOVERNANCE

John R. Lynch was born in Concordia Parish, Louisiana in 1847. His mother was enslaved, and his father was an Irish-born overseer on a large cotton plantation. While in bondage Lynch toiled as a field hand and as a domestic servant. During the Civil War he worked as a cook for Union soldiers, and in the late 1860s as a photography assistant. With the onset of Radical Reconstruction and the enfranchisement of African American men, Lynch joined a local political club and began to distinguish himself as a community leader. Adelbert Ames, the military governor of Mississippi, appointed him to the office of justice of the peace in Natchez in 1869. Less than a year later, Lynch was elected to the Mississippi House of Representatives, and the following year he ascended to Speaker of the House. In 1872, at the age of 26, he was elected to the first of his three terms in Congress. His district bordered the eastern bank of the Mississippi River from one end of the state to the other and included a substantial majority of African American voters, nearly all of whom voted Republican.[20] In addition to his public service, Lynch helped to build the state Republican Party, holding numerous leadership posts, including head of the state party from 1881 to 1892. At the Republican National Convention in June 1884, he was elected temporary chairman, the first African American to hold such a position in any major party. But after fraud, intimidation, and redistricting stymied his further attempts to win elective office, he moved into the federal bureaucracy, accepting appointments from Republican presidents to positions such as fourth auditor of the US Treasury and major in the US Army. In short, few contemporaries had as large a range of experiences and personal contacts from which to assess Reconstruction, from both a local and a national perspective.[21]

One of Lynch's main arguments was that Reconstruction benefited the South, not least because it established true democracy for the first time. Reconstruction state governments, wrote Lynch, "were the best governments those States ever had before or have ever had since" because they were "based upon the consent of the governed." They were not "perfect" by any means, but they were "a decided improvement" since they gave ordinary citizens, especially ex-slaves, a voice in government and a measure of equality in public affairs.[22] To defend his argument in favor of Reconstruction, Lynch attacked key tenets of the white supremacist ideology. He also downplayed the more radical changes during Reconstruction, while highlighting biracial cooperation and comity among political leaders. In particular, he addressed three myths in his book: the myth of corrupt Republican governments, the myth of "Negro Domination," and the idea that black Republicans drew the color line.[23]

Using Mississippi, his home state, as an example, Lynch took direct aim at the white supremacist charge that southern Republican governments were rife with corruption. In contrast to the prevalent view that uneducated African

Americans and dishonest carpetbaggers exploited government offices for personal gain, Lynch asserted throughout *The Facts of Reconstruction* that southern Republican governments were effectively administered and that experienced Republicans, both white and black, served the public honorably. He used his own participation in government and his conversations with national political figures as evidence to counter the racist stereotypes that black politicians were incompetent upstarts in the legislative chambers. This behind-the-scenes approach was intended to establish his authority as an expert on politics while simultaneously dispelling the myth of black incompetence.

In response to the charge that Republicans had squandered taxpayer dollars, Lynch offered a detailed analysis of Mississippi's finances and his own expertise as a member of the legislature. In a rare use of documentary evidence, Lynch quoted extensively from a state treasurer's report, demonstrating that Adelbert Ames's administration in two years' time had reduced the state debt by 37 percent *and* decreased the property tax rate by nearly half.[24] In contrast, subsequent Democratic regimes reversed these trends, increasing both indebtedness and taxes. "During the whole period of Republican administration," Lynch proudly asserted, "not a dollar had been misappropriated, nor had there been a single defalcation."[25]

While Republican governance had kept the fiscal house in order, at least in Mississippi, Republican legislators had also greatly increased and shifted the burden of taxation. Knowing full well that Reconstruction acquired a terrible reputation in part from its association with high taxes, Lynch contextualized the problem. He ignored the progressive tax system that Republican governments instituted, which shifted the tax burden from the shoulders of landless laborers to wealthy property owners. Instead he focused on the use of tax revenues to fund a new public school system. Very few school buildings existed in Mississippi after the Civil War, and those that stood needed substantial repairs. Moreover, the new state constitution mandated free public school education for all Mississippi children, prompting the legislature to launch an extensive campaign to build schools and provide classrooms all across the state, even though the state's economy had yet to rebound from the war years. Acknowledging the encumbrance that these new taxes placed upon landowners, Lynch explained that the state's credit rating was so poor that it could not borrow the funds necessary for school construction. Thus, "a higher rate of taxation had to be imposed," Lynch contended, but it was only a temporary increase. Once the school buildings were constructed (a one-time expense) and with the appreciation in taxable property as a result of a revived economy in the 1870s, state revenues increased, which allowed the debt to be paid down while reducing property taxes.[26]

The charge of Republican corruption had bite not merely because of fiscal issues but because Reconstruction had dismantled the ruling oligarchies in the South and established a biracial democracy. Reconstruction, Lynch noted, "meant the destruction of the power and influence of the Southern aristocracy."[27] The enfranchisement of African American men led to the creation of new state constitutions that shifted power away from the landed elite toward the masses, both white and black. Lynch, who had experienced enslavement, was emblematic of the rise of a new generation of Republican officeholders and the decline of the old slaveholding elite. This new generation did not merely look different and come from a different social class, they set about to restructure southern society along more egalitarian lines. Radical Republicans established a permanent public school system, balanced the tax burden, spurred economic growth through railroad construction, facilitated equal access to public spaces and the justice system, and integrated ordinary people into the structures of governance. In just a few short years, Lynch and fellow radicals undermined racial and class hierarchies and altered the relationship between citizens and their government.[28] Yet the specifics of this restructuring and Lynch's role in it are noticeably absent in his book.

Contrary to the passive image portrayed in *The Facts of Reconstruction,* Lynch played a major role in breaking down social and political distinctions. He, along with other African American congressmen, spoke movingly about the need for an enhanced federal civil rights law. During debate on the bill, Lynch assailed the arguments used to justify white supremacy and denounced the attacks upon African Americans as they went about their daily lives, even going so far as to describe the limits of his own patriotism. "The only moments of my life when I am necessarily compelled to question my loyalty to my Government or my devotion to the flag of my country," he thundered from the floor of the House of Representatives in 1875, "are when I read of outrages having been committed upon innocent colored people and the perpetrators go unpunished." In short, he insisted that the federal government protect "human rights" and guarantee "the enjoyment of public rights."[29] Congress complied with a civil rights law that aimed to protect black people's access to public restaurants, theaters, transit, and other accommodations. The law, however, lacked sufficient mechanisms to protect African Americans' rights as citizens because it placed the burden of enforcement on those subjected to public discrimination. Perhaps the weak enforcement provisions, and the fact that the Supreme Court struck down the law eight years after its passage, explain why Lynch ignored the Civil Rights Act of 1875 in his book.[30]

Lynch's reticence on equal rights might also have reflected the speed with which these far-reaching measures dismantled entrenched aristocratic power and ushered in a new era of radical governance. By focusing on the fiscal responsibility of Reconstruction governments and the creation of a public school system, Lynch offered a less inflammatory approach to Reconstruction history. If he had emphasized how Radical Republicans broke down deep-rooted racial and class barriers, it would have made his task more difficult, as he was writing in an era when white supremacist ideologies and practices were broadly accepted.[31] And so by moderating Reconstruction's impact and highlighting the least controversial attributes of Republican governments, Lynch hoped to make his overall argument more acceptable to the American public.

## BLACK POLITICAL POWER

A second major theme in *The Facts of Reconstruction* is the myth of "Negro Domination." Lynch repeatedly claimed that African Americans never had a "disposition to rule or dominate the whites," nor did they ever hold a majority of offices.[32] He pointed out that, at least in Mississippi, carpetbaggers never "had absolute control" of any level of government; that black legislators never held a majority in any state legislature; and that only a handful of African Americans were ever elected to federal office.[33] The charge of "Negro Domination" was particularly insidious because white Democrats used it to justify the violent overthrow of Republican governments and later the disfranchisement of African American voters. But Lynch was wrong—knowingly wrong—about black political power at the county and municipal level.

"The colored men never at any time had control of . . . any county or municipality," he claimed, and yet in his home city of Natchez and in the surrounding counties, African American leaders dominated political affairs and offices.[34] From 1871 to 1875, African Americans held four of the five seats on the Adams County Board of Supervisors—the chief administrative body in the county.[35] In Natchez, voters elected four black Republicans to the eight-member board of aldermen, one of whom was Lynch's brother, and they propelled Robert H. Wood, a freeborn African American and a longtime friend of Lynch's, to the mayor's office—the only elected black mayor in nineteenth-century Mississippi.[36] In Lynch's place of birth, Concordia Parish, Louisiana, black Republicans held thirteen of eighteen offices in 1874, including state legislator, coroner, all the justices of the peace, and all the constables.[37] Scores of African American men served in public office in his district and hometown.[38] Most notably, a handful served as sheriff—the most powerful and influential office in the day-to-day lives of county residents—including two of Lynch's friends, Wood and William McCary.[39]

The extraordinary political power of African Americans in Lynch's hometown owed something to the unique demography and history of the region. In the Natchez District, black people outnumbered white people by substantial margins, so much so that the district ranked as one of the greatest concentrations of African Americans in the nineteenth-century South, comparable to the Mississippi Delta, the Louisiana sugar regions, and the South Carolina and Georgia lowcountry. Between 1860 and 1890 the Natchez District's black population varied from 65,000 to 88,000 people, and as a percentage of the total population, it ranged from 80 percent to 82.5 percent.[40]

In addition to holding offices, African Americans controlled local Republican organizations as well. For every one hundred Republican votes, each precinct in Adams County was allotted one delegate to the county party convention (and an additional delegate for remainders over fifty votes), and it fell to the neighborhood clubs to select delegates.[41] Because of the large demographic imbalance in the rural precincts, every delegation was composed almost entirely of African American men. At the 1873 Adams County Republican convention, nineteen of twenty-four delegates—most of whom were farmers or farm laborers—were African Americans, and these delegates selected an African American candidate for sheriff.[42] The power of the black voter in the rural areas was further reflected in party leadership circles. Six of the seven members of the Adams County Republican executive committee in

1872 and twenty-three of twenty-four Concordia Parish party leaders in 1877 were African American.[43]

Thus, Lynch underplayed the extent of black political power during Reconstruction in the Natchez District. African American politicians did not dominate the political system as whites did later in the Jim Crow era, but they did control municipal and county government and party positions in many localities across the South.[44] Lynch—savvy political operative that he was—knew this; indeed, his elevation to Congress came as a result of a majority of African American delegates endorsing his nomination. But to write about the history of black power at the local level would likely have raised howls among a white public that equated black office holding with corruption and unpopular social reforms. The memory of black political power and of the successful administration of government by rural working-class African Americans was of little use to Lynch in 1913. His goals were much more limited—for white authorities to protect African American political and civil rights and to find a way to contest the hegemony of white supremacy. A southern grassroots democracy in which most local offices were held by African American men was almost unimaginable to most whites in Jim Crow America.[45]

## BIRACIAL POLITICS AND ELECTORAL VIOLENCE

A third myth that Lynch sought to debunk was that African American politicians drew the color line and thus deserved some of the blame for the pervasiveness of racial segregation in the turn-of-the-century South. He argued, instead, that black and white people worked together in mutual accord throughout Reconstruction. "There was and still is a bond of sympathy between the two races at the South," wrote Lynch, "a bond that the institution of slavery with all its horrors could not destroy, the Rebellion could not wipe out, Reconstruction could not efface, and subsequent events have not been able to change."[46] He was his own best evidence on this account. Republicans and Democrats, whites and African Americans, considered him to be an excellent legislator, orator, and leader.[47] And he went out of his way in his book to portray white Republicans with whom he worked, as well as prominent white Democrats, as honorable men.

To demonstrate interracial harmony, Lynch recounted a series of meetings with prominent white politicians, such as Speaker of the House James G. Blaine, Secretary of the Interior Lucius Q. C. Lamar, Secretary of State Walter Q. Gresham, and Presidents Ulysses S. Grant and Grover Cleveland. He quoted extensively from these conversations, but the quotations should be considered only approximations of the actual dialogue that took place decades before. It is hard to believe, for example, that the lengthy exchange with Lamar (nearly three thousand words of direct quotation) is a verbatim account of their private meeting in 1885.[48] For Lynch, the precise words of each exchange (the authentic reconstruction of the past) were not as important as his memory of the event and its meaning for the present. He acknowledged as much by admitting that some direct quotes were conjecture.[49] The tone and substance of the conversations portray an alternative history, one of biracial and even bipartisan politics.

In a meeting with President Grant soon after the infamous and corrupt Mississippi election of 1875, Lynch demanded to know why the president refused to send federal troops to protect Republican voters from marauding bands of "white liners" and other violent Democrats. Grant explained that he feared Ohio would turn Democratic if he used force in Mississippi, and thus Republicans would lose the White House in 1876. But as Lynch probed the former general-in-chief of the Union army, he was able to extract an admission from the president that his failure to send troops had been a mistake. "I admit that you are right," Grant supposedly told the 28-year-old congressman.[50] This conversation, and others, allowed Lynch to demonstrate that he (and by extension other African American politicians) did not mindlessly follow the dictates of white Republican leaders, and that powerful white officeholders respected and carefully considered the political opinions of these politicians. Indeed, Lynch prefaced the story with an account of how he persuaded the president to fire an insufficiently Republican postmaster from southern Mississippi.[51] The encounter with Grant also demonstrates how Lynch carefully used the words of national political figures to critique the course of American politics over the previous thirty-five years. According to Lynch's recollection, Grant predicted that some of the greatest achievements of the Civil War would be "lost," specifically that federal power would diminish and "National citizenship" rights would be ignored.[52] Grant's prophecy described all too well the cultural milieu that Lynch and his readers inhabited, one in which the "Lost Cause" dominated interpretations of the war, while African American demands for federal protection of citizenship rights fell on deaf ears. The remorseful words of a former president allowed Lynch to indirectly blame white Democrats for besmirching the sacrifices of war.

Not all white supremacist Democrats, however, were scorned by Lynch. He trumpeted his friendly relationship with Lucius Q. C. Lamar to underscore his argument that biracial and bipartisan comity was quite common in the Reconstruction era. Lamar served in Congress prior to the Civil War, but resigned his seat to lead Mississippi's secession effort and then raised a regiment for the Confederate army. He returned to Congress the same year that Lynch was elected, was later elevated to the US Senate, and before he was appointed to the Supreme Court, he served as secretary of the interior.[53] In the mid-1870s, Lamar was one of the most prominent opponents of Radical Reconstruction and owed his Senate seat to the white counter-revolution, even as he privately lamented the electoral fraud and violence.[54] In 1885 Lamar, as secretary of the interior, met with Lynch to discuss federal appointments. In recognition of unspecified "favors in the past," Lamar offered him an appointment as a "special agent of public lands" in the Dakota Territory, but Lynch declined because, as a good Republican, he could not contemplate working for a Democratic administration.[55] Nonetheless, the offer suggested a degree of mutual respect between black and white political rivals that was hard to imagine in 1913.

Also hard to imagine was the request that Lynch laid before Lamar. While in Congress, Lynch helped many young black men and a few white Republicans secure clerkships in the Pension Bureau. With a new Democratic administration, Lynch feared that these men would be fired, so he asked, as a personal favor, if Lamar would retain these clerks. Lamar agreed, except in two situations where the clerks were involved in interracial marriages. Lynch fought these exclusions and was able to convince Lamar to keep an African American man who had married a white woman, but he could not save the job of a white lawyer who was married to an African American teacher. Lamar's supporters in Mississippi knew of this latter relationship and demanded that the clerk, a former Union army officer who later became the Republican sheriff of Yazoo County, be fired. Although Lynch did not mention his name in the text, the clerk in question was Albert T. Morgan.[56] Lamar explained to Lynch that he did not have any problems with the clerk or his marriage, but he did not wish to risk his political future over one controversial clerk.[57] And so Morgan lost his job, but the African American clerks retained their positions. Thirty years later, it was difficult to find any federal official, let alone an avowed white supremacist, who was willing to protect African American employees. By 1910 President William H. Taft had recently abandoned the Republican tradition of appointing African Americans to southern patronage jobs. The incoming Woodrow Wilson administration in 1913 implemented a new federal segregation policy just as Lynch's book was going to press, and subsequently demoted black civil servants and proceeded to segregate federal workplaces.[58]

Cooperation and goodwill across racial and political lines was not an invented memory, and evidence of it can be found in the documentary record of Reconstruction. "The two races got along well together," boasted Lynch, in the era before the "white leagues" organized in Mississippi. Even "the Democratic [P]arty," he noted before Congress, "sometimes [put] colored men on their own ticket."[59] A northern reporter echoed this general assessment by observing that the black population in Natchez "seems to live on terms of amity with" the whites.[60] Some measure of racial tolerance was also evident in a local Democratic newspaper's plea for steamboats and railroads "to furnish . . . accommodations" to black patrons "equal in every respect to those furnished to white people paying the same rate of fare."[61] And Lynch maintained cordial and friendly relations with the leading Democrats in Adams County, especially William T. Martin, a former slaveholder and Confederate general.[62] Perhaps only the son of a white overseer and enslaved mother, a field hand, but the favorite of an elite planter, could envision a time when, as he expressed in 1876, "race prejudices" would one day "be buried in the grave of forgetfulness."[63]

Lynch's much praised temperament and evenhandedness, however, had their limits. His book fails to acknowledge his interactions with bitter white supremacists and how they ruined his political career. Two-thirds of the way into *The Facts of Reconstruction,* he mentions, almost in passing, that he decided to run for Congress again in 1880 and that he would "again measure arms with Chalmers."[64] Four years before, James R. Chalmers defeated Lynch in an election marked by fraud and violence.[65] In 1880, Chalmers bested Lynch again, using similar methods, but this time Lynch appealed the election results to a congressional committee, which, after a lengthy deliberation, ruled that due to fraud, Lynch should be awarded a seat in Congress.[66] Accounts of these political battles do not appear in the book, and neither does the first name of Lynch's most bitter opponent. Lynch's struggles with Chalmers reveal the violence, intimidation, and deepening racism that were endemic during Reconstruction, a memory that Lynch had little use for in 1913.

Lynch never extended the hand of cooperation to Chalmers—a person so odious that Lynch, uncharacteristically, attacked his character in public speeches. Before Republican audiences during the 1876 electoral campaign, he blasted Chalmers, a former Confederate general, for participating in the Fort Pillow massacre, in which scores of surrendering black soldiers were executed, and for personally ordering the execution of a "negro child."[67] Chalmers's Democratic followers vigorously rejected these charges and condemned Lynch. Upon hearing that the congressman intended to speak at a rally in Port Gibson and that he intended to bring up Chalmers's inglorious past, a column of two hundred armed white men converged on the meeting ground. Fearing an outbreak of violence, Republican leaders adjourned the meeting before Lynch had a chance to speak. Nonetheless, militant white Democrats instigated a riot in downtown Port Gibson on October 21, 1876, which included exchanges of gunfire between black and white residents.[68] At another Republican rally one week later, this time at the small town of Fayette in Jefferson County, Lynch again confronted hostile white Democrats who were particularly incensed at his statements castigating Chalmers. Although hundreds of whites patrolled the streets, armed with rifles and at least one cannon, nearly four thousand freedpeople rebuffed this show of force and proceeded to a church square to hear Congressman Lynch. Soon after he got up to speak, a white Democrat interrupted him, yelling, "You tell a damned lie on General Chalmers." Lynch tried to continue, but each time, Democrats "commenced hooting and hallooing." Finally, Republican leaders called off the meeting.[69]

Lynch alluded to Reconstruction violence in his book, but he never elaborated on it, nor did he discuss how his own life was often at risk while campaigning. At the time, he acknowledged to a *New York Times* reporter that if he had given some of his usual campaign speeches, "it might have been an excuse for a massacre."[70] Fortunately, he was able to escape harm, but many of his supporters were not so lucky. On November 5, 1876, a week after the stifled political rally in Fayette, Democrats executed at least twenty-five black men in rural Jefferson County for participating in a political meeting at a local church. Nevertheless, the massacre did not deter hundreds of black voters, who showed up at the polls on Election Day, where they were met by Democratic officials and armed white supremacists who flaunted their unimpeded access to the ballot boxes.[71]

Lynch was silent about the violence in 1913, but not in 1876. In a speech before Congress, he lambasted the Democratic Party: "Shame upon this once grand, noble, and patriotic organization; it has so degenerated that it can have no nobler aim, no grander object, no higher aspiration than the degradation, humiliation and political subjugation of an innocent, harmless, powerless (as compared to whites) and inoffensive race."[72] Before a congressional committee investigating the political violence, he summed up the events that he witnessed this way: "A perfect reign of terror prevailed during the campaign."[73] By contrast, in his book he used neutral and vague language to describe these events, noting that Democrats "seize[d] the State Government" through "questionable methods" because "it could be safely done."[74] When he did refer to electoral violence, he used opaque terms, such as "sanguinary revolution" instead of bloody revolution, "*vi et armis*" instead of "by force of arms," and "Mississippi methods" for a concerted campaign of violence and intimidation.[75]

Lynch, the historian, failed to explore political violence and offered few explanations for why white Democrats would resort to such brutal methods. He blamed state and federal officials for failing to protect Republican voters, which had the effect of emboldening the white vigilantes in their attacks on African Americans. But it was not just the fecklessness of state and federal power that opened the door to electoral violence. The other side of the issue was the strength of the Republican Party in African American communities. Democrats used massive force because they could not sway Republican voters through legitimate political channels. Since 1867 Democrats had used all manner of economic coercion, social ostracism, and intimidation to prevent African American men from voting with the Republican Party. They nominated moderates and pseudo-Republicans, such as President Grant's brother-in-law Louis Dent, in an attempt to confuse black voters. Wealthy white Democrats appealed to black voters on the basis of presumed paternalistic bonds that were forged under slavery. They offered personal protection and guaranteed employment to those who supported the Democrats. And of those African Americans who supported the Democratic tickets, some were even nominated to run against black Republicans in the hopes of splitting the black vote.[76] Despite these measures, the vast majority of freedpeople, along with perhaps 25 percent of the white population, Lynch estimated, remained committed to the egalitarian principles of the Republican Party.[77] Lynch boasted of this resiliency before Congress, noting that the party was so strong that "nothing short of organized terrorism and armed violence... could crush it out of existence or defeat it at the polls."[78] He was right, of course, and the Democrats did just that.

## A USEABLE PAST

The overthrow of democratically elected governments and the slaughter of friends and allies must have shaken Lynch's faith in the political system and the future of the South. Perhaps we can understand Lynch's neglect of these incidents by viewing his book less as a history focused on "facts" and instead as a constructed memory that offered a useable past to counter the endemic segregation and race-based violence of the early twentieth century. He might not have wanted to reopen the old wounds of the past and confront the painful memories of violence directly, as T. Thomas Fortune did. Revisiting white supremacist hostility and the subversion of democratic elections also might not have been the most effective strategy in convincing contemporary whites of the benefits of equality. To acknowledge the pervasive levels of fraud and explicit acceptance of violent methods among Democrats would undermine Lynch's claim that Democratic leaders were honorable opponents.

Memories of violence and intense political struggles did not suit his purposes in 1913, but in another context and another era, these memories had more value. In his more complete autobiography, *Reminiscences of an Active Life: The Autobiography of John Roy Lynch,* which he composed in the mid-1930s and was published posthumously, he included many recollections of political violence and his struggles against Chalmers. Even though the bulk of the book is largely a reprint of *The Facts of Reconstruction,* he begins with his birth and includes substantial information on his formative years and his life outside of politics. At the end of his life, the violence had more meaning, helping to explain his early departure from elective office and his abandonment of Mississippi after Jim Crow had tightened its grip on his home state. Indeed, he wrote both accounts from the relative safety and security of his new home on the south side of Chicago.[79]

Lynch ignored the sordid details in *The Facts of Reconstruction* because he was at pains to demonstrate that the victims of the Solid South were not just black people. To reach out to his white audience, he placed particular emphasis on southern white Republicans who faced political intimidation from Democrats. Lynch told the story of Colonel James Lusk, a southern aristocrat and a local leader in the Republican Party, who was so ostracized by his white neighbors that he feared that his daughters would be unable to find suitable marriage partners.[80] There was also Joseph Carpenter, a socially prominent Natchez businessman, who withdrew his name as a Republican elector in 1884 after Democrats threatened to boycott his businesses and to harass his children at school.[81] The enormous effort to legally segregate whites from blacks and to prevent African Americans from exercising political influence would not merely leave African Americans "without a hope for the future," Lynch argued, but it also left many white men "intimidated by the Democratic [P]arty" and "prevented [them] from giving effective expression to their honest political opinions and convictions."[82] In this sense, the solidly Democratic South was a "serious menace" to the entire body politic.[83]

The book was also a plaintive plea for Republicans to recognize their foolishness in abandoning their core values. Lynch denounced a series of naïve northern Republicans, from Blaine to Hayes to Taft, who believed that accommodating the Democratic Party's white supremacy would have political benefits.[84] Republicans were still deluded even in the present day, Lynch argued, because they failed to recognize that "the so-called race question" is the "most effective weapon" that Democrats have to "hold the white men in political subjection."[85] He reminded his audience that the Republican Party had once stood with "the middle classes, the laboring people, the oppressed and the slave," a memory that many turn-of-the-century Republicans had forgotten.[86] He asserted that the cardinal principles of the party included "bold and aggressive advocacy and defense of liberty, justice, and equal civil and political rights for all classes of American citizens."[87] And so in 1913, he believed that Republicans could come to their senses and distance themselves from thirty-five years of failed policies toward the South. Writing later in his autobiography after two more decades of Republican inaction against Jim Crow, Lynch reprinted this chapter on the future of the Republican Party in the South, but he notably excised the sentences that referred to the "hope" and "glory" of the Republican Party.[88]

*The Facts of Reconstruction* is an important source for understanding the Reconstruction era, but its silences and obfuscations about African American politics and the violent counterrevolution shed just as much light on life in Jim Crow America. As radical as Reconstruction was in Lynch's 1913 presentation, the history was far more radical than he was willing to acknowledge. He minimized his own record as a strong civil rights advocate. He ignored African American office holding at the local level, as well as African Americans' achievements in establishing a more equitable social order. He minimized white violence against African Americans and overlooked the remarkable political mobilization efforts among black workers. Yet he also accentuated interactions across the color line. In short, he left out many of the radical features of Reconstruction in order to make the case against the scourge of legal racial segregation in early twentieth-century southern society.

While it is impossible to know exactly why he left out these parts, Lynch's constrained memory of Reconstruction seemed to reflect his realistic assessment of contemporary problems and his own hope for the future. He wanted in 1913 to move the public discussion away from the veneration of white supremacy and toward an acknowledgment of African Americans' rights as citizens. The memory of African American men running local governments and the election of black politicians was of little use to Lynch. So, he offered another memory—a counter-memory—one where African Americans and white southerners worked together toward common goals. In this way, Lynch used *The Facts of Reconstruction* to create a site of memory from which all Americans could begin to build a new society.[89]

His book did little in the short run to shift popular white perceptions or to compel white historians to rethink the Reconstruction era, but it did quench the thirst of many African Americans looking for a firm rebuke to the prevailing white supremacist versions of southern history. "Your book," wrote Dr. A. Wilberforce, a prominent black physician and health editor for the *Chicago Defender,* "gives me information I have been searching for over twenty-five years."[90] "Perhaps more than any living man," gushed *The Crisis,* the official magazine of the NAACP, Lynch "knows the truth [of Reconstruction] from the Negro's point of view."[91] Lynch was looking for an opening in the early twentieth century, for a way to undermine Jim Crow ideology, and he hoped that his facts and his memories could accomplish this goal.

## NOTES

Another version of this essay, titled "Facts and Memories: John R. Lynch and the Revising of Reconstruction History in the Era of Jim Crow," was published in *The Journal of African American History* 97 (Fall 2012): 427–48.

1. John R. Lynch, *The Facts of Reconstruction* (New York: Neale, 1913), 10.
2. Lynch, *Facts of Reconstruction,* 9.
3. See, for example, Booker T. Washington's dismissive view of Reconstruction in *Up From Slavery* (1901; repr., Boston: Bedford/St. Martin's, 2003), 76–80. Ordinary African Americans, however, held on to a more positive view of emancipation and Reconstruction. See Geneviève Fabre and Robert O'Meally, eds., *History and Memory in African-American Culture* (New York: Oxford University Press, 1994); David Blight, *Race and Reunion: The Civil War in American Memory* (Cambridge, MA: Harvard University Press, 2001), 300–37.
4. Hilary A. Herbert, et al., *Why the Solid South? Or, Reconstruction and Its Results* (Baltimore: R. H. Woodward, 1890), 333, iii.
5. For Dunning's major works, see William Archibald Dunning, *Essays on the Civil War and Reconstruction and Related Topics* (New York: Macmillan, 1898), and *Reconstruction, Political and Economic, 1865–1877* (New York: Harper, 1907). Of particular importance to this essay is James Wilford Garner, a Dunning student, and his book, *Reconstruction in Mississippi* (New York: Macmillan, 1902).
6. *Birth of a Nation,* directed by D. W. Griffith, Epoch Film Co., 1915.
7. W. E. Burghardt Du Bois, "Reconstruction and Its Benefits," *American Historical Review* 15 (July 1910): 781–99; Rayford W. Logan, "Carter G. Woodson: Mirror and Molder of His Time, 1875–1950," *Journal of Negro History* 58 (January 1973): 7–13; Jacqueline Goggin, *Carter G. Woodson: A Life in Black History* (Baton Rouge: Louisiana State University Press, 1993), 32–36; W. Fitzhugh Brundage, *The Southern Past: A Clash of Race and Memory* (Cambridge, MA: Harvard University Press, 2005), 155. Lynch also contributed two articles to *The Journal of Negro History:* John R. Lynch, "Some Historical Errors of James Ford Rhodes," *Journal of Negro History* 2 (October 1917): 345–68; and Lynch, "More About the Historical Errors of James Ford Rhodes," *Journal of Negro History* 3 (April 1918): 139–57.
8. On Reconstruction historiography, see Eric Foner, "Reconstruction Revisited," *Reviews in American History* 10 (December 1982): 82–100; Thomas J. Brown, ed., *Reconstructions: New Perspectives on Postbellum America* (New York: Oxford University Press, 2008).
9. William C. Harris assessed the book in an introduction to a 1970 reprint of *Facts,* but he did not scrutinize the memory problems in the book or take into account the context of the

times in which Lynch wrote. Lynch, *The Facts of Reconstruction* (New York: Neale, 1913; repr., Indianapolis, IN, and New York: Bobbs-Merrill, 1970), v–lvi.

10. Peter Novick, *That Noble Dream: The "Objectivity Question" and the American Historical Profession* (New York: Cambridge University Press, 1988), 47–85.

11. For scholarly assessments, see George W. Ellis, review of *The Facts of Reconstruction,* by John R. Lynch, *Journal of Race Development* 4 (April 1914): 494–95; J. C. Ballagh, review of *The Facts of Reconstruction,* by John R. Lynch, *Annals of the American Academy of Political and Social Science* 62 (November 1915): 295–96; J. W. Garner, review of *The Facts of Reconstruction,* by John R. Lynch, *The Mississippi Valley Historical Review* 3 (June 1916): 112–13. For popular reviews, see *Chicago Defender,* 16 August 1913, 21 February 1914, 12 December 1914, 19 December 1914, 2 January 1915, 9 January 1915; review of *The Facts of Reconstruction,* by John R. Lynch, *The Nation,* 23 July 1914, 108–9; review of *The Facts of Reconstruction,* by John R. Lynch, *American Missionary,* October 1915, 409–10; George W. Ellis, "Lynch on Southern Reconstruction," review of *The Facts of Reconstruction,* by John R. Lynch, *Chicago Daily Tribune,* 7 March 1914.

12. Laurie F. Maffly-Kipp, "Redeeming Southern Memory: The Negro Race History, 1874–1915," in *Where These Memories Grow: History, Memory, and Southern Identity,* ed. W. Fitzhugh Brundage (Chapel Hill: University of North Carolina Press, 2000), 169–89; Laurie F. Maffly-Kipp, *Setting Down the Sacred Past: African-American Race Histories* (Cambridge, MA: Harvard University Press, 2010).

13. On the use of autobiographies in historical memory, see Paul G. Pickowicz, "Memories of Revolution and Collectivization in China: The Unauthorized Reminiscences of a Rural Intellectual," in *Memory, History, and Opposition Under State Socialism,* ed. Rubie S. Watson (Santa Fe, NM: School of American Research Press, 1994), 127–47; Jacquelyn Dowd Hall, "'You Must Remember This': Autobiography as Social Critique," *Journal of American History* 85 (September 1998): 439–65; Jeremy D. Popkin, *History, Historians, and Autobiography* (Chicago: University of Chicago Press, 2005), 11–56; Kathryn L. Nasstrom, "Between Memory and History: Autobiographies of the Civil Rights Movement and the Writing of Civil Rights History," *Journal of Southern History* 74 (May 2008): 325–64.

14. V. P. Franklin, *Living Our Stories, Telling Our Truths: Autobiography and the Making of the Afro-American Intellectual Tradition* (New York: Oxford University Press, 1995); V. P. Franklin and Bettye Collier-Thomas, eds., "Vindicating the Race: Contributions to African-American Intellectual History," Special Volume, *Journal of Negro History* 81 (1996): 1–144.

15. Shawn Leigh Alexander, "T. Thomas Fortune, Racial Violence of Reconstruction, and the Struggle for Historical Memory," in this volume.

16. Carole Emberton, "The Freedwoman's Tale: Reconstruction Remembered in the Federal Writers' Project Ex-Slave Narratives," in this volume.

17. Lynch, *The Facts of Reconstruction,* 9, 11. By contrast, he took a much harsher tone, with a sprinkling of sarcasm, in his *Journal of Negro History* articles. See, for example, Lynch, "Some Historical Errors of James Ford Rhodes," 345, 360, 362, 366; Lynch, "Communications," *Journal of Negro History* 16 (January 1931): 103, 114–15.

18. For more on the interplay between memory and history, see Paul Connerton, *How Soci-*

*eties Remember* (Cambridge, UK: Cambridge University Press, 1989); David Thelen, "Memory and American History," *Journal of American History* 75 (March 1989): 1117–29; Pierre Nora, "Between Memory and History: *Les Lieux de Mémoire*," in *History and Memory in African-American Culture*, 284–300; Hall, "'You Must Remember This'"; W. Fitzhugh Brundage, "No Deed but Memory," in *Where These Memories Grow*, 1–28.

19. For more on the memory of Reconstruction, see Gaines Foster, *Ghosts of the Confederacy: Defeat, the Lost Cause and the Emergence of the New South, 1865–1913* (New York: Oxford University Press , 1987); Grace Elizabeth Hale, *Making Whiteness: The Culture of Segregation in the South, 1890–1940* (New York: Vintage, 1998), 75–84; Blight, *Race and Reunion*, 138–39, 278; Brundage, *The Southern Past;* Mark Elliott, *Color-Blind Justice: Albion Tourgée and the Quest for Racial Equality* (New York: Oxford University Press, 2006), 165–92; Bruce E. Baker, *What Reconstruction Meant: Historical Memory in the American South* (Charlottesville: University of Virginia Press, 2007).

20. *New York Times*, 17 November 1876. Black voters in Mississippi's Sixth Congressional District outnumbered white voters 100,500 to 30,650.

21. For details on his personal and political life, see John R. Lynch, *Reminiscences of an Active Life: The Autobiography of John Roy Lynch*, ed. John Hope Franklin (Chicago: University of Chicago Press, 1970).

22. Lynch, "More About the Historical Errors of James Ford Rhodes," 144–45.

23. Lynch, *The Facts of Reconstruction*, 92.

24. Lynch, *The Facts of Reconstruction*, 86–91. Lynch cited the state treasurer's 1875 report that the rate of taxation for general purposes had dropped from seven mills to four mills, which was two mills lower in 1875 than in 1910. One mill equals one dollar of tax for each $1,000 of taxable property value, or a 0.1 percent rate. For confirmation of Lynch's figures, see W. H. Gibbs to George S. Boutwell, 19 June 1876, *Report of the Select Committee into the Mississippi Election of 1875*, 44th Congress, 1st Session (Washington, DC, 1876), Doc. Ev., 149. For more on Mississippi taxation, see William C. Harris, *The Day of the Carpetbagger: Republican Reconstruction in Mississippi* (Baton Rouge: Louisiana State University Press, 1979), 626–27.

25. Lynch, *The Facts of Reconstruction*, 165. On Mississippi's indebtedness, which was one of the smallest state debts in the South during Reconstruction, see Harris, *Day of the Carpetbagger*, 704.

26. Lynch, *The Facts of Reconstruction*, 34, 51–52, 86 (quote). See also Christopher M. Span, *From Cotton Field to Schoolhouse: African American Education in Mississippi, 1862–1875* (Chapel Hill: University of North Carolina Press, 2009).

27. *The Facts of Reconstruction*, 101.

28. On the political achievements of freedpeople during Reconstruction, see Steven Hahn, *A Nation Under Our Feet: Black Political Struggles in the Rural South from Slavery to the Great Migration* (Cambridge, MA: Harvard University Press, 2003), 216–64.

29. Rep. John R. Lynch, R-MS, *Congressional Record*, Vol. 3, part 2, 43rd Congress, 2nd Session (Washington, DC, 1875), 943–47. For more on the innovative use of "public rights" by African American and Republican leaders, see Rebecca J. Scott, "Public Rights, Social Equality, and the Conceptual Roots of the *Plessy* Challenge," *Michigan Law Review* 106 (March 2008): 777–804.

30. Bertram Wyatt-Brown, "The Civil Rights Act of 1875," *Western Political Quarterly* 18 (December 1965): 763–75; William Gillette, *Retreat from Reconstruction, 1869–1879* (Baton Rouge: Louisiana State University Press, 1982), 259–79.

31. There are many fine works on turn-of-the-century white supremacy. These include but are not limited to Rayford W. Logan, *The Betrayal of the Negro: From Rutherford B. Hayes to Woodrow Wilson* (New York: Collier Books, 1965); John W. Cell, *The Highest Stage of White Supremacy: The Origins of Segregation in South Africa and the American South* (New York: Cambridge University Press, 1982); Joel Williamson, *The Crucible of Race: Black-White Relations in the American South Since Emancipation* (New York: Oxford University Press, 1984); Neil McMillen, *Dark Journey: Black Mississippians in the Age of Jim Crow* (Urbana: University of Illinois Press, 1989); Glenda Elizabeth Gilmore, *Gender and Jim Crow: Women and the Politics of White Supremacy in North Carolina, 1896–1920* (Chapel Hill: University of North Carolina Press, 1996); Hale, *Making Whiteness;* Leon Litwack, *Trouble in Mind: Black Southerners in the Age of Jim Crow* (New York: Knopf, 1998); Stephen Kantrowitz, *Ben Tillman and the Reconstruction of White Supremacy* (Chapel Hill: University of North Carolina Press, 2000); Marilyn Lake and Henry Reynolds, *Drawing the Global Colour Line: White Men's Countries and the International Challenge of Racial Equality* (Cambridge, UK: Cambridge University Press, 2008).

32. Lynch, *The Facts of Reconstruction,* 94, 107, 115 (quotation).

33. Lynch, *The Facts of Reconstruction,* 94. Contrary to Lynch's assertion, South Carolina had black majorities in the state house from 1868 to 1876, and in the state senate from 1874 to 1876. Thomas C. Holt, *Black Over White: Negro Political Leadership in South Carolina during Reconstruction* (Urbana: University of Illinois Press, 1977), 97.

34. Lynch, *The Facts of Reconstruction,* 93. William C. Harris, in his introduction to the 1970 reprint of *The Facts of Reconstruction,* also pointed out this discrepancy (p. xxv).

35. *Natchez Democrat,* 15 November 1871, 26 January 1873, 11 August 1874.

36. *Natchez Democrat,* 3 January 1871; Vernon Lane Wharton, *The Negro in Mississippi, 1865–1890* (Chapel Hill: University of North Carolina Press, 1947; repr., New York: Harper and Row, 1965), 167.

37. U.S. House, *Contested Election, Spencer vs. Morey, Louisiana,* Vol. 3, Rpt. No. 442, 44th Congress, 1st session (Washington, DC, 1876), 121–22.

38. I have identified over four hundred black men who held political office or party leadership positions. Further details can be found in my Black Politicians Database, http://go.geneseo.edu/BlackPoliticiansDB, and in Justin Behrend, *Reconstructing Democracy: Grassroots Black Politics in the Deep South after the Civil War* (Athens: University of Georgia Press, 2015).

39. McCary was one of two sureties that enabled Lynch to post a bond for his first public office as justice of the peace. See Lynch, *The Facts of Reconstruction,* 29. Lynch never discussed McCary and Wood as sheriffs, nor their political rivalry, in his book or his later autobiography. He did, however, briefly mention them in the first of his *Journal of Negro History* articles. See Lynch, "Some Historical Errors of James Ford Rhodes," 356–57.

40. Historical Census Browser (2004), from the University of Virginia, Geospatial and Statistical Data Center, http://mapserver.lib.virginia.edu/. On regions of high black population concentrations, see Sam Bowers Hilliard, *Atlas of Antebellum Southern Agriculture* (Baton

Rouge: Louisiana State University Press, 1984), 34. In 1870, Concordia Parish had the highest percentage black population in the nation at 93 percent.

41. *Natchez Democrat,* 27 September 1871.

42. *Natchez Democrat,* 13 August 1873.

43. Republican Executive Committee Meeting Memo, 23 September 1872, Natchez Archives, History Department, California State University Northridge (CSUN), Northridge, California; *Concordia Eagle,* 3 March 1877.

44. On extensive black office holding across the South, see Eric Foner, ed., *Freedom's Lawmakers: A Directory of Black Officeholders during Reconstruction,* rev. edition (Baton Rouge: Louisiana State University Press, 1996), and Hahn, *A Nation Under Our Feet,* 216–64.

45. For more on the limits of imagination and the unthinkability of history, see Michel-Rolph Trouillot, *Silencing the Past: Power and the Production of History* (Boston: Beacon Press, 1995), 70–107.

46. Lynch, The *Facts of Reconstruction,* 23.

47. Lynch, The *Facts of Reconstruction,* 66. Even Garner, the Dunningite, conceded the point, but in a typically racist manner. He praised Lynch for being "one of the most intelligent of his race . . . and distinctly Caucasian in his habits." Garner, *Reconstruction in Mississippi,* 296.

48. Lynch, *The Facts of Reconstruction,* 236–48. Nor is it plausible that Lynch faithfully recalled his own precise statements, often running into the hundreds of words, in these conversations from the 1870s. For other examples of copious quotations, see 135, 152–55, 275–77, and 278–81. For direct quotations for which Lynch was not a party to a private conversation, see 64–65, 121–23.

49. Lynch, *The Facts of Reconstruction,* 238, 242. And yet some historians have used these quotations without acknowledging their dubious provenance. See Eric Foner, *Reconstruction: America's Unfinished Revolution, 1863–1877* (New York: Harper and Row, 1988), 555; Brooks D. Simpson, *The Reconstruction Presidents* (Lawrence: University Press of Kansas, 1998), 181, 188; Michael F. Holt, *By One Vote: The Disputed Presidential Election of 1876* (Lawrence: University Press of Kansas, 2008), 22.

50. Lynch, The *Facts of Reconstruction,* 152.

51. Lynch, *The Facts of Reconstruction,* 147–49.

52. Lynch, *The Facts of Reconstruction,* 154–55.

53. Lucius Quintus Cincinnatus Lamar, Biographical Directory of the United States Congress, http://bioguide.congress.gov/scripts/biodisplay.pl?index=L000030.

54. Lynch, "Communications," *Journal of Negro History* 16 (January 1931): 118–19.

55. Lynch, *Facts of Reconstruction,* 236–37. Ten years later, the Cleveland administration again offered Lynch a high-level federal appointment, but again Lynch turned down the offer because, although sympathetic to Cleveland and friendly with Secretary of State Gresham, he could not publicly identify with the Democratic Party. See 277–81.

56. On Morgan's removal from the Pension Bureau, see Garner, *Reconstruction in Mississippi,* 376n1; Albert T. Morgan, *Yazoo: Or, On the Picket Line of Freedom in the South,* intro. Joseph Logsdon (1884; repr., Columbia: University of South Carolina Press, 2000), xlvii.

57. Lynch, *Facts of Reconstruction,* 235–50.

58. Kathleen Long Wolgemuth, "Woodrow Wilson's Appointment Policy and the Negro," *Journal of Southern History* 24 (November 1958): 457–71; Kathleen Long Wolgemuth, "Woodrow Wilson and Federal Segregation," *Journal of Negro History* 44 (April 1959): 158–73; Williamson, *The Crucible of Race,* 356–71.

59. Rep. John R. Lynch, R-MS, *Congressional Record,* Vol. 4, part 6, 44th Congress, 1st Session (Washington, DC, 1876), 5540–43.

60. Edward King, *The Great South* (Hartford, CT: American Publishing Co., 1875), 294.

61. *Natchez Democrat,* 20 February 1873, quoted in Harris, *The Day of the Carpetbagger,* 450.

62. In re *John R. Lynch vs. Board of Commissioners of Election,* 9 October 1896, drawer 432, no. 9, Circuit Court Cases, Adams County, Historic Natchez Foundation, Natchez, Mississippi.

63. Rep. John R. Lynch, R-MS, *Congressional Record,* Vol. 4, part 1, 44th Congress, 1st Session (Washington, DC, 1876), 1005–7.

64. Lynch, *The Facts of Reconstruction,* 191.

65. *New York Times,* 17 November, 22 November, 26 December 1876; testimony of John R. Lynch, *Testimony as to Denial of Elective Franchise in Mississippi at the Elections of 1875 and 1876,* 44th Congress, 2nd Session (Washington, DC, 1877), 123 (cited hereafter as *Denial of Elective Franchise*).

66. U.S. House, *Contested-Election Case of Lynch vs. Chalmers,* Majority and Minority Reports, 47th Congress, 1st Session, House Report No. 931; U.S. House, *Testimony in the Contested Election Case of John R. Lynch vs. James R. Chalmers, From the Sixth Congressional District of Mississippi,* 47th Congress, 1st Session, Misc. Doc. No. 12.

67. Testimony of Thomas Richardson, *Denial of Elective Franchise,* 193. On the accusation against Chalmers, see U.S. House, *Report of the Committee on the Conduct of the War on the Fort Pillow Massacre,* 38th Congress, 1st Session, House Report No. 65, p. 5. For more on the massacre, see Richard L. Fuchs, *The Unerring Fire: The Massacre at Fort Pillow* (Rutherford, NJ: Fairleigh Dickinson University Press, 1994); Andrew Ward, *River Run Red: The Fort Pillow Massacre in the American Civil War* (New York: Penguin, 2005).

68. Testimony of Thomas Richardson, *Denial of Elective Franchise,* 194; *Weekly Clarion* [Jackson, MS], 1 November, 8 November 1876.

69. Testimony of Merrimon Howard, *Denial of Elective Franchise,* 168–69; testimony of John R. Lynch, *Denial of Elective Franchise,* 113–14.

70. *New York Times,* 26 December 1876.

71. Testimony of A. M. Hardy, Merrimon Howard, Peter Hurst, and Lewis H. Ingraham, *Denial of Elective Franchise,* 142–47, 174–87, 896–900, 940–50; Jeannie Dean, ed., *Annie Harper's Journal: A Southern Mother's Legacy* (Denton, TX: Flower Mound Writing Company, 1983), 44; *New York Times,* 15 November 1876.

72. Rep. John R. Lynch, R-MS, *Congressional Record,* Vol. 4, part 4, 44th Congress, 1st Session (Washington, DC, 1876), 3781–84.

73. Testimony of John R. Lynch, *Denial of Elective Franchise,* 109.

74. Lynch, *The Facts of Reconstruction,* 141–42.

75. Lynch, *The Facts of Reconstruction,* 98, 141–42, 159, 165.

76. For more on Democratic efforts to sway black voters, see Behrend, *Reconstructing Democracy,* 107–11, 182–88.

77. Lynch, *The Facts of Reconstruction,* 106.

78. Rep. John R. Lynch, R-MS, *Congressional Record,* Vol. 4, part 6, 44th Congress, 1st Session (Washington, DC, 1876), 5540–43.

79. Lynch, *Reminiscences of an Active Life,* 182–86, 217–33, 293–99.

80. Lynch, *The Facts of Reconstruction,* 121–23.

81. Lynch, *The Facts of Reconstruction,* 230–33. For another example, see 178–80.

82. Lynch, *The Facts of Reconstruction,* 121 (first quote), 318 (second and third quotes).

83. Lynch, *The Facts of Reconstruction.,* 316.

84. Lynch, *The Facts of Reconstruction,* 130–36, 178–85, 224–26, 317–25.

85. Lynch, *The Facts of Reconstruction,* 253.

86. Lynch, *The Facts of Reconstruction,* 292.

87. Lynch, *The Facts of Reconstruction,* 323.

88. Lynch, *The Facts of Reconstruction,* 324–25. Chapter 46 of *Reminiscences of an Active Life* (pp. 458–64) included all of chapter 32 in *Facts,* except for the last seven sentences.

89. For more on sites of memory, see Nora, "Between Memory and History."

90. Wilberforce's statement was included in an advertisement for Lynch's book in *The Crisis,* December 1914, 97.

91. Review of *The Facts of Reconstruction,* by John R. Lynch, *The Crisis,* March 1914, 253–54. On advertisements for Lynch's book in *The Crisis,* see November 1915, 46; December 1915, 98; January 1916, 150; February 1916, 203; March 1916, 271; April 1916, 322.

5

# The Freedwoman's Tale

## *Reconstruction Remembered in the Federal Writers' Project Ex-Slave Narratives*

CAROLE EMBERTON

Hannah Irwin was about twelve years old when the Civil War came to an end. She had been a slave on Ryan Bennett's plantation near Louisville, Alabama, in Barbour County, on the edge of the Black Belt. One of twenty-nine enslaved people on the Bennett place, Hannah labored alongside her mother Hester and father Sam. Her memories of the war and Reconstruction centered on the spectral riders she knew as the "Ku Klux." They made quite an impression on the young girl, who remembered seeing them ride by her cabin one night "when de re'struction was a-goin' on." "Dey wuz all dressed up in white, an' dere hosses wuz white an' dey galloped faster dan de win,'" she recalled. While she thought at first that they were "a whole pack of ghosties," someone else in the cabin informed her of what was going on: "'De Ku Klux is atter somebody.'" In fact, according to Hannah, they were after some freedpeople on a neighboring plantation "dat said dey wuz a-goin' to take some lan' dat warn't deres." The plantation's owner had been killed in the war, Hannah explained, "an' warn't nobody 'ceptin' de mistis en' some chilluns" left on the place. She claimed more than one hundred former slaves "commenced a riot" and drove the woman away in fear. Hannah recalled that the woman arrived at the Bennett house late one night "wid a wild look on her face" and told Ryan Bennett "whut dem niggers is up to." Her old master's response made as much of an impression on her as had the site of the Klan riding up through the trees. Ryan Bennett, by that time approaching sixty years old, "wid out sayin' a word . . . put his hat on and lef' out de do'." It wasn't long after that that Hannah heard the commotion outside her window and looked out to see the Ku Klux. Although she was afraid at first, once Hannah realized that they planned to stop the "riot" on the neighboring plantation and that Mister Bennett was one of them, she "wuz always proud of 'em." Furthermore, the Klan's threats to tie all the freedmen up and leave them to starve in the woods had the intended effect of restoring peace to the community, she believed. "Atter dat dese niggers all 'roun' Louisville, dey kept mighty quiet."[1]

Irwin's memory of the Ku Klux Klan as an effective organization for restoring order contradicts several important aspects of the narrative of Reconstruction that we have come to accept. For modern historians, the desire for land among freedpeople is evidence of their essential American-ness, a quality to be commended instead of derided. Although Hannah's recollections can be read as support for the historiographical consensus that the Klan was a tool for labor control used by planters like Ryan Bennett to ensure their workers' fear and obedience, we are more critical of the subtext of her narrative, namely that the Klan organized to protect white womanhood. Highly attuned to the discursive function of the trope of protection, today's historians have dissected this aspect of the Lost Cause narrative until nothing remains but a skeleton of a once robust tale of romantic vigilante violence. Yet Irwin's stated pride in having a personal connection to the organization through her former master remains unsettling and more difficult to dislodge from its place in her narrative.[2]

It might be tempting to dismiss Irwin's pride as a kind of false consciousness exhibited for the benefit of the white woman who interviewed the ex-slave on her front porch sometime in the mid-to-late 1930s. The racial etiquette of the Jim Crow South made it prudent to tell whites what they wanted to hear—a version of the "tragic era" narrative which at the time dominated the collective white memory of Reconstruction, including most of the historical scholarship on the period. One cannot help but notice how Irwin's description of Ryan Bennett's stoic resolve to right a wrong committed against a white woman could be a scene from *Birth of a Nation.* Perhaps Irwin's advanced age (she was in her eighties) clouded her memory, compromising the accuracy of those recollections and making her nostalgic for her younger days. As the interviewer noted, Hannah Irwin lived alone in "a little one room shack." She was "too old and feeble" to work or go out anymore and relied on the charity of friends for both spiritual and economic sustenance. The old woman appeared to welcome the rare company of the interviewer, who in turn found "Aunt Hannah" to be a quaint relic of bygone days.[3]

As compromised as her memories of Reconstruction might have been, Hannah Irwin's troublesome tale should not be dismissed out of hand because it fails to meet our expectations of what a freedperson should have felt or said in the wake of emancipation. The stories of freedpeople bursting into spontaneous song when they learned of their freedom, the many parades celebrating slavery's demise, or public readings of the Emancipation Proclamation have become emblematic of the black response to freedom. Yet if these kinds of public commemorations characterized one aspect of black popular political culture and collective memory after the Civil War—the Jubilee moment—they did not represent its totality.[4]

A darker dimension of these memories of emancipation and Reconstruction, which has largely gone unnoticed, appears in the testimonies of ex-slaves such as Hannah Irwin. In contrast to the "official" counter-memories of the war and Reconstruction posited by leading black intellectuals, such as Frederick Douglass, William Wells Brown, John Roy Lynch, and in the twentieth century W. E. B. Du Bois, what we might call the black vernacular memories reflected a decidedly less celebratory understanding. The often downbeat accounts of elderly ex-slaves in these interviews, who regularly testified to their attachment to former masters and powerful whites, in general have been dismissed by professional historians. Yet these interviews, based on the personal experiences of vulnerable individuals living in small rural worlds, may provide a more realistic understanding of the lived experience of freedom for many ex-slaves in the aftermath of the Civil War.[5]

Hannah Irwin was exceptional neither in her personal circumstances nor in her troubled memory of Reconstruction. Irwin's story echoes many other similar accounts of misguided attempts to reform the postwar South, all seasoned with declarations of love for their downtrodden former masters, disdain for impotent "Yankees," and sharp criticism for "biggity" freedpeople contained in the more than two thousand ex-slave narratives collected by the Federal Writers' Project (FWP) during the 1930s. And like other testimonies in that collection, she confuses dates and places to the extent that one might conclude that her story is of little value because she gets so many details wrong. From this perspective, Hannah Irwin's tale represents why these narratives are such problematic sources.

The ex-slave narratives collected by an army of mostly white cultural workers during the Great Depression constitute one of the richest yet most controversial archives in American history. Since they were first rediscovered in the 1970s, these narratives have occupied a unique place in American historiography, providing scholars an opportunity to debate not only the usefulness of these particular sources but also larger questions about the nature of memory and the production of historical knowledge. Social historians warn of the racial dynamics of the interview process and the fallibility of human memory. Cultural and oral historians acknowledge these issues but argue that the narratives can illuminate a host of historical questions. Still, even those scholars most sympathetic to the narratives' richness feel the need to continually justify their use of them. Expositions on the narratives proceed like a cautionary tale, forewarning readers about the need to "avoid the pitfalls" and alerting them to the many problems with "authenticity" and "bias." Are any other collections of primary sources labeled with such ominous warnings?[6]

Among the paramount concerns historians have about the narratives have to do with their veracity. Whether or not a particular narrative is "true" or an accurate reflection of established historical knowledge often becomes a kind of litmus test for the usefulness of the entire collection. While many scholars are cautious, others insist that such apprehension is unnecessary. In her study of Appalachian slavery, Wilma Dunaway relied heavily on the narratives and came away "with a deep respect for the quality and the reliability of these indigenous narratives." Compared to many of the other contemporary and even secondary historical sources Dunaway consulted, the memories contained within FWP narratives were no worse in terms of accuracy and reliability and in many aspects fared better.[7]

But what about when they didn't? Do narratives with jumbled chronologies or narrators who misremember key events lack historical value? Does Hannah Irwin simply get her history wrong, or does her tale reveal some important truths about life after slavery? This essay explores Hannah Irwin's seemingly erroneous testimony about an uprising that probably never happened but that nonetheless captured the political turmoil of Reconstruction in ways that more "reliable" sources may not. By triangulating the FWP narratives with contemporary sources and the theoretical insights garnered from the fields of oral histories and memory studies, we can gain a deeper appreciation of how the past lives within the present, and more specifically, how life under

Jim Crow required ex-slaves like Hannah Irwin to manage their memories of Reconstruction in particular ways. This narrative reveals how violence during both the Civil War and Reconstruction required freedpeople to develop political sensibilities that made them hesitant to ally themselves too closely with either Yankees or Confederates, Republicans or Democrats. For Hannah Irwin and her contemporaries, learning how to negotiate whites' expectations of what they should do and say represented one of the first and most important lessons of freedom.[8]

+ + +

Like most oral testimony from former slaves, Irwin's recollections reveal some verifiable "facts" as well as some less demonstrable assertions about black life in the postwar South. A quick search in the eighth and ninth US census finds Ryan Bennett and his holdings. In 1860, the widower lived with his five children on a 200-acre plantation, in addition to owning another 2,100 acres of unimproved land, valued at $12,500. Bennett's personal property, valued at $50,000, included the twenty-nine enslaved people who lived in five cabins on the plantation. The slaves ranged in age from forty-five to six months old. If Hannah's estimation of her age at the time of the war's end was correct, then she was most likely the six-year-old female listed on Bennett's inventory. Bennett survived the war, as he appears again on the 1870 census, albeit in a drastically reduced status. The 1870 count also finds a household of freedpeople, headed by thirty-six-year-old Hannah Mcallister, living nearby. The ages of the household's fifteen residents correspond precisely to the ages of the slaves listed on Bennett's 1860 schedule. Among them was a thirteen-year-old girl named Hannah Irwin. If this is the Hannah Irwin interviewed by the FWP in 1937, then she would have been eight at the war's end in 1865 instead of twelve. Since slave births were rarely recorded, Irwin's confusion over her age was not uncommon. As sociologist Charles Johnson, one of the first scholars to interview ex-slaves in the early 1930s, pointed out, rural blacks born in slavery often depended upon their former owners for a record of their birth. If they moved away from "their white folks," or when their former owners died, their ages were also lost. This seemed not to puzzle Johnson's subjects too much since at the time "ages are only needed at rare intervals, when a census is being taken or for the even less exacting requirement of an obituary and death certificate." Thus, this older generation dismissed the importance of knowing one's age with "the utmost casualness."[9]

Similarly, Irwin's timeline of events, such as when the war ended, likely lacked precision. However, for a person who continued to experience many of the same conditions associated with slavery, such as hunger, deprivation, and physical assault, the temporal line between slavery and freedom may not have seemed clearly drawn. This was the case with Abe Livingston, who clearly recalled that the news of freedom came at about nine or ten o'clock on a Tuesday morning; he and the other slaves on his Texas plantation left the fields and did not return for a week. However, his everyday life changed very little at first. "Freedom didn' mean much to me, 'cause I didn' know the difference," he explained. For Livingston, the "difference" did not become apparent until several years later, when he managed to secure a good job on the railroad.[10]

As with the stories told by Irwin and Livingston, many oral histories contain blurred timelines or confused chronologies. Certain experiences, especially traumatic or extraordinary ones, may take precedence over other seemingly less important ones in an individual's memory, and thus result in a chronological narrative that is out of sequence. This can be disconcerting for professional historians who "do not expect people to drop out of time," according to historian Richard White. White argues that people often measure time in two frames: the everyday and the extraordinary. While the mundane, repetitive events of everyday life may jumble into a blur, extraordinary events stand out and are connected to other extraordinary events to mark the passage of time. This may result in temporally discrete and disconnected events remembered as simultaneous or closer in time than they actually were. In Hannah Irwin's narrative, two extraordinary events take precedence. The "riot" happens and the "Ku Klux" put it down. However, these events may not have occurred in the order that Hannah recalls.[11]

Or they may not have occurred at all. A search in local newspapers fails to turn up any mention of a disturbance in Barbour County like the one Irwin describes. But that does not mean Irwin's story of a riot preceding the Klan ride means that struggles over land did not contribute to the growing violence of the postwar period. In her study of Alabama loyalists, Margaret Storey notes the centrality of land confiscation and redistribution to early plans for Reconstruction, both at the state and national levels. Radical Republican congressman Thaddeus Stevens proposed a controversial plan to treat the former Confederate states, in his words, as "conquered provinces," confiscate the estates of the South's largest landholders, and redistribute the property to freedpeople and loyal Unionists. He believed confiscation was necessary in order to produce realignment in southern society, institutions, and culture. Many Alabama loyalists also backed confiscation as a punishment for those who had persecuted them during the war. Whatever the motivation, the struggle for land played a central role in the grassroots politics of Reconstruction.[12]

Riots and other forms of collective violence helped organize the memories of Reconstruction for many southerners. Two local histories, published in the 1930s, of the area where Irwin lived mention a plot organized by a group of local freedmen to break into the general store, steal weaponry and ammunition, and murder all the white people. Neither of these histories gives dates other than the "Reconstruction period." Both mention the name of a freedman named Alex Hamilton, a carpenter, who betrayed the plotters by informing his former master. As a reward for his loyalty, Hamilton is given a gold watch as well as a parcel of land in town on which to build a house. Hamilton appears in the 1870 census, aged 31, working as a carpenter and owning $1,200 in real estate and $3,000 in personal property—a considerable sum for a freedman. Had the property, indeed, been a reward for his role in revealing a murderous plot? Was the "plot" really anything more than rough talk by local blacks, frustrated and unhappy with their ability to secure land or employment? Did white anxiety about the revolutionary social and political changes wrought by emancipation reach a fever pitch here, as it did in many other places throughout the former Confederacy, giving way to rumor and panic about plots and insurrections? White women wrote both of these town histories, which conform to the typical "Lost Cause" narrative. Yet while history may only partially corroborate the story of an attempted riot, the sense of anxiety, fear, and dislocation that lay at the heart of white memories like these remained an important touchstone well into the twentieth century.[13]

Could Hannah Irwin have been thinking of another event altogether? The most documented and well-known violent confrontation between blacks and whites to occur in Barbour County was the Eufaula Riot of 1874. On November 3 of that year, an Election Day riot in town claimed the lives of at least seven freedmen and wounded as many as seventy more. The climax of a hotly contested election for the position of city court judge, the Eufaula Riot represented the growing strength of white supremacist political organizations throughout the Deep South that year. At the same time the White Man's Party formed in Barbour County to defeat Republican incumbent Elias M. Keils, a native "scalawag," for leadership of the court that oversaw disputes between freedmen and whites, there were similar paramilitary organizations that challenged Republicans at both the local and state levels in Louisiana and Mississippi. The Crescent City White League in New Orleans succeeded in routing the state militia there in September, resulting in a coup of the state government that heralded the dawn of Redemption across the former Confederacy. Witnesses to the Eufaula violence heard whites shouting, "Fall in Company A; fall in Company B," after the first shots rang out. Led by a former Confederate officer who was also Keils's rival for the city judge position, the Barbour County White Man's Party came to the polls prepared to fight. Although black voters had traveled as a large group to guard against intimidation from local whites, they were mostly unarmed, having been advised repeatedly by Republican leadership to avoid anything that might provoke a violent response. Carrying only walking sticks and canes, the black voters were effectively ambushed. Only a few had cast votes when the shooting commenced, and while the polls stayed open throughout the day, no blacks ventured to the polling places when the riot was over. Keils lost the election as well as his teenage son, Willie, who was shot and died two days later.[14]

While Irwin may not have witnessed the riot firsthand, no doubt she heard about it as local blacks retrieved the bodies of the dead for burial and cared for the many wounded. The men in her household and on neighboring farms would have been among those who camped out on the outskirts of town on the Monday night before the election and marched en masse to the polls the next morning. This had been the largest, most flagrant assault against local freedmen since emancipation, and its effects on their political aspirations were profound. Many of the men who survived the attack were forced to leave Eufaula in fear for their lives. Henry Frazer, who had been a steadfast Keils supporter and led a group of 450 black voters into town that morning, moved to Montgomery after the riot. Not only were there death threats, but he also reported that about thirty leading black Republicans had been jailed on trumped-up charges of setting fire to a local saloon. "To-day if you were in Eufaula," he told investigators, "you could not find a half dozen or a dozen really good men who could vote the republican ticket." Likewise, Maurice Seals, who witnessed a white man shoot an unarmed black man and then "jump on him and stamp him and hit him one or two licks with his pistol," also moved to Montgomery. After making it home that day, he talked to many freedmen who passed by his house on their way out of town who said "they did not vote and they were glad that they did not." Whether it was because of the continued threats of violence, outright violence, the inability to get work because they were known Republicans, or being jailed for crimes they did not commit, the black political organization of Barbour County disintegrated.[15]

Could the generalized, everyday struggles between freedpeople and white planters over control of the land throughout Reconstruction and the extraordinary concentration of violence at Eufaula on Election Day 1874 have melded in Irwin's memory? The contest over access to land and working conditions was so routine in the lives of rural blacks in the post-emancipation South that it might be difficult to recall any particular quarrel, but the election riot, although not uncommon for the larger story of grassroots Reconstruction, would appear exceptional to someone like Hannah Irwin whose knowledge of the "big picture" was limited. By using the term *riot,* a word routinely invoked for the events at Eufaula in contemporary accounts and eyewitness testimony, Irwin may have been recalling the political unrest there on November 3, 1874, but by 1937, it was no longer a discrete event. By then, it was bound up with freedpeople's long-term economic struggles and the transformation in personal relationships between whites and blacks on the plantations themselves. Furthermore, the general fear of disorder prevalent during the early years of Reconstruction may have aggregated distinct events into a tangled mass of memory that is impossible to completely unwind.

\+ + +

So, does that mean the Ku Klux Klan did not raid the neighboring plantation? Did Irwin "acquire" this particular memory from stories she heard others tell about the spectral nightriders? How might earlier wartime encounters with mounted men in the area have shaped her narrative about the Klan as an organization that restored order to the neighborhood? Even though she was not a direct target of their terror, the Klan traumatized Hannah Irwin just as it did countless freedpeople in Alabama and across the Deep South in the late 1860s and early 1870s. Although Barbour County did not receive any special attention from congressional investigators in 1871, there is little reason to doubt Irwin's claim to have seen the Klan ride by her cabin or that her former master was a member. William Mudd, a circuit court judge from Jefferson County, Alabama, explained to the investigators that planters encouraged nightriding and sometimes participated in it themselves "to excite something of a terror over the laboring population, so as to compel them to do by fear what they were unable to make them do by law." According to Mudd, it would be impossible for the vigilante group to operate freely without both the knowledge and consent of the area's employers.[16]

But the Klan would not have been the first mounted terror Irwin witnessed. In the last days of the war, Union cavalry raids crisscrossed southeastern Alabama, including Barbour County. As many as four thousand men on horseback, part of the larger campaign known as Wilson's Raid, rode through Louisville near the Bennett plantation on April 28, 1865. Although the war was officially over by then, word of Lee's surrender had not made it to the Confederate hinterland. It was only after General Benjamin H. Grierson arrived in Eufaula that he received a telegram informing him that it was no longer necessary to subdue the hostile population. After delivering the news to the locals, Grierson set up camp across the Chattahoochee River in Georgia, where his men remained for the next few months. Although Barbour County avoided the fate of Tuscaloosa, Montgomery, and Selma, which were devastated by the raids, the fear engendered by the approaching Yankee troops drove residents into sheer panic. Like other plantation owners in the area, Victoria Clayton, as well as her slaves, buried food and other valuables. She ordered the remaining livestock taken to the swamp to avoid confiscation. Members of the Garland family, whose plantation lay on the road Grierson took into Eufaula, hauled away their household furniture in wagons and attempted to hide their animals in the canebrake. Parthenia Hague, the Garlands' governess, quivered at the news that the approaching Yankee cavalrymen were burning some of the outlying areas on their way to town. In the end, Grierson took a different route, bypassing the Garland place altogether. "Eufaula had escaped, by a few days, the physical scars of a civil war," wrote one local historian, "but her people, and all true Confederates, had been left with deep emotional scars which only time might heal."[17]

One need not have been a "true Confederate" to feel the emotional trauma of war. Slaves, too, experienced the deprivation and fear even while they may have looked forward to slavery's end. Treated as "contraband" property, runaways who made their way to Union lines existed in a wartime purgatory somewhere closer to slavery than freedom. The camps into which they crowded were breeding grounds for smallpox and cholera, where many died unattended and forgotten, casualties of a war that did not want them. Men of recruitment age were impressed into service whether or not they wanted to "strike a blow for freedom," as Frederick Douglass envisioned. The others who were unfit for service but were nonetheless "able-bodied" were forced to grow cotton or corn, wash, cook, and serve white soldiers who looked upon the refugees as little more than the slaves they had always been. Those who stayed behind on southern farms and plantations faced down hunger and the Home Guard, becoming objects of Confederate wrath and dejection. The invading "liberators" likewise took certain liberties with confiscated property. When the FWP interviewer asked Henry Jenkins what the Yankees did when they came to his plantation, he replied that the Yankees "seemed more concerned 'bout stealin,' than they was 'bout de Holy War for de liberation of de poor African slave people." When Union soldiers arrived, "they took off all de hosses, sheeps, cows, chickens, and geese, took de swine and de fishes they caught, corn in crib, meat in smoke-house, and everything," and left little for anyone black or white to live on.

Rejoicing could quickly turn to regret. "Us looked for the Yankees on dat place like us look now for de Savior and de host of angels at de second comin,'" recalled Savilla Burrell, who despised her brutal master who sold her siblings away and whipped her mother. "Dey come one day in February. De took everything carryable off de plantation and burnt de big house, stables, barns, gin house and dey left the slave houses," leaving Burrell and her family to taste the bitter along with the sweet. The beef and hams the soldiers ate sometimes failed to satiate other desires. Confederate women's fears of rape were realized on the bodies of enslaved women. Crystal Feimster argues that although historians believe the rape of southern women was rare, the fact that Union soldiers used the threat of sexual violence to subdue a rebellious population made the fear of rape a living reality for both white and enslaved women. At least 250 Union soldiers were court-martialed for rape, and often those acts were committed against enslaved women as a warning to white southern women of the danger of resisting Union demands. Irwin as well as Burrell must have understood freedom as circumstantial and not categorical.[18]

Viola Guntharpe remembered that the Yankees made "a mess out of their lives." Like Jenkins and Burrell, Guntharpe was a slave on a plantation near Winnsboro, South Carolina, just north of the state capital at Columbia. Winnsboro lay in the path of William Tecumseh Sherman's army as he blew through the Carolinas in the winter of 1865. Nearing the end of their long march that began the previous fall in Atlanta, Sherman's troops had just left Columbia in ashes when they headed northward to the upcountry plantations. In search of provisions to keep the army moving, Sherman's commanders dispatched squads of foragers to confiscate food and livestock from area residents. In an area already stretched thin by four years of war, hunger tempered the joy of liberation. "Well, after ravagin' de whole country side," Guntharpe explained, "de army go across old Catawba [River] and left de air full of de stink of dead carcasses and de sky black wid turkey buzzards." She recalled "de picaaninnnies suckin' their thumbs for want of sumpin' to eat" after the troops moved on, leaving the newly freed to scavenge for their survival. "Lots of de chillun die," Guntharpe recounted, "as did de old folks, while de rest of us scour de woods for hickory nuts, acorns, cane roots, and artichokes, and seine de river for fish."

Barnett Spencer, who had been a slave in Alabama, concurred with Guntharpe's recollections of the hardships of war. Their compliance always being controlled through the physical need for food, slaves were accustomed to hunger and deprivation, but the Union invasion heightened an already meager existence. "The Yankees starved out more black faces than white at their stealing," he remembered. After they came, it was hard to find either food or shelter, since many of the buildings on his plantation, including the slave quarters, had been burned. Many ex-slaves "died in piles" from starvation and disease. Hunger left children like Guntharpe and Spencer with an attenuated understanding of freedom that the rest of their lives lived in poverty in the rural South failed to make any more tangible. For Guntharpe, freedom seemed both awesome and superficial. "De Yankees sho' throwed us in de briar patch . . .

all us had to thank them for, was a hungry belly, and freedom—[s]umpin' us had no more use for then, than I have today for one of them airplanes I hears flyin' 'round de sky, right now." Like the airplanes that hovered high above her, emancipation left only the faintest trail in her life. Her hungry belly, on the other hand, grounded her memories in ways that freedom could not.[19]

Did Hannah Irwin confuse Grierson's cavalrymen with the Klan? Perhaps. Klansmen sometimes claimed to be troops and were described as military-like, while occupying troops during Reconstruction were sometimes described by the southern press as Klan-like. Her memory of the Klan's horrifying ride may have resonated with earlier memories of terror on horseback and the deprivation that followed them to her plantation just as it had for Violet Guntharpe. Likewise, her belief that the Klan had stopped a black riot and restored order to the community may have also reflected her attempt to make sense of the disorder first brought to Barbour County by Grierson's men. Irwin's former owner, Ryan Bennett, had seen his fortunes decline considerably in the wake of the war. Once the owner of an impressive farm that produced a bounty of wheat, rye, corn, oats, and cotton, Bennett found his estate reduced from some 2,300 acres to just under 400. His livestock holdings—a crucial marker of wealth for small farmers in any era but particularly in the postwar years—were decimated. The mules, milk cows, cattle, and sheep were gone. All that remained in 1870 was one horse, four oxen, one beef cow, and thirteen swine. In 1860, Bennett had owned sixty swine, enabling him to feed his family well and fulfill his obligations as a slaveholding patriarch. Bennett may not have fed his slaves all that well—few slaveholders did—but as long as the fields, gardens, and livestock remained, so too did their sense of Bennett's mastery. Whether it was because of some of Grierson's soldiers who confiscated Bennett's property; or because he had to slaughter the animals to feed his family while the Union blockade stemmed the flow of goods up and down the Chattahoochee; or because he had been forced to liquidate his holdings for much-needed cash after the war, the comfortable prewar world of the Bennett plantation had been broken. The war stripped Bennett of his former authority, but through his association with the Klan, Irwin may have experienced a reclamation of some of the social power he had formerly possessed. Through their campaign of extralegal violence, the Klan eventually restored a sense of order and predictability in Irwin's mind. Simply put, the Klan helped put things back the way they were. We need not necessarily read this as a commentary on the relative benefits of slavery and the dangers of freedom, as many of Irwin's white contemporaries certainly believed it was. Like the other ex-slaves who recalled how the war upended their lives, for better *and* worse, Irwin attempted to articulate her understanding of the past and the passage of time where upheaval and uncertainty were not always a welcome reality. In her memory, the Klan's ride signified a more familiar and perhaps comfortable normality. Irwin's ties to Bennett probably had less to do with love or pride as much as they did with his ability to perform a prescribed role, but she nonetheless used the language of affect to translate that relationship for the interviewer. That language enabled her to possess a level of personal dignity that obscured her dependence on the Bennett family. In her tale, her relationship with her former master is a matter of choice rather than desperation.

Ultimately, it does not matter that we cannot verify every aspect of Irwin's narrative. Her testimony, along with that of the thousands of others archived in the FWP ex-slave narratives, are valuable not for the reliability of any information about specific people or events they might convey but rather for "the essence of an ineffable experience," to borrow a phrase from Christopher Browning, whose work on the memories of Holocaust survivors offers a more open yet nonetheless critical framework for using this type of oral history. While Browning insists that oral histories can and should be scrutinized for accuracy when using them to piece together a narrative of events, even those that seem less reliable for these purposes remain valuable because they communicate fragments of thoughts and feelings that often remain unspoken in the day-to-day lives of survivors of trauma. Like Holocaust survivors, American ex-slaves carried with them traumas, both great and small, spectacular and commonplace. The pain of family separations, physical abuse, hunger, deprivation, invasion, and even freedom, imprinted patterns on their lives the edges of which may have smoothed out over time but whose texture remained remarkably perceptible decades later toward the end of their long lives. These testimonies lend insight if not conclusive answers to questions about the experience of being newly freed in the rural South that no other sources can give.[20]

+ + +

In particular, the ex-slave narratives reveal the complicated process by which freedpeople struggled to come to terms with the new dynamics of power in the former Confederacy: how they decided whom they could trust, who would and could keep their promises and meet certain expectations, and what the consequences were of placing trust in the wrong hands. Freedpeople experienced great political vulnerability, and as a result the choices they made about whom to support were fraught with anxiety and sometimes led them to make choices that might appear short-sighted, timid, or narrow. First and foremost, it was important to maintain good personal relationships with local whites. Both Hannah Irwin and Molly Scott, a former slave living in Granville, Georgia, stressed the importance of this. According to Scott, "If you be good whose ever place you lives on would keep 'em [the Klan] from harmin' you." Although she acknowledged that freedpeople often had no choice but to steal or starve, in order to "be good" one had to avoid thieving, or at least not get caught. Otherwise the Klan would come after you. Being good also meant avoiding politics. Not only did the Klan target outspoken Republicans and their supporters, planters routinely "turned out" freedmen who refused to vote Democratic.

Local judge William T. Blackford of Greensboro Alabama, explained the risks of black political independence to congressional investigators. Blackford's job required him to adjudicate labor disputes between planters and freedpeople. He testified that "not less than five hundred negroes at various times come and report that 'we cannot vote or go to the election; if we do, we will be turned out of house and home, and we have got nothing to subsist on except what we have got in the field.'" Blackford explained that planters routinely dismissed workers for "trivial causes" in order to avoid sharing the crop at the end of the season. More often than not going to political meetings cost them their jobs and homes. As a result, Blackford reported that freedpeople had become "very much dissatisfied with what [they] term [their] rights," and voting had decreased considerably at the county level. It's no wonder Scott declared, "I say I ain't never voted. Whut in de world I would want er vote for? Let em vote if they think it do em good."[21]

The knowledge of how capricious the Klan could be in choosing its victims might lead scholars to dismiss the belief that "being good" would spare a person from the Klan. Some might also disagree with Scott's definition of what it meant to "be good" and instead award that status to those men and women who refused to bow to the planters' demands to stay out of politics and just keep their heads down and work. It is a sad commentary on black life in the late nineteenth century that a freedman or freedwoman might internalize the political violence they witnessed and take responsibility for it. However, "being good" nonetheless reflected part of a larger worldview among some rural blacks that may help us understand how they navigated the dangerous terrain of Reconstruction. First and foremost, it highlights how ex-slaves' memories were embedded in local conditions and events. The worlds these men and women lived in were quite small and inextricably bound to the physical locations in which they existed and the people with whom they lived, both black and white. As such, the "being good" mentality reveals a certain practical realism by which ex-slaves measured their own vulnerability and determined the most feasible ways to offset it. It was also an implicit acknowledgment that southern whites still wielded considerable power—maybe not in the larger world of national politics but certainly in the daily lives of former slaves in the rural South. And although it cast southern whites in a protective, paternalistic role, "being good" offered freedpeople a semblance of control over their own lives.

Freedpeople paid a high price for their political activity when they backed a party whose local organization failed to match that of the well-armed and drilled opposition. A man like Keils, who could not protect his own child, could not be expected to shield anyone else. According to one witness, Keils advised black voters not to bring any weapons with them to the polls. When some protested, pointing out that whites were typically armed with not one but three or four pistols each, Keils dismissed their worries. "He said here that the men in Eufaula would not as much as shoot a frog," recalled Johnson.[22] If he thought his own ties to the local community would protect him, he underestimated the depths of white rage and the extent to which his opponents would go to destroy not only his political career but also the foundation of black political mobilization in the county. If a local man like Keils could be so naïve, northern emigres could appear downright stupid. Hannah Irwin recalled a Yankee soldier stopping her in the field one day to ask her an important question. He wanted to know what the white flowers growing all around them were called. "You'd think dat a gentmen wid all dem decorations on hisself woulda knowed a fiel' of cotton," she laughed. It might be hard to believe that even the greenest recruit from the far reaches of New England would not recognize a cotton boll, but this part of Irwin's story can be read as a commentary on the liberators' general ignorance of the entrenched nature of power in southern society. How could a man with so little local knowledge be relied upon?

Herein lay the rub for Republicans in the Reconstruction South. Their inability to supplant local power structures, to command obedience if not allegiance among local whites, and to break the planters' economic and social stranglehold made them unlikely, even dangerous, allies for ex-slaves who could hardly afford the alienation such alliances might cost them. How must it have looked to the black voters, as they ran for cover in the streets of Eufaula, to see the captain of ten federal soldiers sent to oversee the election watch the melee from the window of his hotel room, prohibited from sending his measly unit into action by orders from the commander of the Department of the South, who informed him in advance that US troops could only be engaged to enforce revenue, not election laws?[23] Keils's naïveté, coupled with the army's impotency, left local blacks with few choices. One was to withdraw from politics. Another was to maintain close ties to those men who demonstrated their power over life and death. Martin Jackson, a slave from Texas, learned this lesson during the war. Like "lots of the colored boys" he knew, Jackson wanted to run away and join the approaching Union army. His father, however, explained to him the risk in doing so, even if the Yankees won. "He kept pointing out that the War wasn't going to last forever," Jackson recalled, "but that *our forever* was going to be spent living among the Southerners, after they got licked." Seeing the wisdom in his father's advice, Jackson stayed with his master and accompanied him into the Confederate service as a camp servant. Although he secretly supported the Union, Jackson never forgot his father's advice to maintain close ties with local whites.[24]

Local networks of power and authority were difficult to dismantle even though Republicans may have held high offices at the state and federal level. When his former master's father "beat up a Radical nigger," Jesse Williams recalled the sham of a trial that resulted. The courthouse was "packed" that day, according to Williams, as local blacks and whites gathered to see what the outcome would be. The anticipation mounted as the defendant pleaded guilty, but when the judge passed sentence, the farce became apparent to all. The judge gave the defendant the choice of one year in the state penitentiary or a fine of $1. The courtroom erupted; blacks were outraged and whites cheered the judge. "De judge take his silk beaver hat and gold headed cane and march out, while de baliffs holler: 'Make way! Make way for de honorable judge!'" Williams recounted. "Everybody took up dat cry and keep it up long as de judge was on de streets. Oh, how dat judge twirl his cane, smile, and strut."[25]

Charlie Davenport of Natchez, Mississippi, also testified to the enduring strength of local power structures. The "'shawl-strop folks'[26] told the blacks they could go to all the balls and 'tainments' that white folks did," Davenport said. But when "a bunch o' uppity Niggers" went to Memorial Hall for a performance, "all the white folks got up and left an' lef' dem Niggers a-settin' in a empty hall." White indignation did not stop there, however. The next night, according to Davenport, "the "Kloo Kluxes . . . grabbed ever' Nigger what walkded down dat aisle . . ." the night before and showed them what northern promises were really worth. Like both Irwin and Scott, Davenport placed blame squarely on the shoulders of those blacks, including himself, who had been "bit by de freedom bug" and were naïve enough to believe that the northerners among them possessed the power to protect freedpeople from white backlash.[27]

Sometimes it was a case of "better the devil you know." Yankees could be deceitful as well as impotent. Gabe Hines and his new wife, Anna, were "gittin' use to being free" when a northern man offered them a new job with "big wages an a fine house to boot." It was a tempting offering, but Gabe and Anna were unsure about leaving their home and kin behind. They did not know this man, but he seemed to be a "gen'ulman," and a well-dressed and well-spoken gentleman surely could be trusted. They talked about it for two days before finally deciding to take the risk. Then Gabe and Anna packed up what belongings they could carry, for the northern gentleman would not allow them to take any baggage—a possible sign of trouble, but they accepted it. With some clothes and household items tied into handkerchiefs and slung over sticks, Gabe and Anna made their way to Columbus, Georgia, although at the time they were not sure where they were going; their new employer would not tell them. When they arrived at the northerner's plantation, they did not find the big wages and fine house they had been promised. Instead, Gabe was paid only fifty cents a month and "dat fine house tu'ned out to be mo' like a stable." With a bitter taste still in his mouth over fifty years later, Gabe described their disappointment: "Instid of our cabin and garden and chickens and our trees, we had a turrible place, right out under the hot sun wid watah miles away down a hill."

Because the plantation was located at such a considerable distance from their original home, there had been no local knowledge on the place's condition or the reliability of its owner. Most likely, the new planter had trouble securing local workers in and around Columbus, which is why he traveled so far afield to find Gabe and Anna.

If Hines now doubted that his new employer was the gentleman he made out to be, he became certain when the Ku Klux paid a visit one night. They found the man hiding behind Gabe and Anna's cabin and "jes tuk him off somewhar, we nebber knowed whar, but he di'n't come back no mo.'" The man's wife fled town the next day giving the excuse that she could no longer associate with the native whites because they were too poor and ill-mannered. "Dey was po!," Gabe exclaimed. "Dey is no denyin' that. We was all po' caze the Yankees done ruint Columbus. But... de's a big di'ence in bein' po' an' qual'ty an' bein' jes po' white trash." It was clear that he considered his employer to be among the latter group.

Hines blamed himself for being naïve enough to trust in an unfamiliar man with no local connections. "I nebber will be able to tell myself whut made us do hit," he confessed, still harboring much regret over leaving the security and happiness he associated with the time before they accepted the northern man's offer. Feeling deceived and manipulated, Gabe resented the Yankee who promised far more than he could ever deliver. Broken and unfulfilled promises make up a common theme in the ex-slaves' memories of Reconstruction. "Dey promise to give every'body forty acres o' lan' an' a mule," said Nettie Henry of Meridian, Mississippi. "A lot of 'em [freedpeople] didn' have no better sense dan to believe 'em. Dey'd go 'head an' do what de Yankees 'ud tell 'em," she lamented. "Well, dey didn' give 'em nothin,' not even a rooster. Didn' give 'em nothin' but trouble." For Henry and others living in Meridian, trouble included a riot in 1871 that left as many as thirty black residents dead. Like Hannah Irwin, Henry did not address the riot directly, but the incident could hardly have escaped her notice. The Yankees' broken promises cost everyone. Louis Meadows believed that such big talk had gotten President Lincoln killed. "He los' his life 'cause he promised more dan he could ever rightly hope to do."

Whether they were intentionally deceitful or just overly confident in their own abilities to transform both the material and cultural conditions of life in the rural South, northerners asked a lot of freedpeople. They asked them to forfeit the long-standing relationships that provided both security and stability and to trust in an unknown and unproven set of ideals and networks. While those older relationships may have reeked of servitude and dependency, the alternatives often bore the dangerous scent of imprudence. Suspicions that blacks may have harbored that their liberators were less than willing and/or capable of protecting their new constituency turned into certainty when the Klan came calling. Faced with the ever-present threat of violence for making the wrong choice, some freedpeople remembered the violence in a way that not only confirmed their own decision to stay out of the fray but also helped remake a confusing, chaotic, and cruel world into a more predictable, controllable, and hopefully safer place to be.

+ + +

By the 1930s, when the FWP interviewers arrived at Hannah Irwin's doorstop, Reconstruction was long over, but many dangers remained. Irwin told her story of the Klan putting a stop to black misbehavior at a time when white mobs continued to extract obedience from rural black workers in ways that marked a continuum with past racial violence. In this way, Irwin's narrative, along with the other testimony that reads as obsequious or pandering to the expectations of white interviewers, may reflect the narrators' implicit acknowledgment that direct challenges to the racial order remained as risky in 1937 as they were in 1867. As Pete Daniel reminds us, "the violence that attended peonage sent tentacles of dread throughout the entire black community."[28]

White mob violence wed past to present for rural black southerners. The National Association for the Advancement of Colored People (NAACP) estimated that between 1889 and 1918 over 2,500 African Americans were lynched nationwide, the vast majority of them in the South. According to the Tuskegee Institute's tabulations, at least 273 people were lynched in Alabama from 1871 to 1920. All but one of them was black.[29] Lynchings were a community affair, often drawing hundreds and in some cases thousands of spectators to witness the mutilation and murder of people accused of some heinous transgression, but most often whose only real guilt lay in having black skin.

These spectacular orgies of violence and the impunity with which whites engaged in public murder formed the principal ritual in what Mississippi native Richard Wright called his "baptism of racial emotion." At a young age, Wright explained, black children in the South were forced to learn, first and foremost, how to get along with whites and avoid the threat of physical violence that overshadowed even the most benign interactions. As a result, black parents stressed, sometimes with fists and belts, the necessity of holding one's tongue and suppressing anger and resentment as well as pride and sometimes even joy—anything that might attract a vengeful or sadistic white gaze. "In this perilous world," recalled Benjamin Mays, the longtime president of Morehouse College, "if a black boy wanted to live a halfway normal life and die a natural death he had to learn early the art of how to get along with white folks." Or leave the South altogether, as Wright did.[30]

Although the overall frequency of lynchings declined in the first two decades of the twentieth century, mob murder continued to plague the South. There was a noticeable spike in lynchings in 1930, prompting the Commission on Interracial Cooperation (CIC), an Atlanta-based antilynching and uplift organization, to create the Southern Commission on the Study of Lynching. Under the direction of sociologist Arthur Raper, the commission issued a report on the twenty-one documented lynchings of 1930, which urged Congress to pass additional legislation to force state authorities to prosecute lynch mobs and those in law enforcement who knowingly aided their murderous rampages. Included with the recommendations were detailed accounts of each lynching, including the killings of four blacks near Emelle, Alabama, in Sumter County on July 4–5. What began as a supposed altercation over a second-hand car battery ended in a two-day-long "extended manhunt" involving a mob of whites from neighboring Mississippi that prompted local plantation owners to advise their tenants to take cover in their cabins until the danger passed. But Raper's investigation revealed that when Esau Robinson, his father Tom, and two brothers armed themselves to confront and ultimately kill a white man named Grover Boyd, it was not simply because Robinson refused to pay Boyd for the car battery. According to local blacks, the real reason had to do with Boyd's "stepping out" with some of the Robinson women. Unable to stifle his indignation any further, Robinson chose confrontation over conciliation and paid with his life as well as the lives of his uncle and two innocent bystanders caught up in the manhunt, including a pregnant woman. Tom Robinson later received a death sentence for his role in the violence, bringing the final death count for area blacks to five.[31]

The Emelle lynchings were not a singular event in 1930s Alabama. White mob violence remained a defining feature of the decade but so were demonstrations of resistance from local blacks. In the spring of 1931, nine black youths were charged with raping two white girls on a train near Scottsboro in northern Alabama. The trial of the Scottsboro Boys made national headlines in part because of the involvement of the International Labor Defense (ILD). A branch of the Communist Party, which had been working to organize industrial and agricultural American workers, including black workers in the South, the ILD participated in the antilynching movement and publicized the brutality of other forms of Jim Crow justice. The ILD's involvement with the Scottsboro case endeared them to many black Alabamans and helped galvanize the nascent Alabama Sharecroppers' Union (ASU), which formed in the summer of 1931. The ASU advocated for a number of reforms in the tenant-owner relationship, including the right of tenants to sell crops directly instead of going through owners; the right to keep small garden plots; cash payments for crops; and the establishment of nine-month elementary schools for tenants' children. The ASU also called for the immediate release of the Scottsboro Boys. An estimated six hundred people, mostly black sharecroppers, joined the ASU by 1932.[32]

Despite these rather modest numbers, the ASU's organizing efforts met with stiff resistance from local planters and law enforcement. In July 1931, sheriff's deputies in Tallapoosa County attempted to break up a union meeting at Camp Hill, killing one farmer and inciting another "extended manhunt" reminiscent of the Emelle lynchings. The ILD called it "a deliberate slaughter" and charged the Sheriff's Department with "hunting and shooting down Negroes in several towns in that section, as well as raiding and shooting tenant farmers in their homes." In all, thirty-five farmers were jailed. Although all of them would be released by the fall of 1932, the ASU withered in Tallapoosa County as a result of the "Camp Hill Riot." A second attempt to organize later that year was met with similar repression. When the ASU's local leader, Ned Cobb, stood in the way of deputies attempting to repossess a union member's property, a shoot-out ensued, leaving Cobb severely wounded and another farmer dead.

Cobb served twelve years in prison for attempted murder, and soon the ASU stalled after violent white repression in other Black Belt counties forced the union to retreat from its radical vision of "factories in the field" and accept the more modest, capitalist reforms of New Deal agencies like the Farm Security Administration.[33]

It was within this context of ongoing racial violence as well as increasing black radical resistance from the antilynching movement and the ASU that Hannah Irwin narrated her life story to the FWP interviewer in 1937. The "riots" at Emelle, Camp Hill, and Tallapoosa County, as the white press called them, constituted the present in the past for Irwin. It is possible that these events helped bring to mind and perhaps even shape Irwin's memory of ex-slaves plotting to take over her master's land, and the Klan's role in suppressing that "riot." But because individual memory is not a storage cabinet, to borrow an analogy from historian Michel-Rolphe Trouillot, where past events are clearly labeled and neatly organized, it is impossible to know for certain the extent to which the agrarian protests of the 1930s may have influenced Irwin's recollections of Reconstruction, an earlier period of great agrarian unrest. Yet while there is no irrefutable evidence that directly connects Hannah Irwin to either the riot she recalls in the 1860s or the agrarian violence surrounding her in the 1930s, we cannot assume that no connections existed. Rather than see past and present as independent places whose connections are clearly linear, Trouillot argues that historians should see them as relational positions whose meanings are derived from each other. "The past is only past because there is a present," he writes, "just as I can point to something *over there* only because I am *here*. But nothing is inherently over there or here. In that sense, the past has no content." Only in relation to the present does the past have any meaning. For Trouillot, it would be impossible to conclude that the agrarian violence of the 1930s bore no relation to Irwin's recollections of the 1860s and '70s, regardless of whether we can verify what she did or did not know about Emelle, Camp Hill, or Tallapoosa.[34]

If we wish to understand how and why Hannah Irwin constructed her troubling narrative in the way that she did, then it is imperative to understand the context within which she remembered. Just as scholars reconstruct the historical context of any primary source, historians should give the FWP ex-slave narratives a fuller consideration of their historicity and not simply a dismissal of their importance because they do not tell a straightforward or "accurate" story, or because they contradict our conception of the "truth" of Reconstruction. Hannah Irwin's belief in the power of "being good" reflected her present as much as it did her past. Esau Robinson and Ned Cobb eschewed being good, and look where it got them: dead or in prison. The lessons Irwin claimed to have learned about Reconstruction reflected the realities of rural black life in the South during the 1930s.[35]

By "being good," freedpeople like Hannah Irwin, Molly Scott, and Nettie Henry had, in their minds, ensured their own survival, and by the late 1930s, when the FWP came to collect their memories, their survival made them the focus of an immense national project that they may have little understood. Yet for the first time since Reconstruction, the government—albeit in an amorphous form with very little if any tangible political power—turned its attention to the invisible lives of rural ex-slaves. For a brief moment, these elderly men and women seized a unique opportunity to make their lives legible not only for the interviewers and future readers who might one day encounter their words in print but also for themselves. As such, the FWP ex-slave narratives were not simply an exercise in memory but also in self-making. The selves that emerged from those interviews may not always conform to historians' expectations, but they are nonetheless important if we are to engage with the full meaning of emancipation.

## NOTES

1. Interview with Hannah Irwin, in *Born in Slavery: Slave Narratives from the Federal Writers' Project, 1936–1938: Alabama Narratives, Vol. 1,* http://memory.loc.gov/cgi-bin/ampage?collId=mesn&fileName=010/mesn010.db&recNum=224&itemLink=S?ammem/mes nbib:@field%28AUTHOR+@od1%28Irwin,+Hannah%29%29, hereafter cited as *Born in Slavery.* In the interview, Irwin only refers to her master as Mr. Bennett. I used the 1860 US Census and slave schedules to identify him as Ryan Bennett and determine the size of his estate. United States of America, Bureau of the Census, *Eighth Census of the United States, 1860* (Washington, DC: National Archives and Records Administration, 1860). M653.

2. On the dominant narrative of Reconstruction today, see, among many others, Eric Foner, *Reconstruction, 1863–1877: America's Unfinished Revolution* (New York: Harper & Row, 1988); Steven Hahn, *A Nation Under Our Feet: Black Political Struggles in the Rural South from Slavery to the Great Migration* (Cambridge: Belknap, 2003); W. E. B. Du Bois, *Black Reconstruction in*

*America, 1860–1880* (New York: 1935; repr., New York: Touchstone, 1995). Stephanie McCurry discusses the importance of the protectionist trope to the making of the Confederate nation in *Confederate Reckoning: Power and Politics in the Civil War South* (Cambridge: Harvard University Press, 2010), 94. With regard to Jim Crow, see also Jacqueline Dowd Hall, *Behind the Mask of Chivalry: Jesse Daniel Ames and the Women's Campaign Against Lynching,* rev. edition (New York: Columbia University Press, 1993); Glenda Gilmore, *Gender & Jim Crow: Women and the Politics of White Supremacy in North Carolina, 1896–1920* (Chapel Hill: University of North Carolina Press, 1996); and more recently, Crystal N. Feimster, *Southern Horrors: Women and the Politics of Rape and Lynching* (Cambridge: Harvard University Press, 2009), among others.

3. Interview with Irwin, *Born in Slavery.*

4. On black commemorations of emancipation, see Mitch Kachun, *Festivals of Freedom: Memory and Meaning in African American Emancipation Celebrations, 1808–1915* (Amherst: University of Massachusetts Press, 2003); Kathleen Clark, *Defining Moments: African American Commemoration and Political Culture in the South, 1863–1913* (Chapel Hill: University of North Carolina Press, 2005); William Blair, "Celebrating Freedom," in *Lincoln's Proclamation: Emancipation Reconsidered,* ed. William A. Blair and Karen Fisher Younger (Chapel Hill: University of North Carolina Press, 2009), 195–220.

5. My understanding of official versus vernacular memories comes from John Bodnar, *Remaking America: Public Memory, Commemoration, and Patriotism in the Twentieth Century* (Princeton, NJ: Princeton University Press, 1992), 13–17. On Douglass, see Blight, *William Wells Brown;* Lynch, *The Facts of Reconstruction;* Justin Behrend, "Facts, Memories, and History: John R. Lynch and the Memory of Reconstruction in the Age of Jim Crow," in this volume; and Du Bois, "The Propaganda of History," in *Black Reconstruction in America.*

6. For a recent warning about the narratives pitfalls from a scholar who believes they are useful sources, see Sharon Ann Musher, "The Other Slave Narratives: The Works Progress Administration Interviews," in *The Oxford Handbook of African American Slave Narratives,* ed. John Ernest (New York: Oxford University Press, 2014), 101–38. For more on the long debate about the narratives' representativeness and usefulness, see C. Vann Woodward, "History from Slave Sources," *American Historical Review* 79 (1974): 470–81; John Blassingame, "Using the Testimony of Ex-Slaves: Approaches and Problems," *Journal of Southern History* 41, no. 4 (November 1975): 473–92; Norman Yetman, "Ex-Slave Interviews and the Historiography of Slavery," *American Quarterly* 36, no. 2 (Summer 1984): 181–210; Donna Spindel, "Assessing Memory: Twentieth-Century Slave Narratives Reconsidered," *Journal of Interdisciplinary History* 27 (1996): 247–61; and Stephanie Shaw, "Using the WPA Ex-Slave Narratives to Study the Impact of the Great Depression," *Journal of Southern History* 69, no. 3 (August 2003): 623–58.

7. Wilma Dunaway, *Slavery in the American Mountain South* (Cambridge: Cambridge University Press, 2003), 12. See also Woodward, "History from Slave Sources."

8. Richard Wright, *Black Boy: A Record of Childhood and Youth,* anniversary edition (New York: Harper, 2007), 7.

9. Charles S. Johnson, *Shadow of the Plantation* (Chicago: University of Chicago Press, 1934), 17–18. Johnson and a team of assistants interviewed former slaves living in Macon County,

Alabama, for this study. One of the pre-WPA oral history projects, Johnson's work at Fisk University, along with similar projects headed by John Cade at Southern University and Prairie State College, anticipated the larger studies conducted by the federal government a few years later.

10. Eighth and Ninth Census of the United States; Interview with Abe Livingston, in *Born in Slavery.*

11. Richard White, *Remember Ahanagran: Storytelling in a Family's Past* (New York: Hill and Wang, 1998), 35. See also Terri L. Snyder, "Suicide, Slavery, and Memory in North America," *Journal of American History* 97, no. 1 (June 2010): 39–62. Snyder argues that ex-slaves tended to "compress" memories of discrete events into longer memory narratives.

12. Margaret Storey, *Loyalty and Loss: Alabama's Unionists in the Civil War and Reconstruction* (Baton Rouge: Louisiana State University Press, 2004), 208–210.

13. Mattie Thompson, *History of Barbour County Alabama* (Eufaula, AL: n.p., 1939); Eugenia Persons Smartt, *History of Eufaula, Alabama* (1933; repr., Eufaula, AL: J. S. Clark, 1995).

14. Melinda M. Hennessy, "Reconstruction Politics and the Military: The Eufaula Riot of 1874," *Alabama Historical Quarterly* 38 (Summer 1976): 112–25; Alabama Election.

15. 43rd Cong., 2nd Sess., "Affairs in Alabama," House Rep. no. 262, 261, 815.

16. *Condit. of Affairs,* pt. 10, v. 3, Alabama: 1758.

17. Victoria Clayton, *White and Black under the Old Regime* (1899; repr, New York: Books for Libraries Press, 1970); Pathenia A. Hague, *A Blockaded Family* (1888; repr., Freeport, NY: Books for Libraries Press, 1971); Robert H. Flewellen, *Along Broad Street: A History of Eufaula, Alabama, 1823–1984* (Eufaula, AL: Robert H. Flewellen, 1991), 89. See also James Pickett Jones, *Yankee Blitzkrieg: Wilson's Raid Through Alabama and Georgia* (Lexington: University Press of Kentucky, 2000) and *The War of the Rebellion: A Compilation of the Official Records of the Union and Confederate Armies,* Ser. 1, Vol. 49, Part I (Washington, DC: 1897), 137.

18. For more on contraband camps, disease, and danger, see Jim Downs, *Sick from Freedom: African American Illness and Suffering during the Civil War and Reconstruction* (New York: Oxford University Press, 2012); Thavolia Glymph, "The Liberty to be Free: The Problem of Freedom as a Problem of American Exceptionalism," paper given at the Gilder Lehrman Center 13th annual conference, 11–12 November 2011; and Glymph, "Gender and Trauma in the American Civil War," paper given at the University at Buffalo Humanities Institute, 28 March 2014. On impressment and the coercive nature of military life, see Carole Emberton, "'Only Murder Makes Men': Reconsidering the Black Military Experience," *Journal of the Civil War Era* (September 2012): 369–93; and interview with Savilla Burrell, in *Born in Slavery.* On the rape of enslaved women, see Crystal Feimster, "'How Are the Daughters of Eve Punished?': Rape during the Civil War," in *Writing Women's History: A Tribute to Anne Firor Scott,* ed. Elizabeth Anne Payne (Jackson: University of Mississippi Press, 2011), 64–81.

19. Interviews with Violet Guntharpe and Spencer Barnett, in *Born in Slavery.* On the use of food as a method of control on slave plantations, see Walter Johnson, *River of Dark Dreams: Slavery and Empire in the Cotton Kingdom* (Cambridge: Harvard University Press, 2013), 178–80.

20. Christopher Browning, *Collected Memories: Holocaust History and Postwar Testimony* (Madison: University of Wisconsin Press, 2003), 38. Michael Gomez makes a similar case for the

ex-slave narratives in *Exchanging Our Country Marks: The Transformation of African Identities in the Antebellum South* (Chapel Hill: University of North Carolina Press, 1998), 199.

21. *Condit. of Affairs,* pt. 9, v.2, Alabama, 1290.

22. HR 262, 808.

23. Hennessy, "Reconstruction Politics and the Military," 120–21.

24. Interview with Martin Jackson, in *Born in Slavery.* Italics mine.

25. Interview with Jesse Williams, in *Born in Slavery.*

26. "Shawl-strop" is another name for "carpetbagger" and refers to the way in which northern emigres would carry their belongings tied up with a leather belt or shawl strap.

27. Interview with Charlie Davenport, in *Born in Slavery.* Justin Behrend provides additional context for understanding the event Davenport describes in *Reconstructing Democracy: Grassroots Black Politics in the Deep South after the Civil War* (Athens: University of Georgia Press, 2015), 131–33.

28. Pete Daniel, *The Shadow of Slavery: Peonage in the South, 1901–1969* (Urbana: University of Illinois Press, 1972), 29.

29. NAACP, *Thirty Years of Lynching in the United States* (1919; repr., New York: Negro University Press, 1969); Robert Moton, *Record of Lynchings in Alabama from 1871 to 1920* (Tuskegee, AL: Tuskegee Normal and Industrial Institute, 1921). It should be noted that these tabulations were not comprehensive. The researchers relied primarily upon newspaper reports, and since not all lynchings were reported in the papers, or records were scant, especially for earlier years, it is likely that the count of 273 is an underestimation.

30. Wright, *Black Boy,* 7; Benjamin Mays, *Born to Rebel: An Autobiography,* rev. edition (Athens: University of Georgia Press, 2003), 22. Leon Litwack chronicles the psychological toll of Jim Crow in *Trouble in Mind: Black Southerners in the Age of Jim Crow* (New York: Vintage, 1998).

31. In all, six people died in the two days of violence, including Grover Boyd and a member of the white mob who was killed by "friendly fire." Arthur R. Raper, *The Tragedy of Lynching* (1933; repr., Mineola, NY: Dover, 2003), 59–84.

32. Robin D. G. Kelley, *Hammer and Hoe: Alabama Communists During the Great Depression* (Chapel Hill: University of North Carolina Press, 1990); Lowell K. Dyson, *Red Harvest: The Communist Party and American Farmers* (Lincoln: University of Nebraska Press, 1982).

33. Theodore Rosengarten, *All God's Dangers: The Life of Nate Shaw* (New York: Vintage, 1974), 560–61.

34. Michel-Rolphe Trouillot, *Silencing the Past: Power and the Production of History* (Boston: Beacon Press, 1995), 14–15.

35. Irwin's narrative represents what historian Robert McGlone terms an "aphoristic memory," which he defines as a "distinctive class of reminiscences [that] confirm one or more cherished truths about the rememberer's sense of self or about his or her understanding of life in general." See McGlone, "Deciphering Memory: John Adams and the Authorship of the Declaration of Independence," *Journal of American History* 85, no. 2 (September 1998): 411–38, 412.

# III

# RECONSTRUCTION AND THE CREATION OF AMERICAN EMPIRE

6

# The Lessons of Reconstruction

## *Debating Race and Imperialism in the 1890s*

MARK ELLIOTT

Remembering the era of Reconstruction has always been more than a matter for historians. One of the ideological pillars of the era of rigid Jim Crow segregation and disfranchisement was the repudiation of the policies of Reconstruction and the searing sense of aggrievement among white southerners for all they had been forced to endure. "The Southerner will regularly bring forward the horrors of the Reconstruction governments and of 'black domination,'" Gunnar Myrdal commented in 1944. "These memories are in a sense to be cherished. They serve as a vital defensive function to the white South... [which] needs to believe that when the Negro voted, life was unbearable."[1] Blacks must be kept from the polls because history taught that black voting had brought all manner of corruption, chaos, and disorder. A belief in the injustices of Reconstruction was felt deeply by white southerners because they emotionally justified the harsh strictures of segregation and disfranchisement.

Northerners were complicit in allowing the mythology about the "horrors of Reconstruction" to flourish. This chapter examines a crucial moment of political reconciliation between North and South in which conflicting memories and meanings given to Reconstruction played a prominent role. At the outset of the 1890s, northerners remained deeply divided about the violation of black rights in the South, and the Republican Party remained committed (rhetorically, at least) to the interests of its black constituency in the South. Reconstruction may have ended, but the *principle* of full black citizenship and voting rights had not been vanquished.[2] The most influential and memorable sources of anti-Reconstruction mythology had yet to be produced: the Reconstruction novels of Thomas Dixon Jr. and Thomas Nelson Page, the scholarship of the Dunning school, the film *Birth of a Nation,* and Claude Bowers's propagandistic *The Tragic Era: The Revolution After Lincoln* (1929). All of these infamous cultural productions were creations of the era of legally sanctioned Jim Crow segregation that was about to be born.

At the centerpiece of my analysis are two major conferences held in upstate New York in 1890–1891, on the shores of Lake Mohonk, which brought together white southerners and northerners to discuss the so-called "Negro Question." An unprecedented meeting of former antagonists, the two Lake Mohonk Conferences on the "Negro Question" foreshadowed the culture of reconciliation that would truly flower only after the Spanish-American War of 1898. While the conferences failed to create the consensus on the topic they were called to address, the conversation generated at Mohonk provides a unique window into the process of public memory in formation. The conferences were initiated by a small group of liberal-minded northerners who reached out to white southerners in an effort to put sectional discord behind them. Disheartened by the failure of Reconstruction, these Republican Party leaders believed that a new model for "racial uplift" of African Americans should harmonize with strategies for Indian assimilation in the American West. Conceding a great deal to the southern perspective on Reconstruction, they sought the support of white southerners for their educational and missionary efforts, arguing that a gradual approach would ease the hostility toward black material advancement in the South. They readily agreed that Reconstruction had been a mistake from which the nation had to learn. But the ideological reconciliation they sought had unintended results. Rather than improve race relations in the South, the kind of concessions made at Mohonk merely encouraged the coming of disfranchisement and legalized segregation. Perhaps unforeseeable in 1890, the "lessons of Reconstruction" would help guide American internationalism in the age of imperialism, as Natalie Ring shows in another essay included in this volume. The Jim Crow era would also be the era of empire, and the distorted public memory of Reconstruction would be relevant in both contexts.

## REVIVING RECONSTRUCTION

When the Republican Party won a majority in both congressional houses, along with the presidency, in the elections of 1888, it gained control of the federal government for the first time since Grant's presidency. Soon after convening in early 1889, the Fifty-first Congress revisited long-deferred proposals to exercise federal power to protect black voting rights in the South, and provide federal funding for black public education. For Republican leaders like William E. Chandler, Henry W. Blair, George Frisbee Hoar, Thomas B. Reed, and Henry Cabot Lodge, these measures sought to finish the job that Reconstruction had started. By protecting black voting rights with federal supervision of elections, they hoped to secure a foothold for the Republican Party in the South, making southern elections competitive again. By supporting black schools with special federal funds, they hoped to reduce racial antagonism in the South and allow blacks to achieve greater social acceptance and economic advancement. For southern Democrats, however, these proposals amounted to a wholesale return to Reconstruction.[3]

Of these two proposals, Democrats most vociferously attacked the Federal Elections Bill, and they turned directly to the history of Reconstruction for ammunition. Alabama congressman Hilary A. Herbert was so convinced that the lessons of Reconstruction spoke conclusively against black voting rights that he quickly enlisted Democratic leaders from all of the Reconstructed states, plus Missouri and West Virginia, to help him compile a full-length history of the era, which appeared in 1890 as *Why the Solid South? Or Reconstruction and Its Results.* While Herbert denied that the book's purpose was political, nothing could have been more evident considering its haste of construction and its authorship by leading congressional Democrats such as Senator Zebulon Vance writing on North Carolina and Henry Gray Turner on Georgia. Promising "impartial" and "accurate" history, Herbert dedicated his book to the "businessmen of the North" whose investments in the South, he suggested, would be put at risk by the prospect of a return to political instability and rampant corruption. Ultimately, four chapters from the book would be submitted as evidence in the senatorial debates over the Federal Elections Bill.[4]

Senators Wade Hampton and John Tyler Morgan, who led the fierce Democratic minority opposition in the Senate, amplified the themes from Herbert's book in two contributions in *The Forum.* In an article entitled "What Negro Supremacy Means," Hampton decried what he saw as a travesty of corruption and extravagance inflicted on wholesome taxpayers by poor, unlettered black politicians during the dark days of Reconstruction in South Carolina. "Devoid of principles and incapable of shame," Hampton said of black public officials, "the sole object of their public acts was to enrich themselves at the expense of the tax-payers of the state." To support these historical claims, Hampton excerpted long passages from James S. Pike's 1874 propaganda piece *The Prostrate State: South Carolina Under Negro Government,* and assured readers that "the picture he gives is not overdrawn. No colors were too dark to portray that hideous scene: no language strong enough to denounce it."[5]

Senator Morgan, the outspoken Alabamian, echoed his colleague in his own article in *The Forum,* which unapologetically argued for ballot restrictions to prevent "Negro Majorities" from ruling over whites. "The southern people are not mistaken as to the dangers of the ballot in the hands of the Negro race," Morgan warned, "eight years of the horrors of enforced Negro rule has demonstrated to them that a relapse into that condition would be the worst form of destruction."[6] Both of these leaders leaned heavily on their racially charged memories of Reconstruction to unabashedly excuse southern extralegal methods of excluding blacks from the ballot box as a means of "self-defense." Now that the threat of "black rule" had returned, both senators concluded that the time had come to impose a literacy, property, or "moral" restriction on the ballot to neutralize the black vote in a manner that circumvented the Fifteenth Amendment prohibitions against racially defined restrictions. While Democratic senators floated these proposals, the State of Mississippi did not wait for Congress to act on its Federal Elections Bill. Democratic legislators there called a Constitutional Convention that began in August of 1890 to discuss the imposition of a literacy test and a poll tax to "protect" the ballot. Before the end of the year, these preemptive measures would become Mississippi law, making inconsequential the threat posed to white supremacy by the Federal Elections Bill and initiating a wave of similar changes that swept through the South over the next decade.

Positions had long been established on Republican senator Henry W. Blair's bill for federal aid to education.[7] Though passed by previous Republican Senate majorities, and discussed for a decade, it provoked a new reaction this time. Senator Matthew Butler of South Carolina presented an alternative bill to provide federal funds for the emigration of blacks out of the country rather than spend the federal surplus on education. Drawing upon an elaborate treatise by Carlyle McKinley, assistant editor of the Charleston *News and Courier,* Butler argued that federal money would be better spent carrying out a program of voluntary expatriation for southern blacks. Senator Butler did not consider this a serious proposal, introducing the issue as a diversion tactic to derail Blair's measure and antagonize Republicans. To his surprise, the issue gained traction. First, Senator Morgan argued passionately on the Senate floor in favor of the Butler Emigration Bill, subsequently joined by Zebulon Vance of North Carolina, Wade Hampton, and other leading southern Democrats. Secondly, and more surprisingly, Bishop Henry McNeal Turner, the outspoken AME church leader with a long-standing interest in colonization, drummed up support among his followers for Butler's proposal, to the delight of Democrats. Faced with this multifaceted attack on their legislative plans, Republican leaders were on the defensive.[8]

Some Republicans responded with their own counter-memories of Reconstruction. Responding to Hampton's article in *The Forum,* New Hampshire senator William E. Chandler refuted the historical portrayal of Reconstruction in such political tracts as *The Prostrate State,* which he said was full of "exaggeration and caricature." Reconstruction may have been a time of social disorder and strife, but Republicans like Chandler placed the blame for that at the feet of southern white Democrats. Chandler recalled the acts of violence by southern whites, calling them "bloody deeds planned and incited by cruel and brutal men who yet claimed to be civilized and refined." Chandler disdained leaders like Hampton who gained power through violence and fraud, yet "even now consider themselves to be the only natural rulers of free America." By contrast, Chandler praised the blacks for their perseverance and adherence to peaceful methods despite being a "race of slaves, unaided, despised and hated by their unrepentant and unsubdued late masters."

If Reconstruction was a "failure," who was to blame for it? Senator Chandler admitted that Reconstruction governments had been guilty of "corrupt practices" but insisted that on the whole, black politicians had performed "as well and as nobly as they could their new duties as freedmen and citizens," and the faults of a few corrupt men should not overshadow the great progress made in those years. Having learned valuable lessons from their misplaced trust in unscrupulous men, he predicted, black voters and politicians would not be susceptible to the same mistakes again:

> The failure, if it be such, of the first experiment will not be repeated under new conditions and better auspices. The charge that the two races cannot live side by side in the Southern states in political equality, the voters of each freely participating in all elections, has not been proved. It is mere clamor raised to excuse the suppression of the Negro vote in order to obtain partisan power in state and nation.[9]

Chandler, it seemed, was ready to try again at achieving the goals of Reconstruction.

A full-throated defense of Reconstruction came from Richard P. Hallowell, Boston lawyer and former abolitionist whose brother had commanded black soldiers in the 54th Massachusetts. On March 12, 1890, Hallowell discussed black suffrage before the Harvard Historical Society in a presentation entitled "The Southern Question, Past and Present," in which he offered a markedly different historical account than Hampton's and Morgan's. Revisiting the sequence of events that led to congressional Reconstruction and the Fifteenth Amendment, Hallowell made clear that these were no rash acts but carefully considered remedies imposed on the South only after the former Confederate states proved determined to resurrect as much of the institution of slavery as possible. Listing a host of progressive reforms introduced during Reconstruction, Hallowell insisted the "Negro" had fully "demonstrated his capacity for self-government" by advancing democracy and public education in the South, despite having their "private property destroyed," their "schoolhouses burned," and being "ostracized, defrauded, persecuted, mobbed, flogged, and murdered by native whites." Yet all of their accomplishments were being overturned by Democrats who came to power by force. Hallowell had particularly harsh words for Wade Hampton, whose 1876 gubernatorial campaign in South Carolina, he said, "was, in reality, a ruffianly, murderous onslaught upon the lives, the rights and the liberty of the negro and the white men who stood by him." Hallowell condemned the "wiseacres of today who carp at and criticize" Reconstruction, calling for blacks to be deported to Africa. What critics were determined to label a "race problem," he suggested, was really a "southern" problem: specifically, the problem of how to deal with the unrepentant disloyal men of the South who were determined to defy the Constitution. "Negro Suffrage was one of the logical and inevitable results of the Civil War," he concluded, "and until accepted in entire good faith there can be no lasting peace."[10]

Memories of Reconstruction thus remained polarized among prominent figures in the two political parties as the Fifty-first Congress undertook its work in 1889–1891. For Democrats, black suffrage was a diabolical and discredited scheme to advance the Republican Party's interests in the South. For Republicans, suppression of the black vote was a disgraceful continuation of slavery and a well-worn Democratic Party strategy to preserve undue southern influence in national politics. Both appealed to the history of Reconstruction to support their points. The Lodge Federal Elections Bill passed the House in July of 1890, but would stall in the Senate where the Democrats launched the longest filibuster in US history to help defeat it by January 1891.[11] The Blair Bill went down to an early defeat in the Senate in March of 1890, though attempts to revive it in the House would persist for several months.[12]

While Washington roiled with angry partisan debates in June 1890, a cross-sectional gathering of religious, political, and educational leaders came together that June to discuss the "Negro Question" at a mountain resort on Lake Mohonk outside of Poughkeepsie, New York. For three days, they deliberated on the very same issues being discussed in Washington, guided by the Quaker ethic of open and genial discussion. Partisanship and "politics" were disdained. This high-profile conference brought together former slaveholders and abolitionists, Confederate and Union soldiers, Democrats and Republicans, and it revealed a great deal about the shifting ideological sands of the early 1890s. Whether or not it contributed to the subsequent defeat of the Federal Elections Bill (the Blair Bill was already dead), the debates pointed the way toward a new consensus on the lessons to be learned from the "failure" of Reconstruction.

## FROM THE "INDIAN PROBLEM" TO THE "NEGRO PROBLEM"

To fully apprehend what occurred at the Mohonk conferences in the summers of 1890 and 1891, one must first appreciate its connection to Western expansion and imperialist ideologies of "civilization" and "uplift." Annual "policy" conferences at Lake Mohonk were initiated by a wealthy Quaker, Albert K. Smiley, who served on the Federal Board of Indian Commissioners in the administration of Rutherford B. Hayes. In the late 1870s, Smiley found that the array of educational and missionary organizations operating among Indians in the West was racked with confusion and conflicting viewpoints. To bring about a more unified approach, Smiley organized annual gatherings of white leaders in the field of "Indian uplift" at his family-owned resort hotel at Lake Mohonk. Formalized in 1883, and lasting until 1916, the "Friends of the Indian" conferences served as influential think tanks, bringing together over two hundred leaders annually and forging a broad consensus in Washington on Indian policy where discord previously had reigned.[13] The first Mohonk Indian Conferences of the 1880s helped to produce a profound shift in federal Indian policy with the Dawes Severalty Act of 1887. The striking continuity between the conferences on the "Indian Problem" of the 1880s and the two conferences on the "Negro Question" in 1890–1891 has drawn little attention from historians who have written about these meetings.[14]

General Samuel Chapman Armstrong, one of the key figures at the Mohonk Indian Conferences, brought his personal experience with Reconstruction directly to bear on the "Indian Question." Armstrong attended all of the Indian Conferences in the 1880s and tirelessly promoted his unique vision of freedmen's education as the singular best way to achieve "racial uplift." Armstrong was born and raised in Hawaii, where his parents, missionaries from Massachusetts, established schools for native Hawaiians that stressed the morally uplifting influence of manual labor. Armstrong's father taught him that acquiring industrious work habits was the first step toward "civilization." As his biographer Robert Eng has shown, Armstrong adapted his father's missionary technique to the circumstances of Reconstruction and made it the centerpiece of his particular version of "industrial education."[15] After commanding a black regiment during the Civil War, and serving as a Freedmen's Bureau agent, Armstrong became the headmaster at Hampton Institute in Virginia in 1869 and subsequently separated his school from the American Missionary Association so that he could shape the curriculum and promote Hampton as a distinct model for freedmen's education.

Hampton Institute expanded its mission to include Indian education when Armstrong controversially began to enroll American Indians in 1877. Soon, he established a reputation as a visionary educator for Indians. "Civilization," Armstrong told the 1886 Mohonk Conference, "incorporates people who are industrious. If you think there is any hardness in this, remember that it is done with a feeling that we must save them [the Indians] from themselves."[16] Praising Indians' capacity for civilization, he told the Mohonk conferees of the great strides made using the Hampton method, alongside black teachers and students. Armstrong called this mixing "biracial education"—an innovative notion that blacks and Indians ought to be educated together.[17] Through the Mohonk Conferences, Armstrong became a friend and confidant of Albert Smiley, whom he placed on the Board of Trustees at Hampton. Armstrong's career neatly links Reconstruction in the South to missionary work in the West and overseas in the Pacific.

Despite its secluded location, Smiley's Mohonk retreat was no ivory tower. Stacked with men of power and influence, the 1885 and 1886 Mohonk meetings virtually served in place of congressional hearings for the Dawes Severalty Act, one of the most monumental pieces of legislation on Indian affairs of its era. Hailed as the "Indian's Magna Carta" by its sponsor, Massachusetts senator Henry Dawes, the Dawes Act opened a path to citizenship for Indians who accepted a 160-acre allotment of reservation land, to be held in trust by the government for twenty-five years. As Republican chairman of the subcommittee on Indian Affairs, Dawes used the Mohonk deliberations to establish an aura of nonpartisan expertise around the bill, which discouraged opposition from Democratic president Grover Cleveland. The Act reflected the assimilationist views of Armstrong and others who advocated for Indians to become "self-supporting Citizens" by giving up tribal life and operating small family farms.[18] But unlike the policies of Reconstruction that assimilated the freed people on the basis of equality and full citizenship rights, the Dawes Act required that Indians earn full citizenship by demonstrating their worthiness first. Full citizenship rights were used as an incentive—a promised reward in a distant future.

Historian Cathleen Cahill has emphasized the influence of Reconstruction on the Mohonk reformers, and the continuity between their educational efforts among freedmen during Reconstruction and their program for Native Americans. But Cahill overlooks the significant differences that had taken hold based on the "lessons of Reconstruction."[19] Senator Morgan from Alabama, for one, recognized that the Dawes Act reflected a departure from the "rash experiment" of Reconstruction. In his *Forum* article, "Shall Negro Majorities Rule?," Morgan observed that the Dawes Act adopted a wiser method of assimilating Indians into citizenship than Republicans had applied to blacks in the South. "Our process of enfranchising the Indian is just the reverse of [Reconstruction]," he remarked. Whereas the Fifteenth Amendment had bestowed the right to vote on freedmen en masse, Morgan wrote, "we make citizens of [Indians], man by man, and upon the condition of their proving their capacity for citizenship by dissolving their tribal relations and taking lands in severalty." In light of this new approach, Morgan concluded that "we are repenting at our leisure having dealt with this political and temporary question in the heat of our national animosities," and he charged Republicans with having the Fifteenth Amendment "thrust into the Constitution with inconsiderate haste."[20] In Morgan's view, the Dawes Act indicated how the problem of enfranchising blacks might have been dealt with by a cool-headed deliberating body, removed from the narrow pressures of the partisan politics that shaped Reconstruction. Unbeknownst to Morgan, the architects of the Dawes Act were, in fact, about to consider how its approach might be applied to the post-Reconstruction South.

Fresh from their triumph with the Dawes Act, the Mohonk regulars were eager for new challenges. Ex-president Rutherford B. Hayes suggested to his former appointee Smiley that a new annual conference be convened to consider the condition of southern blacks and to propose measures to aid their "rise to the full stature of American citizenship."[21] Hayes's reputation remained tarnished by the bitter criticism he received from fellow Republicans for allowing the final collapse of Reconstruction. For instance, Senator Chandler had eviscerated him in 1877 in an influential open letter that accused him of abandoning southern blacks in exchange for the White House. Richard Hallowell remarked in his presentation to the Harvard Historical Society that he would "always believe" the overthrow of Republicans in South Carolina "was effected by a conspiracy between Wade Hampton and President Hayes."[22] These widely held judgments stung Hayes, who maintained that excessive federal intervention had served only to increase political turmoil during Reconstruction and remained convinced that his noninterventionist policy toward the South had improved the situation. Far from signaling abandonment, he believed his policy had provided a "cooling off" period that allowed blacks a respite from white hostility, which allowed them to advance in wealth and education. Perhaps sensing Hayes's desire for vindication on this issue, Smiley appointed him as honorary chair of the first annual Mohonk Conference on the "Negro Question."

Without a doubt, Hayes and Smiley hoped to foster a new consensus on the troublesome "Negro Question" as they had on Indian policy. The organizers were not seeking to reassure black southerners or to shore up the Republican Party in the South. To the contrary, Hayes and Smiley intended to reach out to southern whites and to forge a common ground with them. Consulting with Armstrong, Smiley carefully compiled a list of southern invitees, emphasizing "broadminded" members of the clergy, educators, and politicians. But he also reached out to southern extremists: Senators Hampton and Morgan were invited, along with Supreme Court Justice L. Q. C. Lamar, Virginia governor Phillip McKinney, and Reverend Thomas Dixon (who was not yet widely known for his racial views). Careful not to antagonize their southern guests, Smiley's invitation promised that matters purely political would be forbidden as a topic of conversation, as he told one invitee: "we wish it to be entirely without reference to and free from knotty political questions."[23] He hoped leaders of both sections would speak in a "spirit of courtesy and consideration of each other's feelings; that there may be no rash words spoken . . . and that at the close of our three days' deliberations we shall be able to arrive at some general conclusions which shall command the confidence of the country."[24] Interestingly, of the prominent Republicans invited, the Reconstruction partisans who had attacked Hayes personally, Chandler and Hallowell, were left off the list, while other politicians, including Senator Hoar and ex-governors Daniel Chamberlain and Rufus Bullock, were included.

One organizational decision by Smiley created a firestorm of controversy: he did not include any black leaders on his invitation list. Fearing that an integrated meeting would diminish southern white involvement and might inhibit the "frankness" of the conversation, Smiley catered to southern white prejudices by not inviting black participants. Once it became public knowledge that blacks were to be excluded, scathing criticism began to appear in the black press that alienated some white sympathizers too. George Washington Cable, the preeminent southern racial progressive of the moment whose *The Negro Question* (1890) was perhaps the most thoughtful contribution to the political debate, turned down the invitation after failing to change Smiley's mind on the matter.

General Armstrong wished to see his protégé invited—Booker T. Washington, whom he had recommended to Smiley as "the most trusted Negro in the country."[25] But Smiley stuck to his guns and kept the same policy for the second conference in 1891, even going so far as to invite southern extremists again (though none attended either meeting). Armstrong called the decision a "great pity" but ultimately defended Smiley, explaining to *The Southern Workman* upon his return from the first conference that "in order to get the Southern white men to come, [Smiley] decided not to invite any colored people." "He is a warm friend of the colored race. His whole object was for their benefit," Armstrong continued, "but he thought it best to do one thing at a time."[26] Booker T. Washington was sorely disappointed and accurately foresaw that "the exclusion of colored men will in large degree cripple the influence of any deliverance the conference may make."[27] Indeed, the cloud of controversy that surrounded Mohonk as a white-only gathering is what scholars most remember the conference for even today.

Scholars should also recognize these conferences as a significant chapter in the evolving public memory of Reconstruction. Roughly one hundred participants came to Mohonk in each of the two "Negro Question" conferences. Few of the invited politicians attended. Only one-fifth of those attending in 1890 can be identified as "southerners," but that number rose to one-third the following year. Southern participants were made to feel welcome, and they repeatedly expressed surprise and delight at the kindness with which their opinions were received by their old abolitionist and Republican foes. An impressive list of Republicans who were active in Reconstruction were in attendance, including General Oliver O. Howard, former head of the Freedmen's Bureau; General Eliphalet Whittlesey, commissioner of the Freedmen's Bureau in North Carolina and later a professor at Howard University; Albion W. Tourgée, Reconstruction-era judge and popular author of novels about Reconstruction; Ednah Dow Cheney, former secretary of the Freedmen's Aid Society; Edward L. Pierce, head of the "Port Royal experiment" in South Carolina in 1862, and later a biographer of Charles Sumner; and Elizabeth Hyde Botume, a teacher in the colored schools in Port Royal since 1864 and author of *First Days Among the Contraband*.[28] Some would defend the past, but that was not their purpose. Most came to discuss what, if anything, remained to be done for the "Negro."

## THE DEBATE AT MOHONK

By framing the debate as a question about "the Negro" and discouraging the discussion of politics, Hayes and Smiley tried to direct the conversation toward the theme of "industrial education." Rather than define the question in regional terms as Hallowell and George Washington Cable had in calling it the "Southern Question," or as the "Race Problem" which might address white racism in both North and South as a central topic, they sought to assess "Negroes" themselves. Both the 1890 and 1891 conferences began, after introductory remarks by Smiley and Hayes, with a presentation that touted "industrial education" as a proven method of uplift that had been solving the racial strife in the South by earning the respect and support of white southerners.[29]

Armstrong himself delivered the first presentation at the 1890 conference, speaking on the theme that all "civilization" began with a belief in the dignity of labor. But because slavery had stigmatized labor as undesirable drudgery, blacks had not yet learned to value hard work over idleness. The foundations of good character and moral habits were being laid at Hampton, he explained, by rewarding student manual labor with wages. In addition to classroom learning, students had to work their way through school, while learning trades that could support them later. Armstrong postulated that, at the outset of Reconstruction, "the great trouble with the Negro was not ignorance: it was deficiency of character. You can feed and clothe the Negro, build his home and give him knowledge but that does not necessarily build up character." The policies of Reconstruction, in his view, had failed to appreciate that. Interestingly, Armstrong insisted that the path to becoming civilized is the same for all peoples, and applied universally across humanity: "The conditions of character and manhood and citizenship for all people are simple and clear . . . this method applies to the Indians and to white men as well as to the Negro. He has got to work to succeed."[30] The discourse of "civilization," as Armstrong employed it, simultaneously declared all people equal and condemned blacks and Indians for their deficiencies as a people.[31]

The logic of Armstrong's "industrial education" implied criticism of Reconstruction by suggesting that, just like the Indians, black people ought to have been educated and "civilized" before becoming full citizens. Whites had attained "character," "manhood," and the capacity for democratic citizenship only after centuries of preparation. A mere quarter-century removed from slavery, were blacks ready for those privileges? Armstrong's answer to this was made clear when he commented: "the Negro is back in the iron age [while] the white race is in its golden age."[32] It seemed that blacks were thousands of years behind whites in their development. Armstrong's arguments about the need for "industrial education" thus accomplished a neat trick. Without repudiating the principle of racial equality—all races, he insisted, were equally capable of attaining "civilization and manhood," and the process was the same for all peoples—he met white supremacy halfway by placing the actual fulfillment of that equality for blacks to be far off in a distant future.

Reverend Armory Mayo from Massachusetts, head of the Federal Bureau of Education, also spoke at the outset of the First Mohonk Conference in 1890, and he stated the problem bluntly. "The pivotal question on which this vast problem turns is, 'Has the Negro, in his American experience, demonstrated a capacity for self-developing American citizenship?'" Northerners and southerners, he believed, had always answered this question differently. Mayo believed that, since the war had ended, blacks had demonstrated that southern paternalism was predicated on a falsehood:

> If the Negro, as so many Southern people believe, is only a perpetual child . . . destitute of the capacity for "the one thing needful" that lifts the subject of paternal[ism] up to the citizen of a republican government, then the thing to do is to leave him to the care of his superiors in the South who certainly know this side of him far better than the people of the North.

But Mayo firmly rejected this "southern" view. In light of the experience since emancipation, he said that the evidence "is all on the side of the final elevation of the Negro to the essential rights and opportunities of American citizenship."[33] But when?

Mayo spoke at length about his admiration for black achievements and their capabilities, and felt they had been harshly judged by northerners who had too "lofty expectations" for the freedmen that were impossible for any people just emancipated from slavery to fulfill. Nevertheless, he surprisingly expressed sympathy for a color-blind educational qualification on suffrage that applied to all races, noting that such a literacy test had been in effect in Massachusetts since 1857. Mayo predicted that the final integration of blacks into southern society would be achieved in a distant future when southern whites softened their prejudice.[34] "I have no doubt that the race problem will finally be solved, in the South, largely through the agency of the Southern Anglo-Saxon people, —not over their heads, but with their thorough co-operation," Mayo mused.

Appealing to his southern participants at the Conference, he asked: "Will the Anglo-Saxon Southern people, at present nine-tenths of the entire white population, in due time appreciate this opportunity, and join hands with all good men and women, at home and abroad, in this, the grandest crusade of all the ages[?]" Mayo put the issue into a global perspective and observed that a "great convergence of opinion" was taking place everywhere that nonwhite peoples could be educated and assimilated into civilized society. "Hostile theories" to the contrary, he believed, would inevitably fall away.[35]

One might call this the foundational "progressive" consensus on race matters: *time,* plus the proper tutelage, would erase the inequalities of the present for blacks (as well as Indians and other nonwhite peoples). Permanent inequality was unthinkable. "Progress," once instilled as an ideal and set in motion, would solve all. As one northerner put it, "every citizen of this republic must have, sooner or later, his full rights, and equal rights with his fellow-citizen. Till that day arrives, the question of civil rights will not be settled."[36] Which only left to be answered—would it be sooner or later? And, if later, how much later? Surprisingly few commentators addressed evolutionary theory or discussed biological differences between the races. "It needs now no argument to prove that the American Negro is capable of civilization," Edward Pierce of Massachusetts observed, "[he] is adapted to civilized life, and has moral and religious instincts, and that in a condition of freedom he does well as soldier and laborer. All this is settled."[37] Indeed, no one debated these points. A common refrain of both conferences was that the "Negro problem" was really "only the problem of humanity" and that the solution was to treat blacks the same as any other group in the same condition, without special consideration or prejudice. Reconstruction policies, therefore, had not been mistaken in their objective, only in their methods, which had served to antagonize relations between the races instead of ameliorating them, and failed to ask whether blacks were ready for full citizenship.

Mayo addressed the history of Reconstruction directly. Responding to its critics, he denied that the "exaltation of the Negro to full American citizenship was either an act of sectional revenge, a narrow and ferocious partisan policy or the reckless experiment of an excited sentimentalism." Rather, Mayo celebrated Reconstruction as a noble effort to live up to the nation's founding ideals. He effused:

> If ever a people, in a great national emergency, acted under a solemn sense of responsibility to God, humanity, patriotism, and republican institutions, I believe the conviction of the loyal Northern people that shaped the acts of reconstruction, is entitled to this judgment, and will so abide in history. It was the most memorable testimony of a national government, just rescued from desperate peril, solemnized by the death of its venerated leader, to its faith in popular institutions, recorded in the annals of mankind.[38]

While defending the motives behind Reconstruction as selfless and noble, he conceded that the "daring experiment" was not a complete success. "I do not defend any injustice, tyranny, reckless experimenting with government itself, that followed that act," he said of the Republican State governments, "no thoughtful man defends such things today." In retrospect, "the act that conferred highest earthly distinction of the full American citizenship on a nation of newly emancipated slaves, of an alien race, involved a penalty of a great injustice to its object." Too much, it seems, was asked from people not yet ready for the demands of citizenship. Ultimately, Mayo was more concerned with vindicating the purity of the motives of the white architects of Reconstruction, than the record of the southern Republican governments themselves.

Several northern participants echoed Mayo's views of Reconstruction as a well-intentioned but flawed effort toward racial justice. Samuel Barrows of Boston discussed the ill effects of Reconstruction on blacks that he observed in the South in the 1860s, explaining that "in the early days the Negro expected a great deal of help from political measures. Instead of climbing the ladder, he expected to be carried up by a political steam elevator, a Negro politician holding and sometimes pulling the wire rope." But Barrows found evidence of "progress" since Reconstruction in the fact that "the Negro has discovered that he can do a great deal more for himself than politics can do for him."[39] In a spirit of sympathy and generosity toward their southern countrymen, many northerners, especially boosters of "industrial education" like Barrows, were willing to concede much to the past grievances of white southerners. One southerner marveled at the genial atmosphere of the conference: "it is the first time that I have ever felt that I could speak with perfect freedom with Northern men, and that, notwithstanding our divergence of views, that it was possible for us to interchange ideas with that mutual consideration, without which the solution of any problem would be impossible."[40]

In the idyllic surroundings of Lake Mohonk, with a Quaker spirit of friendship and forbearance pervading the gathering, very few participants ventured to speak about white political violence against blacks either during Reconstruction or at the present. Even General Howard, without naming the Ku Klux Klan, only briefly made reference to the burning of schools and churches by the opposition in the 1860s to prevent blacks from receiving education. When Howard made this remark, in fact, it sparked a moment of embarrassment and tension significant enough to be mentioned in the press. Howard was chided in one paper for his "impetuous" manner because his remarks sharply disagreed with a former slaveholder who touted the benevolence of former masters. The tension was diffused when General Brinkerhoff—a Democrat of southern upbringing—offered his hand to Howard and the men shook in agreement about the need for northerners and southerners to cooperate. Ex-president Hayes applauded this gesture and expressed delight at the sight of a Democrat and a Republican cooperating (or at least agreeing on the principle of cooperation).[41]

No one spoke in defense of the political side of Reconstruction. All sides, however, praised the efforts of northern missionaries and philanthropists—and even the Freedmen's Bureau—in blazing a trail for black advancement through the educational institutions. Several teachers spoke about their experiences during Reconstruction, for which they were praised, even by white southerners who belatedly found much to admire in those northern women who taught in southern black schools. Even more praise was heaped upon freedpeople themselves, whose accomplishments and advancements were described in various presentations, prompting Bishop Lyman Abbott to wonder whether "the Negro race had made more progress in the last twenty-five years than any people since Adam."[42] Measuring the "progress" of southern blacks invited all manner of comparison, often favorable, to other peoples lacking in "civilization," including Africans, Indians, Chinese, native Hawaiians, Irish Catholics, and poor southern whites.[43]

While all agreed that education was a good thing, disagreements remained over who had the responsibility to provide financial support for it. Whether the taxes of southern whites, the donations of northern philanthropical societies, or blacks themselves had borne, or should bear, the largest burden for educating southern blacks was the source of divided opinion. John Jay of New York, grandson of the first US chief justice, politicized the discussion by calling upon the conference to adopt a bold resolution that urged the president and the Congress to adopt a bill providing sufficient federal aid to public schools to maintain a permanent public school system for all. Reasserting the hopes of the nation's founders, he argued that it was a national responsibility to "secure all children, native or of foreign birth, an elementary education fitted for their rights and duties as American citizens."[44] To Jay's dismay, his resolution was watered down with vague and compromised language that called upon the "people of the United States," rather than the federal government, to support common schools and fulfill their "sacred duty to educate the seven million of Negroes" in the country. The Second Mohonk Conference voted to adopt a more specific resolution calling for "the aid of public education by the national government, for the special benefit of those sections in which illiteracy most prevails."[45] Still, this resolution was buried in the eighth position in a list of nine resolutions, and it lacked the dramatic appeal to the president and Congress that Jay proposed.

Wading into the controversial issue of federal government funding of public schools threatened to upend the sectional harmony sought at the conference. At the First Mohonk, Albion W. Tourgée addressed at length the merits of the recently failed Blair Bill. A longtime critic of the measure from a Radical Republican perspective, Tourgée's own writings had promoted the cause of federal aid to education as an alternative means to accomplish the goals of Reconstruction in two popular novels, *A Fool's Errand* (1879) and *Bricks Without Straw* (1884), and a policy treatise *An Appeal to Caesar* (1884). No author was more identified with efforts to revive Reconstruction with new measures. Nevertheless, he expressed emphatic opposition to the Blair Bill because it had become too compromised to guarantee sufficient aid to black schools. Tourgée pointed out that the Blair Bill left the disbursement of the federal money to the southern state governments with no means of ensuring that colored schools would receive their fair share, if any at all. At the risk of offending southern white participants, he remarked that he did not trust southern state governments when it came to black advancement: "I do not believe that God ever made a people good enough to be entrusted with another people's rights and interests."[46] Passionately in support of national funding of public schools, while opposing the compromised Blair Bill, Tourgée's comments illustrated the challenge of passing effective legislation on the issue.[47]

With the possibility of federal support rapidly fading, the self-supporting, "by-your-own-bootstrap" message of "industrial education" was poised to win cross-sectional support. Yet Armstrong's philosophy elicited some sharp critiques previewing debates that would persist for decades. Joseph E. Roy, secretary of the American Missionary Association, titled his paper "The Higher Education of the Negroes No Mistake," and he aggressively defended his own organization against the implied criticism of Armstrong and his supporters. His presentation cited many examples of black academic leaders—including one "W. E. Dubois of Fisk now at Harvard"—whose achievements served as examples to "stimulate the mass of their people to rise in enlightenment" by inspiring others to seek higher education.[48] Roy echoed John Jay by linking higher education directly to the exercise of citizenship, including the right to suffrage. He claimed higher education was needed "to protect his suffrage, in order to the maintenance of his freedom and of his citizenship, he needs a measure of the larger discipline of education."[49] More than simply reading the names on the ballot, blacks needed the ability to comprehend the issues and to produce their own political leaders. In Roy's view, industrial education was beneficial, but not sufficient, to the larger task of participatory democracy. Many others joined Roy in giving industrial education its due but refused to let it assume pride of place over other educational endeavors.

Outspoken feminist Ednah Dow Cheney went further than anyone else in her criticism. She recommended the racially integrated public schools of Boston as a better model for the nation than any segregated schools, including the industrial ones. She joined with Lyman Abbott in pointing out that segregated and specialized schooling was not likely to achieve assimilation, but rather to perpetuate separation and stigma. But Cheney pushed the need for integration even beyond the classroom. "The first thing is to do away with the prejudice in our own hearts and in our own manners," she insisted. "I am afraid that very few of us can say that we are absolutely free from it . . . we have got to live with him [the 'Negro'] on terms of amity and equality in every respect." Challenging the taboo over "the sexual amalgamation of the races," Cheney proclaimed that social integration should be encouraged: "I do believe that every law forbidding intermarriage should be swept from the statutes."[50] Albion Tourgée similarly called for white churches and houses of worship in the North as well as the South to demonstrate true Christian principles by welcoming blacks and integrating their congregations.

Both Cheney and Tourgée identified the "Negro problem" in the racist culture of white America and called upon whites to change their behavior. "I am inclined to think that the only education required is that of the *white* race. The hate, oppression, the injustice is all on our side," Tourgée said of the "industrial education" panacea. Satirizing Armstrong's philosophy, he mused, "Praise God and make money seems to be a fair paraphrase of the advice given him here. I doubt the good results of the prescription." Blacks understood thrift and self-reliance already, he maintained, having learned to survive on far less sustenance than any of their white teachers could imagine. "The race needs heroes and patriots and martyrs rather than millionaires," Tourgée believed, to lead their struggle for acceptance and equal treatment.[51] Only these two participants sought to reframe the discussion around white oppression.

Meanwhile, the largest political elephant in the room, the Federal Elections Bill, was never named directly but lurked just beneath the surface of the discussion. Rather than defend blacks' constitutional right to suffrage, or lament its suppression, many speakers questioned the wisdom of the Fifteenth Amendment in the first place. W. H. Hickman, president of Clark University in Atlanta, described the Fifteenth Amendment as almost a reckless experiment in democracy that posed "an unparalleled risk to the republic." The enfranchisement of men who had only known government "by force" and had no experience with self-government, Hickman believed, was historically unprecedented, and he remarked, "the wonder is that we have succeeded in this experiment as well as we have."[52] Ironically, Hickman's comments on the Fifteenth Amendment came in a presentation entitled "The Co-Education of the Races" in which he argued that racially integrated schooling was essential to fully assimilate blacks into American citizenship and to achieve political and economic equality (though, unlike Edna Cheney, he reassured his audience that social equality would never result from integrated schooling).[53]

Support for educational or literacy restrictions on the ballot kept finding its way into the comments of both northern and southern participants. "You made him a citizen," a self-described representative of the "old Confederate South" reminded Republicans at the Second Mohonk. While acknowledging Republicans' good intentions, he could not help but complain, "If we could have a moral, an educational, and a property qualification, we would be the better for it; but we are to have universal suffrage."[54] It seemed that many northerners sympathized. The former president of Cornell University, Andrew D. White, made a case for ballot restrictions as progressive reforms. White noted that "we have tremendous questions at the North, quite as serious as those at the South. We have coming in upon us a flood of people who, by all their traditions and habits, are unfitted as yet for the high duties of a republic like this." In fact, the New York State Legislature as far back as the 1870s explored proposals to restrict suffrage by imposing a literacy test as a means to clean up corrupt urban governments supported by immigrant voters. Though this movement failed, President White evidently believed that the moment was auspicious to try again:

> It would be well if the South would establish an educational test for suffrage. Such a course would doubtless disfranchise temporarily a large proportion of the colored population, and indeed a part of the white population. The South might temporarily lose some electoral votes, but it would gain in strength and respect throughout the Union. More than that, I believe that the results of such a course would be so good that it would eventually spread to most, if not all, of the Northern States. I confess to the hope that the time will come when, not only in the North, but in the South, there will be a simple educational test for suffrage.[55]

White imagined that the South could be the testing ground for ballot restrictions that would ultimately become national. Evidently, he did not foresee that a literacy test might be administered in such a way as to purposely exclude nearly all blacks on a permanent basis, but rather envisioned it as an incentive to achieve a degree of literacy that would make voters less susceptible to manipulation by others.

With their former antagonists backtracking on the policies of Reconstruction, some southerners could not resist pushing the historical discussion even further into the past. If Reconstruction and black suffrage were not entirely right, perhaps slavery was not entirely wrong. Picking up on the theme of gradualism, several southerners sought to integrate the history of slavery into the "progressive" narrative of gradual racial uplift. "I did not like slavery any more than General Howard did, and I would not have it again," Reverend A. W. Pitzer insisted. Yet, he pointed out that slavery had its benefits: "but for the fact that these people were compelled to labor for two hundred years they would not be as far advanced as they are today. Enforced labor has placed the American Negro far higher in the scale of civilization than his African brother."[56] One after another, southerners expressed relief at emancipation, praised Lincoln, and even praised abolitionists, while at the same time defending slavery's record as a benevolent civilizing institution. A few northerners began to echo these sentiments. "With all the gigantic evils of slavery, which many Southern men are now the freest to acknowledge," Samuel Barrows offered, "we must admit that through the power of an overruling Providence it was one of the greatest foreign missionary agencies ever devised" because, he said, it brought more Africans into contact with civilization than any foreign mission could ever hope to.[57] The Mohonk debates indicate that, in reaching out to southerners, it was impolitic to dwell too much on the "gigantic evils" of racial oppression in the South, whether past or present.

With the conference having downplayed the importance of black political rights, lamented the mistakes of Reconstruction, and accommodated proslavery ideology, its tone gave Republicans in Washington little encouragement to undertake a renewed intervention in the South. The press coverage of the Mohonk debates highlighted the "spirit of optimism that pervaded all the addresses" and left an impression that problems in the South were well on their way to being solved without new measures. The press also noted the strong support for industrial education among many participants of the conference. At the conclusion of each conference, a series of resolutions were adopted and at both conferences greater support for industrial schooling was recommended. But these resolutions fell short of a resounding endorsement. The first of six resolutions adopted at the concluding session of the first conference recommended "increased facilities for industrial training" but added that "all school authorities . . . use industrial training, not in order to make the Negro a mere toiler, but to evoke a nobler manhood and womanhood by the discipline of intelligent labor."[58] The second conference merely recommended "the great extension of industrial education for both men and women."[59] Neither resolution recommended it to the exclusion of other forms of education, nor claimed a superiority of results from it.

When the Second Mohonk Conference concluded on June 5, 1891, the participants expected to be invited back for the third annual conference slated for June 1892. The invitations never came. For reasons he did not wish to explain, Albert K. Smiley abandoned his plans to make the "Negro Question" meetings a permanent forum as he had done with the Indian Conferences. Black newspapers, like T. Thomas Fortune's New York *Age,* remained harshly critical of it, and pressure was mounting to integrate the meeting.[60] The phenomenon of lynching was gaining more press attention, and it was becoming harder to be sanguine about the future in the face of the white reactionary ascendance in the South. Tourgée joined George Washington Cable's boycott of the second conference because of its exclusionary policy, and William Lloyd Garrison Jr. was planning to boycott the third conference. Meanwhile, potential black allies like Booker T. Washington and William S. Scarborough felt alienated. Contrasting with the optimistic tone at Mohonk, Wilberforce professor Scarborough criticized the conference in the *Arena,* stating, "if social equality were feared by these [progressive whites], then there is little hope for the future. Catering to the prejudices of men only prolongs the conflict, and if the negro's friends expect to really aid them in their struggle upwards, then they need to change their *modus operandi* and adopt a different system of tactics."[61] If black "progress" depended upon lessening the friction and agitation of race relations, then the conference itself was failing to advance this.

The conference also brought criticism as well as praise to industrial education, bringing to the surface serious philosophical differences among educators on the issue. Perhaps the supporters of "industrial education" were taken aback by the criticism that an open dialogue allowed. Despite the naysayers, true believers like ex-president Hayes would continue to work behind the scenes to raise funds and promote schools like Hampton and Tuskegee, which would attract the lion's share of charitable donations from the North by the turn of the century. Hayes, for one, believed that Armstrong had all the answers, as he wrote on January 5, 1892: "So far as I can judge General Armstrong stands next to Lincoln in effective work for the negro. His work, like Lincoln's, is for his whole country also, and for all mankind. It hits the nail on the head. It solves the whole negro problem."[62] As the 1890s unfolded, many more would come to share Hayes's viewpoint through the extraordinary advocacy of Armstrong's disciple Booker T. Washington.

## THE LEGACIES OF MOHONK

The opportunity for federal legislation on the South was effectively dead by the summer of 1892. Republican Senate majority leader George F. Hoar, who carried on the mantle of Charles Sumner as the "conscience" of New England in the Senate, understood the political lessons of the defeat. He had been outmaneuvered in the Senate by the Democrats' delaying tactics, betrayed by some of his own caucus, and unnerved by the ferocity of the opposition. Hoar had never received so much hate mail as when he led the effort to pass the elections bill, he later reminisced, calling it the greatest public "outburst of anger" during his long tenure in the Senate. Looking back, he concluded that no more efforts could be undertaken to secure black voting rights until "a considerable change of opinion in the country, especially in the South" took place, and until the issue ceased to be a "matter of party strife."[63] This would not be the case in the fall 1892 presidential election, where the aftershocks of the federal elections debate haunted the Republicans, and southern Democrats continued to stir up fears of a return to the days of Reconstruction.

Smiley chose to discontinue the "Negro Question" conferences after Harrison's defeat, but Booker T. Washington attempted to pick up the pieces in a major conference series of his own. In February of 1892, Washington hosted the first "Tuskegee Negro Conference," which was attended by over four hundred black farmers, teachers, and ministers from throughout the Deep South. The purpose of the conference was to gather information about black communities and to spread the gospel of "industrial education" throughout the South. Instead of relying on white experts, Washington sought to ask blacks themselves what their needs were. As Washington explained to General Armstrong, he had invited only "the best in each community" who represented the "bone and sinew of the race" in order to discover their "actual moral, industrial and educational conditions." The Tuskegee Conference in some ways resembled a "black Mohonk." As had been done at Mohonk, Washington kept a transcript of the conference proceedings, adopted a series of resolutions at its conclusion, and invited the press to publicize his cause. Unlike at Mohonk, there were no prepared speeches or debates about the past. Focusing on immediate needs, Washington sought material progress through the spread of agricultural and industrial skill training led by Tuskegee and its graduates, who would be hired as teachers in communities across the South. Reporters from the *Independent, Christian Union, Advance, Congregationalist,* and Chicago *Inter Ocean* described the great enthusiasm evident at the First Negro Conference and praised Washington's initiative. The following year, more than eight hundred invitees attended the second Tuskegee Negro Conference, which fast become an annual signature event of the Tuskegee Institute.[64]

Washington would eventually make the "Hampton-Tuskegee idea" into an ideology of racial uplift more powerful than it had ever been in Armstrong's lifetime. After his famous address in 1895 before the Cotton States and International Exhibition in Atlanta, Washington became a national icon. The Mononk conferences might be seen as an important precursor to that influential speech. At Mohonk, the "industrial education" philosophy was proposed by Armstrong and others not merely as the answer to particular educational needs in the black community, but as a solution in Hayes's words to "the whole negro problem." This came at a moment when the Congress was debating whether to take measures to secure black suffrage and stand by the policies of Reconstruction. As is clear from his correspondence with Albert K. Smiley, Washington studied the transcripts of the Mohonk debates closely—his name was mentioned in them more often than any other black American's—and he viewed them as a bellwether of white progressive racial attitudes.[65]

All of the major themes of the Mohonk debates were echoed in Washington's Atlanta speech. First, he repudiated Reconstruction by lamenting that "in the first years of our new life [after Emancipation] we started at the top instead of the bottom," and he belittled black involvement in political life and desire to hold political office. Second, he spoke of the need for blacks to "learn to dignify and glorify common labor," and he dismissed the relevance of higher education, saying, "there is as much dignity in tilling a field as writing a poem." Third, he called for cooperation with southern whites, saying to his all-white audience, "I pledge that in your effort to work out the great and intricate problem which God has laid at the doors of the South you shall have at all times the patient, sympathetic help of my race." Finally, he emphasized that "progress" was taking place among blacks—as evidenced by the achievements on display at the Exposition, which were partly the fruits of their labor—but that it would take an extended period of time to catch up to whites. "Progress," he observed, "in the enjoyment of all the privileges that will come to us must be the result of severe and constant struggle rather than of *artificial forcing*."[66] In his carefully measured words, Washington was reassuring whites that equality would not be demanded any time soon and that "artificial forcing" through governmental policies, such as Reconstruction, was detrimental to the cause.

Turning the page on Reconstruction was a central element in Washington's appeal. One of the things that made the speech so remarkable for southern whites is that a black leader had agreed with them that Reconstruction was a mistake. Again and again, Washington would repeat this point in subsequent speeches and writings. In his celebrated autobiography, *Up From Slavery*, and in his telling of black history, *The Story of the Negro*, Washington made extended commentary on how the misguided policies of Reconstruction led blacks astray and set back their progress. "My race was being used as a tool with which to help white men into office" and to "punish Southern white men," Washington charged. "I felt that the Reconstruction policy, so far as it related to my race, was in large measure on false foundation, was artificial and forced."[67] Whether Washington's statements reflected his true beliefs, or a calculated concession to earn the support of whites, matters little. Adding his voice to the growing chorus of those who looked back on that period as a grave lesson to be learned in racial progress, Washington helped set the agenda for a new era. The meaning of Reconstruction was important not just as a matter of history, but as a guide for the future.

Washington's model of racial uplift had been imported from Hawaii through Armstrong, tested in the American South at Hampton, refined at the Mohonk Indian Conferences, and was about to be exported into the new American empire. Several commentators at Mohonk saw the connection between the American South and missionary work elsewhere. Reverend Craighead of Howard University asked at one point:

> Is there anything peculiar or different in the problem of Negro evangelization that forbids the employment of the same methods which have proved so efficient among other peoples, and in other lands? . . . No one will claim this. Why not, then, adopt the same means to secure for the colored race instruction in morals and religion as our wisest missionaries have employed, for a like purpose, among all other races?"[68]

Craighead believed the "Negro Question" in the American South ought to be brought into line with missionary work everywhere. When the great debate over empire took place in the wake of the Spanish-American War in 1898–1899, the lessons would be applied by the McKinley administration to the new territories coming under American control.

As Natalie Ring shows in her essay in this volume, the Spanish-American War conjured the memory of Reconstruction for many American commentators. Fearing that the defeat of Spain would bring Cuba into the United States, E. L. Godkin spoke against the war, warning that American rule in Cuba would only result in "the opening of fresh fields to carpetbaggers, speculators, and corruptionists," and worse yet, could lead to "the admission of alien, inferior, and mongrel races to our nationality."[69] Anti-imperialist Moorfield Storey raised the same concern: "Shall we establish in Cuba a carpet-bag government, like those upon which we look back with such pride?" he asked sarcastically. "Remember . . . we could not give our Southern fellow-citizens, speaking our language and close at our doors, a reasonably honest government. Can we hope to succeed better with Cuba . . . a people wholly unfitted by race and by education for self-government?"[70] Godkin and Storey seemed unable to imagine Cubans in any other capacity than as helpless tools for white exploitation and a burden for Americans to govern.

After the war, McKinley answered these concerns by judging each of Spain's colonial possessions on a sliding scale that measured their progress along the road to civilization. Cuba was granted a nominal independence, having demonstrated its "readiness" for self-government in its struggle against Spain (although the terms of the 1901 Platt Amendment gave the United States a right to intervene that limited Cuban sovereignty in actual fact). Puerto Rico and the Philippines, however, would remain territories of the United States, with their populations subject to American military governance until they were deemed capable of self-rule. Couching military occupation in the language of racial uplift, McKinley termed his plan for the people of the Philippines "benevolent assimilation," which promised extensive American aid in the form of schools, missionaries, and other civilizing agents. Emphasis was placed on industrial training for the masses, and civics training for the ruling classes. At first, suffrage would be strictly limited and the Philippine Assembly would be merely an advisory body to the American governor William Howard Taft, who considered it a "school of politics [for] educating the Filipinos in the science and practice of popular representative government."[71] The lessons of Reconstruction had been learned: the administration of empire would start from the presumption that an extended, open-ended period of white tutelage had to precede self-government.

Coincidentally, five days before McKinley issued his "benevolent assimilation" proclamation, he made a historic visit to Tuskegee Institute at the invitation of Booker T. Washington. Months before, Washington had anticipated the relevance of the "Hampton-Tuskegee idea" to the project of empire in a letter to the editor of the *Unitarian Register,* which he titled, "Industrial Education for Cuban Negroes." Washington called for donations to help his institution take part in the project of educating blacks in both Cuba and Puerto Rico. "I believe all will agree that it is our duty to follow the work of destruction in Cuba with that of construction," Washington wrote (notably avoiding calling it "*re*construction"). Because half the inhabitants of Cuba were black, he suggested, "in the present depleted condition of the island, industrial education for the young men and women is a matter of the first importance. It will do for them what it is doing for our people in the South."[72] Within a few years, Tuskegee was taking many students from Cuba and Puerto Rico who would then return to their countries to establish schools of their own based on the Hampton-Tuskegee model.

By 1904, the annual Tuskegee Negro Conference had grown to 2,500 attendees, representing blacks from Cuba, Puerto Rico, Africa, and elsewhere throughout the diaspora. As Andrew Zimmerman has detailed, Washington assisted the German Empire in its colonization of Togo by sending Tuskegee representatives to help establish cotton plantations there. While Washington sought to uplift Africans through Tuskegee methods and extend the influence of his institution, the Germans sought to make their colony profitable and put Africans to work. Their purposes dovetailed well. In 1912, Washington hosted a three-day "Tuskegee International Conference on the Negro" that focused especially on missionary work in Africa. Representatives from twenty-five missionary societies and eighteen different countries (or colonies) came to Tuskegee, increasing its fame and the influence of its message of economic self-help in places like South Africa. Across the globe, Washington continued to receive acclamation for having provided a "solution" to the problem of racial uplift.[73]

The Mohonk Friends of the Indian Conferences likewise perceived the relevance of their work for the peoples of America's new colonial possessions. Philanthropists interested in the assimilation of Indians were naturally drawn into the project of "benevolent assimilation" in the Philippines. After several years of panels on conditions in the colonies, the conferences officially renamed themselves the "Mohonk Conferences for the Friends of the Indian and Other Dependent Peoples" in 1904.[74] A leaflet describing the decision to expand the conferences' scope assured readers that their discussions would retain their traditional nonpartisanship by excluding discussion of the anti-imperialist movement: "topical firebrands such as the so-called imperialistic policy of the government are excluded from the programme." Rather, the conference would concentrate on the practical work of uplift. Questions "such as those relating to the economic, industrial, and educational needs and conditions of our fellow-citizens in Porto Rico and the Pacific Islands" and other matters of "intensely vital and of practical moment" would occupy their time.[75] While excluding politics was a convenient way to cultivate an aura of scholarly expertise, it also fit well with the presumptions that had guided the Indian conferences since their inception in the 1880s. Assimilation should come before political rights.[76]

The historical "lessons" of Reconstruction were vital to the discourses that supported segregation, disfranchisement, and empire. The conventional wisdom of the Anglo-American world held that political equality and self-rule would be achieved one day for all colonial peoples. The danger of granting these too soon, however, could be calamitous and therefore the day of their fulfillment therefore could be postponed indefinitely. The memory of Reconstruction drove this lesson home for Americans, and these lessons based upon tales of "black misrule" facilitated the subordination of peoples of the new territories overseas. Ironically, the organizers of the Mohonk conferences of 1890 and 1891 sought to speed up "progress" for black Americans by placating their white oppressors and fostering support for the goal of black advancement. They could not have foreseen that the decade to follow would bring deeper oppression for southern blacks than they had known since Reconstruction, nor could they have anticipated the new lands and foreign cultures that would come under American sovereignty. Nevertheless, the era of Jim Crow and imperialism might have begun at the start of the 1890s when northern progressives decided to turn their back on Reconstruction's promise of equal rights and participatory democracy.

## NOTES

1. Gunnar Myrdal, *An American Dilemma: Vol. 1. The Negro Problem and Modern Democracy* (1944; repr., New Brunswick, NJ: Transaction, 1996), 446–48. More recent scholarship has followed up on Myrdal's insight and explored the centrality of memory to the ideology of segregation. See especially Grace Elizabeth Hale, *Making Whiteness: The Culture of Segregation in the South, 1890–1940* (New York: Random House, 1995); W. Fitzhugh Brundage, *The Southern Past: A Clash of Race and Memory* (Cambridge: The Belknap Press of Harvard University Press, 2005); Bruce E. Baker, *What Reconstruction Meant: Historical Memory in the American South* (Charlottesville: University of Virginia Press, 2007).

2. On the persistence of sectional politics, see Caroline E. Janney, *Remembering the Civil War: The Union and the Limits of Reconciliation* (Chapel Hill: University of North Carolina Press, 2013).

3. The history of these Republican proposals is covered in Rayford Logan, *The Betrayal of the Negro: From Rutherford B. Hayes to Woodrow Wilson,* new edition (New York: Collier Books, 1965); and Stanley P. Hirshon, *Farewell to the Bloody Shirt: Northern Republicans and the Southern Negro, 1877–1893* (Bloomington: Indiana University Press, 1962).

4. Hilary A. Herbert, *Why the Solid South? Or Reconstruction and Its Results* (Baltimore: R. H. Woodward, 1890). Herbert's volume was the most comprehensive historical account of Reconstruction to appear before the "Dunning school" scholarship, and its interpretations would influence the more scholarly writings that followed over the next several decades. See John David Smith and J. Vincent Lowery, eds., *The Dunning School: Race and the Meaning of Reconstruction* (Lexington: University Press of Kentucky, 2013), 13–15.

5. Wade Hampton, "What Negro Supremacy Means," *The Forum* (June 1888): 5; James S. Pike, *The Prostrate State: South Carolina Under Negro Government* (New York: D. Appleton, 1874).

6. John Tyler Morgan, "Shall Negro Majorities Rule?," *The Forum* (1889): 595; see also Thomas Adams Upchurch, "Senator John Tyler Morgan and the Genesis of Jim Crow Ideology, 1889–1891," *Alabama Review* 57, no. 2 (2004).

7. On the "Blair Bill," see Gordon B. McKinney, *Henry W. Blair's Campaign to Reform America from the Civil War to the U.S. Senate* (Lexington: University Press of Kentucky, 2013), and Daniel W. Crofts, "The Black Response to the Blair Education Bill," *Journal of Southern History* 37 (February 1971): 41–65.

8. Upchurch, "Senator John Tyler Morgan," 25–38; Carlyle McKinley, *An Appeal to Pharaoh: The Negro Problem and Its Radical Solution* (New York: Ford, Howard, and Hulbert, 1890).

9. Quotations from William E. Chandler, "Our Southern Masters," *The Forum* (1888): 517, 520. On Chandler's career, see Leon B. Richardson, *William E. Chandler, Republican* (New York: Dodd, Mead, 1940).

10. In the 1880s, Hallowell began offering his legal services to fight for the constitutional rights of black men in the South who had their right to vote denied, and he continued to defend the Fifteenth Amendment until his death in 1904. Richard P. Hallowell, *The Southern Question, Past and Present* (Boston: Press of Samuel Usher, 1890), 20. See also Richard P. Hallowell, *Why the Negro Was Enfranchised: Negro Suffrage Justified* (Boston: G. H. Ellis, 1903); Richard P. Hallowell Papers, 1888–1902, David M. Rubenstein Rare Book and Manuscript Library, Duke University, Durham, North Carolina.

11. Thomas Adams Church, *Legislating Racism: The Billion Dollar Congress and the Birth of Jim Crow* (Lexington: University Press of Kentucky, 2004), 151–85.

12. Gordon B. McKinney, *Henry W. Blair's Campaign to Reform America From the Civil War to the U.S. Senate* (Lexington: University Press of Kentucky, 2013), 126–29.

13. *Proceedings of the Annual Lake Mohonk Conference of Friends of the Indian* (New York: Lake Mohonk, 1883–1916), Quaker Collection, Guilford College, Greensboro, North Carolina. Also see Larry E. Burgess, *The Lake Mohonk Conferences on the Indian, 1883–1916,* PhD diss., Claremont Graduate School, 1972.

14. Two scholarly analyses of the Mohonk conferences provide excellent coverage of the "Negro Question" conferences, but neither compares the content of those debates with the previous discussions of Indians in the West. See Leslie Fishel, "The 'Negro Question' at Mohonk: Microcosm, Mirage, and Message," *New York History* (July 1993): 277–314; Ralph E. Luker, *The Social Gospel in Black and White: American Racial Reform, 1885–1912* (Chapel Hill: University of North Carolina Press, 1991).

15. Robert Francis Eng, *Educating the Disfranchised and Disinherited: Samuel Chapman Armstrong and Hampton Institute, 1839–1893* (Knoxville: University of Tennessee Press, 1999).

16. Quoted in Burgess, *Lake Mohonk Conferences,* 28.

17. This "experiment" began unexpectedly when Captain Richard Henry Pratt sent General Armstrong a group of captured Indian warriors whom he had himself begun to educate in a Florida military prison. Donald F. Lindsay, *Indians at Hampton Institute, 1877–1923* (Urbana: University of Illinois Press, 1994).

18. Burgess, Lake Mohonk Conferences; C. Joseph Genetin-Pilawa, *Crooked Paths to Allotment: The Fight over Federal Indian Policy after the Civil War* (Chapel Hill: University of North Carolina Press, 2012).

19. Cahill's valuable discussion notes the extensive roster of Mohonk participants who had experience with the project of "uplifting" African Americans during and after the Civil War. But she does not recognize how much Armstrong's educational philosophy represented a departure from that of the mainstream educators such as those of the American Missionary Society and was, in fact, premised on a critique of Reconstruction. See Cathleen D. Cahill, *Federal Fathers & Mothers: A Social History of the United States Indian Service, 1869–1933* (Chapel Hill: University of North Carolina, 2011), 26–30.

20. John T. Morgan, "Shall Negro Majorities Rule?" *Forum* 6 (September 1888): 597.

21. Isabel C. Barrows, ed., *The First Mohonk Conference on the Negro Question* (George H. Ellis, 1890), 7.

22. Hallowell, "The Southern Question," 20; William E. Chandler, *The Letters of Mr. William E. Chandler Relative to the So-Called Southern Policy of President Hayes* (Concord, NH: Monitor and Statesman Office, 1878).

23. Albert K. Smiley to Rev. Dr. J. L. M. Curry, 31 October 1889, Box 2, Collection 1113, Smiley Family Papers, Special Collections, Haverford College Library.

24. Armstrong to Smiley, 4 December and 31 December 1889, and 10 February 10 1890, Box 2a, Smiley Family Papers; Barrows, *First Mohonk,* 8.

25. Armstrong to Smiley, 10 February 1890, Box 2a, Smiley Family Papers; Fishel, "The 'Negro Question' at Mohonk," 283–86. As a possible ironic consequence of this controversy, the Mohonk Indian Conference quietly began inviting Indian participants to its annual "Friends of the Indian" conference for the first time in 1890.

26. *The Southern Workman* 29 (July 1890): 77.

27. Booker T. Washington to George Washington Cable, 7 April 1890, in Louis R. Harlan, ed., *The Booker T. Washington Papers* (Urbana and Chicago: University of Illinois Press, 1974), 3:45.

28. First Mohonk, 140–42. A complete invitation list, and copies of correspondence with invitees, can be found in Box 2, Smiley Family Papers.

29. At the Second Conference, Samuel Barrows of Boston delivered a presentation on "The Situation of the Negro" to begin the conference, which described his visits to Hampton and Tuskegee. Isabel C. Barrows, ed., *The Second Mohonk Conference on the Negro Question* (George H. Ellis, 1891), 10–12. For an insightful discussion of "othering" of the South and the Mohonk Conferences, see Natalie Ring, *The Problem South: Region, Empire and the New Liberal State, 1880–1930* (Athens: University of Georgia Press, 2012).

30. *First Mohonk,* 13.

31. The elasticity of "civilization" as a discourse has been demonstrated by other historians. Gail Bederman, for instance, memorably showed how Ida B. Wells-Barnett turned this discourse back against white southerners in her antilynching campaign of the 1890s in *Manliness & Civilization: A Cultural History of Race and Gender in the United States 1880–1917* (Chicago: University of Chicago Press, 1995). See also Mary A. Renda, *Taking Haiti: Military Occupation and the Culture of U.S. Imperialism, 1915–1940* (Chapel Hill: University of North Carolina Press, 2001).

32. *First Mohonk,* 13.

33. *First Mohonk.,* 39–40, 49.

34. During the Know-Nothing Party's brief ascendance in the mid-1850s, Connecticut and Massachusetts adopted literacy tests that required voters to demonstrate literacy by writing their own names and reading a passage from the Constitution. The law was intended to keep immigrant voters, especially Irish Catholics, from the ballot box, but it was also justified as providing an incentive for all to get educated. Alexander Keyssar, *The Right to Vote: The Contested History of Democracy in the United States* (New York: Basic Books, 2000), 86.

35. *First Mohonk,* 48.

36. This statement was made by President W. H. Hickman of Clark University. *Second Mohonk,* 62.

37. *First Mohonk,* 52.

38. *First Mohonk.,* 37.

39. *Second Mohonk,* 12.

40. *First Mohonk,* 121.

41. Undated clipping from *The Republican,* Box 2a, Smiley Family Papers; First Mohonk, 126.

42. *First Mohonk,* 82.

43. For example, see *Second Mohonk,* 58–59.

44. *First Mohonk,* 77.

45. *Second Mohonk,* 109; Jay's disappointment is described by Fishel in "The 'Negro Question' at Mohonk," 303.

46. *First Mohonk,* 114. Tourgée's speech is also reproduced in Mark Elliott and John David Smith, eds., *Undaunted Radical: The Selected Writings and Speeches of Albion W. Tourgée* (Baton Rouge: Louisana State University Press, 2010), 152–70.

47. Despite its flaws, black leaders remained largely supportive of the Blair Bill. See Crofts, "The Black Response."

48. *First Mohonk,* quotations on 89 and 90.

49. *First Mohonk,* 91.

50. *First Mohonk,* 126–27.

51. *First Mohonk.* All Tourgée quotes on 108. Tourgée's speech at Mohonk and its reception is discussed at more length in Mark Elliott, *Color-Blind Justice: Albion W. Tourgée and the Quest for Racial Equality from the Civil War to Plessy v. Ferguson* (New York: Oxford University Press, 2006), 246–48.

52. *Second Mohonk,* 60.

53. *Second Mohonk,* 60.

54. *Second Mohonk,* 19.

55. *Second Mohonk,* 120.

56. *First Mohonk,* 71.

57. *Second Mohonk,* 8.

58. *First Mohonk,* 131.

59. *Second Mohonk,* 109.

60. See Fishel, "The 'Negro Question' at Mohonk," 284–88, 306.

61. William S. Scarborough, "The Race Problem," *The Arena* 2 (October 1890): 564.

62. Rutherford B. Hayes to Edward Everett Hale, 5 January 1892, quoted in Eng, *Educating the Disfranchised,* 159–60.

63. Georg F. Hoar, *Autobiography of Seventy Years* (New York: Charles Scribner's Sons, 1903), 2:158.

64. Booker T. Washington, "How I Came to Call the First Negro Conference," *A.M.E. Church Review* 15 (April 1899): 802–8.

65. See Washington correspondence in Box 2 and 2a, Smiley Family Papers.

66. My emphasis. Booker T. Washington, *Up From Slavery, An Autobiography* (1901; repr., New York: Page, Doubleday, 1907), 84.

67.Washington, *Up From Slavery*, 84.

68. *First Mohonk,* 38.

69. E. L. Godkin, editorial, *The Nation,* 13 January1898, 23.

70. Moorfield Storey, "Nothing to Excuse Our Intervention: President's Speech at the Meeting of the Massachusetts Reform Club, April 8, 1898," *Advocate of Peace* 60 (May 1898).

71. Quoted in Julian Go, "The Provinciality of American Empire: 'Liberal Exceptionalism' and U.S. Colonial Rule, 1898–1912," *Comparative Studies in History and Society* 49 (January 2007): 80.

72. Booker T. Washington, "Industrial Education for Cuban Negroes," *Christian Register* 18 (August 1898): 6–7. See also *Booker T. Washington, An Autobiography. A Story of My Life and Work* (Atlanta: J. L Nichols, 1901), 222–23, 239–42. For an insightful discussion of Washington's ideology, see David Sehat, "The Civilizing Mission of Booker T. Washington," *Journal of Southern History* 73 (May 2007): 323–62.

73. Andrew Zimmerman, *Alabama in Africa: Booker T. Washington, the German Empire, and the Globalization of the New South* (Princeton, NJ: Princeton University Press, 2012); Manning Marable, "Booker T. Washington and Black Nationalism," *Phylon* 35 (1974): 398–406.

74. Walter L. Williams recognized the ideological continuity between Indian policy and imperial policy, and noted the expansion of the Mohonk conference in "United States Indian Policy and the Debate over Philippine Annexation: Implications for the Origins of American Imperialism," *Journal of American History* 66 (March 1980): 814–15.

75. Quoted from L. A. Maynard, "Indians and Other Dependent Peoples: A Conference on their Behalf at Lake Mohonk" [1904]. Box 2a, Smiley Family Papers.

76. Truman Clark, "Educating the Natives in Self-Government: Puerto Rico and the United States 1900–1933," *Pacific Historical Review* 43 (May 1973): 220–33.

# 7

# A New Reconstruction for the South

NATALIE J. RING

Do we love our ruins only as ruins? Have we no hope of a future: Is it to be Backward, look backward, O South in the night, until doomsday? Has the clock stopped: Such a long, long, night! And how the children cry! Oh, for a New Day in Dixieland a day of adjustment and reconstruction! When shall it be Onward, strive onward, O South, for the right."

—*The New Day in Dixieland,* Elizabeth Denty Abernathy

On August 16, 1915, an angry mob hanged Leo Frank, a Jewish supervisor in the National Pencil Company in Atlanta, for the accused rape and murder of thirteen-year-old Mary Phagan two years prior. Sensationalist news reports filled with lurid details appeared repeatedly in the southern press, and the crime and subsequent lynching garnered more national attention than many other localized crimes. The *New York Times* described one of the mob's participants howling in fury, lunging and convulsing in a paroxysm of frustration with his hands raised until the corpse was lowered from the tree, at which point the man's "hate" grew "louder and shriller" until he could grind "his heels upon the face in a climax of arch-savagery."[1] Two days after the *New York Times* reported on the feral behavior of the lynch mob, the editors of the New York City–based periodical the *New Republic* urged Americans to be magnanimous and patient with the southern state of Georgia, much as they would be with Haiti and "the more primitive Balkan states" of southeastern Europe: "We shall have to recognize that here is a people suffering from slavery, from a false reconstruction, from too sudden contact with a higher civilization." The magazine warned that the state appeared to have "self-government" but was "not yet fit for it," and only a very small portion of the citizens had "risen to the normal civilization of the Western world." The remainder were "primitive," "uneducated," and "burdened with a citizenship" they were ill-equipped to handle. The editors advocated building more schools to remedy the problem but declared that ultimately Georgia would require "the guidance of comparatively more advanced people" if it was to overcome its savagery and social backwardness.[2]

The *New Republic*'s choice to make an analogy between a southern state and the Caribbean nation of Haiti may seem peculiar at first glance. However, several weeks before the Leo Frank lynching the United States Marines had invaded Haiti and set up an occupation government that would endure for the next nineteen years. Both the invasion of Haiti and the explosion of southern violence in Georgia occupied the same temporal and printed space. The *New Republic* made a calculated decision to use the powerful rhetoric of colonialism to draw attention to the barbaric un-American behavior of the Leo Frank lynch mob. Even while noting that some citizens of the state had expressed "public regrets" and showed a "national conscience," the *New Republic* defended its "sanction" of the rest of the state for exhibiting a "savagery which is barely concealed by Georgia's pretences to civilization." Coming on the heels of decades of US expansion overseas that included the acquisition of colonies and protectorates such as the Hawaiian Islands, Puerto Rico, Guam, and the Philippines, words and phrases such as *primitive, savagery,* and *higher civilization* would have resonated with a majority of Americans.[3] Yet the establishment of the new colonial infrastructure in Haiti generated more than just a sustained use of imperial discourse; much as in other countries subject to American control, the Haitian project involved the construction of roads, bridges, and schools, public health improvement, and the development of commercial agriculture.[4] In the late nineteenth and early twentieth centuries, the US South also had undergone many of the same reforms found in the overseas colonies. The effort to uplift the southern population, including poor whites, was in many ways a domestic civilizing mission. These reform projects were sometimes referred to or understood as the "New Reconstruction" or more commonly "readjustment."

Northern philanthropies, a small coterie of southern liberals, and the federal government interested in reconstructing the South targeted the region for what they described as uplift and readjustment. The first of these terms evoked ideas about evolutionary (and racial) progress, colonialism, and global reform. The latter summoned memories of Reconstruction and referred to perceived lingering racial problems, entrenched poverty, and a commitment to rehabilitate the South in the image of the North. The fact that Georgia was saddled with the legacy of slavery and plagued by "a false reconstruction," according to the *New Republic,* made it a legitimate focus for uplift and readjustment. The similarities drawn between Haiti and Georgia underscore how the memory of the failure of Reconstruction in the South and the exigencies of American imperialism fit together. Questions about whether certain groups (nonwhite peoples in such places as Hawaii or the Philippines, African Americans, or poor whites) could be educated or made fit for American citizenship drew attention to the fact that Reconstruction had not solved the "race problem" or transformed the region into a position to modernize and make economic gains that might benefit the nation as a whole. Memories of the Old Reconstruction invoked in the context of southern readjustment are reflective of an embryonic turn-of-the-century soft liberalism undergirded by imperialism. As Peter Schmidt asserts in his book on "Jim Crow colonialism," "Progressivism involved a *federal* attempt to reconstruct the meaning of Reconstruction, correcting its 'mistakes' while appropriating, containing, and redefining its key ideals, and methods, especially regarding the making of new citizens via educational and other reforms."[5]

From roughly 1890 through World War I, the South and North are said to have reunited with a shared belief in the supremacy of the white race, a universal commitment to encouraging southern racial and industrial harmony, and a dedication to national patriotism buoyed by imperialism and military ventures overseas. The traditional historical narrative of the post–Civil War South also emphasizes the way in which the two regions engaged in collective mythmaking and memory building about the meaning of the Civil War and Reconstruction.[6] David Blight, for example, explains how "three overall visions of Civil War memory collided and combined over time" until the "white supremacist vision" ultimately merged with the "reconciliationist vision" and overtook the "emancipationist vision." Blight's story of this national project of reunion culminates with the Gettysburg reunion in 1913, some fifty years after the end of the Civil War, when Union and Confederate soldiers engaged in a commemorative "remembrance" of the war that stressed brotherhood and a collective white American identity devoid of sectional animosity. In addition, this collective memory of the Civil War offered a particular interpretation of Reconstruction.[7] In 1915 D. W. Griffith issued his national blockbuster *Birth of a Nation,* which captured on film this white supremacist memory of Reconstruction. It portrayed the era as a colossal mistake dominated by the corruption of Radical Republicans and their promotion of "Negro rule," which could only be overturned by the heroic efforts of the Ku Klux Klan intent on restoring white southern home rule. The film finished its three-hour run with the double marriage of two couples representing the reconciliation of North and South. One intertitle card in the film read: "The former enemies of North and South are united again in common defence of their Aryan birthright." This popular collective memory of Reconstruction also paralleled the historiographical interpretation of Reconstruction advocated by Professor William Dunning of Columbia University, which developed in the early twentieth century. The "Dunning School," which included many of the professor's students, became the reigning framework in academia and textbooks used by American schoolchildren for decades.

However, David Blight's three frameworks of "Civil War memory" do not adequately capture the nonsentimental ways in which Americans remembered the postwar era. As Caroline Janney suggests, the stories veterans and their families told about the war "reveal that the categories of those who recalled a Unionist, Emancipationist, Lost Cause, or Reconciliationist memory of the ware were never clear-cut, nor did they remain static. Though Civil War commemorations reached a high point of visibility between the 1880s and 1910s, the understandings and interpretations of the conflict and its meaning were continually being created, negotiated, and renegotiated."[8] While Blight and Janney are at odds over the degree to which divisive memories of the Civil War persisted, neither scholar considers how broader social and political changes in the late nineteenth and early twentieth centuries, such as the Progressive movement and American imperialism, influenced the memory of the war and Reconstruction. Regardless of whether a static or contested commitment to cultural reunion existed, how do we understand the simultaneous appearance in 1915 of *Birth of a Nation*—celebrating sectional reconciliation and the Dunning School's understanding of Reconstruction—with a northern magazine's contention that white southerners suffered from a "false reconstruction" and were ill-equipped to exercise their rights of citizenship like "primitive" Haitians? The analogy between Haiti and Georgia drew on a widespread belief that both the South and the overseas colonies suffered from an array of social problems that existed on an evolutionary continuum, and in the wake of the

Old Reconstruction the southern states had not adequately resolved a set of inherent deficiencies that all modernizing areas around the globe faced; some of these difficulties included illiteracy, economic backwardness, and racial tensions between what were considered to be the civilized and savage races.

Thus the readjustment of the South in the late nineteenth and early twentieth centuries is not a story about the meaning of Reconstruction embodied in the "social memory" of white supremacists or how the culture of sectional reconciliation trumped the "emancipationist vision" so eloquently expressed by African Americans such as Frederick Douglass.[9] The story of readjustment involved a federal, state, and local depoliticized process designed to restructure the South economically and socially. A significant part of this effort included alleviating an allegedly deteriorating irrepressible "race problem" through the use of philanthropy and social scientific action, even while viewing segregation and disfranchisement as necessary. Framing the South as in need of readjustment and reconstruction enabled northern and southern liberals to discuss southern backwardness and the devastation wrought by the institution of slavery and war in an oblique fashion, leaving space to critique certain aspects of Reconstruction if necessary. As one northern philanthropist who described reform in the region as "mainly of the missionary character" lamented, "This whole question in the South is delicate, difficult and so vast as to be comprehended by very few."[10] Ironically, many reformers conceded that the Old Reconstruction had been a mistake in practice and theory, yet they believed the South was still troubled by lingering deficiencies that could be resolved through a repurposed program of reconstruction. This enabled them to skirt accusations of fomenting sectionalism and in most instances kept them above the fray of the Dunning School interpretation of Reconstruction, which, if challenged, could easily slide into a partisan debate about the merits of African American civil and political rights and the South's culpability in starting the Civil War.

+ + +

As early as the 1880s a group of southern and northern critics began to question the mythology of the New South and the Lost Cause and the alleged cultural reunion between the formerly hostile sections. These uneasy detractors identified what came to be known as the "southern problem" or the "southern question" and advocated widespread reform of such southern deficiencies as illiteracy, economic backwardness, "racial friction," waning Anglo-Saxon superiority, and widespread disease. Southern and northern liberals abandoned a strictly political interest in the region and began to focus on the social and economic weaknesses that had not been resolved as a result of Reconstruction. In the beginning, this criticism and concern was faint. Strains of this nascent disapproval reflected the former northern objectives of Reconstruction as well as the interest of a few southern white liberals and black intellectuals with the courage to speak out against the overwhelming tide of New South optimism. By the first decade of the twentieth century, and pushing into the following decade, discussion on how to resolve the "southern problem" reached a crescendo and embodied a strain of what Gary Gerstle has identified as "strong state liberalism." This was a moment in which "liberals turned to the state as an institutional medium capable of reconstructing society and of educating citizens in the task of intelligent living."[11]

The readjustment of the South through the use of the regulatory state and guided by social scientific theory did not include the use of military troops or the implementation of grand pieces of legislation. Yet it was no less a process of reconstruction. James McCulloch, a clergyman and social reformer from Alabama speaking at the 1914 meeting of the Southern Sociological Congress, noted in the introductory remarks of the published conference proceedings that the state of affairs in the region was precarious at best, coming on the heels of Reconstruction, and that despite the "chivalrous spirit" at work for a "nobler civilization" in the New South, much still needed to be accomplished. "Readjustment has been so rapid that the march of progress is irregular," he continued. "The new civilization is lacking in symmetry. Many zones of danger and infection exist."[12] The New Reconstruction would involve the transformative initiatives of the federal government and the efforts of northern philanthropies working in collaboration with a nascent liberal movement in the South. This included northern philanthropists such as Robert C. Ogden and John D. Rockefeller Jr.; northern academics like Albert Bushnell Hart of Harvard University and Frank Tannebaum of Columbia University; government reformers such as Seaman A. Knapp; and southern liberals such as George Washington Cable, Edgar Gardner Murphy, Walter Hines Page, Charles W. Dabney, Samuel C. Mitchell, John Spencer Bassett, Edwin Mims, William O. Scroggs, and Edwin A.

Alderman. Indeed their reformist discourse and material action provided a subtle counter to the belief that some of the social goals of Reconstruction were an abject failure broadly speaking. Reformers called for widespread educational and rural reform to address lingering problems that had not adequately been resolved after the Civil War. Critics of southern problems did not typically promote the elimination of segregation and disfranchisement, but they believed that southern race relations had reached a state of extreme discord and any ensuing conflict between the races could only be resolved through philanthropic and social scientific action.

Thus participants in the conversation found themselves revisiting some of the familiar questions of Reconstruction: How easily could the South be incorporated into the nation-state? What place would the African American population have in the South or the American nation? Would the region's economy wind up weakening or fortifying the national and international economies? How would illiteracy be eradicated in the South and to what end? Reformers and federal authorities raised new questions too, such as: What should be done with the growing population of backward poor whites? How could one resolve the growing "mulatto problem" as a result of several centuries of interracial sex? In particular, Emancipation and Reconstruction had failed to resolve completely the question of race, and despite the powerful forces of cultural reunion the issue continued to press upon the American national imagination. In short, the wider question being considered was: How does one incorporate a backward region or colonial possession, and at what status, into a modernizing nation?

The concept of readjustment reflected the difficulty reformers and observers felt with their observation that not all areas of the South suffered equally, and indeed the region was understood to be wrapped in a paradox of poverty and progress. Holland Thompson, one of William A. Dunning's former students writing in a volume dedicated to his mentor, observed many incongruities in the New South. He noted, "It is a puzzling region, full of contradictions and sharp contrasts. The population is predominantly rural, and yet industrialism is growing with marvelous rapidity. The people are religious—for there is more of Puritanism surviving in the South than anywhere else—and yet instances of lawlessness are frequent. They are kindly, but occasional manifestations of cruelty shock the world. They believe in race purity, and yet we see the mulatto."[13]

These observers frequently couched their descriptions of the process of southern readjustment within the discourse of civilization and its emphasis on progress, evolutionary development, and Anglo-Saxon masculine ideals. The concept of southern readjustment grew out of an intellectual conundrum that Victorian exponents of the philosophy of progress tried to resolve in the nineteenth century: If everyone was moving forward linearly toward some better state of being, what accounted for the persistent inequalities between various cultures, races, and civilizations in the world? For that matter, what accounted for the difference in backwardness between regions? The answer to the paradox lay in the remarkable metaphorical flexibility of sociocultural evolutionary theory. The theory could easily be adapted to explain inequalities of class, race, or gender and the disparities evident in the progress of civilization. The paradox provided resolution with its focus on evolutionary movement, which included horizontal movement through time, toward a unified nation or people; and vertical movement, governed by a sense of hierarchy, since not all rungs of the evolutionary ladder were necessarily equal at any given moment.[14] This intellectual paradigm, of course, easily fit with imperial imagery and language invoked to justify conquest abroad.

Consequently Americans used the discourse of civilization and readjustment not only to mark racial and cultural boundaries but also to mark regional boundaries. References to the South's lack of civilization or adjustment to modernity in journalists' reports, reformers' assessments, and contemporary intellectual thought were ubiquitous.[15] The Southern Sociological Congress, the reform organization led by James McCulloch who warned of the dangers of irregular "readjustment" during the process of southern advancement, dedicated itself to solving "the Southern problem of civilization."[16] Many detractors complained that the New South (often intentionally) lacked a certain level of refinement and civilized life, an attribute that set it apart from the rest of the modern industrial nation. A northern woman traveling in the region reported that what caught her attention the most was southerners' "determined resistance to the inroads of civilization."[17] Even a transplanted foreigner residing in the South for twelve years proclaimed that the region "as a section, does not seem fully to appreciate the importance of the inevitables in civilization—the fixed and unalterable laws of progress." He concluded that there exists "a disposition to plead exception from the operation of universal principles of growth which have proven their inevitableness everywhere else."[18]

Southern liberals, many of whom became expatriates due to their criticism of the region, frequently expressed concern about southern advancement. Edgar Gardner Murphy, a clergyman, child labor opponent, and educational reformer from Alabama, was one of the first to articulate the concept of "southern readjustment" in his book *The Problems of the Present South* (1903). He described how the industrial, educational, and political problems of the region were "phases of the essential movement toward a genuinely democratic order." Murphy stressed that the problems would never be "solved in any mathematical or final sense," only that the effort to resolve them would be part of the process of "southern readjustment." Either life would adjust to these problems or "their conflicting or complementary elements" would "find a working adjustment with one another," since there would occasionally be "recurrent periods of acute antagonism."[19] These periods of "antagonism" might temporarily slow down southern progress, but they were only part of the natural scheme of social development toward a higher state of civilization. Murphy agreed with the assertion that the "peculiar problems of the South" were "sectional in their form"; however, he did not see this assertion as inconsistent with the contention that every problem in every section of the country was important to the "Nation's life."[20]

Although southern liberals like Murphy exhibited a guarded optimism, many detractors conceded that the southern problem of readjustment was due to the inescapable consequence of slavery, which they viewed as the precise antithesis of progress. David Brion Davis has shown how in the Western intellectual tradition, conceptions of slavery and progress have always been juxtaposed with one another. Western thought widely regarded slavery as a liberal progressive force until the late eighteenth century, when intellectuals and abolitionists began to view the institution of slavery as retrogressive, barbarous, and unchristian. Following this momentous ideological shift from the notion of "progressive enslavement" toward the notion of "progressive emancipation," slavery was deemed incompatible with civilization.[21] Later generations would declare that slave societies impeded modernization and industrial capitalism. Concerned observers of the southern situation referred to slavery as "an insuperable obstacle to general industrial advance," described how the "blight of slavery" had left southerners two generations behind northerners, explained how "slavery gagged the South," and dubbed the institution the "great incubus" that had been thrown off.[22] Walter Hines

Page, one of the leading liberal southern proponents of reform who became a national philanthropic figure, journalist, and editor, noted wryly that slavery had "pickled all Southern life and left it just as it found it." Page, like many others, believed that slavery had kept the "social structure stationary" in the South longer than any other region of English-speaking people in the world and that virtually every "undemocratic trait" now evident in the southern people could be accounted for by the institution of slavery.[23]

Walter Hines Page's criticism of southern problems, particularly the region's lack of evolution forward, began as early as the 1870s and 1880s and marked the beginning of a nascent liberal discourse about the New Reconstruction that reached a peak in the second decade of the twentieth century. His critique of the weight of the Lost Cause and the South's backwardness can be seen in his letters to the *Raleigh State Chronicle,* his editorial forays at the *St. Joseph Gazette* in Missouri, his first big piece in the *Atlantic Monthly,* and later articles based on his travels through the South. In the May 1881 *Atlantic Monthly* article titled "An Old Southern Borough" (later identified as his home town of Cary, North Carolina), Page noted that a person could walk from one part of the town to the other and find oneself moving "backward or forward some half a dozen centuries." "The whole town has a languid and self-satisfied appearance. There is little animation in man or beast," he explained. "The very dogs look lazy... the streets are neglected, and in places almost impassable." With regard to intellectual curiosity, Page noticed that "no original arguments, or even phrases, are brought forth" and that most people in the town had no desire for a better life or any future ambitions. In short, Page reported that these "ancient Southern towns" were marked by "an idleness and dullness" that contributed to a perpetual feeling of stagnation and decay.[24]

One month later, the North Carolinian began a several-months-long journey through the Confederate South and penned weekly letters with the intention of sending them to prominent northern newspapers such as the *Boston Post* and the *New York World.* The bulk of Walter Hines Page's reports reiterated much of what he had written in "An Old Southern Borough." Early on in his travels Page stumbled upon Jefferson Davis living quietly on an estate in Biloxi, Mississippi, likely rejoicing in the recent publication of his book *The Rise and Fall of the Confederate Government* (1881). John Milton Cooper Jr. described Davis as "alert and hospitable" and referred to Walter Hines Page as the "reporter" probing the former Confederate president for an assessment of the present state of the South. “Can the visitor escape a certain depression?” Page queried. “Everywhere in the South men are looking to the future. Cotton mills and railroads are of more consequence than battlefields where the fathers of this generation fell.”[25] The divide was startlingly clear. Page, who questioned whether there was much left to cherish in the Old South and became a leading figurehead in advocating a New Reconstruction of the region, stood in stark contrast to Davis, who remained behind to bemoan the supposed tragic turn of the Old Reconstruction while dreaming of gallant Confederate soldiers in more youthful days. Thirty years later, in an editorial entitled “The New Reconstruction,” the editor of the *Southern Workman* published by Booker T. Washington’s Hampton Institute praised Walter Hines Page’s efforts to promote educational reform in the South. He wrote, “It is really what Dr. Page calls it, a work of reconstruction. This word is not popular in the South, for it is associated with some endeavors at reconstruction just after the war which were not altogether wise, but the work that is now being carried on commands the cordial support of all the best people of the South.”[26] The “best people” referred to liberal southerners dedicated to solving southern problems who were not burdened by a decades-old allegiance to Confederate ideals and were interested in repurposing the word *reconstruction* to defend their call for transformation.

In addition, advocates for the New Reconstruction could successfully distance themselves from bitter sectional tension by framing the problems of the South in a broader context that included drawing comparisons between the region and overseas colonies or other countries. By the late nineteenth century, educators, some philanthropists, and social scientists began to frame their discussion of southern readjustment, both implicitly and explicitly, in the context of colonialism and transnational reform. A New Reconstruction of the South would entail domestic civilizing missions at home that were informed by work done abroad. Likewise, men seeking to uplift nonwhite people in the imperial outposts overseas would use the South as a training ground or blueprint for uplift. In her work on the practice of comparison in North American history and postcolonial studies, historian Ann Stoler notes, “Category making produced cross-colonial equivalencies that allowed for international conferences and convinced their participants—doctors, lawyers, policy makers, and reformers—that they were in the same conversation, if not always talking about the same thing."[27] During this period a global movement of peoples, patterns of governance, reform practices, racial ideologies, and social scientific theories circulated between the United States and other countries including the overseas colonies. This transnational discussion cast the South as a distinctive place in relationship to the rest of the country even as this reform and rhetoric drew attention to the similarities between the region and transoceanic locales in the context of imperialism. Thus it is not surprising that the editors of the *New Republic* moved to compare Haiti with the state of Georgia and viewed both as suffering from a "false reconstruction" and in need of the guidance of civilized reformers.

The experience of Reconstruction in the United States encouraged experts on the South to consider that period as an example of early colonialism on domestic soil as well as to accept the existence of an early twentieth-century "southern problem." Some reformers made a concomitant pledge to newly reconstruct the region as a colonial template. In a think piece meditating on the end of the Spanish-American War in 1898 and what it meant to govern countries separate from the United States and populated with people of color, Walter Hines Page explained how colonial rule was a new problem for Americans but certainly not for the British. Page suggested the answer could be found close by. He advocated using the "process of reconstruction of the local governments of the Southern States" as a blueprint for colonial rule since, "in principle," the similarities were many. Colonial administrators, he argued, should look to the South's experience with a long military occupation following the Civil War and the way in which the federal government determined that the states had established and tested a "competent local government."[28] Over the course of the next two decades Page's participation in the Southern Education Board's effort to reduce southern illiteracy and his service on the board of the Rockefeller Sanitary Commission to Eradicate Hookworm in the southern states was influenced by the transnational connections he made between reconstructing the South in the early twentieth century and the concerns of colonial administrators seeking to uplift peoples in foreign locales.

Regardless of whether Progressive reformers or politicians embraced an imperialist or even anti-imperialist position, they often grafted the vocabulary of Reconstruction onto discussions about educational and sanitary reform in the colonies. One year after Page's meditation on the meaning of the Spanish-American War, Albert Shaw, an unofficial advisor to President Theodore Roosevelt, a classmate of Woodrow Wilson, and the editor of the American version of the *Review of Reviews,* crafted a series of editorials in a section of his monthly magazine, *The Progress of the World,* that elided the rhetoric of Reconstruction with the discourse of imperialism. Shaw explained how Americans had "a very especial reason for taking seriously to heart the lessons of the reconstruction period after our Civil War" because they now faced "four new problems of reconstruction": Hawaii, Puerto Rico, Cuba, and the Philippines.[29] In a cluster of editorials in the February 1899 issue, Shaw struggled to balance his belief that the native peoples of these colonies should be given the authority to govern themselves, particularly in the wake of oppressive Spanish colonial rule, with competing assertions that the United States might have to occupy these countries and assist with reconstruction until the colonies could adopt a true form of self-governance.

Referencing Thomas Nelson Page's novel *Red Rock: A Chronicle of Reconstruction,* Shaw embraced the dominant mythology of the time that Reconstruction involved northern seizure of local control from the southern people through a "*régime* of military occupation" and had been a colossal harmful mistake.[30] He warned that "the faintest symptoms of carpet-bag rule in Porto Rico [*sic*] or in Hawaii should be viewed with alarm" and portrayed the "Spaniards as the 'Carpetbaggers' in Cuba" who had provided substandard education and questionable moral instruction to the Cubans.[31] On one level, Americans played the role of southerners fighting an imperial northern power signified by the Spanish people. However, on another level in a second editorial titled "Reconstruction Work for Cuba," Shaw viewed Americans as northern in character and advised that for the unforeseeable future they would have to oversee the "restoration of order" with a replacement "military occupation" until Cubans could take care of their own affairs and substitute a local army.[32] "Sanitary Reconstruction" of the seaports in Cuba "such as the construction of sewers, the filling up or draining of marshes, the dredging of foul harbors, the improvement of municipal water-supplies, and whatever else may be necessary in every part of the island to reduce to a minimum the danger of yellow fever and other epidemic diseases," he declared, could only be accomplished with the controlling hand of the American military.[33] In his pledge to support a New Reconstruction of the colonies, Shaw failed to note the irony of labeling the

Spaniards "Carpetbaggers" while simultaneously reasoning that Americans must engage in using their own military force to insure that the colonies would meet the imperatives of reform.

The impulse to think about the old or new Reconstruction in the South in the context of American imperialism persisted after the Spanish-American War, particularly in public health efforts to eradicate such diseases as malaria and hookworm in the southern states. In 1912 Walter Hines Page used his widely distributed magazine *World's Work* to draw attention to the problem of hookworm in the "disease belts" of the world with an essay titled "The Hookworm in Civilization" that moved back and forth between stories about hookworm infection in Virginia, North Carolina, Puerto Rico, Louisiana, the Philippines, Ecuador, British Guiana, India, Mississippi, and Ceylon, among other places. He described how both public health work in the US South and these various global locales seemed likely to lead to "the reclamation of other tropical peoples and the utilization of their lands." Whether Page called the effort to eradicate hookworm a matter of reclamation, readjustment, or reconstruction, the intention of public health reformers and southern liberals who supported this effort was clear; rather than relying on northern finance or technology alone, making human bodies in the New South healthy would jump-start progress, overcome southern backwardness, and reduce the number of chronically lethargic weak laborers. Page also explained that "it is the same disease that has for centuries made a large part of all tropical and semi-tropical peoples anemic" and even theorized that "the hookworm has probably played a larger part in our Southern history than slavery or wars or any political dogma or economic creed." "If there had been no hookworm victims in our Southern states," he asserted, "it is certain that national history would in some way, perhaps in many ways, have been very different."[34] By imagining that the absence of disease in the South might have eliminated sectionalism, changed the course of the Civil War, and perhaps circumvented the failure of Reconstruction, Page used a counterfactual narrative to underscore just how vital it was for the nation to invest in reconstructing the early twentieth-century South.

In addition to public health reform, southern and northern reformers pledged to resolve educational deficiencies that had never been fully dealt with in the years after the Civil War. Efforts to revive the quality of southern education and reduce the level of civic decline began as early as Reconstruction when northern churches and philanthropists entered the region to educate the freed slaves.[35] Edgar W. Knight, professor of education at Trinity College (later Duke University), explained how the South during this period was "looked upon as a vast missionary field."[36] When the federal government pulled its last federal troops out of the South in 1877, public education suffered tremendously because of the Redeemer governments' policy of retrenchment. State appropriations for public schools were appallingly low, and the average length of the school term in the South decreased by 20 percent. A minority of local southern reformers and northern supporters continued to advocate better educational opportunities in the region, but they lacked state support and had to search for alternative funding, often from philanthropic support in the North.[37]

In general, the southern educational reform movement initiated during Reconstruction had focused exclusively on reducing illiteracy rates among the newly freed slaves, and in the years immediately following Reconstruction, white philanthropists continued to direct most of their efforts at African Americans. These groups included the Jeanes Foundation, the George Peabody Foundation, the John F. Slater Fund for the Education of Freedmen, and the Rockefellers' General Education Board. After serving in the Union army and working with the Freedmen's Bureau, General Samuel Chapman Armstrong founded Hampton Institute in Virginia, an internationally recognized school of industrial training based on his experience with mission schools in Hawaii and a belief that there were similarities between African Americans and Hawaiians.[38] Booker T. Washington, a graduate of Hampton Institute, went on to found Tuskegee Institute, another institution that attracted liberal white support and the attention of colonial administrators looking for solutions to global problems.

Yet by the turn of the century philanthropic support began to swing toward eradicating the problem of white illiteracy. In 1901, speaking before an audience of reformers in Salem, North Carolina, Charles W. Dabney, a prominent educational reformer and president of the University of Tennessee, declared, "Believing that the Southern people have at last overcome most of the financial and political results of war and Reconstruction, I hold that the time has come when we must begin seriously upon the work of reconstructing Southern society in all its departments, and that the first thing to do is to establish schools for all the people."[39] That same year the Southern Education Board was founded to promote white and black rural education, and over the years the board included well-known philanthropists and reformers such as Walter Hines Page, Charles W. Dabney, Edgar Gardner Murphy, George Foster Peabody, Robert C. Ogden, Edwin A. Alderman, and Hollis B. Frissell.

Indeed, the scale of white illiteracy was often deemed shocking when compared to those of African Americans and the indigenous inhabitants of the overseas colonies. William H. Skaggs, an ex-Populist, three-time mayor of Talladega, Alabama, and southern expatriate in New York wrote a letter to the editor of the *Birmingham Age-Herald* regarding the deplorable educational facilities and lack of opportunities in his home state. The paper printed the letter with the following byline: "INDICTMENT OF THE SOUTH'S EDUCATION GROWS APPALLING. Wm. H. Skaggs, Former Talladega Man, Presents Some Gruesome Facts. SEES DARK AHEAD FOR OUR WHITE CHILDREN. Says Educational Conditions Among Southern White People Are the Most Deplorable in the Civilized World." Skaggs had collected documentation after making a personal investigation of the educational situation in the southern states and reported that he could "furnish evidence of ignorance, poverty and physical and civic degeneracy" among the white class. He warned that what he had discovered would make every person in the state "stand aghast." In fact, Skaggs noted that not only were blacks rapidly accumulating more property and becoming more literate than poor whites but also that Puerto Rico was "making greater progress than the South." The former mayor explained how children attended public school 200 days out of the year in the Philippines, 165 days out of the year in Puerto Rico, but only 113.3 days in his home state of Alabama. What he found particularly disturbing was Congress's relative lack of interest in southern educational problems as compared to the educational problems of the colonies. He described how William Jennings Bryan had undertaken a combined tour of the southern states and the West Indies and had only reported to the House Committee on Insular Affairs on the grave need for schools, better roads, and hookworm eradication programs in Puerto Rico but not in the US South. Skaggs chastised Bryan for neglecting the region, which had voted for Bryan in substantial numbers during the presidential election of 1908.[40] Charles W. Dabney encouraged southern states to consider accepting national aid for education in the South by appealing to patriotic sensibilities within the context of imperialism. He stressed how white southerners had willingly served their country in defense of the "Cuban people" and died in a "war for aliens" and thus were entitled to national support for their own children. Like Skaggs, he noted the incongruity between establishing schools for Puerto Ricans and Filipinos and neglecting white southern children at home.[41] Skaggs's and Dabney's decisions to compare poor whites with Filipinos and Puerto Ricans highlighted the dreadful repercussion of the southern problem, and the uncanny commonalities between a large group of southern whites and nonwhites overseas.

A transnational circuit of educational reformers and ideas created opportunities for men who were seeking to reconstruct nonwhite people abroad to use the South as a training ground or blueprint as well as, conversely, to seek answers to southern solutions in distant countries. Puerto Rico not only proved to be an analogous social laboratory for hookworm eradication but also one for educational uplift. The secretary of the National Child Labor Committee promised Edgar Gardner Murphy that he would transmit notes on Murphy's experience with the Southern Education Board (SEB) to the new commissioner of education in Puerto Rico with the hope "that the good work of the Southern Education Boards may be extended that far South."[42] The concept of a broader global South incorporating the US South with the colonies in the Caribbean included the commitment to uplift all unenlightened people. Robert C. Ogden, a wealthy businessman from New York City, a partner of the department store magnate John Wanamaker, and a trustee at the Hampton Institute, donated thousands of dollars to the cause and financed a series of train excursions to the South that carried a diverse collection of northerners fascinated with southern educational problems. Some of these train trips included visits to Hampton Institute as well as rural white schools deemed in need of uplift. Hampton Institute enrolled a small number of students from Puerto Rico with the intention of training them in American habits of discipline and frugality, and in 1900 the governor of the island colony petitioned Ogden personally suggesting that he could offer "representative children, bright and alert" who would benefit from attending.[43] In 1904 Ogden received a letter from a graduate student at Harvard University, who was getting ready to head to the Philippines to work under Governor-General Cameron Forbes, to inquire whether he could join one of Ogden's journeys as preparation for his service in the colonial government.[44] As Samuel C. Mitchell wrote after Ogden's death, "It is noteworthy that, just at the time when Mr. Ogden became identified with the popular movement for education in the South, the American people were led, as the result of the war with Spain, to undertake the training of backward peoples in the Philippines, Porto Rico [*sic*] and Hawaii. Here was projected upon a world stage the same task and the same principle of education in the making of a race which the South was at that time exemplifying." He added, "The meaning of this social effort will be lost unless it is realized that the principle and process used here are applicable in every country that aspires to progress under democratic freedom."[45] These reformers' promotion of industrial training and moral uplift linked together southern white schools, colonial schooling in the Philippines, Puerto Rico, and Hawaii, and black institutions such as Hampton Institute and Tuskegee Institute. The rhetoric of uplift and reconstruction tied together a shared set of ideas about industrial democracy, preparation to exercise the rights of citizenship, and economic progress.

However, drawing similarities between poor white people and poor people of color could prove to be thorny when discussing educational programs of uplift. As Edgar Gardner Murphy stressed, "the racial heritage of the white man must be clearly accepted and recognized" when it involved industrial training.[46] While these reformers did not utilize the language of race-baiting southern demagogues, they still remained committed to an idea of democracy that included the social separation of the races and black disfranchisement. Robert Ogden was critical of southern demagogues who hindered the small but "best South" from speaking publicly about the region's educational needs.[47] These were the "best" white southerners, who included Walter Hines Page and whom Booker T. Washington's newspaper the *Southern Workman* had praised for advocating a New Reconstruction. The philanthropic interest in black education, at such places as Hampton Institute and Tuskegee Institute, did not wane entirely at the turn of the century but it remained devoid of any hint of political activism or the call for civil rights. Robert Ogden laid out the problem this way: "The great present need of the South is the uplift of its backward populations.... Through the country the urgent need is for a white civilization that the black man can respect. Only this can eliminate the dangers of the future."[48] Ogden and his supporters viewed education as the key to racial harmony in a segregated system, because if poor whites could be taught to meet the standards of civilized life than blacks would learn to defer to them.

At times, the proponents of southern education were apprehensive about the ability of poor whites to better themselves and noted that African Americans, unlike lower-class whites, never had to be persuaded to send their children to school.[49] Some members of the SEB petitioned for the public advocacy of compulsory attendance laws for whites, whom they insisted without prodding would continue to drag the region down and contribute to enduring racial tensions.[50] In a piece endorsing compulsory education in the southern states, Erwin Craighead from Mobile, Alabama explained how in a democracy, "the primary object of education [was] to make good, intelligent, loyal sovereigns." Without education white southern people would be unable to develop into an "intelligent, prosperous, and orderly citizenship."[51] The language used by Craighead could have easily been used by colonial administrators to describe Filipinos or Hawaiians, although Ogden and his compatriots had faith that poor whites would reach a state of self-government more quickly than the inhabitants of the overseas colonies. Overall the focus on educational revival in the first decade of the twentieth century was a crucial piece of the new reconstruction in both the southern states and the colonial possessions.

+ + +

Although World War I was the largest foreign policy issue the United States faced in the second decade of the twentieth century, the concept of the New Reconstruction continued to flourish in the following decade, fueled in part by the American excursion into Haiti and the evolution of southern liberalism in the 1910s with its attendant interest in the "race problem" and issues such as education. A series of philanthropically funded studies of African American education, the evolution of the Southern Sociological Congress which spawned the University Commission on Southern Race Questions (UCSRQ) in 1912, and the formation of the Commission on Interracial Cooperation (CIC) in 1919 moved those interested in southern problems to rely heavily on social science and to adopt a more critical stance toward the region. The same year the *New York Times* and *New Republic* attacked the Leo Frank lynching, and the latter magazine drew comparisons between the uncivilized nature of Georgia and Haiti. Walter O. Scroggs, an associate professor of economics and history at Louisiana State University, spoke before the students of the University of

Virginia about "The New Reconstruction." Scroggs was one of eight academics, reformers, and self-proclaimed experts on southern race relations invited by the trustees of the Phelps-Stokes Fund to give a series of lectures to the UVA student body from 1912 to 1915. The group included Clarence Poe, Alfred Holt Stone, James H. Dillard, and Ulrich B. Phillips, among others.

While the speakers did not necessarily agree with one another on the nature of the problem or whether a feasible solution existed, their participation underscored a mounting commitment to the professional and scientific study of race relations rooted in sociological practices and theories. By the time these men had gathered to lecture at the University of Virginia thousands of books, periodical articles, editorials, travelers' accounts, sermons, and sociological studies had already been published that documented and discussed every possible aspect of the "race problem" (sometimes also referred to as the "race question," "Negro Question," and "Negro Problem"). Even as early as 1901 a kaleidoscope of dialogue on the "race problem" so dominated the national press, the lecture circuit, and the publishing world that the topic prompted Kelly Miller, the founder of sociology at Howard University and a prolific writer, to remark: "The national opinion concerning the negro is formed and re-formed with such startling rapidity that only the process of instantaneous photography can preserve its shifting phases."[52]

William O. Scroggs was a member of a group of faculty who came together at the first meeting of the Southern Sociological Congress in Nashville, Tennessee to answer Dr. James H. Dillard's call to establish the UCSRQ. The purpose of this organization was to target eleven southern state universities and "aim especially to influence Southern College Men to approach the subject with intelligent information and with sympathetic interest."[53] The vice president of the University of Florida, Professor James M. Farr, thought that each university should "organize a class in sociology to study the race problem, largely by the laboratory method, using the town and county in which the university is located as the field for investigation."[54] At the University of Virginia and the University of Georgia, students under the auspices of the Young Men's Christian Association engaged in a systematic study of the "race problem" outside of their regular coursework.[55] Working in connection with the Phelps-Stokes Fund, the UCSRQ also issued several published letters addressed to these students encouraging them to promote the education of African Americans; engage in interracial collaboration on solving "vital community problems" such as public health reform, building schools and roads, and friendly business relations; and speak out against the "contagious social disease" of lynching, which not only led to the death of its victims but also "lynch[ed] law and justice and civilization."[56] Included in the letters was a shorter version of Scroggs's articulation of the "New Reconstruction."

In the University of Virginia lecture he gave in 1914 (which was published in 1915), Scroggs outlined the platform of the "New Reconstruction" in relationship to "racial adjustment." He explained how the "New Reconstruction" had no resemblance to the "so-called reconstruction of a past generation" because it eschewed political and legal solutions that inherently involved governmental force, demagoguery, and political manipulation. Scroggs proclaimed that the "New Reconstruction . . . is a movement for better education for both whites and blacks, for higher moral ideals, and a socialized religion, for increasing cooperation between the best elements of the races, and for greater publicity for those whose views are based on reason rather than on prejudice and tradition." The key to a successful "New Reconstruction," Scroggs explained, was "not by way of governmental fiat, but by the gradual process of evolution."[57] Thus any readjustment in the South must proceed gradually and prove less disruptive than the process initiated during the "Old Reconstruction," which did not follow the predictable teleological path of progress.

Scroggs did not explicitly situate his call for a "New Reconstruction" in the context of Haiti, but as a social scientist he was certainly aware of the transnational nature of "racial adjustment." Black and white social scientists, intellectuals, and reformers had long considered the study of race relations as inherently global in orientation, especially as it pertained to the development of democracy. British liberals such as Viscount James Bryce, Goldwyn Smith, and Charles Pearson from Oxford and Cambridge visited the United States during and after the Civil War to study American political issues including the "Negro Problem." They conferred with Americans such as Charles Elliot Norton, a social critic; Wendell Phillips, a Boston abolitionist with ties to William Lloyd Garrison; and Herbert Baxter Adams, a professor of history at Johns Hopkins with a doctorate from a German university and a secretary of the American Historical Association. The development of what Marilyn Lake and Henry Reynolds call a transnational "racial regime" involving England and the United

States animated questions about empire, the nature of citizenship, and national sovereignty. These transnational intellectuals viewed Reconstruction in the United States as a catastrophic failure and asked themselves, "How could the two races coexist in a democratic republic?"[58] At the heart of that question was a paradox that theorists such as Bryce and others struggled with: how did one reconcile faith in the creed that "all men are created equal" with the belief in the inferiority of nonwhite races? Bryce argued that the "Negro Problem" was the gravest problem American democracy faced, and in his work *The Relations of the Advanced and Backward Races of Mankind* (1902) he described contact between white and nonwhite races as "a crisis in the history of the world, which will profoundly affect the destiny of mankind."[59] Other Europeans and Americans tackled this dilemma in such books as W. P. Livingstone, *The Race Conflict: A Study of Conditions in America* (1911); John Moffat Mecklin, *Democracy and Race Friction: A Study in Social Ethics* (1914); Maurice S. Evans, *Black and White in the Southern States: A Study of the Race Problem in the United States from a South African Point of View* (1915); and Basil Mathews, *The Clash of Colour: A Study in the Problem of Race* (1925).[60] These self-proclaimed and academic race experts viewed the contact between the white and nonwhite races not only as a new problem evident in the existence of four million emancipated slaves in the southern states but also as one engendered by the inevitable spread of empire. In their minds, segregation was a possible solution and perhaps a necessary piece of the evolutionary path toward resolution.

Like many of these transnational amateur and professional social scientists, William O. Scroggs acknowledged that although the "New Reconstruction" advocated "racial readjustment" it did not seek to overturn the social separation of the races despite the inherent contradictions embedded in such a system. "While this segregation may sometimes result in practices that do not square with our theories of democracy, and may even cause the whites at times to appear illogical and inconsistent," he declared, "it is nevertheless the means by which the race responsible for the nation's past, present and future achievement has maintained its integrity." Scroggs tolerated ambiguity and contradiction even as he made the case that those involved in the "New Reconstruction" should aim to "eliminate those features of the negro's civic status which seem antagonistic to the spirit of a just government."[61] Like many, he believed in the philosophy of "separate but equal" articulated in *Plessy v. Ferguson* (1896), and this enabled him and other early liberals to focus on improving conditions on streetcars, schools, and black neighborhoods as well as targeting lynching, mob violence, and demagogues as antithetical to reasoned conversation. Scroggs remained optimistic that reformers could balance seemingly contradictory facts surrounding the question of race and democracy as long as the process moved forward toward a realignment of society, albeit with an unidentified end point.

At the end of World War I Kelly Miller issued his own pamphlet about "The Negro's Place in the New Reconstruction" from the point of view of an African American sociologist who had written many books on the "race problem" as it related to education, crime, politics, Christianity, the black middle class, interracial sex, and the resulting "mulatto." Like other social scientists, Miller identified the innate contradiction between an "abstract philosophy of human rights," the fight for world democracy, and the status of African Americans in the South. He viewed World War I as a crucial turning point in the "New Reconstruction," since this global war had drawn attention to the inherent democratic rights of humankind. Moreover, Miller reminded his readers that African Americans in the South were keenly aware of the American hypocrisy of fighting an international war for "world democracy" while denying black citizens their universal "manhood rights." The Howard University sociologist made an analogy between the Civil War and World War I, asserting that the Confederacy had been founded upon the principle of "human inequality" much like the German nation-state had championed an immoral undemocratic cause. The older process of Reconstruction had failed, Miller explained, due to the abrupt attempt by one region to force its will on that of another region, but he was hopeful that African Americans would take up the cause of "the new democratic spirit" and seek to make "the program of social justice and human opportunity" their own through the new program of reconstruction. Miller also underscored the transnational component of the "New Reconstruction" in his plea that the United States seize control of the African colonies held by Germany as a way of providing "an example to the world of how a backward people can be governed without exploitation, and lifted to higher planes of civilization under the guidance of the democratic spirit." Just as the United States had assumed control of the Philippines and Puerto Rico under the mantle of "benevolent assimilation" so must it "assume responsibility for the future welfare" of the African colonies that had formerly belonged to Germany.[62]

Although the term *New Reconstruction* was not used widely, it can be tied to the evolution of late nineteenth- and early twentieth-century liberalism, particularly in the South. The concept stood apart from the more familiar Dunning interpretation of Reconstruction, and liberals found it a constructive way to discuss lingering problems in the South without addressing questions about politics or law that many reformers found themselves facing in the immediate years after the Civil War. It proved to be a limited form of liberalism that did not challenge deep structural inequalities such as segregation and disfranchisement but advocated for a soft form of interracial cooperation and benevolent improvement. The discourse of the new reconstruction also reveals that imperial expansion and social reform in education, public health, and economic reform were mutually constitutive. Terms such as *reconstruction, readjustment,* and *uplift* could be substituted for one another and underscored a collective understanding of the modernization of allegedly backward locales in both domestic and foreign settings.

However, it would take a second world war for the discourse of Reconstruction to evolve in yet another direction. The changes wrought by World War II in conjunction with the modernization of agriculture and urbanization paved the way for a grassroots uprising of African Americans demanding their civil and political rights with the support of sympathetic white liberals. This wide-scale movement drew attention to the inherent paradox of American democracy and contributed to the eventual demise of segregation in the South. The twentieth-century movement underscored a more radical commitment to civil rights than the "New Reconstruction," as imagined by individuals such as Walter Hines Page, William O. Scroggs, and Kelly Miller, and was deemed the "second reconstruction" by another liberal southerner named C. Vann Woodward in a set of three lectures given in 1955 at the University of Virginia. Woodward eventually published those lectures as *The Strange Career of Jim Crow,* an influential book that Martin Luther King once referred to as "the historical bible of the Civil Rights Movement."[63] He explicitly designed the lectures for a southern audience, much as William O. Scroggs had in his 1914 lecture at the University of Virginia, except that Woodward's commitment to the promise of the "Second Reconstruction" included lecturing before an integrated audience. Just one year later in *Commentary* Woodward offered his take on the significance of *Brown v. Board of Education* and the growing civil rights movement, this time labeling it a "New Reconstruction."[64] Later in *The Burden of Southern History,* another book that involved several revisions with additional essays added in 1968 and 1993, the Yale professor expressed doubt that the "Second Reconstruction" was as successful as some liberals insisted. Woodward described the cycle of "revolutionary upheavals" as a process of "rise, climax, decline, and retrenchment" and speculated that historians and activists might contemplate the need for a "Third Reconstruction" in the face of a period of reaction. In light of the Vietnam War, black nationalism, and uprisings such as Watts, Woodward added, "Veterans of the Second Reconstruction and planners of a Third would do well to face up to the fact that the one is now over and the other is still struggling to be born."[65] Indeed political scientists Hanes Walton Jr., Josephine A. V. Allen, Sherman C. Puckett, and Donald R. Deskins Jr. have argued that Woodward's bona fide "Third Reconstruction" began with the election of President Barack Obama in 2008.[66] The various articulations of the word *reconstruction* show us that the representation of Reconstruction is malleable and dynamic, able to lend symbolic power to the rhetoric of liberalism as it has waxed and waned throughout the course of the twentieth century and into the twenty-first.

## NOTES

Note to epigraph: Southern Education Board Records, Box 8, Folder 205, Subseries 2.4, Southern Historical Collection, Wilson Library, University of North Carolina at Chapel Hill.

1. "A Regrettable Incident," *New York Times,* 19 August 1915.

2. Editorial, *New Republic,* 21 August 1915, 56. For an excellent account of the Leo Frank case and its regional significance, see Nancy MacLean, "The Leo Frank Case Reconsidered: Gender and Sexual Politics in the Making of Reactionary Populism," *Journal of American History* 78 (December 1991): 917–48.

3. See Gail Bederman, *Manliness and Civilization: A Cultural History of Gender and Race in the United States, 1880–1917* (Chicago: University of Chicago Press, 1995).

4. Mary A. Renda, *Taking Haiti: Military Occupation and the Culture of US Imperialism, 1915–1940* (Chapel Hill: University of North Carolina Press, 2001).

5. Peter Schmidt, *Sitting in Darkness: New South Fiction, Education, and the Rise of Jim Crow Colonialism, 1865–1920* (Jackson: University of Mississippi Press, 2008), 13.

6. See David W. Blight, *Race and Reunion: The Civil War in American Memory* (Cambridge, MA: Harvard University Press, 2000); Nina Silber, The *Romance of Reunion: Northerners and*

*the South, 1865–1900* (Chapel Hill: University of North Carolina Press, 1993); Edward J. Blum, *Reforging the White Republic: Race, Religion, and American Nationalism, 1865–1898* (Baton Rouge: Louisiana State University Press, 2007); Grace Elizabeth Hale, *Making Whiteness: The Culture of Segregation in the South, 1890–1940* (New York: Pantheon Books, 1998); Dewey W. Grantham, *Southern Progressivism: The Reconciliation of Progress and Tradition* (Nashville: Vanderbilt University Press, 1983); Paul Gaston, *New South Creed: A Study in Southern Mythmaking* (New York: Alfred A. Knopf, 1970); Gaines M. Foster, *Ghosts of the Confederacy: Defeat, the Lost Cause, and the Emergence of the New South, 1865–1913* (New York: Oxford University Press, 1987); Charles Reagan Wilson, *Baptized in Blood: The Religion of the Lost Cause, 1865–1920* (Athens: University of Georgia Press, 1982).

7. Blight, *Race and Reunion,* 2–3, 381–97. Blight states the "emancipationist vision" never entirely died, only to reemerge in the "last third of the twentieth century."

8. Caroline Janney, *Remembering the Civil War: Reunion and the Limits of Reconciliation* (Chapel Hill: University of North Carolina Press, 2013), 10. Janney prefers to think of four categories of Civil War memory as noted by Gary Gallagher in *Causes Won, Lost, and Forgotten: How Hollywood and Popular Art Shape What We Know About the Civil War* (Chapel Hill: University of North Carolina Press, 2013), 2.

9. See Bruce E. Baker, *What Reconstruction Meant: Historical Memory in the American South* (Charlottesville: University of Virginia Press, 2007); and Blight, *Race and Reunion.*

10. Robert C. Ogden to Charles Richardson, Esq., 30 March 1904, Robert Curtis Ogden Papers, "Special Correspondence," Box 14, Library of Congress, Manuscript Division, Washington, DC.

11. Gary Gerstle, "The Protean Character of American Liberalism," *Journal of American History* 99 (October 1994): 1046.

12. James McCulloch, "Introduction," in James McCulloch, ed., *Battling for Social Betterment: Southern Sociological Congress, Memphis, Tennessee, May 6–10, 1914* (Nashville, : Southern Sociological Congress, 1914), 3.

13. Holland Thompson, "The New South, Economic and Social," in James W. Gardner, *Studies in Southern History and Politics: Inscribed to William Archibald Dunning* (New York: Columbia University Press, 1914), 315.

14. See Peter J. Bowler, *The Invention of Progress: The Victorians and the Past* (Oxford: B. Blackwell, 1980); and George Stocking, *Victorian Anthropology* (New York: Free Press, 1987).

15. For a competing literary analysis of how the discourse of civilization was employed to make sense of the New South, see Jeremy Dwight Wells, "Civilization and the South: Southern Writers and American Empire, 1866–1907" (PhD diss., University of Michigan, 2000). Wells states that texts about the postbellum South were obsessed with the idea of civilization, but this discourse in the South functioned differently in the immediate years following the Civil War than it did at the turn of the century. Wells argues that early on, the region was criticized for its lack of civilization but in conjunction with the spread of empire overseas, writers almost always celebrated the greatness of southern civilization. However, liberal southerners, northern philanthropists, and government experts often wrote and spoke about the *absence* of southern civilization in the early twentieth century. See Jeremy Wells, *Romances of the White*

*Man's Burden: Race, Empire, and the Plantation in American Literature, 1880–1936* (Nashville: Vanderbilt University Press, 2011), for an expansion on his dissertation.

16. Dr. John E. White, "The Significance of the Southern Sociological Congress," in James McCulloch, *The South Mobilizing for Social Service: Addresses Delivered at the Southern Sociological Congress, Atlanta, Georgia, April 25–29, 1913* (Nashville: Southern Sociological Congress, 1913), 16.

17. "Free Speech in the South," *Independent* 55 (January 15, 1903), 131.

18. Rev. John E. White, "The True and False in Southern Life," *South Atlantic Quarterly* 5 (April 1906): 101.

19. Edgar Gardner Murphy, *Problems of the Present South* (New York: Macmillan, 1904), vii, ix, 199.

20. Murphy, *Problems of the Present South,* x.

21. See David Brion Davis, *Slavery and Human Progress* (New York: Oxford University Press, 1984).

22. Charles B. Spahr, "America's Working People, Part II: The New Factory Towns of the South," *Outlook* 61 (March 4, 1899), 514; William W. Ball, "The Industrial Revolution in South Carolina," *Sewanee Review* 19 (April 1911): 9; and Samuel Chiles Mitchell, "Robert Curtis Ogden: A Leader in the Educational Renaissance of the South," Robert Curtis Ogden Papers, Box 27, Folder 1. For examples of references to slavery as an incubus, see Richard H. Edmonds, *Facts about the South* (Baltimore: Manufacturer's Record, 1902), 1; and William P. Trent, "Dominant Forces in Southern Life," *Atlantic Monthly* 79 (January 1897), 47.

23. Walter Hines Page, *The Rebuilding of Old Commonwealths: Essays Toward the Training of the Forgotten Man in the Southern States* (New York: Doubleday, Page, 1902), 121, 138.

24. Walter Hines Page, "Study of an Old Southern Borough," *Atlantic Monthly* 47 (May 1881), 648, 652–53, 655, 657–58.

25. John Milton Cooper Jr., *Walter Hines Page: The Southerner as American, 1855–1918* (Chapel Hill: University of North Carolina Press, 1977), 57.

26. "The New Reconstruction," *Southern Workman* 40 (July 1911): 389.

27. Ann Laura Stoler, "Tense and Tender Ties: The Politics of Comparison in North American History and (Post) Colonial Studies," *Journal of American History* 88 (December 2001): 863.

28. Walter Hines Page, "The End of the War, and After," *Atlantic Monthly* 82 (September 1898), 430–31. Pushing the southern blueprint for colonization back even further, Burton J. Hendrick, the editor of Walter Hines Page's correspondence, wrote that the North Carolina reformer believed the solution to the colonial problem in the Philippines could be solved by extending Thomas Jefferson's principles of uplifting the common man in remote areas. Hendrick himself made comparisons between Virginia and the Philippines. He encouraged colonizers to train the Filipinos in the "essentials of self-government" as Jefferson did in eighteenth-century Virginia, including teaching them to read and write, training them in agriculture, trades, and mechanic arts, and encouraging them to practice proper sanitary habits and build roads and highways. See Hendrick, *The Training of an American: The Earlier Life and Letters of Walter Hines Page, 1855–1913* (Boston: Houghton Mifflin, 1928), 268.

29. "Our New Reconstruction Tasks," *American Monthly Review of Reviews* 19 (February 1899): 132.

30. "The Fruits of 'Reconstruction,'" *American Monthly Review of Reviews* 19 (February 1899): 131–32.

31. "Our New Reconstruction Tasks," *American Monthly Review of Reviews* 19 (February 1899): 133, and "The Spaniards as Carpet-Baggers' in Cuba," *American Monthly Review of Reviews* 19 (February 1899): 135.

32. "Reconstruction Work for Cuba," *American Monthly Review of Reviews* 19 (February 1899): 133.

33. "The Duty of Sanitary 'Reconstruction,'" *American Monthly Review of Reviews* 19 (February 1899): 135.

34. Walter H. Page, "The Hookworm and Civilization," *World's Work* 24 (September 1912): 504, 509.

35. For a general history of black education during Reconstruction, see Robert C. Morris, *Reading, 'Riting, and Reconstruction: The Education of Freedmen in the South, 1861–1870* (Chicago: University of Chicago Press, 1981); Ronald E. Butchart, *Northern Schools, Southern Blacks, and Reconstruction Freedmen's Education* (Westport, CT: Greenwood Press, 1980); and Donald G. Nieman, ed., *African Americans and Education in the South, 1865–1900* (New York: Garland, 1994).

36. Edgar W. Knight, "Some Fallacies Concerning the History of Public Education in the South," *South Atlantic Quarterly* 13 (October 1914): 373.

37. For a history of the Peabody Fund, see Earle H. West, "The Peabody Education Fund and Negro Education, 1867–1880," in Nieman, *African Americans*. For a history of the Slater Fund, see Roy E. Finkenbine, "'Our Little Circle': Benevolent Reformers, the Slater Fund, and the Argument for Black Industrial Education, 1882–1908," in Nieman, *African Americans*.

38. Natalie J. Ring, *The Problem South: Region, Empire, and the New Liberal State, 1880–1930* (Athens: University of Georgia Press, 2012), 266n110.

39. Charles W. Dabney, "The Public School Problem in the South," Charles W. Dabney Papers, subseries 5.2, Box 25, Folder 319, Southern Historical Collection, Wilson Library, University of North Carolina at Chapel Hill.

40. "Some Newspaper Articles Regarding the Educational Situation and Other Civic Matters in the Southern States: Alabama in Particular," Hoole Alabama Collection, W. S. Hoole Special Collections Library, University of Alabama, Tuscaloosa, 5, 10, 16–17.

41. Untitled typescript, Charles W. Dabney Papers, subseries 5.2, Box 26, Folder 1, Southern Historical Collection, Wilson Library, University of North Carolina at Chapel Hill.

42. Samuel M. Lindsay to Edgar Gardner Murphy, 9 December 1904, Edgar Gardner Murphy Papers, Box 1, Folder 2, Southern Historical Collection, Wilson Library, University of North Carolina at Chapel Hill.

43. Governor Charles H. Allen to Robert C. Ogden, 8 December 1900, Robert Curtis Ogden Papers, Special Correspondence, Box 6, Folder "1900."

44. W. A. Locke to Robert C. Ogden, April 1, 1904, Robert Curtis Ogden Papers, Special Correspondence, Box 7, Folder "April 1–5, 1904."

45. Samuel C. Mitchell, "Robert Curtis Ogden: A Leader in the Educational Renaissance of

the South," Robert Curtis Ogden Papers, Box 27, "Speeches, Writings, and Related Materials," vii, 173.

46. Edgar Gardner Murphy, "The Task of the South: An Address before the Faculty and Students of Washington and Lee University, Lexington, Virginia, December 10th, A.D. 1902," Hoole Alabama Collection, 24–25.

47. See Robert C. Ogden to John Spencer Bassett, 16 November 1903, "Special Correspondence," Box 13, Robert C. Ogden Papers; Robert C. Ogden to Oswald Garrison Villard, 3 December 1903, "Special Correspondence," Box 13, Robert C. Ogden Papers; Robert C. Ogden to Prof. S. G. Atkins, 21 December 1903, "Special Correspondence," Box 13, Robert Curtis Ogden Papers.

48. Robert Ogden to Col. Archibald Hopkins, 6 May 1903, "Special Correspondence," Box 13, Robert C. Ogden Papers.

49. "Compulsory Attendance Laws," Box 18, Folder "Education in the South," Robert C. Ogden Papers.

50. "Summer Meeting of the Southern Education Board, 5–8 August 1907, Box 17, Folder "Education in the South, 1907," Robert C. Ogden Papers.

51. Erwin Craighead, "Compulsory Education and the Southern States," *Sewanee Review* 16 (July 1908): 298.

52. Kelly Miller, "The Negro and Education," *Forum* 30 (February 1901): 693.

53. University Commission on Southern Questions, *Minutes,* 5.

54. University Commission on Southern Questions, *Minutes,* 5, 9, 11.

55. Charles Hillman Brough, "Work of the Commission of Southern Universities on the Race Question," *Annals of the American Academy of Political and Social Science* 49 (September 1913): 48–49.

56. See Trustees of the John F. Slater Fund, *Five Letters of the University Commission on Southern Race Questions* (Charlottesville: Michie Company Printers, 1927).

57. William O. Scroggs, "The New Reconstruction," *Lectures and Addresses on the Negro in the South* (Charlottesville: Michie Company, Printers, 1915), 57, 59, 64, 69.

58. Marilyn Lake and Henry Reynolds, *Drawing the Global Colour Line: White Men's Countries and the International Challenge of Racial Equality* (New York: Cambridge University Press, 2008), 6–9, 53–55, 61. Also see Paul Kramer, "Empires, Exceptions, and Anglo-Saxons: Race and Rule Between the British and United States Empires, 1880–1910," *Journal of American History* 88 (March 2002): 1315–53 for another history of this British-American exchange at the turn of the twentieth century.

59. James Bryce, "Thoughts on the Negro Problem," *North American Review* 153 (December 1891): 641; and James Bryce, *The Relations of the Advanced and Backward Races of Mankind* (Oxford: Clarendon Press, 1902), 7.

60. W. P. Livingstone, *The Race Conflict: A Study of Conditions in America* (London: S. Low, Marston, 1911); John Moffat Mecklin, *Democracy and Race Friction: A Study in Social Ethics* (New York: Macmillan, 1914); Maurice S. Evans, *Black and White in the Southern States: A Study of the Race Problem in the United States from a South African Point of View* (London: Longmans,

Green, 1915); and Basil Mathews, *The Clash of Colour: A Study in the Problem of Race* (Edinburgh: Edinburgh House Press, 1925).

61. Scroggs, "The New Reconstruction," 63.

62. Kelly Miller, *The Negro's Place in the New Reconstruction* (Washington, DC: Howard University, 1919), 8, 17–18, 21, 22–23.

63. "Afterword" by William S. McFeely, in C. Vann Woodward, *The Strange Career of Jim Crow. A Commemorative Edition with a New Afterword by William S. McFeely* (New York: Oxford University Press, 2002); Woodward, *The Strange Career of Jim Crow,* 221.

64. C. Vann Woodward, "The 'New Reconstruction' in the South: Desegregation in Historical Perspective," *Commentary,* June 1, 1956, 501–8.

65. C. Vann Woodward, *The Burden of Southern History* (Baton Rouge: Louisiana State University Press, 1960, 1968, 1991, 1993), 172–73, 177, 178. In 1984 sociologist Manning Marable wrote *Race, Reform, and Rebellion: The Second Reconstruction in Black America, 1945–1982* (Oxford: University Press of Mississippi, 1984), in which he borrowed Woodward's language to argue that structural inequalities in the economy and urban life demonstrated a period of retrenchment following the "Second Reconstruction."

66. See Hanes Walton Jr., Josephine A. V. Allen, Sherman C. Puckett, and Donald R. Deskins Jr., "Woodward's New Intellectual Stream: The Enfranchisement of the Freed Slave Population," in Angie Maxwell, Todd Shields, and Jeannie Whayne, *The Ongoing Burden of Southern History: Politics and Identity in the Twenty-First Century South* (Baton Rouge: Louisiana State University Press, 2012), 162.

# 8

# "A Bitter Memory Upon Which Terms of Peace Would Rest"

## *Woodrow Wilson, the Reconstruction of the South, and the Reconstruction of Europe*

SAMUEL L. SCHAFFER

"It would be an irony of fate," Woodrow Wilson remarked to a friend upon being elected president in 1912, "if my administration had to deal chiefly with foreign problems, for all my preparation has been in domestic matters."[1] Fate did have a sense of irony: within eighteen months of Wilson's arriving in Washington, DC, a Serbian nationalist killed the Archduke Franz Ferdinand, Austro-Hungary declared war on Serbia, Russia mobilized in response, Germany, France, and Great Britain followed, and the Great War had begun. Although Wilson had studied British and German government as a political scientist, he was right: he had little preparation for foreign affairs. His New Freedom was a significant domestic achievement that he, his cabinet, and his Democratic Congress had plotted, campaigned on, sweated over, and mostly enacted in his first year and a half in office. But the European conflict caught him off guard. "I find the President singularly lacking in appreciation of the importance of this European crisis," his advisor Edward House worried in his diary in the fall of 1914. "He seems more interested in domestic affairs, and I find it difficult to get his attention centered upon the one big question."[2]

Wilson did have little diplomatic experience. However, as a southerner born in 1856 he had firsthand experience with war and what followed. Five years old when Confederate troops fired on Fort Sumter, and twenty-one years old when federal troops were withdrawn from the South in 1877, he had been eyewitness to the American Civil War and to the reconstruction of the South. Those experiences affected him deeply, and when he did center his attention upon the "one big question" of the European war, the memory of the Civil War and particularly of Reconstruction pointed the way. Of course, other factors shaped Wilson's foreign policy: he had a keen political mind, and he worked hard to grasp international demands. But as he came to grips with the European conflict and its meaning, he could not help but view it through the lens of a southern-crafted worldview. As a young man and later as an author of American history texts, Wilson had described Reconstruction in the South as a "damnable cruelty and folly." It was a disastrous time, he pronounced, when the victor had imposed unreasonable terms on the vanquished and when the natural political and racial order had been upended.[3] Fifty years later, as he struggled to keep the United States neutral, as he called for a "peace without victory," and as he sought to ensure lasting peace through a League of Nations, Woodrow Wilson applied these same lessons. Wilson's foreign policy, as it turned out, had very domestic, historical roots.

+ + +

As it was for any white southerner born in the 1850s, the Civil War was important to Woodrow Wilson. His first memory, he recalled, was of "standing at my father's gateway in Augusta, Georgia, when I was four years old, and hearing . . . there was to be war."[4] He had seen wounded rebel soldiers when his father's church was turned into a hospital.[5] He had gazed up into Robert E. Lee's face as a young lad and watched Jefferson Davis's ignominious post-capture march through town.[6] But if the Civil War left psychological wounds, they were buried deeply. "To *me* the Civil War and its terrible scenes," he wrote later, "are but a memory of a short day."[7]

Certainly, Wilson told a group of historians in 1896, Confederate soldiers had fought with valor, and the South, he continued, had "nothing to apologize for."[8] But more important to him than the causes or the course of the war were its consequences. Like so many other young men of his generation, he called for a forward-looking, industrialized, and educated New South to rise out of the conflict's ashes, a New South restored, he wrote, to "eminence in national counsels."[9] Therefore, he wished good riddance to the outdated doctrine of state rights and the economic burden of slavery that had been at the heart of the Confederacy's existence.[10] To be sure, the South had suffered terrible human loss in the war, and he grieved for this devastation. But the Civil War, by forcing white southerners to envision a new South in place of the old, had hastened his native land's entry into the modern world. Significantly, Woodrow Wilson was a southerner, not a Confederate. "*Because* I love the South," he declared as a young man, "I rejoice in the failure of the Confederacy."[11]

Because he loved the South, Wilson saw Reconstruction as an unmitigated disaster. He had spent the immediate postwar years in Augusta, before moving in 1870 to Columbia, South Carolina, where his father had taken a position at the seminary and where charred chimneys still served as silent reminders of Sherman's visit.[12] Wilson left few personal recollections of his time in South Carolina, which, with more African American officeholders than any other southern state and with federal troops within its borders until April of 1877, was, in the words of one historian, the "crucible of Reconstruction."[13] But after embarking upon an academic career—he earned his doctorate in history and political science from Johns Hopkins in 1886 and began a teaching and writing career that eventually led him to Princeton in the 1890s—Wilson made his feelings about the period clear. On at least four different occasions he published about Reconstruction, and while his emphasis shifted depending on his audience, his overall message was consistent. Reconstruction was, as he wrote in his 1902 best-selling textbook *A History of the American People,* "the corruption and destruction" of southern society, "a reign of ignorance, a regime of power basely used, . . . [a] burden and [a] nightmare."[14]

The reasons for Reconstruction's failure were clear to Wilson. First of all, it had been discharged under vengeful circumstances. The passions of the Civil War, he wrote in an essay for the *Atlantic Monthly,* had brought "the dangerous intoxication of an absolute triumph upon the side that won" and "the bitterness of death upon the side which lost."[15] Victorious Republicans—whose emotions soon reached a "pitch of ecstasy"—viewed southern states as conquered territories.[16] These Radical Republicans did not know the South, nor did they care about it.[17] Their goal, Wilson concluded, was "not the rehabilitation of the southern governments." Rather, it was to punish the South, to enfranchise the Negro, and to establish permanently their own political power.[18] They were, he concluded, "bent upon bringing the South to utter humiliation."[19]

Second, Wilson argued, Reconstruction was a political and racial revolution—and not of the good sort. In his mind, the wrong people had been placed in power. Encouraged and protected by federal troops, white Republicans and their black allies replaced white southern Democrats in the polling booths and in offices of power. "The most influential white men were excluded from voting," Wilson lamented in his textbook *Division and Reunion,* "while the negroes were all admitted to enrollment."[20] This was a problem, he asserted, because blacks—"a race so recently slaves"—were "unfit to exercise their new liberty."[21] They were, in his words, "a host of dusky children untimely put out of school."[22] As a result, "unscrupulous adventurers" swarmed south, set up shop as politicians, duped these "ignorant" Negro voters to elect them, and oversaw the "ruin of the South."[23] The result was moral and political chaos, Wilson argued, a social order turned upside down. Reconstruction was, simply put, a "perfect work of fear, demoralization, disgust, and social revolution."[24]

The end of Reconstruction, according to Wilson, came about only when the right political and racial order was restored: white southerners in charge, Yankee Republican carpetbaggers banished, and blacks returned to the fields. This happened, Wilson wrote in *Division and Reunion,* when newly elected President Rutherford B. Hayes "very wisely ordered the removal of the federal troops from the South," enabling a "concerted effort by the whites of the South to shut the Negro out."[25] Sometimes this happened by hook and by crook. At others, by noose and firebrand. But while Wilson regretted the violence of the Ku Klux Klan, its members had simply been, he explained, "aroused by the mere instinct of self-preservation."[26] And the benefits were incontrovertible: the removal of the "incubus of that ignorant and hostile vote" allowed the "natural, inevitable ascendency of the whites, the responsible class."[27]

The best result, in his mind, was that the end of Reconstruction cleared the way for sectional reunion. The South's economic resources were freed, and the North welcomed her back into the Union. "The national spirit was aroused and conscious now at last of its strength," Wilson concluded. "The stage was cleared for the creation of a new nation."[28] And here, in Wilson's telling, was the beauty and power of American democracy. As long as it remained a white democracy, it could withstand a mistake like Reconstruction.

This was, of course, a manufactured memory of Reconstruction. It erased African American achievements and grossly distorted Republican governance. It spoke not of the promise of equal citizenship for all races but of a social order turned upside down, not of the stifling of black freedom but of the trampling of white folks' rights, not of a paltry force of Union soldiers and a scattering of African American officeholders but of widespread, unjust federal occupation and "Negro Domination."[29] How much of this came from Wilson's personal recollection is unclear, but he claimed the experience as his own. "The only place in the country," he once told a North Carolina crowd, "the only place in the world, where nothing has to be explained to me is the South."[30] And in writing about it the way he did, Wilson joined a host of other writers, many of them southerners—from Hilary A. Herbert to William A. Dunning to Thomas Dixon—who were cementing this white supremacist version of Reconstruction in national collective memory.[31]

Reconstruction—and the process of writing about it—thus led Wilson to two important conclusions. It showed what happened when harsh terms were foisted upon a loser, and it showed what happened when the right political and social order was turned upside down. The result in the South after the Civil War, he declared, was the "veritable overthrow of civilization."[32] Reconstruction's lessons shaped Wilson's worldview, and its memory stuck with him, even as he left academia for politics, and even as his politics turned from the domestic to the diplomatic.

+ + +

President Wilson's reaction to the guns of August 1914 was, above all, to keep the United States neutral. His thinking was simple. "There are two reasons why I am resolved to keep our country out of this war," he fretted to Secretary of the Navy Josephus Daniels. "1. If we go to war thousands of young men will lose their lives. . . . 2. Every reform we have won since 1912 will be lost."[33] As to the former, Wilson had quickly become aware of the new standard of slaughter the war in Europe was introducing. "War, before this one, used to be a sort of national excursion," he wrote. Now, "the big striking thing . . . [is] the untold human suffering."[34] He had seen war's destruction with his childhood eyes, and his appeals to Americans therefore drew on his own experience as well as the nation's collective memory. "We think our own Civil War one of the bloodiest wars in history," he told a crowd in Kansas City in 1916. "But all the suffering of all the four years of that war are as dust in the balance as compared to the losses and sufferings and sacrifices which are being witnessed in Europe."[35]

He therefore cringed to think of what might happen to the nation's servicemen on Europe's killing fields. "It wrings my heart when I think of the thousands of American boys that we are going to send to their death," he confided to one cabinet member. "There is nothing I wouldn't do to avoid such a catastrophe."[36]

The second reason for neutrality struck Wilson just as deeply. His administration had fought tooth and claw to achieve the New Freedom, and he did not want to take the chance of unraveling its hard work. Going to war would place the very corporations he had fought to curb—with the New Freedom's tariff, currency, banking, and trust legislation—back in the seat of power. "We will be dependent in war upon steel, oil, aluminum, ships, and war materials," he told Daniels. "Neither you nor I will live to see government returned to the people. Big Business will be in the saddle."[37] Indeed, American entry into the Great War would bring on great domestic disorder, he told Georgia congressman William C. Adamson, an "era of recklessness and crime . . . [a] saturnalia of exploitation, profiteering and robbery."[38] Moreover—and perhaps more importantly—picking up the pieces after the war would be difficult and time-consuming. He had learned firsthand how long it took to revive a society after war. "It would require a generation," he knowingly told Adamson, who had grown up during Reconstruction just a few counties over in Georgia, "to restore normal conditions."[39]

However, Wilson did not see neutrality as nonaction. True, keeping the United States out of the European conflict would save American lives and protect against the unraveling of the New Freedom. But neutrality also offered Wilson an opportunity to play a role on the world stage. Under his leadership, he believed, the United States could negotiate a peace between the Central and Allied Powers. And playing the role of mediator offered the country important benefits. It would boost the United States' authority in the world. It would give Wilson a chance to implement his own healing vision of a new world order, a vision based on democracy, negotiation, and progressive principles.[40] By remaining on the sidelines now, Wilson proclaimed to a 1916 audience, the United States would be ready to serve as "trustees to repair the world when the damage is done."[41]

Wilson made clear the circumstances under which this future peace would have to be negotiated. And here Reconstruction's lessons emerged most strikingly. To create a context in which a new world order could best be propagated, Wilson understood, the victor could not impose harsh terms on the vanquished.

Thus, he wanted nothing more than a stalemate between the Central and Allied Powers. "The President hopes for a deadlock in Europe," reported a *New York Times* correspondent after an interview with Wilson. "The chance of a just and equitable peace," the president had told him, "will be happiest if no nation gets the decision by arms." Wilson understood well what would happen if the opposite came true. "The danger of an unjust peace," he had continued, "will be if some one nation . . . succeeds in enforcing its will upon the others."[42]

As Wilson steered the precarious course of nonintervention, he hammered this point home. In November and December of 1916, Wilson went through multiple drafts of a "peace note" to send to the warring nations. The combatants must emerge from the conflict as equals, he urged, to pave the way for future growth. "Hopes of peace and of the willing concert of free peoples will be rendered vain and idle," he penned, "if resentments must be kindled that can never cool."[43] The United States would be ready to help ensure future peace—particularly through joining a league of nations that would guide this process—but only if the belligerent nations would settle their differences without creating these resentments. "Upon a triumph which overwhelms and humiliates cannot be laid the foundations of peace and equality and good will," he counseled the combatants. "An irreparable damage to civilization cannot promote peace."[44]

Wilson's warnings have traditionally been seen as idealistic proposals rooted in his vision for the world's future peace.[45] However, his rhetoric suggests a deeper-seated source. True, Wilson wanted to lead the negotiations and to end the war before the United States was dragged in. True, it would be easier to fulfill his dream of a league of nations if the belligerents came to the table on equal status. True, this was a noble vision. But Wilson wasn't speaking just from idealism. Nor was he speaking just from common sense. He was speaking from experience, and his language reveals as much. "Humiliation" . . . "resentment" . . . "one nation forcing its will upon the other" . . . "irreparable damage to civilization"—these were the exact same terms he had used to describe the results when avenging Radical Republicans had descended on a conquered South. Words were important to Wilson—he had made a living skillfully wielding them—and he used the same language to describe what might happen in the European aftermath as he had to describe what did happen in the reconstruction of the American South.

Taken in this light, Wilson's famous speech calling for a "peace without victory" seems practically lifted from his *History of the American People*'s description of Reconstruction. After sending his peace note through diplomatic channels, Wilson decided to take his thoughts to the public. Speaking to the Senate in late January 1917, Wilson laid out for the first time publicly his vision of a new world order. Lasting peace was the goal, he asserted, and it would be based on such principles as freedom of the seas, arms limitations, and a community of power based on the equal rights of nations. There was only one path, however, to this lasting peace. "It must be," he proclaimed, "a peace without victory." And while the eloquence of this phrase rightly deserves prominence, the words Wilson chose to explain his reasoning are equally significant. "Victory would mean peace forced upon the loser, a victor's terms imposed upon the vanquished," he explained. "It would be accepted in humiliation, under duress, at an intolerable sacrifice, and would leave a sting, a resentment, a bitter memory upon which the terms of peace would rest."[46] Wilson was speaking to the US Senate in 1917. But he may as well have been speaking to the US Senate fifty years earlier.

Wilson never explicitly made the connection between Reconstruction and World War I. But he wouldn't have. Although he was a born-and-bred southerner, and half his cabinet hailed from below the Mason-Dixon, he was wary of giving the impression, as he told a friend, "that the South is seeking to . . . take possession of the administration."[47] He was a nationalist, as he saw it, who happened to hail from the South. Indeed, many in the nation had interpreted his election as the first southern president since the Civil War as a moment of national reunion: "Induction of Wilson Cements National Ties," the *New York Tribune*'s headline had announced the morning after his inauguration.[48] As the debates over American entry into World War I intensified, then, Wilson was more worried about the threat to national unity that partisan and ethnic tensions represented.[49] Reminding the nation of old wounds—and his own southern origins—would not serve his current purposes.

But Wilson took seriously the lessons of history. He often read aloud passages of his *History of the American People* to explain his domestic policies to friends.[50] And he hoped to apply a historical lens to the current European conflict: "I have tried to look at this war ten years ahead," he told an interviewer in 1916, "to be a historian at the same time I was an actor."[51] The concrete examples he offered sometimes referenced the punitive territorial and financial demands following the Franco-Prussian War of 1870: taking away Germany's colonies, he warned in his peace note, "would rankle in her breast as did the rape of Alsace-Lorraine to the French."[52] But the Great War was the biggest challenge of his presidency, and the only way he could fully grasp it was through the lens of the biggest events in his own life. Thus, the warnings against having a winner and a loser and, more importantly, the emotional language of "humiliation" and "resentment"—the heart of his appeals for a peace without victory—these emerged from his memory of the American Civil War and Reconstruction.

+ + +

Throughout the war and its aftermath, Wilson held true to his belief that a punitive peace was detrimental to a lasting peace. When the United States entered the conflict in April of 1917, he prosecuted the war to the fullest, urging Americans to devote their hearts, minds, and resources to the war's cause. "The world," Wilson told Congress, "must be made safe for democracy."[53] But even as the Food Administration urged wheatless Mondays and meatless Tuesdays to support the troops, as the attorney general prosecuted American citizens under the Espionage and Sedition Acts, as two million American doughboys set foot on the European continent, Wilson maintained that only moderate terms for the war's loser would result in the world's future peace. In January of 1918, he outlined more precisely what he thought these terms should be. "The day of conquest and aggrandizement is gone by," he told Congress in his annual message. "The world [must] be made fit and safe to live in." The specifics of his proposal, as he outlined them in fourteen enumerated points, would include such elements as open covenants, open trade, arms reductions, and even-handed adjustment of colonial claims. Its spirit, though, remained one of a peace between equals, one that would avoid resentments on either side. "We have no jealousy of German greatness," Wilson asserted. "We do not wish to injure her or to block in any way her legitimate influence or power." "We wish her only," he concluded, "to accept a place of equality among the peoples of the world . . . instead of a place of mastery."[54]

After the Allies forced Germany to an armistice in November of 1918, in no small part because of these offerings of a healing peace, Wilson broke presidential tradition and decided to attend the peace conference himself. No sitting president had ever been to Europe, but for Wilson, shaping the terms of peace—the world's future, as he saw it—was just too important.[55] His reception in Europe was pandemonium: leaflets welcoming the "Savior of Humanity" showered down on his touring car, two million cheering Parisians choked the streets to see him, the streets in Rome were sprinkled with golden sand.[56] Wilson made clear in the early weeks that he held to the approach outlined in the Fourteen Points—and their underlying assumption of moderation toward the losers. He wanted to guarantee lofty principles such as freedom of the seas and equality of nations through a league of nations, he assured people. He wanted to avoid military occupation and stiff reparations.[57] And it seemed to him that the peoples of Europe agreed with him. Their acclaim, he told a friend on his first day in Paris, was "based upon the trust that I will stand fast to the principles and purpose which I have avowed."[58]

Unfortunately for his cause, he may have misunderstood the cheers. The leaders of the other nations at the conference were certainly feeling less charitable—and certainly less concerned with Wilson's "principles and purpose." Britain and France had suffered deeply at the hands of the Central Powers, and their leaders were bent on making Germany pay. They also wanted Wilson to know just how bad the destruction was: during the days before negotiations began, the French tried to arrange for a battlefield visit. "They were trying to force him to go to see the devastated region," one of his confidantes recounted, "so that he might see red and play into the hands of the governments of England, France, and Italy."[59] But Wilson was not to be swayed. Lasting peace would only come if he didn't see red. "Even if France had been entirely made a shell hole," he told a friend, "it would not change the final settlement."[60] The first conflict that arose in the halls of Versailles, then, was over the indemnities Germany would be forced to pay. And the other Allied nations were adamant. "Reparation for acts committed," proclaimed French prime minister Georges Clemenceau in his opening remarks as the conference's premier, "is due to all of us."[61]

Wilson's main counterpart at Versailles, it turned out, would be Clemenceau, who—in a remarkable historical twist—also had deep ties to the American Civil War and Reconstruction. In the spring of 1865, Clemenceau had traveled to the United States to work as a physician for the Union army. Arriving too late to serve, he stayed for the next five years as a political correspondent for the liberal Paris newspaper *Le Temps*. Thus, at the very same time that Wilson was absorbing the myths of Negro Reconstruction in Georgia and South Carolina, Clemenceau was sending glowing descriptions of Radical Reconstruction from New York City to his French audience.[62] He praised the abolition of slavery and the extension of citizenship rights to blacks. He lauded the Fifteenth Amendment.[63] He wrote a stirring obituary of Radical leader Thaddeus Stevens—the same man whom Wilson had castigated in his textbook as author of the Republican "Policy of Rule or Ruin."[64] Clemenceau's final piece in *Le Temps* in 1870 spelled out the most important lesson he had learned. "As long as justice is disregarded, the avenging spirit lives on," he wrote. "There can be only one way of ending all questions: that is to solve them in accordance with justice."[65]

So as the southern-born Democrat Wilson squared off against the Republican-sympathizing Clemenceau fifty years later, the echoes of Reconstruction might yet be heard in the halls of Versailles. There is no indication that Wilson knew of Clemenceau's background and no evidence that the specific topic of Reconstruction ever arose in their long hours of negotiations.[66] However, the South's state after the Civil War was certainly on Wilson's mind—and it certainly helped frame his understanding of Europe's condition. "I was born in a conquered and devastated country," he told Clemenceau and other leaders in a conversation about the possible French occupation of the German Saar river valley. "That has helped me, believe it, to understand the questions which are asked here."[67] Moreover, both Clemenceau's and Wilson's worldviews had been in large part fashioned during the reconstruction of the American South: it dominated the formative years of Wilson's youth, of course, and Clemenceau had journeyed to the United States during a particularly poignant time in his own life, writing a friend that he would return to France "when I shall have become a big boy."[68] And the core beliefs they had acquired then reemerged at Versailles. Wilson was concerned with a healing peace and order. Clemenceau was concerned with reparations—over 1.6 million Frenchmen, after all, had died in the conflict—and justice.

Although the resulting Treaty of Versailles went Clemenceau's way—the Germans were forced to pay billions in reparations, relinquish their colonial possessions, and admit guilt in causing the war—Wilson was willing to make these concessions for the sake of the League of Nations.[69] The League, in his mind, would take care of any of the Treaty's defects by replacing a "balance of power" achieved by entangling international alliances with a "community of power" based on the equality of nations.[70] It would thus provide a democratic solution to the war's causes. It would also provide a democratic solution to the world's future, because it would guarantee order. The League's purpose, after all, Wilson wrote in his draft of its covenant, was "to secure peace, security and orderly government."[71] And here was a solution rooted in Wilson's conclusions about the United States at the end of Reconstruction. Just as American democracy had absorbed the mistakes of Reconstruction—the "national spirit" that emerged when it was all over—the League of Nations could correct the mistakes of the Treaty of Versailles.[72]

Wilson made this connection explicit in a Memorial Day speech at Suresnes Cemetery in May 1919. "The League of Nations is a covenant of governments that these men shall have not died in vain," Wilson told his audience. He liked to think that the spirit of those American soldiers who had fallen in the Civil War would mingle with the souls of these who had succumbed in Europe. "As those men gave their lives in order that America might be united," he intoned, "these men have given their lives in order that the world might be united."[73] The American experience pointed the way to the world's future. Even if crippling reparations would make for a more difficult rebuilding of Germany, a new world order might emerge from the Great War, just as a new nation had emerged from the Civil War.

But if the League brought order and democracy, it was an order rooted in racial hierarchy and a democracy that mirrored the white democracy Wilson had defended in the American South. And nowhere did this emerge more clearly than in his plans for the former colonies of the Central Powers. All along, Wilson had proclaimed that the world's peoples had the right to determine their own government under the League's oversight.[74] But as it turned out, this "self-determination" came with restrictions: different peoples were differently qualified to choose their political fates. What he envisioned was less-developed peoples—read: darker-skinned ones—achieving nationhood only eventually, and only under the guidance of more civilized ones.[75] The League covenant made provisions for the colonies of the Central Powers with this process in mind. "The tutelage of . . . such peoples not yet able to stand by themselves," read Article 22, would "be entrusted to advanced nations."[76] Some of these peoples, particularly those formerly under the Ottoman Empire, would be fast-tracked to independent nation status. Others—and the covenant specified those of Central and Southwest Africa—would become League "mandates" to be tutored in self-government.[77]

Once more, then, in the League's mandate system, Reconstruction's lessons surfaced. On the one hand, Wilson supported the system because he saw it as a way to keep the colonies from simply being annexed by the victors—"dividing the swag," he called it.[78] On the other, as he had learned in Reconstruction, dark-skinned peoples untrained in freedom could not be left on their own. Mandates, therefore, offered a paternalistic solution to stave off racial and political disorder. As some historians have rightly pointed out, the hierarchy that emerged in these regions—the countries were classified as A, B, and C mandates, depending on their "stage of development"—derived in part from Wilson's graduate training in Germanic racial theories.[79] However, it also fit the racial lessons he had learned firsthand in the Reconstruction South. African Americans freed from slavery had needed guidance, not rights. "It was a menace to society," he had written in his *History of the American People,* "that negroes should . . . be set free and left without tutelage."[80] Africans freed from colonialism would need the same, from more advanced nations. "Under their tutelage," Wilson told the assembly at Versailles—using the same words again—"the helpless peoples of the world will come into a new light."[81]

Thus, even though Wilson believed these former colonials would eventually govern themselves, the League covenant simply produced racial hierarchy under another name. In the same way that freedom was denied to emancipated African Americans through Jim Crow and disfranchisement, Africans freed from colonialism were not allowed to determine their own self-government. The League of Nations, in Wilson's mind, provided democracy and order. But national self-determination was not for everybody, just yet, and the democracy of nations certainly was not the equality of all peoples. Indeed, when the Japanese representatives at Versailles introduced an amendment calling for racial equality, Wilson balked. He only offered half-hearted support to a watered-down version, later telling the League Commission that he wanted matters of racial equality "forced as much as possible into the background."[82] If African Americans were not yet qualified to vote in the American South, darker-skinned peoples around the world—"the poor, naked fellows in the jungles of Africa," he called them at one point—were hardly ready for democracy.[83]

+ + +

Many geopolitical, economic, and national concerns shaped how Woodrow Wilson came to think about American entry into World War I and how to construct the peace that followed. He was worried about American lives and the fate of his progressive domestic program. He thought deeply about military matters and international political systems. He had a vision for a new world order and America's place in it. He read memos and listened to advisors and treated with ambassadors. But he was also a historian, and he was a southerner, and he had grown up during the United States' most cataclysmic events. As his scholarly writings and best-selling textbooks revealed, these events—and coming of age in the South as they came to pass—shaped his understanding of American history. And as his policies as president revealed, his understanding of American history shaped his understanding of international affairs. Wilson's beliefs in the world's future derived from his interpretations of the past.

Recognizing Wilson's approach to the Great War and the Versailles Treaty as one seen through a white southerner's Civil War– and Reconstruction-tempered worldview, then, offers important insights into Wilson's role in the conflict. Much, of course, has been written about Woodrow Wilson's internationalism and its roots in his moral convictions, Christian values, belief in progressive history, commitment to national self-determination, or idealism.[84] Much has recently—and rightly—been written about the segregation of the federal government under Wilson's administration and its roots in his southern background.[85] And a growing number of scholars have begun to connect the two: to point to Wilson's southern background—particularly his racism—as a factor in his approach to foreign policy.[86] However, Wilson's racial beliefs stemmed from more than being born in the South, and his liberal internationalism stemmed from more than idealism. Wilsonian internationalism also derived from his interpretation of southern history. Examining Wilson's decisions through his Civil War– and Reconstruction-shaped lens, with its deep convictions about racial hierarchy, the relationship between winners and losers, and the need for political order, thus provides a richer, more textured understanding of Wilsonianism. When we think about diplomatic history and international relations, it is important to consider too the historical understandings of the individuals involved.

Ultimately, using this memory-shaped lens points to broader historical connections. It links in important ways the nineteenth and twentieth centuries. It ties the Civil War to the Great War. It draws significant parallels between emancipation in the American South and decolonization in Africa. It also gives new meaning to familiar phrases like "peace without victory" and revises the way we see the relationship between Wilson and Clemenceau. Although separated by half a century—and vast oceans, among other things—the two conflicts and their aftermaths were connected by a generation of men who, as young men, witnessed one and, as leaders, directed the other. Other factors certainly came into play, but through the worldview and memory of Woodrow Wilson, the ghosts of the Reconstruction of the South hovered over the reconstruction of Europe.

NOTES

1. Ray Stannard Baker, *Woodrow Wilson: Life and Letters* (New York: Doubleday, Doran, 1931), 4:55.

2. Diary of Edward M. House, 28 September 1914, Edward M. House Papers, Manuscripts and Archives, Yale University Library.

3. Woodrow Wilson, "John Bright," 6 March 1880, *The Papers of Woodrow Wilson,* ed. Arthur S. Link (Princeton, NJ: Princeton University Press, 1966–1994), 1:619 (hereafter cited as "*PWW*").

4. Woodrow Wilson, "An Address in Chicago on Lincoln," 12 February 1909, *PWW,* 19:33.

5. August Heckscher, *Woodrow Wilson* (New York: Scribner's, 1991), 13.

6. Woodrow Wilson, "An Address on Robert E. Lee at the University of North Carolina," 19 January 1909, *PWW,* 18:635; Baker, *Wilson: Life and Letters,* 1:52.

7. Woodrow Wilson, "Marginal notes on James E. Therold Rogers, ed., *Speeches on Questions of Public Policy by John Bright* (vol. 1)," [19 July 1880], *PWW,* 1:664–65.

8. Woodrow Wilson, *Division and Reunion, 1829–1889* (New York: Longmans, Green, 1893), 239, 252; Woodrow Wilson, *A History of the American People* (New York: Harper & Brothers, 1902), 4:312; quotation from "Remarks by Prof. Woodrow Wilson," *Annual Report of the American Historical Association for the Year 1896* (Washington, DC: Government Printing Office, 1897), 1:296.

9. Woodrow Wilson, unpublished "Letters from a Southern Young Man to Southern Young Men," 21 March 1881, *PWW,* 2:33–36.

10. On state rights as outdated, see Wilson, *History,* 5:128–30. On slavery as a burden, see Wilson, *Division and Reunion,* 298; Wilson, *History,* 4:194–95, 5:116.

11. Woodrow Wilson, "Essay on John Bright," 6 March 1880, *PWW,* 1:618 [emphasis added].

12. For background on Wilson's early life, see John M. Cooper, *Woodrow Wilson: A Biography* (New York: Alfred A. Knopf, 2009); Arthur S. Link, *Wilson: The Road to the White House* (Princeton, NJ: Princeton University Press, 1947); Heckscher, *Woodrow Wilson.*

13. Bruce E. Baker, *What Reconstruction Meant: Historical Memory in the American South* (Charlottesville: University of Virginia Press, 2007), 10.

14. Wilson, *History,* 5:78.

15. Woodrow Wilson, "The Reconstruction of the Southern States," *Atlantic Monthly* 87, no. 519 (January 1901): 12.

16. Wilson, *History,* 5:6.

17. "They did not know the region with which they were dealing," he wrote. They "were ignorant of the South"; Wilson, *History,* 5:50.

18. Wilson, *History,* 5:78; Wilson, *Division and Reunion,* 281.

19. Wilson, *History,* 5:38.

20. Wilson, *Division and Reunion,* 268.

21. Wilson, *Division and Reunion,* 261.

22. Wilson, "Reconstruction of the Southern States," 6.

23. Wilson, *Division and Reunion,* 273; Wilson, *History,* 5:58, 5:82, 5:52.

24. Wilson, *History,* 5:49.

25. Wilson, *Division and Reunion,* 286, 274. See also Wilson, "Reconstruction of the Southern States," 12.

26. Wilson, *History,* 5:58.

27. Wilson, *History,* 5:137; Wilson, *Division and Reunion,* 273.

28. Wilson, *Division and Reunion,* 287.

29. For Reconstruction—and its memory—see, among others, Eric Foner, *Reconstruction: America's Unfinished Revolution* (New York: Harper and Row, 1988); Steven Hahn, *A Nation under Our Feet: Black Political Struggles in the Rural South from Slavery to the Great Migration* (Cambridge: Harvard University Press, 2003); Thomas J. Brown, ed., *Reconstructions: New Perspectives on the Postbellum United States* (New York: Oxford University Press, 2006); Baker, *What Reconstruction Meant.*

30. Wilson, "Address on Robert E. Lee," *PWW,* 18:631. Although Arthur Link and John Cooper offer reasonable challenges to the complete nature of Wilson's southern-ness, Wilson spent his first thirty years in the South, and he claimed it, defended it, and appealed to it throughout his life. See Arthur S. Link, "Woodrow Wilson: The American as Southerner," *Journal of Southern History* 36, no. 1 (February 1970): 3–17; Cooper, *Woodrow Wilson.* For Wilson as a southerner, see, among others, Michael Dennis, "Looking Backward: Woodrow Wilson, the New South, and the Question of Race," *American Nineteenth Century History* 3, no. 1 (Spring 2002): 77–104; Michael Dennis, "Race and the Southern Imagination: Woodrow Wilson Reconsidered," *Canadian Review of American Studies* 29, no. 3 (1999): 109–131; Anthony Gaughan, "Woodrow Wilson and the Legacy of the Civil War," *Civil War History* 43, no. 3 (September 1997): 225–42.

31. Wilson's language and message echoes such works as James Pike's *The Prostrate State: South Carolina under Negro Government* (1874), and he cites such books as Hilary A. Herbert,

*Why the Solid South? Or, Reconstruction and Its Results* (1890), John W. Burgess, *Reconstruction and the Constitution, 1866–1876* (1902), William A. Dunning, *Essays on the Civil War and Reconstruction and Related Topics* (1898), and William Garrott Brown, *The Lower South in American History* (1902). Dixon—who sat across the aisle from Wilson in their first year of graduate school—made sure to quote and attribute Wilson's *History* in the intertitles of his racist epic film *Birth of a Nation* (which, not coincidentally, Wilson screened in the White House in 1915). For the white supremacist version of Reconstruction, see Baker, *What Reconstruction Meant,* 14–16, 21–38.

32. Wilson, *History,* 5:49.

33. Josephus Daniels, *The Wilson Era: Years of Peace, 1910–1917* (Chapel Hill: University of North Carolina Press, 1944), 582. See also Arthur S. Link, *Wilson: The Struggle for Neutrality, 1914–1915* (Princeton, NJ: Princeton University Press, 1960), 51–53.

34. Woodrow Wilson, "An Unpublished Prolegomenon to a Peace Note," 25 November 1916, *PWW,* 40:67–68.

35. Woodrow Wilson, "An Address on Preparedness in Kansas City," 2 February 1916, *PWW,* 36:109. See also Gaughan, "Wilson and the Legacy of the Civil War," 239.

36. Ray S. Baker, "Interview with Albert Sidney Burleson," 17 March 1927, Box 102, Folder "Burleson, Albert," Ray Stannard Baker Papers, Manuscripts Division, Library of Congress, Washington, DC.

37. Daniels, *Wilson Era: Years of Peace,* 582.

38. "Adamson Memorandum," Box 99, Folder "Adamson, William C.," Baker Papers.

39. "Adamson Memorandum," Box 99, Folder "Adamson, William C.," Baker Papers.

40. Heckscher, *Woodrow Wilson,* 421–25.

41. Wilson, "An Address on Preparedness," 2 February 1916, *PWW,* 36:109.

42. H. B. Brougham, "Memorandum of an Interview with the President, Dec. 14, 1914," in F. Fraser Bond, *Mr. Miller of "The Times": The Story of an Editor* (New York: Charles Scribner's Sons, 1932), 142.

43. Woodrow Wilson, "An Appeal for a Statement of War Aims," 19 December 1916, *PWW,* 40:275.

44. Woodrow Wilson, "Draft of a Peace Note," 25 November 1916, *PWW,* 40:72–73.

45. See, for example, Arthur S. Link, *Wilson: Campaigns for Progressivism and Peace, 1916–1917* (Princeton, NJ: Princeton University Press, 1965), 165–289; Cooper, *Woodrow Wilson,* 315–19, 362–73; Heckscher, *Woodrow Wilson,* 390–93, 419–27. Link had noted that Wilson held a "fundamental conviction . . . that victory by either side would produce resentments," but he did not pursue the source of Wilson's conviction; Arthur S. Link, "That Cobb Interview," *Journal of American History* 72, no. 1 (June 1985): 10.

46. Woodrow Wilson, "An Address to the Senate," 22 January 1917, *PWW,* 40:536.

47. Woodrow Wilson to Oscar W. Underwood, 21 January 1913, *PWW,* 27:66–67.

48. "Induction of Wilson Cements National Ties," *New York Tribune,* 5 March 1913.

49. Gaughan, "Wilson and the Legacy of the Civil War," 238. See also Woodrow Wilson, "An Appeal to the American People," 18 August 1914, *PWW,* 30:393–94; "Campaign Address at Madison Square Garden," 2 November 1916, *PWW,* 38:601. For the Great War threatening

sectional reunion, see Woodrow Wilson, "An Address to the Grand Army of the Republic," 28 September 1915, *PWW,* 34:534–35; "Reflections on Memorial Day at Arlington Cemetery," 31 May 1915, *PWW,* 33:287–88.

50. Diary of Edward M. House, 30 September 1914, House Papers.

51. Ida M. Tarbell, "A Talk with the President of the United States," *Collier's* 58, no. 7 (28 October 1916): 6.

52. Woodrow Wilson, "An Unpublished Prolegomenon to a Peace Note," *PWW,* 40:69. See also Brougham, "Memorandum of Interview," 142.

53. Woodrow Wilson, "Address to a Joint Session of Congress," 2 April 1917, *PWW,* 41:525.

54. Woodrow Wilson, "Address to a Joint Session of Congress," 8 January 1918, *PWW,* 45:536, 538–39.

55. John Cooper argues convincingly that Wilson's Fourteen Points shortened the war; Cooper, *Woodrow Wilson,* 451–53. For Wilson's decision to go, see Cooper, *Woodrow Wilson,* 454–58; Thomas J. Knock, *To End All Wars: Woodrow Wilson and the Quest for a New World Order* (Princeton, NJ: Princeton University Press), 190–93.

56. Knock, *To End All Wars,* 194–95.

57. Cooper, *Woodrow Wilson,* 441–75; Heckscher, *Woodrow Wilson,* 489–93.

58. Woodrow Wilson to H. B. Brougham, 17 December 1918, *PWW,* 53:412. Wilson told the Italian parliament on a goodwill visit that the duty of the conference was to "organize the friendship of the world"; Woodrow Wilson, "Speech to the Italian Parliament," 3 January 1918, *PWW,* 53:598. See also Cooper, *Woodrow Wilson,* 465.

59. Diary of Edith Benham, 10 January 1919, *PWW,* 53:707. See also Margaret MacMillan, *Paris 1919: Six Months That Changed the World* (New York: Random House, 2001), 22.

60. Diary of Edith Benham, 20 January 1919, *PWW,* 54:175.

61. "Protocol of the Plenary Session of the Paris Peace Conference," 18 January 1919, *PWW,* 54:130.

62. Georges Clemenceau, *American Reconstruction, 1865–1870, and the Impeachment of President Johnson,* ed. Fernand Baldensperger, trans. Margaret MacVeagh (New York: MacVeagh, 1939), 13–31; J. Adam Tooze, *The Deluge: The Great War and the Remaking of Global Order, 1916–1931* (New York: Viking, 2014), 63–64; David S. Newhall, *Clemenceau: A Life at War* (Lewiston, NY: Edwin Mellen, 1991), 41–54; J. Adam Tooze, "From Brest Litovsk to Versailles, 1917–1919: The Making of a Modern Peace," circulated paper, Yale University, November 2010, 34–35.

63. Clemenceau, *American Reconstruction,* 37–41, 62–63, 277–80. Clemenceau wrote in praise of the Fifteenth Amendment, "There is only one method of ending all difficulties, and that is justice, not force"; Clemenceau, *American Reconstruction,* 295.

64. Clemenceau, *American Reconstruction,* 224–27; Wilson, *History,* 5:49–50.

65. Clemenceau, *American Reconstruction,* 300.

66. Tooze, *The Deluge,* 63; Tooze, "From Brest Litovsk to Versailles," 35.

67. "Mantoux's Notes of a Meeting of the Council of Four," 11 April 1919, *PWW,* 57:246.

68. Newhall notes that Clemenceau's sojourn in America coincided with a period of mental and emotional "growing up"; Newhall, *Clemenceau,* 45–47, quotation 45. Clemenceau even

remarked years later, to a New York audience, "I looked around and I learned what Europe hadn't taught me—to help myself.... [Today I] express my thanks for the good and practical education that I received"; *New York World,* 22 January 1922, in Newhall, *Clemenceau,* 46.

69. Knock, *To End All Wars,* 194–226, esp. 224–26; Joseph Fry, *Dixie Looks Abroad: The South and U.S. Foreign Relations, 1789–1973* (Baton Rouge: Louisiana State University Press, 2002), 169; Cooper, *Woodrow Wilson,* 454–505.

70. Woodrow Wilson, "An Address to the Senate," 22 January 1917, *PWW,* 40:536.

71. Woodrow Wilson, "A Draft of a Covenant," 8 January 1919, *PWW,* 53:678. Lloyd Ambrosius notes that Wilson saw order as integral to American democracy and that his understanding of democracy was critical to his vision of the League; Lloyd E. Ambrosius, *Wilsonian Statecraft: Theory and Practice of Liberal Internationalism during World War I* (Wilmington, DE: Scholarly Resources, 1991), 1–2, 8–10.

72. Wilson, *History,* 5:129, 5:299.

73. "Soldiers Hear President," *New York Times,* 31 May 1919; Woodrow Wilson, "Remarks at Suresnes Cemetery on Memorial Day," 30 May 1919, *PWW,* 59:608.

74. From speeches to peace organizations to his Fourteen Points to his drafts for a League covenant, Wilson maintained peoples' rights to sovereignty; Woodrow Wilson, "An Address in Washington to the League to Enforce Peace," 27 May 1916, *PWW,* 37:115; "Address to a Joint Session of Congress," 8 January 1918, *PWW,* 45:537; "Second 'Paris Draft' of the Covenant," 18 January 1919, *PWW,* 54:145.

75. For Wilson and the idea of (national) self-determination, see Erez Manela, "Imagining Woodrow Wilson in Asia: Dreams of East-West Harmony and the Revolt against Empire in 1919," *American Historical Review* 111, no. 5 (December 2006): 1327–51; Erez Manela, *The Wilsonian Moment: Self-Determination and the International Origins of Anticolonial Nationalism* (New York: Oxford University Press, 2007); Lloyd E. Ambrosius, *Wilsonianism: Woodrow Wilson and His Legacy in American Foreign Relations* (New York: Palgrave Macmillan, 2002), esp. 125–43; Betty Miller Unterberger, "The United States and National Self-Determination: A Wilsonian Perspective," *Presidential Studies Quarterly* 26, no. 4 (December 1996): 926–41.

76. *The Paris Covenant for a League of Nations* (New York: League to Enforce Peace, 1919), 12–13.

77. For analysis of the racial dimensions of the League mandates and Wilson's relation to them, see Lloyd E. Ambrosius, "Woodrow Wilson and *The Birth of a Nation:* American Democracy and International Relations," *Diplomacy and Statecraft* 18 (December 2007): 689–718; Lloyd E. Ambrosius, "Democracy, Peace, and World Order," in *Reconsidering Woodrow Wilson: Progressivism, Internationalism, War, and Peace,* ed. John M. Cooper (Baltimore: Johns Hopkins University Press, 2008), 225–49, esp. 239–40; Ambrosius, *Wilsonianism,* 21–29; Manela, *Wilsonian Moment,* esp. 24–26; Knock, *To End All Wars,* 201–4.

78. Diary of Dr. Cary T. Grayson, 28 January 1919, *PWW,* 54:308; "Hankey's Notes of a Meeting of the Council of Ten," 28 January 1919, *PWW,* 54:330.

79. Ambrosius, *Wilsonian Statecraft,* 1–28; Ambrosius, *Wilsonianism,* 21–26; quotation, *Paris Covenant for a League of Nations,* 13. Manela also points to Wilson's southern background as important in shaping his international vision; Manela, *Wilsonian Moment,* 27–28.

80. Wilson, *History,* 5:18. Wilson also used the word *tutelage* to defend the Reconstruction-era black codes, passed by white southern Democrats during the months before Radical Reconstruction, which put the freed slaves back into virtual slavery; Wilson, *History,* 5:18–22.

81. Woodrow Wilson, "An Address to the Third Plenary Session of the Peace Conference," 14 February 1919, *PWW,* 55:177; "Woodrow Wilson on the League's Constitution," *Current History* 9, no. 3 (March 1919): 400. Wilson referred to the mandatory countries as "trustees" of the colonized peoples; see, for example, Woodrow Wilson, "An Address in the Tabernacle in Salt Lake City," 23 September 1919, *PWW,* 63:458; "An Address to the Columbus Chamber of Commerce," 4 September 1919, *PWW,* 63:15.

82. Woodrow Wilson, "Remarks," 11 April 1919, *PWW,* 57:268. See also Cooper, *Woodrow Wilson,* 472–73, 489–90; Paul G. Lauren, *Power and Prejudice: The Politics and Diplomacy of Racial Discrimination* (Boulder, CO: Westview, 1996), 76–101; Knock, *To End All Wars,* 249. For House's account, see Diary of Edward M. House, 4 February 1913, 9 February 1913, and 13 February 1913, House Papers.

83. Woodrow Wilson, "An Address in Reno," 22 September 1919, *PWW,* 63:435.

84. See, for example, John M. Cooper, *Breaking the Heart of the World: Woodrow Wilson and the Fight for the League of Nations* (New York: Cambridge University Press, 2001); Lloyd E. Ambrosius, *Woodrow Wilson and the American Diplomatic Tradition: The Treaty Fight in Perspective* (New York: Cambridge University Press, 1987); Knock, *To End All Wars;* Ambrosius, "Democracy, Peace, and World Order"; Manela, *Wilsonian Moment;* Robert W. Tucker, *Woodrow Wilson and the Great War: Reconsidering America's Neutrality, 1914–1917* (Charlottesville: University of Virginia Press, 2007); John Morton Blum, *Woodrow Wilson and the Politics of Morality* (Boston: Little, Brown, 1956); N. Gordon Levin, *Woodrow Wilson and World Politics: America's Response to War and Revolution* (New York: Oxford University Press, 1968); Arthur S. Link, *Woodrow Wilson: Revolution, War, and Peace* (Arlington Heights, IL: AHM, 1979).

85. See, for example, Eric S. Yellin, *Racism in the Nation's Service: Government Workers and the Color Line in Woodrow Wilson's America* (Chapel Hill: University of North Carolina Press, 2013); Gary Gerstle, "Race and Nation in the Thought and Politics of Woodrow Wilson," in *Reconsidering Woodrow Wilson: Progressivism, Internationalism, War, and Peace,* ed. John M. Cooper (Baltimore: Johns Hopkins University Press, 2008), 93–124; Nicholas Patler, *Jim Crow and the Wilson Administration: Protesting Federal Segregation in the Early Twentieth Century* (Boulder: University Press of Colorado, 2004).

86. See, for example, Mary A. Renda, *Taking Haiti: Military Occupation and the Culture of U.S. Imperialism* (Chapel Hill: University of North Carolina Press, 2001); Tooze, *The Deluge;* Manela, *Wilsonian Moment;* Ambrosius, "Woodrow Wilson and *The Birth of a Nation.*"

# IV

# REMEMBERING RECONSTRUCTION IN THE POST–CIVIL RIGHTS ERA

# 9

# The Cultural Work of the Ku-Klux Klan in US History Textbooks, 1883–2015

ELAINE PARSONS

It may seem unnecessary to ask why the Ku Klux Klan[1] has a prominent place in US history textbooks. In their reign of terror from 1867 to 1871, Ku-Klux groups threatened, robbed, attacked, raped, disfigured, and killed thousands of freedpeople and their white allies in many parts of the South. This was an important element of the postwar effort by white Democrats to deprive freedpeople of the use of their newly won political, economic, and social rights. Part of the work of any national history narrative is to make itself appear to have been inevitable. Yet the inclusion of actors or events in the national narrative has always been contentious and contingent, reflecting the interested understandings of those writing, selecting, and reading history textbooks. The Reconstruction-era Klan became a canonical episode in US history for very different reasons than those for which many today agree that it belongs there. The people who chose to put the Klan into the national story saw it as representing white southerners' unified determination to institute a stern but necessary solution to the problem of black freedom. Committed to white supremacy, and at a moment of high imperialism, these historians were accustomed to benefiting from others' violence while retaining a distance that allowed them to consider it distasteful. The figure of the Klan allowed Progressive-era historians to naturalize racial violence, and sometimes to romanticize it as well, even while they displaced it temporally as well as spatially from their own lives. Talking about racial oppression through the figure of the Ku-Klux suggested that postwar racial violence was unrelated to more proximate claims of oppression that might require political response. It made white-on-black violence into a spectacle and a fascinating narrative rather than an enduring problem that demanded a political response.

The Progressive generation passed away, but through the deeply racist twentieth century and up to the present, the Klan has maintained and expanded the position they had carved for it in the national narrative. Even though the civil rights era would see the transvaluation of the Klan—tragic or romantic until the 1950s, then consistently portrayed in negative terms by the later twentieth century—many generic elements of the Ku Klux narrative in high school history textbooks are remarkably consistent from its first appearance in 1883 to the present. Textbook authors decided what stories to tell and how to tell them, and they edited their account of the Klan in large ways and small in response to them. Yet the continuities in Klan passages across the political and regional spectrum and over time are as telling as the distinctions. Textbooks often claimed in their prefaces to represent a new and better way of telling the national story, but their content, structure, and wording were usually remarkably similar to those of their period, and of the periods before and after. US history textbooks had a life of their own: their always-overlapping stories become the expected story, and the worst of the atrocities and catastrophes they enumerated became comfortingly familiar as inevitable things we had suffered and overcome to become ourselves. Textbook writers could only tweak and massage the dominant narrative of recent works.

This paper, based on a review of the passages about the Klan in a large selection of textbooks in Harvard's Gutman Library, traces the remarkable continuities and notes the slow changes in the national textbook narrative over time. Even as the valuation of the Klan transformed in the mid-twentieth century, many of the basic structural elements of the Progressive-era textbook Klan narrative have persisted. The four most troubling and tenacious of these persistent tendencies are: (1) to sensationalize the Klan as mysterious, entertaining, or beyond critical comprehension; (2) to present white people as active agents and black people as passive and helpless; (3) to depict the Klan as radically discontinuous with other forms of racial oppression occurring before, after, or alongside it; and (4) to make the Klan stand in for all white-on-black violence, allowing the reader to believe that such violence had geographic and social limits, a beginning, and, most comfortingly, an end.

History textbook narratives have long operated at the intersection of the scholarly, the popular, and the political. They are authorized (and, since the Progressive era, usually authored) by trained professional historians who want to reflect scholarship in their field; selected and purchased by school administrators who represent and at times are closely observed and guided by local political sentiment; and read by students whose willingness to engage with them may depend upon their connection to popular cultural tropes, or their "relevance" to contemporary ideas and forms. Successful textbooks have navigated a treacherous course among these constituencies, which make conflicted, heterogeneous, and changing demands on their historical narratives.

Any textbook has had to address professional academics, as they have the ability to lend or deny credibility to the book. And dominant professional understandings of the Reconstruction era have shifted dramatically over time. Those who have explored the historiography of the Reconstruction era have usually divided it into a "traditional" period that celebrated white Democrats' triumph over "vindictive" efforts of white Republicans to "fasten black supremacy" upon them; the emergence of a more complex and sympathetic portrayal of Reconstruction's failure in the 1920s and 1930s; and a dramatic revision in the 1960s that highlighted Reconstruction's achievements, followed immediately by more skeptical "post-revisionists" who doubted the radicalism of Reconstruction and its dramatic and lasting effects.[2] The Klan found a home in all of these phases of historical interpretation. And Reconstruction-era history has always been contentious. Exasperated review essays have proliferated through the twentieth century. Francis B. Simkins, in his 1939 "New Viewpoints of Southern Reconstruction," threw up his hands at the Reconstruction narrative's deep implication in popular politics and almost irreducibly ideological nature. Howard K. Beale's 1940 "On Rewriting Reconstruction History" condemned the continued sectional and racial partisanship in the field.[3] John Hope Franklin in 1948 powerfully critiqued the persistence of the Dunning School, as exemplified by the strikingly racist work of E. Merton Coulter, who chose to ignore "records of contemporary articulate Negroes" and worked to create an image of the Reconstruction South with "a particular kind of atmosphere, in which federal troops stride over the South with a merciless vengeance, irresponsible Negroes exhibit a complete lack of restraint in their new freedom, and Southern whites writhe under the heel of Negro-Scalawag-Carpetbag rule."[4] Franklin returned to survey the field many years later, in 1980, with hardly more optimism.[5] Bernard A. Weisberger, in "The Dark and Bloody Ground of Reconstruction Historiography" (1959), bemoaned the persistence of the "operatic" version of Reconstruction history, in which Congress and southern black people "debauched and plundered a proud but helpless people until finally, desperately harried whites responded with their own campaigns of violence and persuasion."[6]

Historians have often taken note of how the ideas in their field were applied or neglected in textbooks. Lawrence Dunbar Reddick, in a 1934 article in the *Journal of Negro History,* critically reviewed representations of race in southern history textbooks, identifying and dissecting the racial stereotypes that pervaded the textbooks' Klan apologetics.[7] Van S. Allen, in 1971, wrote a brief review of the elementary and middle school textbooks of the 1960s, finding them deeply inadequate in their recognition of black Americans' humanity, but improving over the course of the decade.[8] Thomas Holt, in 1995, began with the indisputable claim that "The traditional narrative of the Reconstruction era tends toward incoherence." Explaining what he saw as a strangely fractured picture of historical change in seven textbooks from 1989 to 1993, he called for a more nuanced engagement with recent scholarship.[9] Most recently, Anthony L. Brown has explored efforts of black scholars in the Progressive era to challenge the racial depictions in that period's textbooks.[10] In a separate project, written together with Keffrelyn D. Brown, he analyzed depictions of racial violence in contemporary textbooks; they determined that today's texts "discuss [violence] in ways that ignore, undermine, or misrepresent the larger institutional/structural ties that supported [and] benefited from, their enactment."[11] These scholars recognized the representation of the Reconstruction era in the simplistic format of the textbook as a fraught moment in our national narrative, and as a privileged though often incoherent location for the negotiation of race. Textbook authors and publishers had to keep one eye on this culturally powerful though internally inconsistent group.

The demands of local and statewide school officials could be as dynamic as those of academic scholars. Local expectations varied regionally. Southern school districts, regularly controlled by white southerners, demanded histories told from a "Southern perspective." From the Progressive era through the present, interested groups have regularly protested or advocated representations of the Ku Klux Klan in textbooks. Pressure from white southern apologists (including, particularly during the 1920s, Klan groups themselves) was strongest from the beginning of the twentieth century through the outbreak of the

Second World War. The NAACP and other antiracist groups and individuals protested celebratory representations of the Klan from the beginning, but their voices became influential only with the civil rights movement. After the 1960s, the politics of Klan inclusion in the national narrative have shifted, as antiracists have called for serious and sustained engagement with the forces of racial oppression and therefore advocated substantial focus on the Klan.

The Klan's position in popular culture shifted as well over the century. Public interest waxed and waned, tracking both major popular cultural texts and increased Klan activity. Popular interest in the Klan continued after its suppression into the 1880s, declined in the 1890s, then rose again around 1905 with the publication of *The Clansman* and other popular treatments of the Klan. Klan mentions dramatically increased coincident to the release of *Birth of a Nation* in 1915, peaking in 1925 (at a substantially higher rate than they had ever reached in the Reconstruction era). Public interest in the Klan continued to fluctuate dramatically in the following decades. It increased during the Second World War (as the war against European fascism raised concerns about right-wing organizations in this country), then peaked in 1967 with the Klan's resurgence.[12]

The tone of the popular discussion of the Klan also fluctuated: competing representations of the Klan coexisted in every period, and Klan representations of any sort were sure to provoke popular outrage. In films, comic books, plays, short stories, and popular novels just as in textbooks, the sober insistence on the Klan's tragic necessity so dominant in the late nineteenth century became more purely celebratory in the interwar period, took on a dark tone as dangerous and subversive in the 1940s, and evolved into a posture of pure condemnation in and after the civil rights era. Yet even as the tone changed, and as contemporaries challenged competing representations, audiences expected, and usually received, certain consistent images and story lines when they read or viewed Klan-themed entertainment.

It was not immediately apparent to nineteenth-century textbook authors that the Ku-Klux Klan should be part of the story of Reconstruction at all. Indeed, while textbooks generally covered material up to a year or so before their publication date, the Klan (which became nationally known in early 1868) was not generally included in history textbooks until around the turn of the century. Of the forty textbooks among those surveyed that were published between 1872 and 1893, only five mentioned the Klan.[13] Textbooks in those years covered several events in the early Reconstruction era: Johnson's impeachment, Grant's election and reelection, several Indian conflicts including the Modoc War, and the militant Fenianism of 1866–1870, but made no mention of the Ku-Klux Klan. Even those writers whose strong partisanship might have made the idea of the Ku-Klux Klan of particular interest did not integrate it into their accounts. Two of these were not included in the survey of materials in the Gutman collection, but are interesting because of the political significance of their authors: Thomas Wentworth Higginson (abolitionist and postwar transcriber of spirituals) and Alexander Stephens (vice president of the Confederacy and postwar apologist) each published a textbook that included coverage of the period in which the Klan was active: Stephens in 1872, Higginson in 1875. Higginson did not refer to the Klan at all. Stephens mentioned the Ku-Klux Act (actually the passage of the act is the last event mentioned in the textbook, and Stephens suggests that if unchecked, it would undo all of the national development chronicled by the rest of the textbook) but not the Klan itself.[14] In a later edition of the text, published in 1883, Stephens again referred to the injustice of the Ku-Klux Acts and added an additional mention of the Klan, explaining that the cause of the acts was "bitter partisans, attributing the homicides [of black men in South Carolina] to the Ku-Klux Klan." But these are his only references: the Ku-Klux Klan is first absent in his narrative, then explicitly defined as nonactors.[15]

One reason most textbooks published through the 1890s did not mention the Klan may be that their narratives focused on biographical accounts, and on the federal level. So, for instance, John Ridpath's influential 1880 *History of the United States* is organized largely around important national figures: Andrew Johnson, U. S. Grant, and Horace Greeley. Ridpath's coverage of affairs in the South from 1866 through 1872 describes congressional debates, legislation, and constitutional amendments pertaining to the region: conflicts between Johnson and Congress over readmission, the Civil Rights Act, and amnesty. His text sometimes strays beyond Washington: he covers the Chicago Fire and the Modoc War. But the closest he comes to noting what anyone in the South is doing during Reconstruction is his claim that "the elevation of the negro race to citizenship was regarded with apprehension."[16] John Anderson's *A Popular School History of the United States* (1880) deals even less with the conquered

South. It touches on the Reconstruction amendments and the impeachment, but says nothing about events on the ground in the South: it is more interested in the acquisition of Alaska and the normalization of diplomatic relations with Great Britain.[17]

Some scholars were beginning to think about the Klan as a force worth mentioning in the Reconstruction era. Pioneering black historian George W. Williams, in his neglected two-volume *History of the Negro Race in America 1619–1880,* published in 1883, was one of the first to integrate the Klan into the national narrative. His mention was brief: "But after a while a gigantic Ku Klux conspiracy was discovered. This organization sought to obstruct the courts, harass the negroes, and cripple local governments. It spread terror through the South and made a political graveyard of startling dimensions."[18] But Williams's work would only become influential on its rediscovery years later. When the Klan first began to make its way into the historical narrative, it was mainly at the invitation, and due to the influence, of white professionalizing historians. These historians sought to depict white southerners as the ones driving history forward at a time when black southerners appeared to substantially share formal political power; making the Klan central to their accounts allowed them to imagine formal systems of government in the South (and to a great extent in the North) as hopelessly impotent, and informal groups of disfranchised whites as remarkably powerful. As W. E. B. Du Bois later wrote, "The real frontal attack on Reconstruction . . . came from the universities and particularly from Columbia and Johns Hopkins."[19] Emphasizing the Klan was one of few plausible ways to project collective white agency into the Reconstruction-era South. The more closely the author of a history textbook in this era was tied to research institutions involved in the project of professionalizing historical scholarship, the more likely he (or occasionally, she) was to refer to the Klan.

The first mention of the Ku-Klux in the textbooks in this survey is in Arthur Gilman's 1883 *A History of the American People.* While Gilman, a banker, was a gentleman historian from an earlier era, he was near the heart of the professionalization of the social sciences: he lived in Cambridge and was involved in founding the women's institution that became Radcliffe College. His close proximity to professional history is suggested, above all, by his early adoption of "notes, which are placed for convenient reference at the bottom of the pages to which they refer."[20] Gilman writes:

> In 1867 the Governor of Tennessee, William G. Brownlow, called upon the United States military to suppress violent demonstrations in that State that had been traced to an organization known as the "Ku-klux Klan [*sic*]." It appears that at the close of the war a number of secret political societies were formed in the Southern States, the objects of which were to offset, as was claimed by the people of the section, the acts of certain other societies formed through the agency of intriguers from the North, who were exciting the Negro population to acts of violence, and endangering their homes and social relations. It has been reported that five hundred thousand members united the Ku-Klux Klan, of whom forty thousand were in Tennessee. Congress ordered an investigation in April 1871, and the result was published in twelve volumes. The organization died out afterwards, partly because the relation of the North and South were becoming more harmonious, and the passions engendered by war were growing weaker.[21]

This is not an entirely sympathetic portrayal, and shows distaste for violence: by attributing the Klan's end to the decline of the "passions engendered by the war," the author expresses distance from the Klan. And the passage was constructed around a posture of neutrality, balancing reports of Klan violence with reports of freedpeople's violence. Yet it does some important cultural work: it portrays the Klan as organized and powerful, while black southerners were helpless dupes of northern white instigators. It claims to represent the voice of the "people of the section" as justifying the Klan, therefore naturalizing it. It does not contextualize the Klan in relationship to any older, later, or concurrent types of violence, and it allows the Klan to stand in for white-on-black violence generally. And it cleanly places the Klan in the past: the Klan faced state scrutiny, and, the passage neatly specifies, it "died out."

Alexander Johnston made a second mention of the Klan in his 1885 *A History of the United States for Schools*. A professor of jurisprudence and political economy at Princeton University, his monograph in Herbert Baxter Adams's *Johns Hopkins University Studies in Historical and Political Science* placed him at the red-hot center of early professional history. He described the Klan as

> a secret society of whites, extending all through the Southern States. It was originally formed as a sort of police, to keep the freedmen in subjection. It then

> attacked the white Republicans, the "carpet-baggers" or "scalawags." Finally it seems to have gone into the work of committing murders for pay or spite, so that the better class of whites were compelled to aid in putting it down. Before this took place, Congress passed a number of severe laws, intended to put an end to the society and its practices of riding by night in masks and disguises to terrify, whip, or murder freedmen and white Republicans.[22]

This passage is less extensive than Gilman's, and more critical. It introduces a claim common in textbooks up through the 1950s that while the Klan might have been justified in the beginning (Johnston had spent the previous few paragraphs describing the chaos of Negro rule), it quickly became unjustifiable as less elite white men moved in. Yet even in this fairly critical passage, the Klan emerges as an organized response to black ineffectiveness, stands in for white-on-black violence generally, and is not presented as part of a longer pattern or tradition of racial oppression.

George F. Holmes's *New School History of the United States,* a year later, included a still briefer mention. Holmes was an adopted southerner and a professor at the University of Virginia.[23]

> A strange, secret, and undiscoverable body, called the Ku-Klux Klan, excited much alarm among the freedmen of the more Southern States, and provoked rigorous proceedings on the part of the majority in Congress. The Military Enforcement Act was the most stringent of these measures.[24]

This passage, with its use of the word *strange,* is the first to introduce the important theme of the Klan's inscrutability. A less Klan-sympathetic textbook published by the California State system in 1888 was the fourth in the collection to mention the Klan, as a secret society formed to "keep the negroes in subjection," which was violent but was soon suppressed by the federal government and better class of southern whites.[25] One by John Fiske, an instructor at Harvard, was the fifth. It reiterated that the Klan emerged as a response to black misgovernment, "sometimes committed deeds of violence," and disappeared when the better southern whites stepped up to end it.[26] Not surprisingly, a year ahead of Fiske, Woodrow Wilson's 1893 text, *Division and Reunion* had apparently been at the cusp of mentioning the Klan. The name "Ku Klux" appears nowhere in his text, nor does he mention that a particular organized entity was involved, but he has an (approving) section on white-on-black political violence, and whoever placed subheadings along the sides of the text labeled this section "Ku-Klux Movement."[27] Wilson would more than rectify the omission in his extensive treatment of the Klan in his 1902 *A History of the American People.*[28]

Progressive-era historians continued to build on this foundation. A little under two-thirds of textbooks published between 1894 and 1913 mentioned the Klan. The themes common in the earliest narratives—white agency and black powerlessness; the Klan as synecdoche for all white-on-black oppression; and the Klan as decontextualized from earlier, later, and concurrent forms of oppression—continued to pervade the narratives. The fourth, spectacularizing the Klan, also became increasingly important. While one might expect that the fact that professional historians were gaining market share would lead to a less dramatic and sensationalizing narrative tone, early professionals spectacularized the Klan shamelessly. As Francis B. Simkins complained a few decades later of historians' treatment of Reconstruction generally, it was "at best the picturesque pageantry of the artist; at worst, the cheap sensationalism of the journalist or the scenario writer."[29]

There was a reason the first generation of professional historians embraced dramatic narration. They spoke of themselves as objective, but they also understood themselves as nation-builders at a time of great transition and great promise. William Archibald Dunning, in his 1913 presidential address to the American Historical Association, "Truth in History," would make a striking defense of the pragmatic value of the sometimes false historical accounts written by the amateur historians his professionals were replacing. While Greece had never been as virtuous and Moses never as just as these amateur historians led people to believe, Dunning insisted, the popular belief in their justice and virtue had enabled the rise of Western culture. Dunning's address was a call for a useable national history, and came strikingly close to suggesting some creativity in producing one. Dunning acknowledged the importance of objectivity but felt obligated to produce a history that would support the political need for national unity and purpose.[30]

It was certainly possible to write accounts of Reconstruction in which the Klan had no role. Former slave John R. Lynch's 325-page *The Facts of Reconstruction* (1913), for instance, does not mention the Ku Klux Klan at all.[31] Yet

Progressive-era historians were drawn to the Klan narrative for all the reasons that have been discussed. In their own time, lofty modern dreams were constantly interrupted by eruptions of lynch mobs, workmen's strikes, and shady foreign anarchists at home, and foreign populations stubbornly unwilling to accept the legitimacy of the rule of their more civilized betters. In writing their histories of Reconstruction, they allowed themselves to imagine embattled white southerners as both virtuous and destined to prevail. Despite the evidence of their own eyes, they told the story of the Klan as though racial violence had been an awkward bump in the road to unchallenged white supremacy.

The typical Progressive-era textbook version of the story was distinct from that of other periods in its tone of stern necessity, combined with an expressed regret, but also in the particularly heavy-handed way in which the Klan was combined with the idea of the unfolding of racial destiny. Committed to the idea that each racial group collectively guided itself so as to conform to its prescripted role (some were intended simply to submit honorably to their betters), they shifted their narratives away from biography toward accounts of collective achievement, truncated older textbooks' epic descriptions of warfare in favor of accounts of institution-building, and abandoned the tone of providentialism so pervasive in older texts in favor of exploring "the undercurrents that move society."[32] A glowing review of Columbia Professor David Saville Muzzey's 1911 textbook insisted, typically, that it covered "social and economic problems" rather than military history or "the careers of men of slight influence in high office."[33]

Many Progressive-era intellectuals found a master explanation for historical change in the mystical idea of "race spirit," in which history moved forward through the unfolding of each race's unique destiny.[34] For many white progressives, the white "race spirit" was to think and to rule; it was inevitable that southern whites, through some (necessarily social) mechanism, would resume that rightful place. This was a particularly appealing idea for those justifying the United States' new global imperialism. As Natalie Ring argues in chapter 7, accounts of imperialism and historical representations of the Reconstruction era drew from one another.[35] Just as Cubans and Hawaiians were destined to fall under US rule, so it was only natural that postwar black southerners had fallen under the rule of whites. As William Dunning's influential scholarly text *Reconstruction: Political and Economic* (1907) typically put it, the Klan was "the inevitable extra-legal protest of the former political people against their subjection to the freedmen and northerners."[36] The story of the Ku-Klux Klan, then, offered itself as a moment in the races' eternal struggle for position, a reassuring example of the natural tendency of the white race to dominate the black, and of its inevitable success.[37] But black scholars explored the idea as well. W. E. B. Du Bois wrote in his controversial early essay "The Conservation of the Races" that "Turning to real history, there can be no doubt, first, as to the . . . universal prevalence of the race idea, the race spirit, the race ideal, as to its efficiency as the vastest and most ingenious invention of human progress. . . . We see the Pharaohs, Caesars, Toussaints, and Napoleons of history and forget the vast races of which they were but epitomized expressions."[38]

Progressive-era textbooks varied in how they valued the Klan; that division often though not always fell along regional lines, with southern-market textbooks tending toward justification and romanticization. When Susan Lee Pendleton published her Richmond-based textbook in 1895, she did not mention the Klan. The "new and enlarged version" published in 1899, however, did so fulsomely: "No high-spirited, courageous people could patiently submit to such a government. . . . The best men at the South took part." This textbook introduces "protect[ing] white women" as a goal of the Klan.[39] Waddy Thompson's very popular 1904 *History of the United States,* which had been written in Atlanta, Georgia, and marketed to the South, claims that "Organizations were . . . formed among the whites for self-protection." Thompson acknowledged that some Ku-Klux "resorted to extreme violence." But he celebrated the Klan, blaming all of the "terrible condition of the South" on "measures employed by Congress in reconstructing the South."[40] Georgia educator Lawton B. Evans's *The Essential Facts of American History* (1909) agreed: "To protect themselves against these idle and lawless negroes, who were often led away by evil white men, a secret order known as the 'Ku Klux Klan' was formed. . . . When they appeared . . . the frightened blacks scurried to their cabins."[41] But northern-authored texts sometimes sang the same tune. Indianians James Albert Woodburn and Thomas Francis Moran's *American History and Government* (1906) first asserted that "Intelligence and property will rule in the long run. . . . Ignorance and vice have no right to rule," then explained that whites, to restore balance, became Ku-Klux to terrify "superstitious and easily frightened" Negroes.[42] Wisconsin-bred Johns Hopkins PhD James Alton James and his collaborator Albert Hart Sanford explained that Klan violence was "such as other countries have witnessed when the oppression of government drove a class to desperation."[43]

A few textbooks, predictably by northerners, denounced the Klan entirely, and many others expressed disapproval mixed with a concession that it was a natural response to the situation in which white southerners found themselves. Ohioan Henry William Elson's *School History of the United States* (1912) sums up the Klan briefly: "The more vicious class formed the 'Ku Klux Klan,' with the object of intimidating the black vote."[44] Washingtonian Edmond S. Meany's *United States History for Schools* likewise dismissed the Klan: "In other [states] forceful intimidation was resorted to, especially by a secret society called Ku-Klux Klan. By ghostly threats and by actual violence, Negroes were kept from voting or holding office. Not a few murders are charged to this movement before it was finally stamped out."[45] A textbook written by future University of Chicago president Harry Pratt Judson, *The Growth of the American Nation* (1895), found the Klan's violence excessive and "demoralizing," but noted that "Men of the Anglo-Saxon race cannot be expected to submit forever to the dominance of ignorance and corruption."[46]

Perhaps because the Klan was a popular story likely to interest student readers, even those textbook writers least sympathetic to the Klan's goals and tactics embraced sensational framing. In talking about the Klan, textbook writers found a unique opportunity to write about ghosts, pranks, devils, and mystery. Accounts of the Klan also provided a space to give accounts of "frightened darkies," a staple of the minstrel stage and early film. Textbook authors and publishers seeking to make their books popular with students found the Klan narrative useful: they dwelled on their Klan accounts, included plenty of anecdote, and made the Klan a frequent subject for illustrations.

Many Progressive-era textbooks both more and less positive about the Klan emphasized that it had emerged because of freedmen incapable of exercising the new powers artificially bestowed upon them by northerners. The Negro race was in an arrested stage of development: though slaves had been prematurely exposed to civilization, they naturally began to revert to type when the institution of slavery ended. As Johns Hopkins history PhDs Albert Woodburn and Thomas Francis Moran put it in their 1906 textbook, "The idle darkies were waiting around, each one looking for his 'forty acres and a mule' and wondering 'when de land was goin' gur to be devided.' Former faithful slaves were becoming good-for-nothing loafers."[47] Yet these "ignorant negroes" were given political power, while "capable white people, the natural leaders of the South, were left out. This was more than human nature could bear."[48] David Muzzey's influential 1911 textbook explained that "the prostrate South . . . should have been well on the way to industrial and commercial recovery, under the leadership of its own best genius."[49] White southern leadership and black compliance were as inevitable as gravity: through the Klan, races (though at the price of regrettable human suffering), found their rightful place.

Including the Klan in their narrative also helped turn-of-the-century textbook writers, whether driven by the latest historical theories or not, make their books acceptable to southern school boards. Southern textbook purchasers in the Progressive era realized the power that came with their market share, and engaged in a vibrant and familiar public discourse (stretching back before the Civil War) about their dissatisfaction with how the South was represented in northern-authored texts. Texas moved to statewide textbook adoption in 1897, in part so that it could command enough market share to influence textbook content.[50] This sort of organized southern response (in which white southerners, of course, had a substantially louder voice than did black) put additional pressure on textbook companies to include stories like that of the Klan.[51]

It is ironic that a movement largely shaped around opposition to southern compliance with northern authority would also play a narrative role in supporting unification. Dunning and his colleagues were invested in this project as well, and the Klan served not only as an expression of the inevitable unfolding of the white racial spirit but as a space through which the particular will of the (white) southern people was revealed as truly part of the national spirit. As a 1907 text written by University of Pennsylvania history professor John Bach McMaster had it, "most of the Southern whites were determined to stop the misgovernment; [they] banded together in secret societies, called by such names as Knights of the White Camellia, and the Ku-Klux-Klan."[52] Southern whites were, at that moment, resisting the North, yet in so doing they were asserting themselves as a key part of the collective white racial project that had been temporarily forgotten. The Klan folded southern whites back into the national narrative, and participated in the ongoing process of cultural reconciliation playing out in popular fiction, music, and commemorations.

The Klan's position in the textbook narrative only became more secure in the interwar period. With the release of *Birth of a Nation* in 1915, the Klan was even more firmly entrenched in popular culture and hegemonic in textbook narratives. Popular interest in the Klan, in this case, could be traced back to academic approaches: Thomas Dixon, the author of *The Clansman* (1905), the book upon which *Birth of a Nation* was based, had studied at Johns Hopkins under prominent progressive scholars Richard T. Ely and Herbert Baxter Adams; his book sometimes took the tone of a history lecture, overflowing with "Teutonic people" and racial "germ theory."[53] Dixon's technical racialist language did not make it into the film; rather, D. W. Griffith's intertitles describing the condition of the South and rise of the Klan after the war reached back to Dixon's Hopkins classmate, Woodrow Wilson, in his treatment of the Klan in *A History of the American People* (1902).[54] *The Clansman* had depicted the Klan as the white response to black aggression, "the challenge of race against race to mortal combat."[55] The Klan was "the spirit of the South . . . the resistless movement of a race, not of any man or leader of men," which "revealed the unity of the racial life of the people."[56] D. W. Griffith enthusiastically took up this frame in the film.

The film was also an important spark to a second Klan, much larger, less violent, and transcending region. Launched in 1915, the second Klan became a significant national force in 1921, when the spectacle it offered was joined to a sophisticated organizational mechanism.[57] National in its scope and respectably mainstream, the Klan of the early to mid-1920s sponsored parades in the thousands, and attracted the public support of mainstream state, local, and national political leaders. It became an important voice on political issues, particularly locally. At its height in the mid-1920s, it is said to have drawn "from two to four million men, women, and children" into the many groups it comprised.[58]

In the 1920s Klan members and supporters played an important role in how the Reconstruction-era history of the Klan was told in textbooks. Klan supporters cared about textbook narratives.[59] Thomas Pegram has argued that, in pursuit of their nativist and racist goals, the Klan in the 1920s "authentically and energetically took up the cause of public school reform," supporting better funding, professionalization, and centralization, often working alongside the National Education Association.[60] Klansmen won seats on school boards and petitioned boards of education, and were influential as purchasers of US history textbooks.[61]

In texts for high school students during this period, a reference to the Klan was still very much the norm: of 86 textbooks from 1914 through 1941, 78 named the Klan. And sections on the Klan were longer than those that had come before, often as much as five hundred words. It was in this era of the Klan's reemergence that textbooks within and beyond the South alike most consistently presented the Klan in the most unambiguously positive light. Most notably, writers in this period highlighted the mysterious and sensational nature of the Klan. As New Yorker Marguerite Stockman Dickson gushed in her 1927 *American History for Grammar Schools,* "Punishment of these daring men was almost impossible, so complete was the mystery in which they concealed themselves."[62] Harvard history PhD Emerson David Fite's 1916 *History of the United States* described in detail two of the Klan's mechanisms for terrorizing their victims, which he sensationally referred to as "grotesque devices."[63] Toledo, Ohio, school superintendent William Backus Guitteau's 1919 text also focused sensationally on the logistics of terror.[64] Western Reserve history professors Henry Eldridge Bourne and Elbert Jay Benton's *A History of the United States* (1919) expanded upon the Klan's disguises: "Some of the disguises which the members of these societies wore were terrifying. Their faces were masked, and they were shrouded in white. Even their horses were covered with long white gowns."[65] One textbook, intended for a southern audience, went so far as to illustrate its section on Reconstruction with stills from *Birth of a Nation.*[66] A 1926 textbook written by Sister Mary Celeste and presumably intended for a Catholic audience (a group hardly pro-Klan in the 1920s) enhanced the usual account of Klan costuming and trickery with a claim that "skulls of sheep and cattle and even of human beings were often carried on [Klansmen's] saddlebow."[67]

Most interwar textbooks continued to naturalize Klan violence as an inevitable response to an impossible situation. W. E. B. Du Bois wrote in 1935 that "There is scarce a child in the street that cannot tell you that the whole effort [of national reconstruction] was a hideous mistake and a perverse determination to attempt the impossible."[68] The Southern Publishing Company's 1920 *A History of the United States for the Grammar Grades* (endorsed by the United Daughters of the Confederacy) explained, "To accomplish [white control], it was necessary that the negro should lose his interest in politics. . . . Often a thorough fright would result in submission, but in the case of serious offenses the Ku-Klux sometimes took the law into their hands and punished the negroes severely."[69] Even Charles and Mary Beard's 1921 *History of the United States* was built on Progressive-era Klan justification, enhanced by post–*Birth of a Nation* enthusiasm.[70] It cited Thomas Nelson Page's 1904 *The Negro: The Southerner's Problem* as an authority, defined the Klan's victims as "obnoxious persons," and elaborated playfully on Klansmen's costumes and pranks, noting that Klan attacks were committed "at the witching hour of midnight." It reiterated Klansmen's understanding of themselves: the Klan "succored the suffering" and so forth.[71]

Some of the most powerful work on constructing a counter-narrative to one focused on the Klan came from black scholars. And many black scholars even in the Klan's heyday had continued to reject the idea that the Klan was a central actor in Reconstruction. When Carter G. Woodson wrote *The Negro in Our History* in 1922, his treatment of the Klan was noteworthy in its brevity, and pointed in its contextualization: "The Negroes therefore were harassed and harried by disturbing elements of anarchy, out of which soon emerged an oath-bound order called the Ku Klux Klan, terrorizing the Negroes with lawlessness and violence."[72] The Klan did not come out of nowhere to address black chaos, but out of preceding white "elements of anarchy."

W. E. B. Du Bois's *Black Reconstruction* (1935), written after the rise and decline of the second Klan movement, similarly deemphasizes the Klan. The 10 or 11 of 737 pages he allots to Klan violence in a book specifically about race and Reconstruction is a substantially smaller share than textbooks of the day would grant the Klan in their narratives of Reconstruction. And when he did discuss it he rigorously contextualized it, presenting it alongside lengthy considerations of non-Klan-related white-on-black violence. He avoided discussion of the performative or sensationalist elements of Klan attacks, mentioning only that Ku-Klux were "masked."[73] Rather than focusing on white agency, writers like Woodson and Du Bois articulated black agency and accomplishments. When they turned to a discussion of black oppression, it was much more rooted in broad "institutional and historical conditions" rather than focused closely on the Klan.[74] Yet their voices were largely unheard beneath the dominant narrative.

After the second Klan's collapse in the late 1920s, some scholars began to look critically at how it had been written into the historical narrative. Lawrence Reddick in 1935 surveyed the depiction of the Reconstruction era in textbooks of his day, and noted the disempowerment of black people in representations of the period, bemoaning the proliferation of images of wide-eyed and terrified freedpeople.[75] And Francis B. Simkins criticized the sensationalism of Klan treatments in 1939, noting that the "Ku Klux Klan is used as either a glamorous or sinister symbol for the arousal of issues of race, religion, and patriotism in which all Americans, radicals and reactionaries, Negro lovers and Negro haters, are vitally concerned."[76] Howard K. Beale, in a published version of his 1939 Southern Historical Association address, castigated contemporary historians for failing to place the racial tensions of Reconstruction in a geographic, temporal, or economic context. In an article outlining the troubling limitations of current scholarship and outlining new approaches, he pointedly ignored the Ku Klux Klan, mentioning it only to note that historians had failed to realize that most white southerners "wanted nothing from politicians but a chance to live their lives undisturbed," dreamed of peace, and therefore hated the Klan as much as the Loyal League.[77]

The period during and after the Second World War saw a newly urgent call for a nationalist American history: one that the Klan would serve less comfortably than it had in the past.[78] Yet the Klan would hold its ground in the narrative. All of the texts in my survey that were published from the US entry into the war in 1941 through the end of the 1950s mentioned the Klan. They would continue to maintain the four key functions of earlier periods: as Mark M. Krug's 1961 survey of US history textbooks revealed, most textbooks "base their account of Reconstruction primarily on the findings of the Burgess-Dunning-Randall and Fleming school," and their discussion of the Klan was consistent with that.[79] These wartime and postwar textbooks continued casually to insist upon white potency and black weakness, trumpeting "the superstitions of the ignorant negroes."[80] They continued to decontextualize the Klan, and to use it to stand in for all white-on-black violence. And the Klan's spectacle lost little of its appeal: texts of the period continued to celebrate Klan performance and elaborate on their "antics." Klansmen, one 1943 text marveled, "were supposed to be able to remove their own heads at will and to float through the air."[81]

But while narrative elements in the Klan account remained stable, the valence of Klan representations shifted from the celebratory tone of the interwar period and became more mixed. The war against fascism had brought racially charged violent private paramilitary organizations dramatically out of favor. By this point, not only the twentieth-century Klan's membership but its popularity had taken a nosedive. From leadership scandals in the mid-1920s to a slew of financial scandals over control of the property of the once-lucrative group in the 1930s through 1950s, when Klansmen appeared in the newspaper in this period it was often as defendants facing charges of unethical behavior. While disapproval of the twentieth-century Klan often did not imply disapproval of the Reconstruction-era Klan, the pressure that modern Klansmen put on textbooks to celebrate the Reconstruction-era Klan collapsed. Textbook Klan narratives in these years deplored violence and lawlessness more vigorously than before, shifting away from their predecessors' cheerful toleration and glorification, and particularly disapproving the Klan's violation of the government's monopoly on violence. When a 1942 textbook invited students to discuss, "Would you have joined the Ku Klux Klan in 1866?," its authors imagined lively and substantial debate.[82] A 1952 textbook's "Can You Draw Conclusions from Facts?" section asked, "What was good about the work of the Ku Klux Klan? What was bad about it?"[83] John D. Hicks, George E. Mowry, and Robert E. Burke's *The American Nation* discussed the Klan's "fiendish torture and outright murder."[84] William Hamm's *The American People* (1942) was circumspect, judiciously putting complaints about freedmen's rule into the mouths of southern whites and condemning the deeds of violence "ascribed to" the Klan; but it expressed relief when the federal government "finally put an end to its activities," "drastically punish[ing] those who attempted in any way to deprive the Negro of his civil rights."[85]

During this period, textbooks stopped criticizing the government for having used inappropriate or excessive force against the Klan: those inclined to defend southerners had to find a way to positively depict both them and the federal forces that suppressed them, rescripting the troubling fact that black southerners and the federal government had been allied against white southerners. Myrtle Roberts's 1953 text sympathizes with the Klan's motives: "By accident, they found they could right some of the wrongs" of the Reconstruction era. But some Klansmen went too far, and "Unfortunately, many abuses continued until it became necessary for Congress to pass very severe laws."[86] In *Story of*

*Our Country* (1954), Minnesotan Ruth West wrote that, fearing violence from vagrant southern blacks, southern whites turned to the Klan, but when some "lawless" men used their power in evil ways, "Finally, the leaders themselves wished to put an end to the organization. Congress passed laws against the Klan and gave the army authority to stamp it out. Fear of the Klansmen, however, was stronger with the Negroes than their faith in Uncle Sam's army, and most of them stopped using their right to vote."[87] In this account, true Klan leaders and the federal government are allied, while freedpeople fail to maintain their alliance with the federal government out of cowardice. Similarly, a textbook by New Yorker Gertrude Van Duyn Southworth and her son John Van Duyn Southworth portrayed the Klan as in sympathy with rather than opposition to northerners. Northern soldiers "did their best," but were unable to suppress the Klan, until "It was due to the increased understanding on the part of the Northerners as well as to the activities of the Ku Klux Klan that the intolerable conditions in the South were gradually improved."[88] Yet if the tone of the Klan textbook narrative was destabilized by the nationalism and law-and-order commitments that the war had spawned, wartime Americans had little reason to doubt that such illegal and violent groups were crucial to moving history forward. Seen through the lens of the Second World War, the Reconstruction-era Klan seemed troubling but all too plausible, and the idea that the strong race could effectively dominate the weak, and in a spectacular and seemingly decontextualized manner, made more sense than ever.

During the 1960s and 1970s, textbooks began to respond to the civil rights movement. The NAACP and other organizations' protests against racist history textbook content, together with years of effort on the part of antiracist historians, finally began to get some traction.[89] In these years, professional Reconstruction-era history went through profound transitions. Revisionist historians like Leon Litwack and Herbert Gutman took the experience of black southern Americans seriously and joined the challenge to latter-day Dunningites like E. Merton Coulter. Some black scholars in this era who retold this history of the Klan continued the long tradition of dismissing it in few words. Important works like Rayford Logan's *The Negro in the United States: A Brief History* (1957) said only that "scores of secret organizations committed such numerous outrages, that Congress" enacted Ku- Klux Acts.[90] Benjamin Quarles's 1964 *The Negro in the Making of America* gave the Reconstruction-era Klan only a page, though that page deviated little from the standard narrative: "highly organized" Klansmen in colorful costumes sometimes did not even have to use violence, relying on "rural Negroes'" "awe and dread."[91]

John Hope Franklin's 1961 *Reconstruction: After the Civil War* took a very different approach, giving much of a chapter to the Klan, in order to make a frontal attack on historical conventions. Franklin's book repeated the sensationalist element of the dominant narrative and took white empowerment seriously: the Klan was highly organized, highly successful, and "terrified Negroes by weird rituals, ghoulish dress and night rides." But it challenged the standard narrative in several ways. Crucially, Franklin refused to decontextualize the Klan as an extraordinary event either in its own time or in relationship to earlier and later periods: the Klan was "a reflection of the general character of Southern life," really a continuation of the bushwhackers and other prewar and wartime violent groups, and one of many similar groups that existed in its day. And Franklin rejected black disempowerment, filling his chapter with accounts of Klan victims' resistance.[92]

White scholars participated in and responded to this changing intellectual climate, but the standard narrative had endurance, and textbooks, and senior scholars, persisted over time. Richard Hofstadter and Clarence Ver Steeg sounded outdated in 1971 as they maintained a studiously neutral tone that would have seemed appropriate as late as the 1950s.

> The Ku Klux Klan was organized in 1866 in Tennessee, and it spread throughout the South. Its members adopted secret rituals; they rode at night dressed in white hoods and sheets, frightening those who supported Radical Reconstruction. They aimed to terrorize blacks, scalawags, and carpetbaggers. Klansmen often whipped and sometimes killed those they opposed.[93]

By then, most texts had begun to condemn Klan violence as part of a more general awareness of racial prejudice in the history curriculum. California in 1966 mandated that history texts should correctly portray the contributions of African Americans: *Land of the Free,* on which John Hope Franklin was a coauthor, and which was written with the California market in mind, characterized Reconstruction-era Ku-Klux as inflexible "reactionaries" (very much a key word in that period) though even that textbook did not include accounts of resistance to the Klan.[94] Frequently, textbooks of the sixties and seventies portrayed Klansmen as being "embittered," a cardinal sin in that period.[95] "Profoundly bitter and disappointed, some Southerners resorted to violence... in order to 'rescue' their states from Congressional Reconstruction."[96] A 1971 text called the Klan "infamous."[97] Another 1971 textbook, *We the People: A History of the United States of America,* captioned an image: "The Ku Klux Klan stood for fear and violence."[98] And even some established textbooks changed their tune: Bernard Weisberger in 1959 had condemned the first edition of Thomas Bailey and David Kennedy's *The American Pageant* as firmly in the Dunning camp and "No doubt... as stirring, for students, as a showing of *The Birth of a Nation.*" But Bailey and Kennedy's sixth edition (1979) calls Klansmen "deeply embittered," and "resent[ful]" and their actions "atrocious" and "savage."[99] The fear generated by the Klan encounter had, by this period, been relocated from the weakness of the powerless and cowardly black man to the terrorism of the desperate and violent white. A 1967 text called Klansmen a "terrorist group," and one from 1968 criticized them for having taken "the law into their own hands and assumed the roles of judge and jury over a person's life."[100] The consensus that freedpeople ought to be either mocked or pitied for their "superstition" and "ignorance" fell apart. Indeed, these terms almost disappeared from Klan descriptions in textbooks after 1960. A 1967 text still referred to the "more superstitious Negro" but also acknowledged that many "saw through the threatening make-believe."[101]

Some textbooks, for the first time, also began to imagine black people in the South as exercising agency: "The Klan, however, did not triumph, for many Negroes did not scare easily."[102] Texan Allan O. Kownslar and Massachusetts' Donald B. Frizzle's *Discovering American History* (1967) discussed at length the competence of black legislators, including their efforts to "raise money to catch and punish the Ku-klux."[103] And while Progressive-era and interwar texts had referred their readers to southern apologist Thomas Nelson Page for further information, at least one 1971 text quoted, at length, Klan foe Albion Tourgée.[104]

Textbooks in the last decades of the twentieth and into the twenty-first centuries have continued this basic change of tone and have addressed many of the racist implications of conventional Klan framing. The Klan, however, still takes substantial real estate in the story of the period. So, for instance, Davidson et al.'s section on the Klan is larger than that on the election of 1868 or on the Fifteenth Amendment. All texts in the past few decades assign a negative value to Klansmen and a positive value to their victims: texts regularly label the Klan as a terrorist group which, always a negative designation, became even more powerfully so in the 1980s and, especially, after 9/11. Joyce Appleby et al.'s teachers' edition encourages teachers to introduce the Klan, and other similar contemporary groups, as "terrorist groups."[105] Lapsansky-Werner et al. refer to the Klan's "terror tactics."[106]

Yet troubling narrative elements persist in recent textbooks: to make the Klan central to the story of Reconstruction is almost inevitably to emphasize white efficacy and deemphasize black agency. Very few sentences in recent textbook treatments of the Klan have a black subject. In one text, "Black Southerners" are listed as one of three groups who called for Klan suppression, but this is an exception: as a rule, in the discussions of the Klan in these texts, black southerners could only be acted upon.[107] Freedpeople's responses to the Klan are not represented in the texts by Davidson et al. or Lapsansky-Werner et al.; Danzer et al. give two accounts of victim resistance to the Klan.[108] Yet even it repeats that Klan violence "frightened the African American majority away from the polls," and includes a sidebar in its teacher's edition on "Resistance to the Ku Klux Klan," ultimately summarizing it as "ineffective" in the face of white violence.[109] And indeed, it is hard to frame black responses to the Klan as effective: when Klan groups were at their most organized and when their attacks were indeed unexpected, victims had few options. But if the textbook writers had chosen to talk about white-on-black violence through a different lens, focusing on the less organized, less clandestine, violence that was more typical of the period than Klan violence, they would have found greater opportunity to discuss victim agency.

Recent texts differ in the success with which they place the Klan in a larger context of violence and oppression. Appleby et al. stand out in this regard, including a paragraph acknowledging that most southern whites wanted to deny rights to black people and prevented them from having jobs, land, and credit, discussing this before bringing in the Klan. Yet Appleby's text still privileges Klan violence, transitioning to the (longer) paragraph on the Klan with the phrase, "A more serious danger to the freedpeople in the South was. . . ."

Danzer et al.'s text also emphasizes that the Klan was after economic as well as political ends, and follows its Klan description with a discussion of nonviolent economic oppression. Yet it persists in reminding students that white-on-black violence was a southern problem that northerners opposed, for instance. A sidebar in Danzer et al. suggests that teachers ask students how they respond to violence or terrorism they read about elsewhere, and to consider how these reactions "compare with reactions of Northerners to murderous acts of the Ku Klux Klan."[110]

The texts are better than earlier texts at indicating that racial oppression persisted after the Klan's end, yet they still are remarkably unsuccessful in presenting the Klan as part of a long and continuous history of white-on-black violence. Danzer et al. are clearest on this: while the Klan's "activities decreased," "individual acts of violence" in response to the Enforcement Acts and "violence against blacks and white Republicans" continued.[111] Appleby et al. note that laws to suppress the Klan "were not always effective," potentially leaving the impression that the Klan itself continued to be responsible for the persistence of post-Klan violence.[112] Lapsansky-Werner et al. also leave the Klan's end vague, claiming that while its "activities lessened somewhat" with federal intervention, the "threat of violence persisted," suggesting that perhaps the Klan itself remained active into later years.[113] Davidson et al. conclude that, "Although the original Klan disbanded, new groups took its place."[114] These texts leave the impression that the important form that racial violence took was private organized terrorism, and that, if the Klan was beaten back, residual Klan groups, or other private terrorist groups, filled the void. They suppress the fact that Klan violence was only one of many forms of white-on-black violence at the time, and that white-on-black violence would continue uninterrupted, in all of these forms, after the Klan's abatement. Although none say that white-on-black violence ceased with the Klan's decline, all leave the impression that the crisis of racial oppression had been substantially, if imperfectly, addressed.

While none of these textbooks' accounts of the Klan are sensationalist, they bring in elements of sensationalism both in their texts and through the abundant use of images. Three of the four textbooks (Appleby is the exception) include pictures of Ku-Klux or Klan costume elements. Davidson and Stoff include an image of a white pointed hood and a wooden coffin, and another of a Nast cartoon representation of a Ku-Klux. Lapsansky-Werner et al. and

Danzer et al. both include images of two men in Ku-Klux costumes. Danzer et al. additionally refer students to extra online material on the Klan.[115] And all comment on Klan costume and performance. Davidson and Stoff claim that Reconstruction-era Klansmen burned wooden crosses. Appleby tells students that Klansmen wore white sheets. Davidson says only that they wore "white robes with hoods that hid their faces." In fact, cross-burning and all-white costumes were not characteristic of the Reconstruction-era Klan (though some all-white costumes existed). Rather, this representation of the Klan originated with Thomas Dixon's *The Clansman* (1905) as popularized by *Birth of a Nation*. The surfeit of images, and the casual use of descriptive text that in fact refers back to a (dangerous) fictive literary tradition rather than to historical evidence, suggest that historical textbook writers still have work before them if they are to escape the racist Klan narrative produced in the Progressive era.

The point is not that textbooks ought to deemphasize the starkly uneven power relationship of Ku-Klux and their victims, nor that they should necessarily avoid all mention or depiction of Klan costumes. Klan attacks were defined by their sensationalism and by their unequal use of force. But it is crucial to contextualize the Klan in relationship to other contemporary white-on-black violence and to white-on-black violence that preceded and followed it. And the discretionary choice textbook writers have made to let the Klan stand in for all racial violence in this era requires both spectacle and a strong emphasis on white agency and black disempowerment, and encourages exceptionalism.

Using the Klan as a synecdoche for all white and black violence in the Reconstruction era is a strange choice. Klan violence was terrible, but never as deadly as many of the other forms of violence that white people inflicted upon black people in those years. The Klan was only significantly active in selected parts of the rural South, only between 1868 and 1871. So focusing on the Klan leaves out white-on-black violence from 1865 to 1867 and after 1872. It leaves out urban white-on-black violence. It leaves out northern white-on-black violence. And even at the Klan's height, most areas in the rural South never saw the emergence of an active Klan. Klans did not tend to appear in areas with large white or black majorities, or in states where white conservatives quickly began to regain formal power. When a Klan did emerge in a given area, it was almost never active for more than a period of months. So while we lack good numbers on Klan violence, we know that most people at most times, even in the rural South during the Klan's four years of activity, faced no actual Klan threat or violence. Klan terror was real, and afflicted even those who would never face a flesh-and-blood Klansman, but even rural southerners at the Klan's height were much more likely to face much more quotidian forms of violence: being beaten or shot by white neighbors or employers, being harassed and attacked by white people in town, or being subjected to illegitimate violence by agents of the government.

The way that textbooks tell the story of the Klan has evolved in the 130 or so years since it first was adopted as part of our national narrative. Most notably, the Klan, after periods of ambiguity and outright celebration, has been revalued as distinctly negative. Still, the Klan appearance in textbooks is still too often decontextualized, allowed to stand in for all racial violence, spectacularized, and used to propagate an image of white men as empowered and blacks as disempowered even at the hopeful moment of black enfranchisement. Much the same narrative that was so attractive to early historians as a racist frame now serves as a powerful lesson on the dangers of racial violence. The Klan narrative has always been compromised, and even now brings with it some of its racist baggage and continues to achieve some of the unwholesome ends for which it was adopted.

Since the Progressive era, the Klan has worked in US history textbooks as a synecdoche for the many people, forces, and institutions that together oppressed freedpeople in the postwar years.[116] Such approximation can make complex material approachable for beginning students. Yet just as a focus on great individuals in a national narrative erases collective and systemic responsibility for historical changes, so the Klan becomes a convenient approximation for the entirety of antiblack violence. It becomes unnecessary to discuss violence used by white neighbors, employers, and police against individual black men, women, and children in the South and other parts of the country, although such informal forms actually represented the lion's share of white-on-black violence.

Using the Klan as a stand-in for these pervasive violent practices also assigns responsibility for black oppression to the subset of southern white men who joined the Ku-Klux. Anthony L. Brown and Keffrelyn D. Brown have powerfully critiqued the "consistent portrayal of violence against African

Americans as deinstitutionalized acts undertaken by 'bad' men or, at best, 'bad' people" in recent textbooks.[117] Agents of black oppression are labeled as "some of the more hot-headed people of the South," "bad men," "bitter people," "the irresponsible," "the poorer and more ignorant white men, who had been reared amid the degrading influences of slavery," "reckless people," "hoodlum[s]" or "gangs."[118] The Klan fills the explanatory space that might otherwise have been shared with or given to widespread private white violence, oppressive local governments, and postwar social disorganization. The Klan narrative "render[s] these events as the acts of autonomous immoral agents rather than systematic acts that had direct and long-term effects."[119]

Using the Klan to represent black postwar oppression serves to make the oppression of black people a uniquely southern phenomenon and one that the federal government fought decisively against. In recent years historians have heroically challenged the entrenched idea of the South as the "opposite other" and the powerfully entrenched understanding that violent racial oppression, or even all racial oppression, was a uniquely southern phenomenon.[120] The Klan was defined, in its own mind and in public opinion, in large part by its southern-ness. Its narrative dominance has effectively erased ways in which northerners engaged in similar activities. To emphasize the Klan as the cause of black oppression is almost necessarily to depict "northerners" as opposed to such oppression. This further obscures violent antiblack attacks north of the Mason-Dixon Line. So, when Arthur Gilman's passage first introducing the Klan to textbooks begins, "at the close of the war a number of secret political societies were formed in the Southern States, the objects of which were to offset, as was claimed by the people of the section, the acts of certain other societies formed through the agency of intriguers from the North," and ends, "The organization died out afterwards, partly because the relations of the North and South were becoming more harmonious," it tidily defines "the North" as black allies.[121] An 1899 text similarly reifies the antiracist "northern man": "To Northern men it seemed that the whole South was conspiring to make national law inoperative, and to rob the negro of his rights."[122] And this narrative persists.

Just as the Klan demarcated black oppression geographically, so it demarcated it chronologically. Jacquelyn Dowd Hall has argued that focusing on a "short" civil rights movement narrative revolving around canonical figures and events from *Brown v. Board of Education* through the Voting Rights Act, decontextualizes the movement and uncouples it from struggles for economic and gender justice, but also imagines that the movement and its work came to a discrete end.[123] Reassuringly, the Klan had a distinct beginning and a distinct end, seemingly foreclosing the possibility of enduring brutality and injustice. And because it was decisively ended, the account of the Klan feeds into a progressive account of race relations. Textbook Klan narratives frequently end with comforting (at least comforting to their intended readership) statements. In an 1883 text, "The organization died out afterwards, partly because the relations of the North and South were becoming more harmonious, and the passions engendered by war were growing weaker."[124] In a 1939 text, "By the end of 1872 the Ku Klux Klan had virtually disappeared."[125] "Finally, when it had served its purpose, it was disbanded by its leader, General Forrest, one of the greatest of the Confederate cavalry commanders."[126] Or, in 1982, "Life began to return to what white southerners defined as "'normal.'"[127] There were some exceptions to this, particularly in texts written in the post–civil rights era: so, in 1967, "After that, the Klan itself went to pieces, but 'Ku Kluxism' (the use of terror for political ends) continued."[128] But even where they hedge, and note that the Klan did not entirely go away, textbooks' representations of the Klan mark it as atypical, rather than as a part of a persistent national injustice.

The still-fundamentally sensational nature of the representations of the Klan presents the post–Civil War period as a time that resists rational analysis, and that needs to be explored in different terms than other historical episodes. Particularly in the Progressive and interwar period, but to a substantial degree up to the present, textbooks have used strikingly different terms to describe the Klan than in other periods, inviting students to engage it through some combination of resigned perplexity and humor with the use of terms like *strange, weird,* and *bizarre* and the frequent claim that little is and can be known about the Klan. One of the earliest textbook mentions of the Klan, George Holmes's *New School History of the United States,* introduces the Klan as "a strange, secret, and undiscoverable body." The book uses the term *strange* on six other occasions: to muse upon the origins of Native Americans (it playfully asks if they were the lost tribe of Israel? The descendants of the lost city of Atlantis? Had they swarmed out of a hole in the earth?); the Mormons, "a strange people with a strange creed and strange usages"; British authority in New York over Dutch inhabitants was "strange rule"; John Brown's Harpers' Ferry attack was "a strange event"; the *Monitor* and *Merrimack* were "strange war monsters"; and China was a "a strange empire."[129] "Strange" in this book, then, usually meant monstrous or foreign. In the case of John Brown, as in the case of the Klan, it meant that it was a thing impolitic to analyze that was therefore best thought of in the same way as the novel and the foreign. "Strange" marks a thing as beyond our understanding and as outside of historical analysis.

The terms *strange,* along with its near-cognates *mysterious* and *weird,* has frequently appeared throughout these textbooks over the years. "No one save the victim saw the mysterious horsemen come or go. No one knew who they were, nor when nor where they went. . . . Punishment of these daring men was almost impossible, so complete was the mystery in which they concealed themselves."[130] Even a careful and non-celebratory passage like this 1975 excerpt, "The *Ku Klux Klan* was the best known of these secret groups. Mounted Klansmen, dressed in white hoods and ghostly robes, took to the highways of the South. They paraded silently by night through village streets and along country roads," pulls the student toward sensational tropes and away from more conventional historical explanations.[131] This sensationalist presentation allows textbook readers to imagine that there is something confusing or unknowable about racial oppression.

Finally, Klan attacks were fundamentally meant to rob their victims of agency. While historians must represent moments of oppression and violence, the choice to make accounts of oppression and violence central to an analysis inevitably presents victims of that violence as lacking agency. LaGarrett J. King, Christopher Davis, and Anthony L. Brown have argued that US history textbooks consistently present African Americans as lacking control and failing to take steps to influence their historical situation. It is difficult to tell the story of the Klan in any other way; black agency continues to be erased in Klan accounts even in the recent textbook segments about the Klan explored here.[132]

Jacquelyn Dowd Hall writes that "remembrance is always a form of forgetting."[133] Particularly in the last few decades, excellent theoretical work has explored the utility of forgetting to collective recovery from traumatic pasts and to the process of nation-building. The master text of deliberate cultural forgetting is the history textbook: the national sins absent from our textbooks would fill countless counter-textbooks. Yet one national shame, the violence committed against freedpeople by the Ku Klux Klan, managed to not only survive, but to thrive in our national narrative for more than a century and a quarter. Indeed, representations of the Klan have often been most robust during periods in which public approval of the oppression of black people has been at its height. The Klan narrative has always been a way to explain away racial violence as "not us now" or even "not us, ever." Remembering the Klan has powerfully enabled other forgetting.

It seems like a convenient trick that historians have been able to revalue the Klan narrative while keeping many elements of it in its place. But narrative structures have an insidious power: we tell the story of the Klan now with the expectation that children will be horrified by its injustice and will empathize with its victims. We carefully frame our narratives so that they will be read in this way. Yet a narrative that has been so cleanly flipped will always be available to be flipped back again: whether, in time, by future textbook authors, or by individual students pursuing a racist agenda.

Today, it is largely conservative forces that are interested in eliminating the Ku Klux Klan from school textbooks. The stench of terrorism is perhaps so strong that the Klan can currently fit comfortably only into the most radical southern apologetics. The Texas school board, in pursuit of conservative, nationalist, and arguably racialist goals, has recently produced a set of standards that seem to limit, or even remove, the role of the Klan. It is tempting to fight them on this, as on a host of other serious problems with their standards. Yet those committed to an interpretation of history that takes full account of the forces undermining racial justice may not be best served by fighting to preserve the substantial space in the national narrative that the Dunningites built for the Klan. Dunning, Burgess, Turner, and the many others who established the basic structure of our discipline shaped it around a fundamentally racialist, and racist, understanding of history. Some of their interpretive choices in consolidating our national narrative have endured, though in sanitized forms that obscure many of their narratives' initial intentions. The Klan in history textbooks conceals more than it reveals; despite having been so sanitized and refigured, it exculpates the perpetrators of racial oppression in much the same way that Progressive-era professionalizers had intended. It stands in the place of a more subtle, extensive, and honest analysis of racial violence in our history.

NOTES

I would like to thank Edward Copenhagen, the special collections librarian at Harvard Gutman Library, for his crucial assistance with this project, and Aaron O'Data and Brian Kutzley, my graduate assistants, who transformed my archival notes into a useable database.

1. The spelling of the Klan's name changed over time. Ku-Klux (or Ku-Klux Klan) was the dominant spelling in the nineteenth century, but in the twentieth century it was Ku Klux Klan. An individual member of the Klan was commonly called a Ku-Klux in the nineteenth century, but a Klansman in the twentieth. Ku-Klux was also used frequently as a verb in the nineteenth century (to Ku-Klux someone). It was also used as a shorthand to describe the group as a whole.

2. Eric Foner, "Reconstruction Revisited," *Reviews in American History* 10, no. 4 (December 1982): 82.

3. Francis B. Simkins, "New Viewpoints on Southern Reconstruction," *Journal of Southern History* 5, no. 1 (February 1939); Howard K. Beale, "On Rewriting Reconstruction History," *American Historical Review* 45, no. 4 (July 1940): 807–27.

4. John Hope Franklin, "Whither Reconstruction Historiography," *Journal of Negro Education* 17, no. 4 (Autumn 1948): 449.

5. John Hope Franklin, "Mirror for Americans: A Century of Reconstruction History," *American Historical Review* 85, no. 1 (February 1980): 1–14.

6. Bernard A. Weisberger, "The Dark and Bloody Ground of Reconstruction Hisoriography," *Journal of Southern History* 25, no. 4 (November 1959): 428.

7. Lawrence D. Reddick, "Racial Attitudes in American History Textbooks of the South," *Journal of Negro History* 19, no. 3 (July 1934): 225–65.

8. Van S. Allen, "An Analysis of Textbooks Relative to the Treatment of Black Americans," *Journal of Negro Education* 40, no. 2 (Spring 1971): 140–45.

9. Thomas C. Holt, "Reconstruction in United States History Textbooks," *Journal of American History* 81, no. 4 (March 1995): 1641–51.

10. Anthony L. Brown, "Countermemory and Race: An Examination of African American Scholars' Challenges to Early Twentieth Century K-12 Historical Discourses," *Journal of Negro Education* 79, no. 1 (2010): 54–65.

11. Anthony L Brown and Keffrelyn D. Brown, "Strange Fruit Indeed: Interrogating Contemporary Textbook Representations of Racial Violence toward African Americans," *Teachers College Record* 112, no. 1 (January 2010): 45.

12. This pattern is pronounced in both a Google n-gram search for the term "Ku Klux Klan" (limited to books published in the United States) and the same search in the *New York Times* newspaper database.

13. This study is based on a reading of 258 textbooks housed in the Historical Textbook Collection at the Monroe C. Gutman Library at Harvard University. The textbooks are orga-

nized by the year in which a particular edition was printed. I selected three per year, if three were available (they almost always were), preferring books that appeared to be professionally produced, books that I had not selected another edition of in recent years, and books that seemed to be generic textbooks rather than having special themes or innovative organization. Harvard's collection itself is hardly representative of all textbooks. It was assembled from donations, and doubtless favors books that were used by school systems of the sort to donate their outdated textbooks to Harvard. Still, textbooks that succeeded in gaining a large market share found their way into the collection, and given its size and breadth, it is a solid basis for this study.

14. Thomas Wentworth Higginson, *Young Folks' History of the United States* (Boston: Lee and Shepard, 1875); Alexander Stephens, *A Compendium of the History of the United States from the Earliest Settlement to 1872* (New York: E. J. Hale and Son, 1872), 475.

15. Alexander Stephens, *A Comprehensive and Popular History of the United States Embracing a Full Account of the Discovery and Settlement of the Country* (Baltimore: Gately and Haskell, 1882), 855.

16. John Clark Ridpath, *History of the United States. Grammar School Ed.* (Cincinnati: Jones Brothers, 1880), 346.

17. John J. Anderson, *A Popular School History of the United States* (New York: Clark & Maynard, 1880), 295–99.

18. George W. Williams, *History of the Negro Race in America 1619–1880* (New York: Arno Press, 1968), 382.

19. W. E. B. Du Bois, *Black Reconstruction in America: An Essay toward a History of the Part which Black Folk Played in the Attempt to Reconstruct Democracy in America, 1860–1880* (New York: Harcourt, Brace, 1935), 718.

20. Arthur Gilman, *A History of the American People* (Chicago: Interstate Publishing, 1883), vii, 558; "Arthur Gilman Dead," *New York Times,* 29 December 1909, p. 9. Professional historians cited Gilman's work, if often to correct its inaccuracies.

21. Gilman, *A History of the American People,* 558.

22. Alexander Johnston, *A History of the United States for Schools* (New York: Henry Holt, 1885), 381–82.

23. George F. Holmes, *New School History of the United States* (New York: University Publishing, 1886), 272.

24. Holmes, *New School History,* 272.

25. *History of the United States: California State Series of School Text-Books* (Sacramento: State Printing Office, 1888), xi, 347.

26. John Fiske, *A History of the United States for Schools* (Boston: Houghton Mifflin, 1894), 399.

27. Melvyn Stokes, *D. W. Griffith's Birth of a Nation: A History of the Most Controversial Motion Picture of All Time* (New York: Oxford University Press, 2007), 199; Woodrow Wilson, *Division and Reunion, 1829–1889* (New York: Longman, Green, 1893), 274.

28. Woodrow Wilson, *A History of the American People,* Volume 5 (New York: Harper Brothers, 1902), 59–64.

29. Francis B. Simkins, "New Viewpoints on Southern Reconstruction," *Journal of Southern History* 5, no. 1 (February 1939): 51.

30. William Archibald Dunning, "Truth in History," *American Historical Review* 19, no. 2 (January 1914): 221.

31. John R. Lynch, *The Facts of Reconstruction* (New York: Neale Publishing, 1913).

32. Joseph Moreau, *School Book Nation: Conflicts over American History Textbooks from the Civil War to the Present* (Ann Arbor: University of Michigan Press, 2004), 44, 49; Henry William Elson, *History of the United State of America* (New York: Macmillan, 1904), 2:v. Fitzhugh Brundage suggests (convincingly) that the collective southern actor also appealed to the social gospel Protestantism of some Klan supporters. W. Fitzhugh Brundage, "Thomas Dixon: American Proteus," in Michele K Gillespie and Randall L. Hall, eds., *Thomas Dixon, Jr. and the Birth of Modern America* (Baton Rouge: Louisiana State University Press, 2009), 26.

33. Review of David Saville Muzzey, *American History Journal of Education* 74, no. 25 (December 1911): 701.

34. John Higham, *History: Professional Scholarship in America* (Baltimore: Johns Hopkins University Press), 97; Dorothy Ross, *The Origins of the American Social Sciences* (New York: Cambridge University Press, 1991), 17. Paul Laurence Dunbar, in his 1898 reflection on the Wilmington Riots, "Recession Never," *Toledo [Ohio] Journal,* 18 December 1898, argues that white-on-black lynching occurs throughout the nation: "The race spirit in the United States is not local but general."

35. Natalie J. Ring, "A New Reconstruction for the South," [173-202].

36. William A. Dunning, *Reconstruction: Political and Economic* (New York: Harper, 1907), 121–22.

37. Higham, *History: Professional Scholarship,* 94.

38. W. E. Burghardt Du Bois, "The Conservation of Races," American Negro Academy Occasional Papers, no. 2 (Washington, DC: American Negro Academy, 1897), 7.

39. Susan Pendleton Lee, *A School History of the United States* (Richmond: B. F. Johnson Publishing, 1895); Susan Pendleton Lee, *New School History of the United States* (Richmond: B. F. Johnson, 1899), 387.

40. Waddy Thompson, *History of the United States* (Boston: D. C. Heath, 1904), 429–30.

41. Lawton B. Evans, *The Essential Facts of American History* (Boston: Benj. H. Sanborn, 1909), 440–41.

42. James Albert Woodburn and Thomas Francis Moran, *American History and Government: A Text-book on the History and Civil Government of the United States* (New York: Longmans, Green, 1906), 440–41.

43. James Alton James and Albert Hart Sanford, *American History* (New York: Charles Scribner's Sons, 1909), 431–32.

44. Henry William Elson, *School History of the United States* (New York: Macmillan, 1912), 394–95.

45. Edmond S. Meany, *United States History for Schools* (New York: Macmillan, 1912), 456.

46. Harry Pratt Judson, *The Growth of the American Nation* (Meadville, PA: Flood and Vincent, 1895), 327.

47. Woodburn and Moran, *American History and Government,* 432.

48. Woodburn and Moran, *American History and Government,* 439.

49. David Saville Muzzey, *American History* (Boston: Ginn & Co., 1911), 487–88.

50. Moreau, *School Book Nation,* 69–70; Fred Arthur Bailey, "Free Speech and the 'Lost Cause' in Texas: A Study of Social Control in the New South," *Southwestern Historical Quarterly* 97, no. 3 (January 1994): 452–77.

51. Moreau, *School Book Nation,* 79.

52. John Bach McMaster, *A Brief History of the United States* (New York: American Book Company, 1907), 389–90.

53. Melvyn Stokes, *D. W. Griffith's The Birth of a Nation: The History of "The Most Controversial Motion Picture of All Time"* (New York: Oxford University Press, 2007), 32.

54. Stokes, *D. W. Griffith's The Birth of a Nation,* 199; Woodrow Wilson, *Division and Reunion, 1829–1889* (New York: Longman's Green, 1893).

55. Thomas Dixon, *The Clansman: An Historical Romance of the Ku Klux Klan* (New York: Grosset & Dunlap, 1905), 274.

56. Dixon, *The Clansman,* 341.

57. Thomas R. Pegram, *One Hundred Percent American: The Rebirth and Decline of the Ku Klux Klan in the 1920s* (Chicago: Ivan R. Dee, 2011), 8.

58. Pegram, *One Hundred Percent American,* 3.

59. "Allen Out to Drive Klan from Kansas," *New York Times,* 30 October 1922, p. 2.

60. Pegram, *One Hundred Percent American,* 96.

61. Pegram, *One Hundred Percent American,* 76–77, 104–105; Jonathan Zimmerman, *Whose America: Culture Wars in the Public* Schools (Cambridge, MA: Harvard University Press, 2002), 25.

62. Marguerite Stockman Dickson, *American History for Grammar Schools* (New York: Macmillan, 1920), 462–63.

63. Emerson David Fite, *History of the United States,* 2nd ed., revised (New York: Henry Holt, 1923), 417–18.

64. William Backus Guitteau, *Our United States: A History* (New York: Silver, Burdett, 1919), 471–72.

65. Henry Eldridge Bourne and Elbert Jay Benton, *A History of the United States* (Boston: D. C. Heath, 1919), 442.

66. Eleanor E. Riggs, *An American History* (New York: MacMillan, 1916), 405. Describing the textbook, *The Nation* noted that it had a southern valence, and that "Probably there is . . . too much freedom in describing the abuse of the carpet-baggers . . . but this is not a bad error." *The Nation,* 4 May 1916, p. 496.

67. Mary Celeste, *American History* (New York: Macmillan, 1926).

68. Du Bois, *Black Reconstruction in America,* 717.

69. R. G. Hall, Harriet Smither, and Clarence Ousley, *A History of the United States for the Grammar Grades* (Dallas: Southern Publishing, 1920), 394–95; Bailey, "Free Speech," 468.

70. Zimmerman, *Whose America,* 41.

71. Charles A. Beard and Mary R. Beard, *History of the United States* (New York: Macmillan,

1921), 382–83. The Beards are drawing from Peter Joseph Hamilton, *The Reconstruction Period,* volume XVI of the *History of North America* (Philadelphia: George Barrie & Sons, 1905), 449.

72. Carter G. Woodson, *The Negro in Our History* (Washington, DC: Associated Publishers, 1922), 256.

73. Du Bois, *Black Reconstruction,* 674–84.

74. Anthony L. Brown, "Counter-Memory and Race," 58.

75. Reddick, "Racial Attitudes," 256.

76. Simkins, "New Viewpoints on Southern Reconstruction," 50.

77. Howard K. Beale, "On Rewriting Reconstruction," *American Historical Review* 45, no. 4 (1940): 814.

78. Ian Tyrell, *Historians in Public: The Practice of American History* (Chicago: University of Chicago Press, 2005), 132–38.

79. Mark M. Krug, "On Rewriting of the Story of Reconstruction in the U. S. History Textbooks," *Journal of Negro History* 46, no. 2 (April 1961): 135.

80. Leon H. Canfield, Howard B. Wilder, Frederic L. Paxson, Ellis Merton Coulter, and Nelson P. Mead, *The United States in the Making* (Boston: Houghton Mifflin, 1939), 410.

81. Ralph Volney Harlow, *Story of America,* rev. ed. (New York: Henry Holt, 1943), 392–93; Jack Allen and John L. Betts. *History: USA* (New York: American Book Company, 1967), 331; Thomas A. Bailey and David M. Kennedy, *The American Pageant: A History of the Republic,* 6th ed. (Lexington, KY: D. C. Heath, 1979).

82. Charles H. Coleman and Edgar B. Wesley, *America's Road to Now* (Boston: D. C. Heath, 1942), 386.

83. Clyde B. Moore, Helen McCracken Carpenter, Laurence G. Paquin, Fred B. Painter, and Gertrude M. Lewis, *Building a Free Nation* (New York: Charles Scribner's Sons, 1952), 348.

84. John D. Hicks, George E. Mowry, and Robert E. Burke, *The American Nation,* 4th ed. (Boston: Houghton Mifflin, 1941), 39–40.

85. William A. Hamm, *The American People* (Boston: D. C. Heath, 1942), 507–8.

86. Myrtle Roberts, *Pattern for Freedom . . . A History of the United States* (Chicago: John C. Winston Company, 1953), 294–95.

87. Ruth West, *Story of Our Country* (Boston: Allyn and Bacon, 1954), 404.

88. Gertrude Van Duyn Southworth and John Van Duyn Southworth, *The Story of Our America* (Syracuse, NY: Iroquois Publishing 1951), 351.

89. For a full discussion of this, see Zimmerman, *Whose America,* 107–29.

90. Rayford Logan, *The Negro in the United States: A Brief History* (Princeton, NJ: D. Vann Nostrand, 1957).

91. Benjamin Quarles, *The Negro in the Making of America* (New York: Collier Books, 1964), 139–40.

92. John Hope Franklin, *Reconstruction: After the Civil War* (Chicago: University of Chicago Press, 1961), 155, 156, 158–59.

93. Clarence L. Ver Steeg and Richard Hofstadter, *A People and a Nation* (New York: Harper & Row, 1971), 367.

94. John W. Coughey, John Hope Franklin, and Ernest R. May, *Land of the Free* (New York: Benziger Brothers, 1969), 367.

95. Lew Smith, *The American Dream* (Glenview: Scott, Foresman, 1977), 188; Richard C. Wade, Howard B. Wilder, and Louise C. Wade, *A History of the United States* (New York: Houghton Mifflin, 1966), 393.

96. Robert F. Madgic, Staley S. Seaber, Fred H. Stopsky, and Robin W. Winks, *American Experience* (Addison-Wesley, 1971), 147–48.

97. Martin W. Sandler, Edwin C. Rozwenc, and Edward C. Martin, *The People Make a Nation* (Allyn and Bacon, 1971).

98. David B. Bidna, Morris S. Greenberg, and Jerold H. Spitz, *We the People: A History of the United States of America,* teacher's edition (Lexington, KY: D. C. Heath, 1971), 215. I believe that this was my own history textbook.

99. Thomas A. Bailey and David M. Kennedy, *The American Pageant: A History of the Republic,* 6th ed. (Lexington, KY: D. C. Heath, 1979), 444–45; Weisberger, "Dark and Bloody Ground," 436.

100. Richard N. Current, Alexander DeConde, and Harris L. Dante, *United States History* (Glenview: Scott, Foresman, 1967), 343; Landis R. Heller and Norris W. Potter, *One Nation Indivisible,* teacher's annotated ed. (Columbus, OH: Charles E. Merrill, 1968), 323.

101. Allen and Betts, *History: USA,* 331.

102. Stephen H. Bronz, Glenn W. Moon, and Don C. Cline, *The Challenge of America* (New York: Holt, Rinehart and Winston, 1968), 488.

103. Allan O. Kownslar and Donald B. Frizzle, *Discovering American History* (New York: Holt, Rinehart and Winston, 1967), 507–10.

104. Martin W. Sandler, Edwin C. Rozwenc, and Edward C. Martin, *The People Make a Nation* (Boston: Allyn and Bacon, 1971), 341.

105. Joyce Appleby, Alan Brinkley, Albert S. Broussard, James M. McPherson, and Donald A. Ritchie, *Discovering Our Past: A History of the United States* (Bothell, WA: McGraw Hill, 2013), 506.

106. James West Davidson and Michael B. Stoff, *America: History of Our Nation: Civil War to Present* (New York: Prentice Hall, 2011), 557; Emma J. Lapsansky-Werner, Peter B. Levy, Randy Roberts, and Alan Taylor, *United States History: Reconstruction to the Present* (Upper Saddle River, NJ: Pearson, 2010).

107. Appleby et al., *Discovering Our Past,* 506.

108. Gerald A. Danzer, J. Jorge Klor de Alva, Larry S. Krieger, and Louis E. Wilson, *The Americans* (McDougall Littell, 2002), 367; Lapsansky-Werner et al., *United States History.*

109. Danzer et al., *The Americans,* 367.

110. Danzer et al., *The Americans,* 368.

111. Danzer et al., *The Americans,* 368.

112. Appleby et al., *Discovering our Past,* 506.

113. Lapsansky-Werner et al., *United States History,* 90.

114. Davidson and Stoff, *America: History of Our Nation,* 557.

115. Davidson and Stoff, *America: History of Our Nation*, 556, 557; Lapsansky-Werner et al., *United States History*, 90; Danzer et al., *The Americans*, 348B, 367.

116. This works similarly to Derrick P. Alridge's discussion of Martin Luther King as the "embodiment of the civil rights movement [allowing] textbook writers and publishers to condense a large body of information within the life of an individual, event, or series of events." Derrick P. Alridge, "The Limits of Master Narratives in History Textbooks: An Analysis of Representations of Martin Luther King, Jr.," *Teachers College Record* 108 (2006): 662–86.

117. Brown & Brown, "Strange Fruit Indeed," 45; Anthony Brown, "Counter-Memory and Race: An Examination of African-American Scholars' Challenges to Early Twentieth Century K–12 Historical Discourse," *Journal of Negro Education* 79, no. 1 (2010): 54–63.

118. Charles H. Coleman and Edgar B. Wesley, *America's Road to Now* (Boston: D. C. Heath, 1942), 386; Andrew C. McLaughlin, *A History of the American Nation* (New York: D. Appleton, 1899), 484–85. Allen and Betts, *History: USA*, 331, refers to "hoodlumism," which implies "hoodlums." Jacques Wardlow Redway, *The Redway School History* (New York: Silver, Burdett, 1910), 351–52; Stephen H. Bronz, Glenn W. Moon, and Don C. Cline, *The Challenge of America* (New York: Holt, Rinehart and Winston, 1968), 488.

119. Brown & Brown, "Strange Fruit Indeed," 56.

120. Jacquelyn Dowd Hall, "The Long Civil Rights Movement and the Political Uses of the Past," *Journal of American History* 91, no. 4 (March 2005): 1239.

121. Gilman, *A History of the American People*, 558–59.

122. Andrew C. McLaughlin, *A History of the American Nation* (New York: D. Appleton, 1899), 484–85.

123. Hall, "The Long Civil Rights Movement," 1233–63.

124. Gilman, *A History of the American People*, 558–59.

125. Fremont P. Wirth, *The Development of America* (Boston: American Book Company, 1939), 415.

126. Mabel B. Casner and Ralph Henry Gabriel, *The Rise of American Democracy* (New York: Harcourt, Brace, 1938), 416.

127. Beverly A. Burrell, Diane P. Detwiler, Marilyn J. Ryan, and Richard E. Gonzales, *America! America!* 2nd ed., teacher's annotated ed. (Glenview, IL: Scott, Foresman, 1982), 408.

128. Current, De Conde, and Dante, *United States History*, 343.

129. George F. Holmes, *New School History of the United States* (New York: University Publishing, 1886), 6, 221, 237, 266.

130. Dickson, *American History for Grammar Schools*, 462–63.

131. Leonard C. Wood, Ralph H. Gabriel, and Edward L. Biller, *America: Its People and Values*, 2nd ed. (Harcourt Brace Jovanovich, 1975), 485.

132. LaGarrett J. King, Christopher Davis, and Anthony L. Brown, "African American History, Race and Textbooks: An Examination of the Works of Harold O. Rugg and Carter G. Woodson," *Journal of Social Studies Research* 36, no. 4 (2012): 359–86.

133. Hall, "The Long Civil Rights Movement," 1233.

10

# Wade Hampton's Last Parade

## *Memory of Reconstruction in the 1970 South Carolina Tricentennial*

BRUCE E. BAKER

On September 2, the Red Shirts were riding their horses proudly down the main streets of Anderson, South Carolina, cheering for their hero, Wade Hampton. The ancient cannon known as the "Old Reformer" had been hauled out and took a prominent place in the parade, reminding the crowd of the determination of white Democrats that the Republican government that had run South Carolina for eight years during Reconstruction would be removed, one way or the other. Speeches were made about the glories of the Palmetto State's history, the perfidy of carpetbaggers, and the meddling influence of a federal government dominated by Yankees who understood little and cared less about how things were done in the South. Children cheered and flashcubes popped, capturing the moment for posterity. Flashcubes? Indeed, for this parade was but a reenactment of the September 2, 1876, parade, and it was held as part of South Carolina's celebration of the state's Tricentennial in 1970, three hundred years since the first settlement at Charles Towne Landing.

Anderson enthusiastically celebrated the campaign of violence, fraud, and intimidation that marked the end of Reconstruction and the end to African American political power in South Carolina in the same week that all the state's public schools were finally integrated. But this essay will not dwell only on commemorations of Reconstruction of this sort, because by the end of the 1960s, they were no longer typical in the state. Certainly, for decades red-shirted men (and women and children, for that matter) had paraded and celebrated Wade Hampton's 1876 campaign across the entire state, and these invocations of Reconstruction were meant, as a kind of historical homeopathy, to ward off the dangers of a second Reconstruction.[1]

But the second Reconstruction came anyway. It changed South Carolina, and, what is perhaps more surprising, it even changed the way South Carolinians came to see and represent the history of their state, at least for a while. The Jim Crow system was justified by what I have described elsewhere as a "white supremacist narrative of Reconstruction," but in the 1970 celebration of the state Tricentennial in South Carolina, that old story had mostly played out.[2] It was not necessarily replaced by a new, celebratory memory of Reconstruction, but even an end to the old ways of commemorating Reconstruction could be counted a success of some sort. For an all-too-brief moment in the 1970s, South Carolina came closer than it ever had before—or has since—to creating a civic culture of racial inclusiveness that drew the support of the public, to having an economic system that was at least further from desperation than usual, and to telling a story of its own past that did not pivot around white unity on the basis of racial exclusion. Political and economic forces tore apart much of the foundation for that change during the 1980s and 1990s, but by then enough had changed that the white supremacist narrative of Reconstruction never found the level of public acceptance and was never officially endorsed by public figures as it had been up to the early 1960s. Perhaps that is all the progress we can hope for when considering the South in the late twentieth century.

By the late 1960s, as plans for the Tricentennial were being formed, South Carolina was in the midst of a period of significant if subtle change. The civil rights movement had played out in dramatic form on the streets of Little Rock in the late 1950s, at lunch counters in Greensboro and around the South in 1960, at bus stations and city parks and university campuses across the Deep South, with prayers and hymns, police dogs and fire hoses and billy clubs, but throughout this, South Carolina had remained relatively calm. Yet changes beneath the surface would disrupt that calm in the last few years of the 1960s. South Carolina was more fortunate than many southern states in that older structures remained strong enough to contain disorder while new, more progressive structures emerged within them. In politics, the old rings and alliances maintained much of their strength, and the reformers and modernizers worked within them. By the time African Americans reentered politics in South Carolina, a fairly orderly transfer of power to a younger generation of Democrats had taken place, while the Republican Party had established itself as the home for those who opposed all forms of desegregation.[3] In the economy as well, the textile industry remained strong, reaching its peak in the early 1970s, but even in this time of success, political leaders took strong steps to diversify the state's industrial base and recruit foreign companies that would replace the "easy come, easy go" jobs of the textile industry when it eventually began to collapse in the early 1980s.[4]

Until the middle of the 1960s, South Carolina's political world had long been defined by a handful of informal political groupings dominated by a few strong figures. The Barnwell Ring was "a loose confederation of small-county legislators who in recent years had drawn their allegiance more from the rural nature of their causes than from the geographic proximity to Barnwell County."[5] Sol Blatt, the long-time Speaker of the House of Representatives, and Edgar A. Brown in the Senate had been the two leading figures of the Barnwell Ring since the 1920s.[6] Cities had different political alliances, and one powerful group was the Broad Street Gang in Charleston, "a political mechanism named for Charleston's elite business and law-firm address."[7] When Robert McNair became governor in 1965 after a term as lieutenant governor, one of the first things he had to deal with was the reapportionment of the state legislature as a result of a federal lawsuit enforcing the one-man, one-vote principle, which ultimately weakened the rural power centers like the Barnwell Ring.[8]

The other major change in the 1960s was the return of the Republican Party and two-party politics to South Carolina. In 1962, Republicans took two seats in the state legislature and led a credible statewide campaign for US Senate, and in 1964, US senator Strom Thurmond very publicly switched from the Democratic Party to the Republican Party.[9] As the Democrats at a national level became tied to the advocacy of civil rights, a space emerged at the state level for a party that would oppose civil rights. While Democrats in South Carolina certainly did oppose civil rights, the leaders of the party, especially Ernest Hollings and Robert McNair, were what one historian has classed as "polite segregationists," preferring to use legal delay tactics rather than rabble-rousing extralegal confrontations. This left the field open for the Republican Party to become the home of die-hard segregationists in the state, especially with Strom Thurmond's leadership after 1964. The Republicans continued to draw in significant political figures in the mid-1960s who hoped to build their political careers on being hard-line segregationists, but in many ways, the time for that political strategy to work in the South had come and gone.[10] Because powerful Democrats such as Hollings, McNair, and Donald Russell took a more conciliatory approach to race and yet maintained powerful ties to the state's traditional political groupings, as long as the Democrats could hold off the Republicans at the polls, the state had a much better chance of desegregating more peacefully than the other states of the Deep South did.

No white person deserves more credit for the improvement in race relations that occurred in South Carolina by 1970 than Robert McNair, though he served as governor during two of the state's most infamous racial conflicts of the civil rights era. Orangeburg was the center of higher education for African Americans in the state, home to both Claflin College and South Carolina State College. As a result, the town had long nurtured an educated and activist black middle class.[11] With the passage of the Voting Rights Act in 1965, the political significance of Orangeburg only increased, and much of the mobilization of the 1960s for African American rights was tied to South Carolina State College. When McNair took office early in 1967, a controversy over leadership of this black institution tested the patience of African Americans in the state. McNair accepted the need for change, and he tried to navigate between the intransigence of much of the South Carolina white establishment, who did not want to yield political control, however slight, to black South Carolinians, and a restive group of African American activists based at South Carolina State College. Eventually, protests over a bowling alley in Orangeburg that remained segregated into 1968 and a lack of coordination and leadership among the state's various law enforcement agencies led to the Highway Patrol shooting dead four unarmed black protesters in the Orangeburg Massacre.[12] Later in 1968, a strike at the hospital of the Medical University of South Carolina in Charleston brought national attention to the low wages and discriminatory treatment faced by the black workers there. The workers affiliated with New York Local 1199 of the Hospital and Nursing Home Employees Union, and later the Southern Christian Leadership Conference, got involved in supporting the strike. McNair and state leaders worked to avert violence, but refused to budge an inch on union recognition. The largest civil rights protests Charleston had ever seen continued for weeks, and eventually, many of the issues of the strike were settled through negotiation, though without union recognition.[13]

McNair opposed civil rights unionism and failed to avoid bloodshed in Orangeburg, but his handling of school desegregation was statesmanlike, especially in comparison to the governors of many other southern states. Many segregationists in South Carolina had assumed that the election of Richard Nixon as president would ease the pressure to obey *Brown v. Board of Education,* but in 1969 it became clear that pressure from the federal government to desegregate would not abate. In *Alexander v. Holmes County,* the Supreme Court announced that "the obligation of every school district is to terminate dual school systems at once and to operate now and hereafter only unitary schools." Two of the twenty-one school districts in South Carolina that were still segregated—Greenville and Darlington—were integrated in the middle of the academic year 1969–1970. Speaking to South Carolinians in a televised address, McNair said, "We have run out of courts and we have run out of time. We must admit to ourselves that we have pretty well run the legal course and the time has come for compliance or defiance. In South Carolina, we have always followed the law. We will continue to do so. We will comply with the court rulings." Aside from a minor riot in one small town, desegregation occurred without incident in the state where the legal fight had started over twenty years earlier.[14]

Things looked fairly promising on the economic front as well. Ernest Hollings had laid the groundwork for economic development during his tenure as governor in the early 1960s, and several German and Swiss companies arrived in the upstate in the late 1960s.[15] The 1960s had been a good time for the textile industry as well, and the "first wave of African American workers [were] hired in the industry in the mid-to-late 1960s." Employment levels in textiles, which accounted for nearly half of South Carolina's manufacturing jobs, continued to increase until 1973.[16]

The optimistic economic environment encouraged approving gazes toward the past, and the third quarter of the twentieth century saw a number of historical celebrations at both the national and state level. The most ambitious was the Civil War Centennial. Authorized by Congress in 1957, the Civil War Centennial was intended primarily as a celebration of American values on the cultural battlefield of the Cold War, but it ran into the sand as the civil rights movement intensified during the Centennial, complicating the goal of celebrating the old-fashioned narrative of the Civil War that failed to account for its emancipatory nature.[17] In the same period, though, any number of states were celebrating the anniversaries of their origins. Texas had celebrated the Centennial of its statehood back in 1945 with a program of events across the state organized by local history societies and schools.[18] In 1957, county committees across Oklahoma sponsored "rodeos, parades, festivals, pioneer days, and Indian ceremonial dances" to mark the fiftieth anniversary of statehood.[19] Minnesota celebrated a Centennial in 1958, Oregon in 1959, and Nevada in 1964.[20] The subject of these commemorations was historical, but part of the argument for them was commercial. As the deputy administrator for the South Carolina Tricentennial explained to the Rotary Club in Greenwood in the early planning stages, "The Tricentennial can mean millions of dollars for South Carolinians" and "could draw millions of tourists who would spend millions of dollars by just spending one night in South Carolina."[21]

The South Carolina Tricentennial Commission was largely a decentralized affair. "The festivities and main expositions will be at the state level," explained Carlee McClendon of the South Carolina Tricentennial Commission (SCTC) in a slightly disingenuous letter to the nation's leading producer of historical pageants, "and are being organized and directed by this Commission's own professional staff."[22] While this was the case for some of the large events, control over how individual communities chose to commemorate the Tricentennial was up to them. McLendon explained that in Cherokee County, "Each South Carolina County or group of counties will develop and carry out special one week events to include tours, special programs in the churches, historic plays, band concerts and other programs of local and national interest."[23] As James M. Barnett, the SCTC's executive director, explained to one correspondent, "Plans for local participation on the county level are completely under the control of the county Tricentennial committees."[24] In this respect, the SCTC was deferring to the power of local elites who controlled historical societies, but we should also see it as part of a broader movement in South Carolina politics of returning control of local affairs to counties, a process culminating in the Local Government Law of 1975.[25] Given the considerable amount of local control ceded to county Tricentennial Commissions, the way various counties across South Carolina celebrated—or simply ignored—Reconstruction tells us something important about the place of Reconstruction in the state's historical memory at the grassroots level.

For the better part of a century, from around 1890 until the late 1950s, public memory of Reconstruction in South Carolina had been used to celebrate Wade Hampton and the overthrow of biracial government, so it is rather surprising to survey the many evocations of state history in 1970 and see so few mentions of Reconstruction. Dillon County's program simply said nothing about the Civil War or Reconstruction, and the brochures for Laurens County listing historic sites and Tricentennial Week activities made no mention of Reconstruction and barely mentioned the Civil War. A brochure for "Historic Winnsboro South Carolina" listed fifty historical sites, mostly houses and buildings, without once mentioning Reconstruction at all.[26] Still, there were bits of the old attitude here and there. In Aiken, some unfortunate students had to dress up as carpetbaggers for their school's "Parade of the Past," while a luckier boy in Gaffney got to portray Wade Hampton in two performances of Alma Elementary School's Tricentennial Pageant.[27] Saluda opened a new museum as part of its celebrations, proudly displaying an original red shirt from Wade Hampton's 1876 campaign.[28]

At the state level, the Tricentennial made a "special effort" to "present a balanced portrayal of the State's past through exhibits in the Tricentennial centers" in Charleston and Greenville that commemorated "the role of Negroes and Indians in the state's development."[29] This inclusive spirit carried over in some places where there was an active effort to integrate black history into the presentation of local history. In Greenville, Sam Zimmerman, a longtime local civil rights activist and the first African American reporter for the *Greenville Piedmont,* published an article in the local newspaper about black dray and hack drivers in the city at the beginning of the twentieth century.[30] Also as part of the Tricentennial, he wrote a booklet titled *Negroes in Greenville County, 1970* that detailed the struggle against Jim Crow there and assessed what else needed to be done to improve the situation of African Americans.[31] The Winnsboro *News and Herald* carried a story about the history of Calvary United Presbyterian Church, which had been established after the Civil War by the Freedmen's Board of the Presbyterian Church, along with a photograph of its pastor, Reverend J. H. Hudson.[32] Blackville, in Barnwell County, used the Tricentennial as an opportunity to establish a county museum, and the chair of that county's Tricentennial Committee "emphasized that the museum was looking for items from Negro citizens 'because they are also a part of the history of Barnwell County.'"[33]

While many South Carolina communities seem to have ignored Reconstruction in 1970, a few did make it a central part of their commemorations. The goal of the Tricentennial was, as David Glassberg says of historical pageants in general, "promoting a sense of local community identity and cohesion amid the pull of competing affiliations."[34] The main idea behind the Tricentennial, of course, was to celebrate the very beginning of the Carolina colony, so that is what most communities focused on. Since all but a tiny part of the state was settled by colonists by the time of the American Revolution, every part of South Carolina had a colonial past of some sort to work with. In a few cases, though, the specifics of local history, and sometimes current events, shifted the focus to Reconstruction instead.

Anderson, in the upstate, was one such example where several layers of history converged to develop a particular local obsession with Reconstruction. The town was founded in 1828 as one of the new courthouse towns, and it lay only a few miles from the village of Pendleton, which had long-standing connections to important state political figures from the Low Country who summered there. When Wade Hampton began his campaign for governor in 1876, the first parade was held in Anderson on September 2, 1876. He was accompanied by Democratic paramilitaries dressed in red shirts, the first appearance of these iconic figures of South Carolina Redemption. In 1926, the state celebrated the semicentennial of the 1876 campaign with a statewide reunion of the Red Shirts in Columbia. When Anderson celebrated the town's centennial two years later, it made 1876 the hinge between the past and the present, the event that made it possible for the area to industrialize and recover from the economic effects of the Civil War and emancipation.[35]

As ever, Anderson's historical celebrations placed most emphasis on Reconstruction and the town's role in resisting and ending it. The Anderson County Tricentennial Celebration Program ran for a full week. On Monday evening and Tuesday afternoon, visitors were treated to a performance of *As You Like It* in Brown Park by the South Carolina Theatre Company.[36] The company was the creation of Milton Dickson, an alumnus of Anderson College.[37] After trying his hand as a magician, Dickson had turned to acting, and in 1964, he had organized the theater company.[38] By 1970, it was "now in its sixth year of touring colleges, universities, community theatres, and high schools throughout the Southeast," specializing in Shakespeare (a later newspaper article described Dickson as "one of the most acclaimed Shakespearean scholars in the United States" and also mentioned that he had "guest starred on such television series as *Perry Mason, Ironside, The Man From U.N.C.L.E., The Man From Atlantis, Get Smart, Bewitched, Hart to Hart, The Dukes of Hazzard,* and *Hawaii Five-O,* among others").[39] The version of *As You Like It* performed in Anderson had been adapted by Dickson to fit the celebration and was set "in the woods of Anderson County, 1876."[40] The themes of *As You Like It* could easily have been adapted to tell the story of 1876, from the traditional point of view of white South Carolinians. It is a story about usurpation, with the rightful rulers of a realm wandering in the forest until the situation is put right.

The printed souvenir program for the celebration continued the emphasis on 1876. There were, predictably, sections on each town in the county, along with headings such as "Our Cultural Heritage," "Our Architectural Heritage," and "Our Industrial Heritage." Along with these broad overviews was only one essay on an individual from the county's history: Wade Hampton. Mary Dodgen Few's essay began by explaining that "During the bitter years from 1865–1876 that followed the War Between the States, the sane voice of reason in South Carolina was that of Wade Hampton." When Hampton returned to the state after the war, he tried to revive his antebellum fortune, but "finding this hopeless under the existing political and financial conditions in the South, he took up the challenge to free his state from oppression and give it again its honored place in the Union."[41] A native of Spartanburg, Few had become interested in the history of the upstate while living in Turkey as a young woman, and she had published a historical novel set in the late eighteenth century in the upstate.[42]

The timing of the entire Tricentennial week in Anderson had more to do with contemporary concerns than historical events: Anderson's public schools finally desegregated in the same week. Schools in next-door Greenville had been integrated in the middle of the previous academic year, but Anderson County and many others had continued to delay until the US Supreme Court decision in *Alexander v. Holmes County* insisted that all public schools start the 1970–1971 school year integrated. Tensions were high in the late summer. When schools in Dillon County had been "instantly integrated" earlier in the year, a mob of two hundred angry, armed whites tried to re-create Little Rock before being driven away by the police.[43] The local media did not improve the racial atmosphere, with the *Anderson Independent* running an advertisement for local radio station WAIM that promised listeners "No Jungle Music."[44] In such a climate, men riding horses wearing red shirts and cheering the leader who put blacks in their place a century before was no mere lighthearted entertainment. It carried a message and a memory of deadly seriousness beneath the surface—and not very far under the surface.

While Anderson had long been dominated by supporters of a white supremacist narrative of Reconstruction, as their Red Shirt parade suggested, Orangeburg had a different experience that reflected the town's historical significance to South Carolina's African American community. Conflict over the Tricentennial at Orangeburg was one small front in a long-running civil rights struggle in the town. While much of the scholarship on the civil rights movement in Orangeburg has focused on the very high-profile campaigns by African American student activists at the two colleges, leading eventually to the Orangeburg Massacre in February 1968, other aspects of the civil rights movement also played out quietly, away from the streets, led not by college students but by their teachers. The South Carolina Tricentennial became part of a behind-the-scenes contest over how to present the county's history and to what extent Orangeburg would integrate not only the present but also the past.

Orangeburg was, as Jack Bass and Jack Nelson observed, "a fountainhead of white ultaconservatism."[45] The leading figures in the Orangeburg Tricentennial Committee were three white men: Thomas R. Wolfe, L. Richard Rhame, and Lawton R. Connor. Rhame was the general manager of the Orangeburg radio station WTND and had been president of the Orangeburg Historical Society since 1955.[46] A 1961 article in the Pittsburgh *Courier* about sit-ins involving students from South Carolina State and Claflin described him as a "pro-segregationist," and he also seems to have been involved in stirring up public opinion in South Carolina against the 1963 desegregation of Clemson University.[47] Another member of the Orangeburg County Tricentennial Committee was Lawton R. Connor. In his mid-thirties, Connor was born at Walnut Grove Plantation at Eutawville, and in 1970, he founded Holly Hill Academy.[48] When schools in Orangeburg County District 3 opened on an integrated basis in September of that year, white parents had the option of sending their children to Connor's school.[49] It would appear that when it came time to form the Orangeburg County Tricentennial Committee, the task was handed to the Orangeburg County Historical Society. The Orangeburg County Historical Society was organized in 1953 "as a social club centered around history," and it "soon assumed the role as protector of Orangeburg's historical heritage." An influential figure in the society's early years was Alexander S. Salley, an Orangeburg native who was the founding editor of the *South Carolina Historical and Genealogical Magazine* and the first state historian.[50]

With members like Rhame and Connor, it is hardly surprising that the Orangeburg County Tricentennial Committee seems to have been uninterested in incorporating African American history into its commemorations. However, with two historically black colleges in town, it was equally inevitable that there would be a cadre of knowledgeable people committed to making African American history part of the story that Orangeburg would tell the world. In February 1968, three African American men met to form the Orangeburg Historical and Genealogical Society.[51] Francis Frederick, an Orangeburg native, was a Claflin graduate and World War II veteran who spent his career as a school principal in the area.[52] The second member of the organization was Dr. Joseph W. Rice Jr., originally from Anderson, South Carolina and a graduate of South Carolina State College who worked as a teacher and educational administrator.[53]

The final founding member of the Orangeburg Historical and Genealogical Society was Dr. Lawrence C. Bryant. A native of North Carolina, Bryant combined training and work as a pastor with an interest in education. He earned a doctorate in education at the University of Virginia in 1959 and taught in Mississippi and Florida before settling in as a professor of education at South Carolina State College in 1960.[54] Bryant had a long-standing interest in genealogy, and once he was in Orangeburg, he turned this interest toward producing biographies of the African American legislators of South Carolina during Reconstruction.[55] Between 1966 and 1970, he published four books of this material and became an important resource for historians studying Reconstruction in South Carolina at this time, such as Peggy Lamson and Sonja H. Stone.[56]

Seeing an announcement of the Orangeburg Historical and Genealogical Society's formation in the newspaper, Rhame wrote to Carlee McClendon, the

SCTC's coordinator of local events, to distance himself and the Orangeburg County Tricentennial Committee from the upstart organization. They were, he pointed out, "connected with the S.C. State College here in Orangeburg and have no affiliation with any local [white] Society." Far from welcoming the involvement of African Americans in the promotion of local history, Rhame admitted to McClendon, "I view the establishment of such an organization with suspicion."[57]

A year later, the preliminary schedule for Orangeburg's Tricentennial week in July 1970 was ready, but Lawton R. Connor complained "that we are not getting to complete cooperation of all areas in our county." "We do regret this," he claimed, "but we have given these areas the opportunity to participate and just haven't been able to generate any interest."[58] Others noticed the gap in the program. Howard G. McClain, the executive director of the Christian Action Council, South Carolina's first racially integrated organization, complained to the executive director of the Tricentennial Commission that "there was *no mention of any recognition of Negroes* in the program. With so much of Orangeburg County's population being Negro and especially with the two black colleges located in the county seat, it seems especially appropriate that some attention be given to Negro history."[59] Segregated by the Orangeburg County Tricentennial Committee, local African American historians nonetheless used the Tricentennial as an occasion to disseminate black history. Dr. Bryant was commissioned to write a book on the topic for the SCTC, but when he submitted the manuscript in 1971, it was rejected because it needed better organization, style, and focus.[60] When *South Carolina Negro Legislators: A Glorious Success, State and Local Officeholders, Biographies of Negro Representatives, 1868–1902* was published three years later, it carried a note at the end of the title: *Commemorating South Carolina Tricentennial, 1970*.

Ultimately, though, the rival organizations in Orangeburg and the pageantry and cod Shakespeare in Anderson was only sound and fury, signifying nothing. South Carolina was changing, and the absence of the white supremacist narrative of Reconstruction from most of the state indicates the readiness of many—most—to accept that. When John C. West took office as governor in January 1971, he used the recent Tricentennial as a way of marking the change that he represented and intended to continue in South Carolina. "Our Tricentennial year," West said, "was a time of reawakening to our history and heritage; it was a time of new awareness of the essential character and strength of the people of this state. It was also a time to gain new understanding of our particular moment in history, and to view the past and future with a new degree of sensitivity and perspective." West carried on, optimistically, "We can, and we shall, in the next four years eliminate from our government any vestige of discrimination because of race, creed, sex, religion or any other barrier to fairness for all citizens."[61] Much was accomplished, maybe not all West hoped for, but more than anyone could have expected a decade or two earlier. Broader changes in national and regional politics and the sad effects of the state's necrotic textile industry by the mid-1980s shifted historical memory yet again and eventually brought back the red shirts and reawakened interest in the white supremacist narrative of Reconstruction, but this does not diminish the importance of the change in historical memory of Reconstruction marked by the South Carolina Tricentennial of 1970.

Stories of Reconstruction had been a constant clamor in the historical memory of South Carolina for generations, but by the 1970s that had turned to stillness. Just at the moment when the work of revisionist scholars was finally winning the argument in the history books, most South Carolinians simply stopped thinking about Reconstruction. Michel-Rolph Trouillot suggests that the past can be silenced at four different points. Events may not be recorded at all, so there are no sources to work with, or the sources may not be gathered into the archives that historians will eventually consult. The third silencing is when facts are retrieved from the archives to craft narratives, and all three of these problems had bedeviled historians of Reconstruction, but by the 1970s, they had been overcome. Instead, I believe, it was Trouillot's fourth silencing that removed Reconstruction from the historical memory of South Carolinians: "the moment of retrospective significance (the making of *history* in the final instance)."[62] If South Carolinians had used memory of Reconstruction for generations as a way to argue about black citizenship, with whites using horror stories about "Negro domination" to ward it off and African Americans holding Reconstruction up as an unfinished revolution, then once African Americans could vote and hold office, could enter public life on an equal basis, and could send their children to desegregated schools, then the salience of memories of Reconstruction was gone, at least for a while.

Nothing illustrates this silencing better than an unnaming that happened in 1970. A hundred years before, B. F. Whittemore, a white Bostonian who had served as a chaplain in the 53rd Massachusetts, had worked for the Freedmen's Bureau to establish schools in eastern South Carolina. One of those he set up in Conway in 1870 was named for him. Whittemore went on to bigger and better things as the congressman for South Carolina's First District. For the next century, Whittemore School, in various guises, was the center of education for African Americans in Horry County. But when integration came, it came on white terms.[63] A federal Department of Education report noted that schools that had been "named after men and women of special significance to the black community" often had their names changed.[64] Horry County was one of the counties that, as historian Anthony Stanonis puts it, "dragged its feet on integration plans in 1970."[65] An article in the Tricentennial edition of the nearby *Florence Morning News* reminded readers that "Whittemore School in Conway was named for B. F. Whittemore, a white carpetbagger from Boston who came South during the Reconstruction period after the Civil War and served as a member of the U.S. House of Representatives from the First South Carolina District."[66] When the county finally was forced to integrate its schools, it changed the names of all six of its black schools, stripping B. F. Whittemore's name from both Whittemore High School and Whittemore Elementary School.[67] The history of one of Reconstruction's most enduring accomplishments for African Americans in Horry County was removed from public memory in one last petulant stroke.[68]

Recent events are a bit more encouraging, though. African Americans in Horry County (known for good reason as the "Independent Republic") refused to forget Whittemore, both the school and the man it was named for. In 2011, the South Carolina Department of Archives and History unveiled a new historical marker at the site of Whittemore School that acknowledged B. F. Whittemore's background in the Union army and the Freedmen's Bureau and noted his service in Congress and the South Carolina Senate.[69] Even the darker aspects of South Carolina's Reconstruction history are getting new attention more recently. In March 2016 a historical marker in North Augusta named and remembered the seven African Americans murdered in the Hamburg Massacre, a turning point in the troubled election campaign of 1876.[70] Perhaps, as the sesquicentennial of Reconstruction proceeds, South Carolina is opening a new chapter of its relationship to its own past.

NOTES

1. Bruce E. Baker, *What Reconstruction Meant: Historical Memory in the American South* (Charlottesville: University of Virginia Press, 2007).

2. Baker, *What Reconstruction Meant,* 6.

3. Jack Bass and Walter De Vries, *The Transformation of Southern Politics: Social Change and Political Consequence since 1945* (New York: Basic Books, 1976), 257–65; Philip G. Grose, *South Carolina at the Brink: Robert E. McNair and the Politics of Civil Rights* (Columbia: University of South Carolina Press, 2006), 1–21; Philip G. Grose, *Looking For Utopia: The Life and Times of John C. West* (Columbia: University of South Carolina Press, 2011), 98–144. Unlike much of South Carolina's history, the post–World War II period is quite neglected, probably because it offers relatively little of the sort of freakery that historians expect from the Palmetto State.

4. Timothy Minchin, *Hiring the Black Worker: The Racial Integration of the Southern Textile Industry, 1960–1980* (Chapel Hill: University of North Carolina Press, 1999), 9–10; Marko Maunula, *Guten Tag, Y'all: Globalization and the South Carolina Piedmont, 1950–2000* (Athens: University of Georgia Press, 2009), 57–73. The phrase "easy come, easy go" to refer to the textile industry's relationship with the Carolina Piedmont comes from David Carlton, "The Rise and Fall of the Textile South: A Retrospective," paper presented at "Our Past Before Us: The Search for the South Carolina Upcountry," Clemson University, 9 March 2007.

5. Grose, *South Carolina at the Brink,* 11.

6. Grose, *South Carolina at the Brink,* 12.

7. Grose, *South Carolina at the Brink,* 93.

8. Grose, *South Carolina at the Brink,*138.

9. Grose, *South Carolina at the Brink,* 106; Joseph Crespino, *Strom Thurmond's America* (New York: Hill & Wang, 2012), 165–84.

10. Philip G. Grose, *Looking For Utopia: The Life and Times of John C. West* (Columbia: University of South Carolina Press, 2011), 124.

11. Jack Bass and Jack Nelson, *The Orangeburg Massacre,* 2nd ed. (Macon, GA: Mercer University Press, 1984), 8.

12. Grose, *South Carolina at the Brink,* 187–97; Bass and Nelson, *Orangeburg Massacre.*

13. Grose, *South Carolina at the Brink,* 241–62.

14. Grose, *South Carolina at the Brink,* 266–81; Crespino, *Strom Thurmond's America,* 230–36.

15. Maunula, *Guten Tag, Y'all,* 59–66.

16. Timothy Minchin, *Hiring the Black Worker: The Racial Integration of the Southern Textile Industry, 1960–1980* (Chapel Hill: University of North Carolina Press, 1999), 5 (quotation), 10.

17. Robert J. Cook, *Troubled Commemoration: The American Civil War Centennial, 1961–1965* (Baton Rouge: Louisiana State University Press, 2007); David W. Blight, *Race and Reunion: The Civil War in American Memory* (Cambridge, MA: Harvard University Press, 2001).

18. "TEXAS CENTENNIAL OF STATEHOOD," *Handbook of Texas Online,* http://www.tshaonline.org/handbook/online/articles/lkt02, accessed 31 July 2014. Published by the Texas State Historical Association.

19. Linda D. Wilson, "Semicentennial of Statehood," *Encyclopedia of Oklahoma History and Culture,* http://digital.library.okstate.edu/encyclopedia/entries/s/se010.html, accessed 31 July 31 2014.

20. David Kludas, "Centennial Exposition of 1959," *The Oregon Encyclopedia,* www.oregonencyclopedia.org/articles/centennial_exposition_of_1959/, accessed 31 July 2014; Minnesota Historical Society, "Statehood Centennial Commission Records," Minnesota Historical Society, http://www.mnhs.org/collections/upclose/centennial.php, accessed 31 July 2014; Nevada, Centennial Commission, *Final Report of the Nevada Centennial Commission* (Reno: Reno Printing Co., 1964).

21. "Each County Can Have A Part In Tricentennial Celebration," Greenwood *Index-Journal,* 28 February 1968, p. 20.

22. Carlee McClendon to Wayne C. Lemmon, 23 August 1968, Miscellaneous Alphabetical File, Local Events Files, 1967–1971, Tricentennial Commission S219002, South Carolina Department of Archives and History, Columbia, South Carolina (henceforth SCTC).

23. "Historic Sites Here Are Visited," *Gaffney Ledger,* 28 June 1968, p. 3.

24. James M. Barnett to Rev. Howard G. McClain, 20 May 1969, Orangeburg folder, County Correspondence, 1968–1971, SCTC.

25. Charlie B. Tyer, "County Government in the Palmetto State," *The South Carolina Governance Project,*
http://www.ipspr.sc.edu/grs/SCCEP/Articles/county%20government.*htm 1 January 2014.*

26. County Correspondence, 1968–1971, SCTC.

27. "Crowning Of May Queens Starts Day's Activities," *Aiken Standard,* 30 April 1970, p.1; "Alma Elementary Pageant Honors State's Birthday," *Gaffney Ledger,* 8 April 1970, p. 5.

28. "Saluda Tricentennial Week To Include Museum Opening," Greenwood *Index-Journal,* 17 July 1970, p. 7.

29. "State Tricentennial Centers," *Florence Morning News,* 12 August 1970, p. 4.

30. Clipping from the Greenville *News,* 26 October 1970, 2D, in Greenville folder, County Correspondence, 1968–1971, SCTC.

31. W. H. Crosby Jr., "Reporter gets top post in S.C. schools," Baltimore *Afro-American,* 26 May 1973, p. 16; Samuel L. Zimmerman, *Negroes in Greenville, 1970: An Exploratory Approach* (Greenville: South Carolina Tricentennial, 1970)

32. Clipping from Winnsboro *News and Herald,* 21 May 1970, in Fairfield folder, County Correspondence, 1968–1971, SCTC.

33. Clipping from Columbia *State,* September 8, 1969, B1, in Barnwell folder, County Correspondence, 1968–1971, SCTC. For the changes the civil rights movement brought to the relationship between African Americans and local historical memory in the South, see W. Fitzhugh Brundage, *The Southern Past: A Clash of Race and Memory* (Cambridge, MA: Harvard University Press, 2005), 270–315.

34. David Glassberg, *American Historical Pageantry: The Uses of Tradition in the Early Twentieth Century* (Chapel Hill: University of North Carolina Press, 1990), 151–52.

35. Baker, *What Reconstruction Meant,* 19, 56–60; Bruce E. Baker, "Devastated by Passion and

Belief: Remembering Reconstruction in the Twentieth-Century South" (PhD diss., University of North Carolina at Chapel Hill, 2003), 258–65.

36. "Anderson County 1670–1970: Fact, Fiction, Fantasy," Anderson folder, County Correspondence, 1968–1971, SCTC.

37. *Anderson College—Columns/Sororian Yearbook—Class of 1970* (Anderson, SC: n.p., 1970), 194.

38. "Excerpts of Plays By Shakespeare Set," *Edwardsville (Ill.) Intelligencer,* 18 April 1972, p. 7.

39. "Drama Pros Perform Thurs.," *Smoke Signals* [Murfreesboro, NC], 28 October 1970; "Fairmount Holds Shakespeare Day," *Calhoun Times and Gordon County News,* 23 April 1986, 5B.

40. *As You Like It* program flyer, Anderson folder, County Correspondence, 1968–1971, SCTC.

41. "Anderson County Tricentennial Celebration" souvenir program, Anderson folder, County Correspondence, 1968–1971, SCTC.

42. "Mrs. Few to Be Guest At OH Dinner," Hendersonville, NC *News-Times,* 21 May 1974, p. 14; Mary Dodgen Few, *Carolina Jewel: A Novel* (Greenwood, SC: Carolina Editions, 1970).

43. Grose, *South Carolina at the Brink,* 276–81.

44. Anderson *Independent,* September 2, 1970.

45. Bass and Nelson, *Orangeburg Massacre,* 7.

46. Charles A. Alicoate, ed., *Radio Annual-Television Year Books, Twenty-Sixth Annual Edition, 1963* ([New York : Radio Television Daily, 1963]), 504; minutes of the Orangeburg City Council meeting of 5 April 1955, p. 2637, available on http://www.orangeburg.sc.us, accessed 27 October 2013.

47. "Hot Battle Over 'Endorsement' of Carolina Sit-Ins," Pittsburgh *Courier,* 17 January 1961, p. 17; H. Lewis Suggs, "Harvey Gantt and the Desegregation of Clemson University, 1960–1963," in Skip Eisiminger, ed., *Integration With Dignity: A Celebration of Harvey Gantt's Admission to Clemson* (Clemson, SC: Clemson University, 2003), 24, 39n26.

48. Obituary for Lawton Rutledge Connor, Columbia *State,* 21 December 2008; Lawton R. Connor, *The Building of Holly Hill Academy* (Orangeburg, SC: Quality Printing, 1971).

49. "More Southern Schools Begin Integrated Classes," Spartanburg *Herald-Journal,* September 6, 1970, p. 3.

50. "Orangeburg History," *Orangeburg County Historical Society,* http://www.orangeburgh.org/who-we-are, 8 January 2014; Brundage, *Southern Past,* 125–26; Charles H. Lesser, *The Palmetto State's Memory: A History of the South Carolina Department of Archives and History* (Columbia: South Carolina Department of Archives and History, 2009).

51. L. Richard Rhame to Carlee McClendon, 19 February 1968 and 28 February 1968, in Orangeburg folder, County Correspondence, 1968–1971, SCTC; Lawrence C. Bryant, *Autobiography of Lawrence C. Bryant* (Orangeburg, SC: Lawrence C. Bryant, 1971), 223.

52. Obituary for Francis Frederick, Orangeburg *Times and Democrat,* 8 May 2011.

53. South Carolina General Assembly, "Joint Legislative Committee Candidate Screening for College and University Boards of Trustees, Tuesday, March 26, 2013," 28–29, http://www

.scstatehouse.gov/CommitteeInfo/Universities&CollegesScreeningCommittee/Transcripts/March26PM2013ScreeningHearingTranscript.pdf.

54. Obituary for Lawrence C. Bryant, Orangeburg *Times and Democrat,* 15 June 2010.

55. Bryant, *Autobiography.*

56. Lawrence C. Bryant, *Negro Legislators in South Carolina, 1865–1894: Preliminary Report* (Orangeburg: School of Graduate Studies, South Carolina State College, 1966); Lawrence C. Bryant, *Negro Lawmakers in the South Carolina Legislature, 1869–1902* (Orangeburg: School of Graduate Studies, South Carolina State College, 1968); Lawrence C. Bryant, *Negro Senators and Representatives in the South Carolina Legislature, 1868–1902* (Orangeburg, SC: n.p., 1968); Peggy Lamson to Lawrence Bryant, 17 October 1969, Box 1, Vol. 4, Lawrence C. Bryant Papers (and other dates); Sonja H. Stone to Lawrence C. Bryant, 27 November 1972, Box 5, Vol. 22, Lawrence Chesterfield Bryant Papers, David M. Rubenstein Rare Book & Manuscript Library, Duke University, Durham, North Carolina (henceforth LCBP).

57. L. Richard Rhame to Carlee McClendon, 28 February 1968, in Orangeburg folder, County Correspondence, 1968–1971, SCTC.

58. L. R. Connor to Carlee McClendon, 17 April 1969, in Orangeburg folder, County Correspondence, 1968–1971, SCTC.

59. Howard G. McClain to James Barnett, 19 May 1969, in Orangeburg folder, County Correspondence, 1968–1971, SCTC.

60. Lawrence C. Bryant to The Probate Judge, New Orleans, 5 March 1970, Box 4, Vol. 15, LCBP; R. K. Ackerman to Lawrence C. Bryant, September 14, 1971, Box 5, Vol. 21, LCBP; Lawrence C. Bryant, *South Carolina Negro Legislators: A Glorious Success; State and local officeholders; biographies of Negro representatives, 1868–1902* (Orangeburg: South Carolina State College, 1974).

61. John C. West, "Inaugural Address, 1971," in John Carl West Papers, Public, Governor South Carolina Political Collections, University of South Carolina, Columbia, SC, http://digital.tcl.sc.edu/cdm/compoundobject/collection/jwest/id/276/rec/2.

62. Michel-Rolph Trouillot, *Silencing the Past: Power and the Production of History* (Boston: Beacon Press, 1995), 26.

63. A very thorough study of Whittemore School is available in Janice Bock Modjeski, "The Whittemore School: An African-American School in Horry County, South Carolina, 1870–1970" (PhD diss., University of South Carolina, 1999).

64. American Friends Service Committee et al., *The Status of School Desegregation in the South, 1970* (Philadelphia: American Friends Service Committee, 1970), 52.

65. Anthony J. Stanonis, *Faith in Bikinis: Politics and Leisure in the Coastal South since the Civil War* (Athens: University of Georgia Press, 2014), 136.

66. "School Is Named For Carpetbagger," *Florence Morning News,* 4 October 1970, p. 4H.

67. American Friends Service Committee et al., *The Status of School Desegregation in the South,* 53.

68. An excellent overview of this transition and the losses incurred is David S. Cecelski, *Along Freedom Road: Hyde County, North Carolina and the Fate of Black Schools in the South*

(Chapel Hill: University of North Carolina Press, 1994). For its effects on historical memory, see Brundage, *Southern Past,* 274–84.

69. Lindsey Theis, "Historical Marker at Whittemore Park Unveiled," *ABC 15 News,* 18 June 2011, http://origin-www.carolinalive.com/news/story.aspx?id=631311, accessed 21 September 2015.

70. James Folker, "Black victims of 1876 Hamburg Massacre get historical marker," *Augusta Chronicle,* 6 March 2016, http://chronicle.augusta.com/news/metro/2016–03–06/black-victims-1876-hamburg-massacre-get-historical-marker, accessed 27 March 2016.

# Contributors

SHAWN LEIGH ALEXANDER is associate professor and graduate director of African and African American Studies and director of the Langston Hughes Center at the University of Kansas. The author of *An Army of Lions: The Struggle for Civil Rights before the NAACP* and *W. E. B. Du Bois: An American Intellectual and Activist,* he has also edited an anthology of T. Thomas Fortune's writings, *T. Thomas Fortune, the Afro-American Agitator* and a collection on the racial violence after the Civil War, *Reconstruction Violence and the Ku Klux Klan Hearings,* and he has written the introduction to a reprint of William Sinclair's classic 1905 study, *The Aftermath of Slavery: A Study of the Condition and Environment of the American Negro.*

BRUCE E. BAKER (coeditor) earned his MA in folklore and his PhD in history at the University of North Carolina at Chapel Hill. His first book was *What Reconstruction Meant: Historical Memory in the American South*, and he has also published widely on lynching, labor history, the cotton trade, and Reconstruction in the South. He is coeditor of the journal *American Nineteenth Century History* and a lecturer in US history at Newcastle University.

JUSTIN BEHREND received his PhD from Northwestern University. His first book was *Reconstructing Democracy: Grassroots Black Politics in the Deep South after the Civil War*, and he has published on slave rebellions, urban history, and the legacies of emancipation. Currently he is an associate professor of history at SUNY–Geneseo.

W. FITZHUGH BRUNDAGE is William B. Umstead distinguished professor of history at the University of North Carolina–Chapel Hill. He has published extensively on southern history and historical memory, including *The Southern*

*Past: A Clash of Race and Memory* and *Lynching in the New South: Georgia and Virginia, 1880–1930.* He has also edited several volumes, including *Under Sentence of Death: Lynching in the South; Where These Memories Grow: History, Memory, and Southern Identity;* and most recently, *Beyond Blackface: African Americans and the Creation of Popular Culture, 1890–1930.*

MARK ELLIOTT is associate professor of history at the University of North Carolina–Greensboro and received his PhD from New York University. His first book, *Colorblind Justice: Albion Tourgée and the Quest for Racial Equality from the Civil War to* Plessy *v.* Ferguson, won the Avery O. Craven Award from the Organization of American Historians in 2007. He is also the coeditor of *Undaunted Radical: The Selected Writings and Speeches of Albion W. Tourgée.*

CAROLE EMBERTON (coeditor) is associate professor of history at SUNY–Buffalo. Her first book, *Beyond Redemption: Race, Violence, and the American South after the Civil War* explored how the cultural logic of Reconstruction-era violence informed the political discourse of freedom, manhood, and citizenship. Her current book project examines the Federal Writers' Project ex-slave narratives and the memories of emancipation.

ELAINE PARSONS is associate professor of history at Duquesne University. Her recent book, *Ku-Klux: The Birth of the Klan after the Civil War* is the first full-length scholarly history of the Reconstruction-era terrorist group since 1971. Her first book was *Manhood Lost: Fallen Men and Redeeming Women in the Nineteenth-Century United States* (2002). Her current project, *Thugs: A Labor History,* traces the experiences and working conditions of violence workers from the Civil War through the Progressive Era.

K. STEPHEN PRINCE is associate professor of history at the University of South Florida and received his PhD from Yale University. He is the author of *Stories of the South: Race and the Reconstruction of Southern Identity, 1865–1915,* which was selected as sole runner-up for the 2015 Book Prize of the Society for U.S. Intellectual History. He is also the author of *Radical Reconstruction: A Brief History with Documents.*

NATALIE J. RING completed her BA in American studies and music at Amherst College and her PhD in history at the University of California–San Diego. She is the author of *The Problem South: Region, Empire, and the New Liberal State, 1880–1930,* which traces the evolution of the idea of the "southern problem" in the context of US colonialism and explains how national reform efforts to modernize the South contributed to the development of early twentieth-century liberalism. Dr. Ring is also the coeditor of *The Folly of Jim Crow: Rethinking the Segregated South.* She is currently associate professor at the University of Texas–Dallas.

SAMUEL L. SCHAFFER is the assistant dean of faculty at St. Albans School in Washington, DC, where he also teaches history, coaches football, and serves as assistant director of college counseling. He received his BA from the University of North Carolina and his PhD from Yale University, where he was also the Cassius Marcellus Clay postdoctoral associate at the Gilder Lehrman Center for the Study of Slavery, Resistance, and Abolition. His manuscript on Woodrow Wilson's generation of white southerners is currently under contract.

JASON MORGAN WARD is associate professor of history at Mississippi State University. He received his PhD in American history from Yale University. He is the author of *Hanging Bridge: Racial Violence and America's Civil Rights Century* and *Defending White Democracy: The Making of a Segregationist Movement and the Remaking of Racial Politics, 1936–1965.*

# Index

*A Fool's Errand* (Tourgée, 1879), 156
*A History of the American People* (Wilson, 1902), 205, 234, 239
Abbott, Lyman, 155, 157
abolitionists, 144, 160, 193, 230
Adams County, Miss., 92, 96
Adams, Herbert Baxter, 193, 232, 239
Adamson, William C., 208
*Advance,* 163
Africa, 44, 214–215
African Americans: as childlike, 71; as politicians, 6, 29, 47, 61, 63–64, 69, 81n36, 84, 91, 101, 105n33, 106n44, 141, 154, 163, 205, 207, 237, 272, 274; database of politicians, 105n38; as primitive, 9, 42; as rapists, 10, 29; as soldiers, 29, 60, 119, 134n18, 146
Afro-American League, 76
"After War Times" (Fortune, 1927), 69, 76–77
*Aftermath of Slavery* (Sinclair, 1905), 77
Aiken, S.C., 268
Alabama Sharecroppers' Union (ASU), 130–131
Alabama, 20, 22, 43–44, 118, 120, 128, 147, 178, 181, 188
Alaska, 231
Alderman, Edwin A., 178, 188
*Alexander v. Holmes County* (1969), 266, 270
Allen, Josephine A. V., 259
Allen, Van S., 228
Alma Elementary School, 268
Alridge, Derrick P., 261n116
Alsace-Lorraine, 211
Ambrosius, Lloyd, 221n71
American Historical Association, 193, 234
American Missionary Association, 146, 157, 169n19
American West, 140
Ames, Adelbert, 88–89
*An Appeal to Caesar* (Tourgée, 1884), 156
Anderson College, 269
Anderson County, S.C., 270
Anderson, John, 230
Anderson, S.C., 10, 262, 269–270, 272
Anglo-Saxon, 26, 28, 62, 152, 178, 180
anticommunists, 42–43
Appleby, Joyce, 247
*Arena,* 161
Arkansas Delta, 36
Armstrong, Samuel Chapman, 146–147, 149–151, 157–158, 161–164, 169n17, 187
*As You Like It,* 269–270
Atlanta, Ga., 129, 158, 163, 173, 236
*Atlantic Monthly,* 46, 182, 205
Augusta, Ga., 204
autobiography, 76, 86, 100, 103n13
Avary, Myrta Lockett, 24
Axis Powers, 45, 48
Aycock, Charles B., 51
Ayers, Edward L., 70

Bailey, Josiah, 35, 39
Bailey, Thomas, 246
Baker, Bruce E., 18, 55n35
Balkans, 173
Ball, William Watts, 38
banditti, 71
Barbour County White Man's Party, 116
Barbour County, Ala., 109, 114–115, 118
Barksdale, Ethelbert, 21, 84
Barnes, Tom, 63–64
Barnett, James M., 267
Barnwell County, S.C., 264, 268
Barnwell Ring, 264
Barrows, Samuel, 154, 160, 170n29
"Bartow Black" (Fortune, 1886), 71–75, 77, 79
Bass, Jack, 271
Bassett, John Spencer, 178
Beale, Howard K., 227, 242
Beard, Charles, 241

Beard, Mary, 241
Bederman, Gail, 170n31
Bennett, Ryan, 109, 113, 121, 132n1
Benton, Elbert Jay, 240
Big Mules, 42
Bilbo, Theodore, 36, 44–45, 49–50
Biloxi, Miss., 182
biracialism, 8, 11, 18, 86, 88, 90, 93, 95–96
*Birmingham Age-Herald,* 188
Birmingham, Ala., 42
*Birth of a Nation* (1915), 9, 42, 47, 60, 85, 139, 175–176, 219n31, 229, 239–241, 246, 249
*Black and White* (Fortune, 1884), 66–67, 71
*Black and White in the Southern States* (Evan, 1915), 194
Black Codes, 22n80
black nationalism, 259
black newspapers, 61, 72
*Black Reconstruction* (Du Bois, 1935), 59, 76–77, 241
Blackford, William T., 123
Blackville, S.C., 268
Blaine, James G., 94, 100
Blair Education Bill, 6, 141–142, 145, 156, 171n47
Blair, Henry W., 141–142
Blatt, Sol, 264
Blight, David W., 62, 175–176
bloody shirt, 11
*Boston Post,* 182
Boston, Mass., 144, 154, 170n29, 275
Botume, Elizabeth Hyde, 150
Bourne, Henry Eldrige, 240
Bowers, Claude, 139
Boyd, Grover, 129, 135n31
Breckinridge, Clifton R., 24
*Bricks Without Straw* (Tourgée, 1884), 156
Brinkerhoff, Roeliff, 155
Britain, 212, 230
British Guiana, 186
Broad Street Gang, 264
*Brown v. Board of Education* (1954), 196, 251, 266
Brown, Anthony L, 228, 250, 253
Brown, Edgar A., 264
Brown, John, 62–63, 252
Brown, Keffrelyn D., 228, 250
Brown, William Garrott, 219n31
Brown, William Wells, 111
Browning, Christopher, 122
Brownlow, William G., 232
Bruce, John E., 61
Brundage, W. Fitzhugh, 60, 257n32
Bryan, William Jennings, 188
Bryant, Lawrence C., 272–273
Bryce, James, 193
Bullock, Rufus, 149
*The Burden of Southern History* (Woodward, 1960), 259
Burgess, John W., 219n31, 242, 254
Burke, Robert E., 243
Burrell, Savilla, 119
Butler Emigration Bill, 143
Butler, Matthew C., 142

Cable, George Washington, 149, 151, 161, 178
Cade, John, 134n9
Cahill, Cathleen, 147
California, 245
Calvary United Presbyterian Church, 268
Cambridge University, 193
Cambridge, Mass., 231
Cameron, Ben, 29–30
Camp Hill, Ala., 130
Carlton, David, 276n4
Carpenter, Joseph, 100
carpetbaggers, 24–25, 37, 41, 43, 45, 47–49, 52n3, 69, 77, 91, 135n26, 165, 186, 233, 268
Cary, N.C., 182
Central Powers, 212
Ceylon, 186
Chalmers, James R., 96–97, 99
Chamberlain, Daniel, 149
Chandler, William E., 141, 143, 148–149
Charles Towne Landing, S.C., 262
Charleston *News and Courier,* 142
Charleston, S.C., 264, 265, 268
Chase, William Calvin, 61
Chattahoochee River, 118, 121
Chattahoochee, Fla., 64
Cheney, Ednah Dow, 150, 157–158
Cherokee County, S.C., 267
Cherokee, 11
*Chicago Defender,* 101
Chicago Fire (1871), 230
Chicago *Inter Ocean,* 163
Chicago, Ill., 22, 100
China, 253

Chipola River, 63
Christian Action Council, 273
*Christian Union,* 163
*The Chronicles of* Aunt *Minervy Ann* (Harris, 1899), 68, 70, 81n36
Civil Rights Act (1866), 230
Civil Rights Act (1875), 70, 91
*Civil Rights Cases* (1883), 70
civil rights movement, 1, 10, 36, 43, 226, 229, 244, 251, 261n116, 263, 277n33
civil rights unionism, 266
*Civil War and Reconstruction in Alabama* (Flemming, 1905), 60
Civil War, 2, 169n19, 177; memory of, 4, 11, 175–176
Civil War Centennial, 266
Claflin College, 265, 271–272
*The Clansman* (Dixon, 1905), 9, 29–30, 41, 47, 60, 85, 229, 239, 249
Clark University, 158, 171n36
*The Clash of Colour* (Mathews, 1925), 194
Clayton, Victoria, 118
Clemenceau, Georges, 212–213, 220n68
Clemson University, 271
Cleveland, Grover, 94, 106n55, 147
Cobb, Ned, 130–132
Cocker, James P., 64
Collier, Tom, 41
Colmer, William, 49
colonies, 166, 174, 184, 188, 191, 213–214; in Africa, 195, 217; of Germany, 211
Columbia University, 18, 48, 85, 176, 178, 231, 235
Columbia, S.C., 40, 120, 205
Columbus, Ga., 126–127
*Commentary,* 196
Commission on Interracial Cooperation (CIC), 129, 191
Communists, 41–43, 130
Compromise of 1877, 7
Concordia Parish, La., 87, 92–93, 106n41
Confederate battle flag, 50
*Congregationalist,* 163
Congress of Industrial Organizations (CIO), 42
Congress, 88, 129
Connecticut, 170n34
Connor, Lawton R., 271, 273
Conservative Manifesto (1937), 39
Constitution, 26, 67, 170n34; amendments, 23, 68; Fifteenth Amendment, 26, 142, 144, 147, 158, 169n10, 213, 247; Reconstruction amendments, 26, 28
constitutional conventions: 1867–1868, 52n4; 1890, Mississippi, 142
Constitutional Education League (CEL), 42
consumers, 8
contraband camps, 119
Conway, S.C., 275
Cooper, John Milton, Jr., 182
Cornell University, 159
corruption, 25, 29, 47, 88, 90, 93, 139, 141, 159, 165, 176
Cotton States and Industrial Exhibition (1895), 163
Coulter, E. Merton, 227, 244
counter-memory, 62, 66, 71, 77, 86–87, 101, 111, 241
Cox, Ernest Sevier, 49
Craighead, Edwin, 191
*The Crisis,* 101
*The Crucible of Race* (Williamson, 1984), 32n5
Crummell, Alexander, 86
Cuba, 8, 165–166, 185, 189, 235

Dabney, Charles W., 178, 187–188
Dabney, Virginius, 46
Dakota Territory, 95
Daniel, Pete, 128
Daniels, Josephus, 207–208
Danville, Va., 68
Darlington County, S.C., 266
Davenport, Charlie, 126
Davis, Christopher, 253
Davis, David Brion, 181
Davis, Jefferson, 182, 204
Dawes Severalty Act (1887), 146–147
Dawes, Henry, 147
DeBardeleben, Charles, 42
debt: in Mississippi, 104n25; during Reconstruction, 89
*Democracy and Race Friction* (Mecklin, 1914), 194
Democratic National Convention (1936), 40
Democrats, 11, 20, 37, 39–40, 84, 86, 98, 100, 106n55, 145, 162, 206; in North, 41; in South Carolina, 263
Dent, Louis, 98

desegregation, 157; of schools in South Carolina, 266, 270–271, 274–275
Deskins, Donald R., Jr., 197
Dickinson, Jonathan Q., 64
Dickson, Marguerite Stockman, 240
Dickson, Milton, 269–270
Dies, Martin, 43
Dillard, James H., 192
Dillon County, S.C., 268, 270
disfranchisement. *See* suffrage
*Division and Reunion* (Wilson, 1893), 206, 233
Dixiecrat revolt (1948), 49–50
Dixon, Frank, 43
Dixon, Thomas, 8, 23, 29, 41–43, 47, 60, 67, 129, 149, 207, 219n31, 239, 249
Douglass, Frederick, 111, 119, 177
Du Bois, W. E. B., 44, 59, 76–78, 85, 111, 157, 231, 236, 240–241
Dunaway, Wilma, 112
Dunbar, Paul Laurence, 257n34
Dunning School, 85–86, 139, 168n4, 176–177, 196, 227, 244, 246, 254
Dunning, William A., 18, 60, 85, 176, 179, 207, 219n31, 234–235, 238, 242, 254
Durham, John, 24

Eastland, James O., 49
Ecuador, 186
education, 144, 156; during Reconstruction, 89–91, 146; reform of, 187
Egypt, Ill., 11
election: of 1868, 230, 247; of 1872, 230; of 1875, 94; of 1876, 1, 40, 97, 144, 262, 268–269, 275; of 1888, 140; of 1892, 162; of 1908, 188; of 1936, 40; of 2008, 197; fraud, 95–96
Elson, Henry William, 237
Ely, Richard T., 239
Emancipation Proclamation, 72, 84, 111
emancipation, 2, 59, 62, 72, 102n3, 111, 132, 160, 163, 179, 213
Emelle, Ala., 129
emigration, 142
empire: American, 8, 164, 167, 172n74, 174, 176; anti-imperialism, 167; German, 166
Enforcement Acts (1870–71), 230, 233, 245, 248
Eng, Robert, 146
England, 193, 212
Espionage Act (1917), 211
*Essays on the Civil War and Reconstruction* (Dunning, 1898), 60, 219n31
Eufala, Ala., 118
Eutawville, S.C., 271
Evans, Lawton B., 236
Evans, Maurice S., 194
evolutionary theory, 180
The *Facts of Reconstruction* (Lynch, 1913), 84–85, 87, 99, 234
Fair Employment Practices Committee (FEPC), 43, 48–49
Farm Security Administration, 131
Farr, James M., 192
fascism, 43, 243
Fayette, Miss., 97
Feimster, Crystal, 119
Feldman, Glenn, 18, 32n5, 52n5
Fenianism, 230
Few, Mary Dodgen, 270
fiction, 8, 18, 25, 69, 75, 139, 150, 156, 229
53rd Massachusetts, 275
54th Massachusetts, 144
filibuster, 39, 43–44
film, 8, 229
Finley, Keith, 55n35
*First Days Among the Contraband* (Botune, 1893), 150
Fisk University, 134n9, 157
Fiske, John, 233
Fite, Emerson David, 240
*Flaming Sword* (Dixon, 1939), 41
Fleming, Walter L., 60, 242
Florida, 61, 69, 169n17, 272
Food Administration, 211
Forbes, Cameron, 189
Forrest, Nathan Bedford, 252
Fort Pillow Massacre, 97
Fortune, Emanuel, 61–63, 65, 69, 75, 77
Fortune, Sarah Jane, 62
Fortune, T. Thomas, 6, 86, 99, 161
Fortune, Timothy, 62
*The Forum*, 141, 147
Fourteen Points, 212, 220n55, 221n74
France, 211–213
Franco-Prussian War (1870), 211
Frank, Leo, 173–174, 191
Franklin, John Hope, 78, 227, 245
fraternal benefit societies, 70

Frazer, Henry, 116
Frederick, Francis, 272
free labor, 3
Freedmen's Aid Society, 150
Freedmen's Board of the Presbyterian Church, 268
Freedmen's Bureau, 63–64, 146, 150, 155, 187, 275
Frissell, Hollis B., 188
Frizzle, Donald B., 246
Frog Level, S.C., 268

*Gabriel Tolliver* (Harris, 1902), 25
Gadsden County, Fla., 63
Gaffney, S.C., 268
Garner, James W., 60, 102n5, 106n47
Garrison, William Lloyd, 193
Garrison, William Lloyd, Jr., 161
Gavagan, Joseph, 39
General Education Board, 187
George Peabody Foundation, 187
Georgia, 35, 41, 48, 118, 141, 173–176, 184, 191, 208, 213, 236
Germany, 8, 49, 195, 211–214
Gerstle, Gary, 178
Gettysburg, reunion in 1913, 175
Gilbert, John, 77
Gilman, Arthur, 231, 251
Gilmore, Glenda, 54n18
Glassberg, David, 269
Godkin, E. L., 165
Google n-gram, 255n12
Grady, Henry W., 18
Granbury, Oscar, 65
Grand Army of the Republic, 11
Grant, Ulysses S., 94, 140, 230
Granville, Ga., 123
Graves, John Temple, 22
Great Depression, 112
Greeley, Horace, 230
Greensborough, Ala., 123
Greenville County, S.C., 266
*Greenville Piedmont,* 268
Greenville, S.C., 268, 270
Greenwood, S.C., 267
Gresham, Walter Q., 94, 106n55
Grierson, Benjamin H., 118, 121
Griffith, D. W., 9, 42, 47, 60, 85, 175, 239
Guadalcanal, Battle of, 45
Guam, 174
guerrilla warfare, 2
Guild, Walter, 21
Guitteau, William Backus, 240
Guntharpe, Viola, 120
Gutman, Herbert, 72, 244

Hague, Parthenia, 118
Haiti, 173–176, 184, 191, 193
Hale, Grace Elizabeth, 18
Hall, Jacquelyn Dowd, 251, 253
Hallowell, Richard, 144, 148–149, 151, 169n10
Hambright, N.C., 24
Hamilton, Alex, 115
Hamilton, Charles M., 69
Hamilton, J. C., 45
Hamm, William, 243
Hampton Institute, 146–147, 161, 164, 170n29, 183, 187, 189–190
Hampton, Wade, 40, 141, 143–144, 148, 262, 268–270
Harper's Ferry, Va., 252
Harris, Joel Chandler, 23, 25, 60, 68, 76, 78, 81n36
Harris, William C., 102n9
Harrison, Benjamin, 162
Hart, Albert Bushnell, 178
Harvard Historical Society, 144, 148
Harvard University, 157, 178, 189, 233, 240
Hawaii, 146, 164, 174–175, 185, 187, 190–191, 235
Hayes, Rutherford B., 61, 71, 100, 145, 148–150, 155, 161, 206
Helena, Ark., 36
Hemphill, John J., 21
Hendrick, Burton J., 199n28
Henry, Nettie, 127, 132
Henry, Nettie 132
Herbert, Hilary A., 20, 24, 141, 168n4, 207, 218n31
Hickman, W. H., 158, 171n36
Hicks, John D., 243
Higginson, Thomas Wentworth, 230
Hines, Anna, 126
Hines, Gabe, 126–127
historians, 204, 225; African American, 9; of civil rights, 44; professional, 8, 9, 18, 44, 85–86, 204–205, 216, 226, 231–232, 234; reactions to textbooks, 228

historical markers, 275
historical memory, historiography of, 4, 13n10
historical narratives, 4
historical pageants, 267, 269–270
historical societies, 267
*A History of the American People* (Wilson, 1902), 210, 215
Hoar, George Frisbee, 141, 149, 162
Hoey, Clyde, 51
Hofstadter, Richard, 245
Hollings, Ernest, 264, 266
Holly Hill Academy, 271
Holmes, George F., 233, 252
Holocaust, survivors of, 122
Holt, Thomas C., 228
Home Guard, 119
hookworm, 186, 188
Horry County, S.C., 275
Hospital and Nursing Home Employees Union, 265
Hotchkiss, Gilbert, 25
House, Edward, 203
Howard University, 150, 164, 1922, 195
Howard, Oliver O., 150, 155, 159
Hudson, J. H., 268
Hunter, Tera, 72

imperialism, 175, 183–184, 188, 225, 235
*Independent,* 163
India, 186
Indian policy, 172n74
Indians, 11–12, 140, 146–147, 149, 151, 153, 169n14, 169n17, 252, 268
industrial education, 151, 154, 157–158, 160–163, 165–166, 190
industry codes, 38
International Labor Defense (ILD), 130
Irish Catholics, 170n34
Irwin, Hannah, 109, 123, 128, 132
Italy, 212

Jackson County, Fla., 63, 69, 77, 79
Jackson, Martin, 125
Jackson, Miss., 47
Jacksonville, Fla., 61
James, James Alton, 236
Janney, Caroline, 176
Japan, 215
Jay, John, 155, 157
Jeanes Foundation, 187
Jefferson County, Ala., 118
Jefferson County, Miss., 97
Jefferson, Thomas, 199n28
Jenkins, Henry, 119
Jim Crow, 17, 86
John F. Slater Fund for the Education of Freedmen, 187
Johns Hopkins University, 193, 205, 231, 236–237, 239
Johnson, Andrew, 230
Johnson, Charles S., 113, 124, 133n9
Johnston, Alexander, 232–233
Johnston, Joseph F., 22
Johnston, Olin, 47–48
Joint Select Committee, 66
journalists, African American, 61
Jubilee, 1
Judson, Henry Pratt, 237

Kamp, Joseph P., 42–43
Kansas City, Mo., 207
Keils, Elias M., 116, 124–125
Kennedy, Craigen, 46
Kennedy, David, 246
Kentucky, 24
King, LaGarrett J., 253
King, Martin Luther, 196, 261n116
Knapp, Seaman A., 178
Knight, Edgar W., 187
Knights of the White Camellia, 238
Know-Nothing Party, 170n34
Kownslar, Allan O., 246
Krug, Mark M., 242
Ku Klux Klan, 10, 29, 30, 36, 45, 60–61, 63–666, 68–69, 71, 73, 77, 80n8, 109, 114, 117, 121, 123, 126–128, 131, 155, 176; 1871 investigation of, 10, 63, 66, 75, 232; Second, 239, 242
*Ku Klux Klan: Its Origin, Growth and Disbandment* (Wilson, 1905), 60

labor unions, 42–43, 70
laissez-faire ideology, 7
Lake Mohonk Friends of the Indian Conferences, 139–172
Lake, Marilyn, 193
Lamar, Lucius Q. C., 94–95, 149

Lamson, Peggy, 272
land redistribution, 48, 109–110, 114, 117, 127, 131, 147
Landon, Alf, 41
Laurens County, S.C., 268
*Le Temps,* 212–213
League of Nations, 204, 209, 212–215
Lee, Robert E., 51, 204
Leech, Jonadeb, 25
*The Leopard's Spots* (Dixon, 1902), 23, 41
Lester, J. C., 60
liberalism, 175, 178, 183, 196; in Britain, 193; in South, 181
Lincoln, Abraham, 1, 160–161; assassination of, 29, 127
Litwack, Leon, 72, 244
Livingston, Abe, 114
Livingstone, W. P., 194
Lodge Federal Elections Bill (1890), 6, 20–21, 31, 141–142, 145, 158
Lodge, Henry Cabot, 20, 141
Logan, Rayford, 244
Louisiana State University, 191
Louisiana, 45, 116, 186
Louisville, Ala., 109–110, 118
Lowcountry, 92, 269
*The Lower South in American History* (Brown, 1902), 219n31
Loyal League, 242
Lusk, James, 100
Lynch, John R., 6, 87, 111, 234
lynching, 10, 17, 19, 32n3, 35, 41, 60, 65, 128–130, 161, 173–174, 191, 193, 235, 257n34; antilynching legislation, 39, 43; antilynching movement, 131, 170n31; statistics, 135n29

Macon County, Ala., 134n9
mammy, 81n36
Marable, Manning, 202n65
Marianna, Fla., 62–66
Martians, 22
Martin, William T., 96
Marx, Karl, 41
Massachusetts, 146, 152, 170n34, 246
Mathews, Basil, 194
Mayo, Armory, 152–153
Mays, Benjamin, 129
Mcallister, Hannah, 113
McCary, William, 92, 105n39
McClain, Howard G., 273
McClellan, James F., 64–65, 77
McClellan, Maggie, 65
McClendon, Carlee, 267, 272
McCulloch, James, 178, 180
McGlone, Robert, 135n35
McKinley, Carlyle, 142
McKinley, William, 165
McKinney, Phillip, 149
McMaster, John Bach, 238
McNair, Robert, 264–265
Meadows, Louis, 127
Meany, Edmond S., 237
Mecklin, John Moffat, 194
Medical University of South Carolina, 265
Memorial Day, 214
memory: aphoristic, 135n35; and group identity, 19; personal, 7, 76
Meridian, Miss., 127
*Merrimack,* 253
Micheaux, Oscar, 8
migration, 129
military occupation, 41, 185, 205
Miller, Kelly, 192, 195–196
Mims, Edwin, 178
Minnesota, 244, 267
minstrelsy, 237
missionaries, 155, 160, 165–166
Mississippi, 21, 23, 26, 35–36, 39, 44–46, 49–50, 66, 84, 94, 99, 116, 129, 142, 186, 272
Mississippi Delta, 92
Mississippi House of Representatives, 88
Mississippi Plan, 45
Mississippi River, 88
Missouri, 141
Mitchell, John, 61
Mitchell, Samuel C., 178, 189
Mobile, Ala., 191
Modoc War, 230
Molotov-Ribbentrop Pact (1939), 43, 54n18
*Monitor,* 253
Montgomery, Ala., 24, 116–118
Moon, Henry Lee, 44
Moore, Ely P., 62
Moran, Thomas Francis, 236–237
Morehouse College, 129
Morgan, Albert T., 95–96

Morgan, B. W., 35
Morgan, Henry, 143
Morgan, John Tyler, 141, 147
Mormons, 252
Mowry, George E., 243
Mudd, William, 118
Murphy, Edgar Gardner, 178, 181, 188–190
museums, 268
Muzzey, David, 235, 238
Myrdal, Gunnar, 139

NAACP, 41, 46–47, 101, 128, 229, 244
Nashville, Tenn., 192
Nast, Thomas, 248
Nat Turner Legion, 42
Natchez District, Miss., 92–93
Natchez, Miss., 88, 91–92, 100, 126
National Child Labor Committee, 189
National Education Association, 239
National Recovery Administration, 38
*The Nation,* 258n66
Nazis, 45
Negro domination, 91, 139, 142, 207, 274
*The Negro Question* (Cable, 1901), 149
*The Negro: The Southerner's Problem* (Page, 1904), 27
Nelson, Jack, 271
Nevada, 267
New Deal, 10, 36–39, 41, 43–44
New England, 162, 203
New Freedom, 203, 208
New Hampshire, 143
New Haven, Conn., 42
New Orleans, La., 116
*New Republic,* 184, 191
New South, 18, 179
New York, 139–172, 155, 188, 252
New York, N.Y., 61, 189, 213, 240, 244
*New York Age,* 161
New York *Globe,* 61
New York State Legislature, 159
*New York Times,* 191, 209, 255n12
*New York Tribune,* 210
*New York World,* 182
Nichols, Matt, 65
Nixon, Richard, 266
Nora, Pierre, 19
Norfolk *Journal and Guide,* 76
North Augusta, S.C., 275
North Carolina, 20–21, 27, 39, 50–51, 141, 143, 150, 186, 199n28, 207, 272
North: abstraction in, 23–24, 26, 30; memory of Reconstruction in, 11, 17
Norton, Charles Elliott, 193

Obama, Barack, 197
Odum, Howard, 46
Ogden, Robert C., 178, 188–190
Ohio, 94
Oklahoma, 267
"Old Reformer," 262
oral tradition, 36
Orangeburg County, S.C., 273
Orangeburg Historical and Genealogical Society, 272–273
Orangeburg Historical Society, 71
Orangeburg Massacre, 265, 271
Orangeburg Tricentennial Committee, 271, 273
Orangeburg, S.C., 10, 40, 265, 271
Oregon, 267
outside agitators, 37, 40, 42, 46, 48, 52n4
Oxford University, 193

Pacific Islands, 167
Page, Thomas Nelson, 25, 27–28, 60, 70, 139, 185, 241
Page, Walter Hines, 178, 181–184, 186, 188, 196
paramilitary organizations, 116
Paris, 212
Paris Commune, 7
patronage, 96, 106n55
Peabody, George Foster, 188
peace, 210–211
Pearson, Charles, 193
Pegram, Thomas, 239
Pendleton, S.C., 269
Pendleton, Susan Lee, 236
Pension Bureau, 95
periodicals, 18
Perman, Michael, 31
Phagan, Mary, 173
Phelps-Stokes Fund, 192
Philadelphia *Tribune,* 76
philanthropists, 187
Philippines, 8, 165, 167, 174–175, 185–186, 188–191, 195, 199n28

Phillips, Ulrich B., 192
Phillips, Wendell, 193
Piedmont, S.C., 29
Pierce, Edward L., 150, 153
Pike, James S., 142, 218n31
Pitzer, A. W., 159
plantation, 72
Platt Amendment, 165
plays, 8
*Plessy v. Ferguson* (1896), 70, 194
Poe, Clarence, 192
poetry, 8, 71–72, 75
political speeches, 63
poor whites, 188, 190–191
Popular Front, 54n18
Populists, 18, 188
Port Gibson, Miss., 97
Port Royal Experiment, 150
Port Royal, S.C., 150
Poughkeepsie, N.Y., 145
Prairie State College, 134n9
Pratt, Richard Henry, 169n17
Prince, K. Stephen, 51
Princeton University, 205, 232
print culture, 17
*The Problems of the Present South* (Murphy, 1903), 181
Progressive Era reform, 5, 7, 176
The *Progress of the World,* 185
property rights, 7
*The Prostrate State* (Pike, 1874), 142–143, 218n31
public health, 185–186, 196
Puckett, Sherman C., 197
Puerto Rico, 8, 165–167, 174, 185–186, 188–190, 195
Purman, W. J., 63, 65, 69, 77

Quakers, 155
Quarles, Benjamin, 245

*Race and Rumors of Race* (Odum, 1943), 46
*The Race Conflict* (Livingstone, 1911), 194
race knowledge, 21–22, 24, 26–27, 30
race war, 46
*Race, Reform, and Rebellion* (Marable, 1984), 202n65
*The Races of Mankind* (Weltfish, 1943), 48
racial etiquette, 110
racial hierarchy, 5
racial purity, 38
racial uplift, 140, 146, 163, 165, 167
Radcliffe College, 231
Radical Reconstruction, 87, 213
radicalism, 87
radio, 271
railroads, 90, 96, 114
*Raleigh State Chronicle,* 182
Randall, James G., 242
rape, 119, 134n18
Raper, Arthur, 129
Readjuster movement, 11
readjustment, 179–181, 193–194
reconciliation, 139
Reconstruction Acts (1867), 52n4
*Reconstruction and the Constitution* (Burgess, 1902), 219n31
*Reconstruction in Mississippi* (Garner, 1901), 60, 102n5
Reconstruction syndrome, 32n5, 52n5
Reconstruction: conservative narrative of, 9; definition of, 1, 22; as experiment, 23, 27, 153–154, 158, 169n17; historiography of, 227–228; memory weakening, 10, 263; radicals' view of, 42; as reform, 6–7; temporal boundaries of, 5; white supremacist memory of, 20, 67
*Reconstruction: Political and Economic* (Dunning, 1907), 235
*Red Rock* (Page, 1898), 25, 70, 185
Red Scare, 42
Red Shirts, 40, 47, 50, 262, 268–269, 274
Reddick, Lawrence Dunbar, 228, 242
Redemption, 1, 49
Reed, Thomas B., 141
regional autonomy, 3
regional development, 39
*The Relations of the Advanced and Backward Races of Mankind* (Bryce, 1902), 194
religion, 179, 257n32
*Reminiscences of an Active Life* (Lynch, 1970), 99
Republican National Convention (1884), 88
Republicans, 3, 20, 23, 31, 37, 61, 78, 84, 86, 88, 92, 98, 100, 139–140, 145, 149, 162, 205, 213, 233, 264; Radicals, 29, 37, 67, 91, 176, 209; white, 11
*Review of Reviews,* 185
Reynolds, Henry, 193

Rhame, L. Richard, 271–272
Rice, Joseph W., Jr., 272
Richmond, Va., 49, 236
Ridpath, John, 230
Ring, Natalie W., 140, 165, 235
riots: Camp Hill Riot (1932), 130; Danville Massacre (1883), 68, 71; Eufala Riot (1874), 115–116, 124–125; Hamburg Massacre (1876), 71, 275; Jackson County War (1869–71), 63–64; Lamar, S.C. (1970), 266, 271; Battle of Liberty Place (1874), 116; Meridian Riot (1871), 127; Port Gibson Riot (1876), 97; Watts Riot (1965), 197; Wilmington Massacre (1898), 26, 255n34
*The Rise and Fall of the Confederate Government* (Davis, 1881), 182
Roberts, Myrtle, 243
Robertson, E. D., 36
Robertson, James, 36
Robinson, Esau, 129, 132
Robinson, Tom, 129
Rockefeller Sanitary Commission to Eradicate Hookworm, 184
Rockefeller, John D., Jr., 178
Rogers, Calvin, 64–65, 75, 77
Roosevelt, Eleanor, 44
Roosevelt, Franklin D., 37, 39–41, 44, 48; court-packing plan, 39; "Roosevelt purge" of 1938, 39; "Roosevelt recession," 39
Roosevelt, Theodore, 185
Roy, Joseph E., 157
Russell, Donald, 265
Russell, Richard, 48Saar River, 213

Salem, N.C., 187
Salley, Alexander S., 272
Saluda, S.C., 268
Sanford, Albert Hart, 236
scalawags, 41–42, 48–49, 116, 233
Scarborough, William S., 161
Schmidt, Peter, 175
scientific racism, 70
Scott, Molly, 123, 132
Scottsboro Boys, 130
Scroggs, William O., 178, 192–194, 196
Scurlock, Wyatt, 64
Seals, Maurice, 117
Second Reconstruction, 10, 37, 41, 43–45, 48, 196–197, 202n65, 263
Sedition Act (1918), 211
segregation, 19, 28, 43–44
Selma, Ala., 118
Seminoles, 62, 82n40
Shady Dale, Ga., 25
Shaw, Albert, 185
Sherman, Joan, 71–72
Sherman, William T., 120, 205; March to the Sea, 38, 42, 48
Simkins, Francis B., 227, 234, 242
Simmons, Furnifold, 21
Sinclair, William, 77, 80n8
Skaggs, William H., 188
Skaggs, William H. 188
slavery, 71, 87, 93, 98, 114, 119, 159–160, 175, 177, 181, 204, 217n10, 237; in Appalachia, 112; history of, 61
Smiley, Albert K., 145, 147–150, 161–163
*Smith v. Allwright* (1944), 47
Smith, Ellison D. "Cotton Ed," 40, 47
Smith, Goldwyn, 193
Smith, William Benjamin, 22
social Darwinism, 59
South Africa, 166
South Carolina, 21, 40, 47, 51, 141–142, 213, 230
South Carolina, Local Government Law (1975), 267
South Carolina General Assembly, 9
South Carolina State College, 265, 271–272
South Carolina Theatre Company, 269–270
South Carolina Tricentennial, 10
South Carolina Tricentennial Commission, 267, 273
Southern Christian Leadership Conference, 265
Southern Commission on the Study of Lynching, 129
Southern Education Board, 184, 187, 189, 191
Southern Historical Association, 242
Southern Publishing Company, 240
Southern Society of New York, 44
Southern Sociological Congress, 178, 180, 191–192
Southern States' Industrial Council (SSIC), 38, 40
Southern University, 134n9
*Southern Workman*, 150, 183, 190
Southworth, Gertrude Van Duyn, 244
Southworth, John Van Duyn, 244
Spain, 165

Spanish-American War, 140, 165 184–186, 190
Spartanburg, S.C., 270
speeches, 18
Spencer, Barnett, 120
*St. Joseph Gazette,* 182
Stanonis, Anthony, 275
states rights, 204, 217n10
steamboats, 96
Stennis, John C., 10, 50
Stephens, Alexander H., 230
Stevens, Thaddeus, 29–30, 67, 115, 213
Stoler, Ann, 183
Stone, Alfred Holt, 22, 26, 192
Stone, Sonja H., 272
Stoneman, Austin, 29–30
Stoneman, Elsie, 30
Stoneman, Phil, 30
Storey, Margaret, 114
Storey, Moorfield, 165
*The Story of the Negro* (Washington, 1909), 164
*The Strange Career of Jim Crow* (Woodward, 1955), 196
*Studies in the American Race Problem* (Stone, 1908), 23
suffrage, 157–158; African American, 20, 23, 86; disfranchisement, 17, 19, 27–28, 35, 44; limitation, 142; limitation by education, 152; limitation by literacy tests, 152, 159, 170n34; limitation by poll tax, 35–36, 44–45
Sumner, Charles, 150, 162
Sumter County, Ala., 129
Suresnes Cemetery, 214

Taft, William H., 96, 100, 166
*Take Your Choice: Separation or Mongrelization* (Bilbo, 1947), 49
Talladega, Ala., 188
Tallapoosa County, Ala., 130
Tallmadge, Eugene, 35, 41
Taney, Roger B., 62
Tannebaum, Frank, 178
taxation, 104n25, 155; in Mississippi, 104n25; during Reconstruction, 89–90
Taylor, A. A., 78
Tennessee, 232, 245
testimony, 76, 113, 122
Texas, 43, 47, 114, 125, 238, 246, 254, 267
textbooks, 8–9, 44
textile industry, in South Carolina, 264, 266, 274
Third Reconstruction, 197
Thompson, Holland, 179
Thompson, Waddy, 236
Thurmond, Strom, 264
Tillman, Benjamin, 21
Togo, 166
Toledo, Ohio, 240
Tourgée, Albion W., 150, 156–157, 161, 246
*The Tragic Era* (Bowers, 1929), 140
*The Traitor* (Dixon, 1907), 41
Treaty of Versailles, 213–214, 216
Trinity College, 187
*The Trojan Horse in America* (Dies, 1940), 43
Trouillot, Michel-Rolph, 131, 274
Truman, Harry S., 49–50
Tulane University, 22
Tunnell, Ted, 24, 52n3
Turkey, 270
Turner, Frederick Jackson, 254
Turner, Henry Gray, 141
Turner, Henry McNeal, 143
Tuscaloosa, Ala., 21, 118
Tuskegee Institute, 128, 161, 163, 166, 170n29, 187, 190
Tuskegee Negro Conference, 162, 166
Tuskegee Negro Conference 166

U.S. Board of Indian Commissioners, 145
U.S. Department of Education, 152, 275
U.S. House of Representatives, 35, 43–45; Committee on Insular Affairs, 188; Special Committee on Un-American Activities, 43
U.S. Senate, 36, 39, 43, 51, 95, 162, 210
U.S. Supreme Court, 47, 91, 95
U.S. Treasury, 88
*Uncle Remus* (Harris, 1881), 23
Uncle Remus, 68
Union army, 119–120, 124–125, 207, 212, 275; graves of, 64; removal from South in 1877, 187, 203
Unionists, 11
*Unitarian Register,* 166
United Confederate Veterans (UCV), 11, 44
United Daughters of the Confederacy, 11, 18, 240
United Service Organizations (USO), 48
University Commission on Southern Race Questions, 191–192

University of Alabama, 46
University of Chicago, 237
University of Florida, 192
University of Georgia, 192
University of North Carolina, 46
University of Pennsylvania, 238
University of Tennessee, 187
University of Virginia, 191–193, 196, 233, 272
*Up From Slavery* (Washington, 1901), 164

Vance, Zebulon, 20, 141, 143
Vardaman, James K., 23, 26
Ver Steeg, Clarence, 245
Versailles, 212–213, 215
Vicksburg, Miss., 45
Vietnam War, 197
Vigilantes, Inc., 35
violence, 6, 11, 63, 71, 74–76, 78, 86, 99, 113, 117, 121, 143–144; against African Americans, 90, 125; by African Americans, 64, 232; depictions of, 228; election, 36, 95–98, 124; by Ku Klux Klan, 66; political, 98–99, 155, 206; psychological effects of, 124, 135n30; during Reconstruction, 6, 9, 62
Virginia, 11, 24, 146, 149, 186, 199n28
Voting Rights Act (1965), 251, 265

Waddell, Alfred Moore, 26
Walker, Susan, 23
Walton, Hanes, Jr., 197
Wannamaker, John, 189
Ward, Jason Morgan, 31
Washington, Booker T., 68–69, 76, 81n36, 102n3, 149–150, 161–164, 166 183, 187, 190
Weisberger, Bernard A., 227, 246
Wells, Jeremy, 198n15
Wells-Barnett, Ida B., 61, 86, 170n31
Weltfish, Gene, 48
West Indies, 188
West Virginia, 141
West, 12, 169n14
West, John C., 273
West, Ruth, 244
Western Reserve University, 240
white counterrevolution, 45
white leagues, 94, 96; Crescent City White League, 115
White Man's Party, 116
white moderates, 46
white primary, 47
White, Andrew D., 159
White, Green, 64
White, Richard, 114
White, Walter, 47
Whittemore Elementary School, 275
Whittemore High School, 275
Whittemore School, 275
Whittemore, B. F., 275
Whittlesey, Eliphalet, 150
*Why the Solid South?* (Herbert et al., 1890), 2, 141, 168n4, 219n31
Wilberforce College, 161
Wilberforce, A., 101
*Williams v. Mississippi* (1898), 70
Williams, George W., 231
Williams, Jesse, 125
Williams, Kidada, 66
Williams, Walter L., 172n74
Williamson, Joel, 32n5
Wilmington, N.C., 26
Wilson, D. L., 60
Wilson, Woodrow, 8, 96, 185, 203, 217, 233, 239
Wilson's Raid (1865), 118
Winnsboro, S.C., 120, 268
Winston, George T., 27
*Within Our Gates* (Micheaux, 1919), 8
Wolfe, Thomas R., 271
Wood, Robert H., 92
Woodburn, James Albert, 236–237
Woodson, Carter G., 85, 241
Woodward, C. Vann, 196
World War I, 8, 50, 175, 191, 195, 203, 207–208
World War II, 10, 35, 38, 45, 49, 196, 229, 244, 272
*World's Work,* 186
Wright, Richard, 129

Yale University, 197
Yazoo County, Miss., 95
Young Men's Christian Association, 192

Zimmerman, Andrew, 166
Zimmerman, Sam, 268
Zip Coon, 9